Size, Risk, and Governance in European Banking

Size, Risk, and Governance in European Banking

Jens Hagendorff, Kevin Keasey,
and Francesco Vallascas

OXFORD
UNIVERSITY PRESS

OXFORD
UNIVERSITY PRESS

Great Clarendon Street, Oxford, OX2 6DP,
United Kingdom

Oxford University Press is a department of the University of Oxford. It furthers the University's objective of excellence in research, scholarship, and education by publishing worldwide. Oxford is a registered trade mark of Oxford University Press in the UK and in certain other countries

First Edition published in 2013

Impression: 1

Published in the United States of America by Oxford University Press
198 Madison Avenue, New York, NY 10016, United States of America

British Library Cataloguing in Publication Data

Data available

ISBN 978–0–19–969489–1

As printed and bound by
CPI Group (UK) Ltd, Croydon, CR0 4YY

Author Biographies

JENS HAGENDORFF

Jens Hagendorff (BA, MA, PhD) is the Martin Currie Professor in Finance and Investment at the University of Edinburgh. He teaches across a range of subjects in banking and investments, including executive and MBA teaching. Jens has previously worked at the Financial Stability Department of the Bank of Spain, University of Leeds, and he was also a visiting fellow at the Federal Reserve Bank of Atlanta. Jens has acted as an invited speaker at various bank regulatory agencies, including the Federal Reserve Bank of Chicago and the Federal Deposit Insurance Corporation.

Jens' work focuses on European banking. Much of his work examines whether bank strategies, corporate governance, and regulation have measurable effects on the riskiness of banks. Further, his ongoing work with the Bank of Spain and the Federal Reserve Bank of Atlanta analyses the performance and risk implications of bank mergers in the European Union.

Jens' work on European banking has been published in highly rated international journals such as *Review of Finance, Journal of Corporate Finance, Journal of Banking & Finance,* and *Journal of Financial Services Research.*

KEVIN KEASEY

Kevin Keasey is Professor of Financial Services, Director of the International Institute of Banking and Financial Services, and Head of the Accounting and Finance Department at the University of Leeds.

Kevin is the author of 12 books, monographs, and edited volumes on corporate governance, financial regulation and financial services, small firm finance and financial markets, and behavioural finance, and is the author of over 115 refereed articles in leading international journals and over 80 other publications (book chapters, reports, etc.). His research covers a range of methodologies from the empirical to the experimental, and in his chosen areas of specialism he has received international recognition. In addition, he is the joint editor of a number of series of edited volumes by leading international authors on specific themes within the corporate governance literature, and is an editor, deputy editor, and on the editorial board of a number of academic journals. He has directed a number of research projects for funding bodies such as the ESRC, ICAEW, CIMA, and the Nuffield Foundation.

Kevin has taught across the range of his research interests and more general accounting and finance topics in a number of leading institutions. He has initiated a range of successful MBA and MA programmes at home and overseas, and, most recently, he has built extensive networks in China, culminating in an agreement with Tsinghua University in Beijing. Kevin is an established teacher of executive programmes and he jointly directed, across the 1990s, the Chancellor of the Exchequer's Financial Sector Scheme for managers from the former Soviet Union (a £2 million-plus scheme). Most recently, in 2009, he has prepared and delivered a course on governance in the NHS for senior medical directors across the UK.

As well as establishing, leading, and building academic units, Kevin has substantial and extensive experience as an entrepreneur, corporate director, and a mentor to senior executives. His director and non-executive positions have included a hi-tech holding company, a fast growth care company, a venture capital company, and PLCs in the IT and telecom sectors. In addition, he founded Ecom Group Ltd and was a founder and chairman of Aquilo PLC until the end of 2006 (AIM listed—£30m turnover and 130 staff in 2006). He is (has been) a fellow of the Royal Society of Arts, the CEO Circle (a group of the leading CEOs in the UK), and the Northern Region Advisory panel of the Stock Exchange.

FRANCESCO VALLASCAS

Francesco Vallascas is Associate Professor of Banking and Finance at the University of Leeds. He teaches across a range of subjects in banking and international finance. Francesco has previously worked as a Lecturer in Financial Intermediation at the University of Cagliari and with the research centre of the European Commission on several research projects.

Francesco's research interests lie in European banking and in banking regulation. His main research examines banking risk and financial stability in European banking. He also examines the effects of mergers and acquisitions on bank risk-taking, and the effectiveness of corporate governance and regulatory mechanisms in limiting risk-taking by banks.

Francesco's work on banking has been published in highly rated international journals such as *Review of Finance*, *Journal of Corporate Finance*, *Journal of Banking & Finance*, *Journal of International Money & Finance*, and *Journal of Financial Services Research*.

Contents

Part V Conclusions and Implications for the Re-regulation of European Banking

List of Figures

List of Tables

Part I
Introduction

1

Introduction

The financial crisis that erupted in 2007 has brought the issues surrounding the size, risk, and regulation of banks to the attention of a wide audience. It is difficult to open a broadsheet or a business magazine without being confronted with some aspect of bank behaviour, be it their risk levels, bankers' excessive rewards, the intertwining of bank and sovereign risk, or how they should be regulated to avoid problems in the future. In Europe, the recent and ongoing crisis has demonstrated that the European Union (EU) was institutionally ill-prepared to manage a financial crisis, especially one involving large cross-border institutions which are systemically important to a number of countries. The creation of a single market for banking services, the introduction of the euro, and successive waves of enlargements have been building blocks for the consolidation and internationalization of European banks. However, one of the unique features of European banking is that, despite the gradual emergence of pan-European banks, there remains great diversity in what banks do and in the structure of banking sectors and supervisory practices across member states.

Policy debates over the future of European banking will, therefore, be shaped by an assessment of the riskiness of banking firms as well as the ways by which the corporate governance of banking firms can resolve some of these issues. Improved corporate governance, for instance, via more active monitoring by shareholders, offers a promising route for the improved monitoring of European banks. Here as well, differences with regard to existing corporate governance practices across the EU mean that the effectiveness of proposals aimed at strengthening corporate governance is likely to vary by country.

The purpose of this book is to integrate and synthesize the various perspectives on the size, risk, and governance of banking as applied to the European market. Academic work on European banking has been scarce relative to US-focused work; this is unfortunate, given the unique institutional factors in Europe and the urgency with which regulatory lessons from the financial crisis which started in 2007 have to be learnt in countries in Europe and other countries outside the US.

To achieve this aim, the book is divided into three parts that focus on size, risk, and governance respectively, with each part being further subdivided into chapters. Each chapter integrates and synthesizes academic studies on European banking that focus on size, risk, and governance; and furthermore, each chapter provides fresh insights based on the new analysis of the empirical questions at hand.

Part II: Size in European Banking

Part II provides an overview of how the size of banking firms affects stability in the European banking sector. The two chapters in this part review the quantitative empirical literature relating to size effects in European banking. The chapters also offer new insights into the issue as to whether or not bank size motivates risk-taking where explicit or implicit 'too-big-to fail' policies shield bank creditors from market discipline.

Chapter 2: *Bank Systemic Size and Systemic Crises*

This chapter analyses the relationship between systemic size, measured as the ratio of bank assets to GDP, and bank risk. Given that the emphasis is on systemic size, we take an international sample of banks to form a backdrop to later chapters and demonstrate that systemic size does not affect bank risk-taking in general. However, and consistent with explanations that systemically large banks maximize the value of the financial safety net, we show that systemically larger banks engaged in more aggressive risk-taking during the recent crisis. Crucially, the risk effect of systemic size during the recent crisis does not extend to other crisis periods. The recent crisis, therefore, appears to have been unique in terms of its behavioural implications for systemically large banks.

Chapter 3: *Increases in Size and Bank Default Risk: Evidence from European Bank Mergers*

This chapter analyses the implications of European bank consolidation on the default risk of acquiring banks. Acquisitions are the most salient means to increase the size of banks and increases in bank size can have important effects on bank risk, as shown in the previous chapter. Risk considerations may be linked to merger strategies, and there may be different outcomes for the riskiness of the resulting institution. Two themes surface in the literature on the risk implications of bank mergers and acquisitions (M&A): consolidation delivers diversification effects (and reduces risk) or, alternatively, the risk effects of consolidation are shaped by regulatory incentives (which may induce an increase in risk). Banks may face incentives to build larger organizations with the intent of becoming 'too-big to fail' in order to extract benefits from the providers of financial safety nets in Europe.

We analyse the implications of European bank consolidation on the default risk of acquiring banks. For a sample of 134 bidding banks, we employ the Merton distance to default model to show that, on average, bank mergers are risk neutral. However, for relatively safe banks, mergers generate a significant increase in default risk. This result is particularly pronounced for cross-border and activity-diversifying deals as well as for deals completed under weak bank regulatory regimes. Also, large deals, which pose organizational and procedural hurdles, experience a merger-related increase in default risk. Our results cast doubt on the ability of bank merger activity to exert a risk-reducing and stabilizing effect on the European banking industry.

Part III: Risk in European Banking

Part III discusses the literature relating to each of the different elements of risk in European banking. The chapters in this section also include new insights from a large dataset of European bank risk in different institutional contexts.

Chapter 4: *The Trends and Composition of Banking Risk across Europe*

This chapter examines the trends and composition of banking risk across Europe since the late 1980s. Particular emphasis is given to trends in European banking risk and the importance of international and European components of that risk. The chapter examines whether the growing integration and internationalization of European banks has increased their vulnerability to cross-country shocks and increased the likelihood of cross-country banking crises.

More specifically, this chapter examines the trends and composition of volatility across European banking systems from January 1988 to December 2010. While there is no evidence of a long-term trend in the average level of banking system volatility, there is a change in its composition resulting from the growing importance of international and European non-financial components, especially in the largest banking systems. We argue that the changing composition of banking system volatility is the effect of a long-term integration process (with a growing importance of cross-border activities) that has not been influenced by the introduction of the euro. Our results highlight the increasing vulnerability of the European banking systems to international and European shocks and an increasing likelihood of cross-border banking crises, and the need for regulatory reforms that focus on effective cross-border crisis management and resolution so as to safeguard the systemic stability of European banking in the near future.

Chapter 5: *The Determinants of European Bank Exposure to Systemic Shocks*

The purpose of this chapter is to analyse whether a European banking system that consists of smaller and more specialized banking firms and is regulated with a larger set of prudential rules than at present is likely to better withstand systemic shocks than current systems. The chapter adopts a novel empirical approach that relates the changes in the risk that a bank fails to changes in the degree of systemic stability. The chapter also examines the role of liquidity in protecting banks against these shocks only when the banking system is under stress. Further, we make the policy recommendation that regulatory interventions that impose constraints on the maximum size of a bank seem the most effective tools to safeguard systemic stability.

Again, more specifically, utilizing a novel empirical approach and an extensive sample of listed European banks, we identify which bank characteristics offer a shelter from systemic shocks and we compare the relative effects of several hypothetical regulatory interventions on a bank's risk exposure. While the results show that restrictions on a bank's leverage ratio and the imposition of liquidity requirements, as in the Basel III Accord, may improve the resilience of a bank to systemic events, they also demonstrate that bank size, the share of non-interest income and asset growth (none of which are at the centre of the new regulatory landscape) are key determinants of a bank's risk exposure. In particular, the introduction of a cap on bank absolute size appears the most effective tool, *ceteris paribus*, to reduce the default risk of a bank given systemic events. Furthermore, in spite of the integration process of the financial industry in Europe, the analysis presented here shows that such a cap should be country-specific and that smaller economies require smaller banks.

Part IV: Corporate Governance in European Banking

Much of the corporate governance literature excludes banking firms on the grounds that they are regulated firms. However, due to the large externalities associated with bank failures and the access of banking firms to public funds which results from this, shareholder monitoring may offer a crucial complement to supervisory scrutiny. The three chapters in Part IV focus on regulation, board monitoring, and opacity in European banking.

To date there are very few studies on bank governance that focus on European banks. One of the reasons is the limited availability of reliable data on the corporate governance of European banks. For instance, data on the remuneration of individual directors and their professional background is not available in a number of countries or has only recently been made available in other countries. That means a meaningful quantitative analysis of governance issues in banking is difficult if we focus on European banks only. For this reason, Chapters 6 and 7, which both make use of a unique and hand-collected dataset on the governance of European banks, also use data on US banks as a benchmark for the European data.

Chapter 6: *Board Monitoring, Regulation, and Performance in the European Banking Industry*

The relationship between bank-level corporate governance and industry regulation remains an open question. In this chapter, we examine the interaction between firm-level monitoring and bank regulatory regimes to influence bank performance in European and US banking. The chapter considers whether board monitoring mechanisms are effective in preventing underperformance under bank regulators of varying stringency. The purpose of this analysis is to evaluate the potential to which the monitoring by shareholders can complement similar efforts by financial regulators.

The specific monitoring effect of boards of directors versus industry regulation is unclear. In this chapter, we examine how the interaction between bank-level monitoring and regulatory regimes influences the announcement period returns of acquiring banks in the US and twelve European economies. We study three board monitoring mechanisms (independence, CEO-chair duality and diversity) and analyse their effectiveness in preventing underperforming merger strategies under bank regulators of varying strictness. Only under strict banking regulation regimes do board independence and diversity improve acquisition performance. In less strict regulatory environments corporate governance is virtually irrelevant in improving the performance outcomes of merger activities.

The results presented in the chapter indicate a complementary relationship between monitoring by boards and bank regulation. The results are the first to report evidence consistent with complementarity by investigating the effectiveness (rather than the prevalence) of governance arrangements across regulatory regimes. The results suggest that attempts to improve the ability of bank boards to critically assess managerial initiatives are most likely to be successful if internal governance is accompanied by strict industry regulation.

Chapter 7: *Executive Pay and Risk-taking in the European Banking Industry*

Few topics in the financial press have generated as much public interest as compensation in the banking industry. This chapter examines a unique and hand-collected dataset of executive compensation by all European bank CEOs of listed banks that publish such data. To further expand the sample of banks, the chapter also includes a sample of similarly sized US banks. Also considered here are the effects of CEO cash bonuses on the level of bank default risk for a sample of US and European banking firms. Specifically, the chapter employs the Merton distance to default model to show that increases in CEO cash bonuses lower the default risk of a bank. However, we find no evidence of cash bonuses exerting a risk-reducing effect when banks are financially distressed or when banks operate under weak bank regulatory regimes. Our results link bonus compensation in banking to financial stability and caution that attempts to regulate bonus pay need to tailor CEO incentives to the riskiness of banks and to regulatory regimes.

The investigation comes against the background of an emerging policy consensus in many European countries that compensation practices and bonus payments in particular have promoted excessive risk-taking at financial firms. For instance, the Committee of European Banking Supervisors (CEBS, 2010) proposes in its draft guidelines on remuneration policies that at least 50 per cent of variable compensation (including bonus payments) should be non-cash. Crucially, our finding that CEO bonuses are linked to lower default risk challenges the view underlying these regulatory guidelines that cash-based executive compensation is linked to high risk-taking in the banking industry.

Chapter 8: *Systemic Risk Potential and Opacity in European Banks*

This chapter focuses on the relationship between systemic risk potential (measured via synchronicity in stock price movements) and opacity in European banks. Regulatory initiatives that enhance the information environment may lower bank opacity and increase the firm-specific information incorporated in stock prices. The chapter examines whether these initiatives lower or increase the risk interdependencies between the largest European banking firms. As such, the findings of this chapter are of significance for the re-regulation of the banking industry.

We examine the impact of opacity on bank stability, measured in terms of stock return co-movement and crash risk, for a sample of European banks. Our results show that less opaque banks have lower co-movements and exhibit a lower probability of stock price crashes. Two major regulatory implications can be drawn from our analysis. First, our results demonstrate that removing bank opacity should contribute to the stability of the financial sector. Second, together with the evidence of a strong positive impact of size on bank exposure to systematic and systemic shocks and on the probability of stock price crashes, these results add support to forms of the re-regulation of the banking industry based on limits on bank size.

Part V: Conclusions and Implications for the Re-Regulation of European Banking

Chapter 9: *Conclusions and Implications for the Re-regulation of European Banking*

The final chapter, Part V, critically reviews the new insights gained from the chapters above, while offering policy implications as regards the role of size, risk and governance in European banking.

Part II

Size in European Banking

2

Bank Systemic Size and Systemic Crises

Introduction

Concerns that large banks exploit their implicit claim on the safety net by taking on more risk have been heightened by the performance of several of the world's most systemically large banks during the financial crisis that erupted from the second half of 2007 (FSB, 2010; BCBS, 2011b). By means of illustration, seven out of the ten systemically largest banks were subject to a taxpayer-funded bailout during the crisis.[1]

The issue of excessive risk-taking by systemically large banks has gained further attention from the fact that the banking industry has seen increasing scale and concentration over the last two decades. Partly in response to deregulation, many banks engaged in mergers and acquisitions, thus causing a rapid growth in bank asset size. This fast-paced consolidation of bank assets has meant that banks have grown rapidly relative to the economies in which they are chartered. This is clearly illustrated by Figure 2.1, which plots the evolution of the ratio of bank assets to GDP for the fifty systemically large banks since 1998. While the average systemic size of these banks was 40 per cent of GDP in 1998, it reached more than 70 per cent in 2007, and exceeded 200 per cent for a number of individual banks in the same year (among them Credit Suisse, Dankse, Fortis, and UBS).

Partly in response to concerns over bank risk-taking, policymakers are currently considering various initiatives aimed at imposing restrictions on the size, capital structure, and income mix of banks. For instance, some policymakers have recently proposed caps on the size of domestic banks. Also, the

[1] In order of magnitude, the ten systemically most important banks (in terms of bank assets to GDP) in our sample during 2007 are (whether they were bailed out during the crisis is indicated in parentheses): UBS (yes), Ageas (yes), Credit Suisse Group (no), Danske Bank (yes), Dexia (yes), Arab Bank (no), Royal Bank of Scotland Group (yes), Nordea Bank (no), Depfa Bank (yes; via parent company), Bank of Ireland (yes).

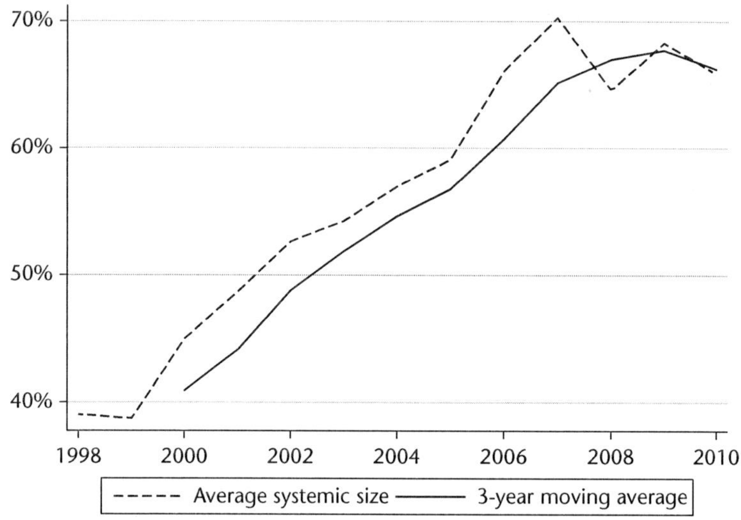

Figure 2.1. Evolution of Systemic Size in the Top 50 Systemically Large Banks as of end-1998

Basel Committee (BCBS, 2011) advises raising the capital requirements pertaining to global systemically important banks (GSIBs), which include numerous systemically large banking firms under the proposed Basel III capital adequacy framework.[2] Also, the Dodd–Frank Act bars US bank holding companies from proprietary trading and certain types of other investments. Similarly, the Independent Commission on Banking has recently proposed that UK banks will need to separate and independently capitalize their retail and investment banking activities.

This chapter examines if the default risk of banks changes as they grow in systemic size during both normal and crisis periods. Empirical research has only recently begun to consider the risk implications linked to systemic size in banking (Demirgüç-Kunt and Huizinga, 2010, 2011). Rather than examine systemic size, previous work on size and risk has focused on stand-alone (or absolute) bank size and found some evidence that larger banks take more risks (e.g. Boyd and Runkle, 1993; Benston, Hunter, and Wall, 1995; Penas and Unal, 2004; De Jonghe, 2010; Gropp, Hakenes, and Schnabel, 2011; Brunnermeier, Dong, and Palia, 2012).

[2] GSIBs are banks that are deemed systemically relevant because of their size, complexity, and interconnectedness with the rest of the financial system. For these institutions, the Basel Committee (BCBS, 2011) proposes increasing the minimum regulatory capital ratio, defined as regulatory capital over risk-weighted assets, by up to 3.5 per cent above the minimum applied to non-systemically important banks. The additional capital is to be held in equity and equity-like financial instruments.

The distinction between stand-alone and systemic size is important, because growth in systemic size affects the risk-and-return profile of banks differently from growth in stand-alone size. Demirgüç-Kunt and Huizinga (2011) show that, while growth in stand-alone size offers banks a trade-off between profitability and risk, growth in systemic size is undesirable as it reduces return without a clear impact on risk. Moreover, the distinction between stand-alone size and systemic size is important, because banks that are small in absolute terms may be systemically large when chartered in a small economy. Bailing out systemically large banks can create substantial fiscal costs (e.g. via asset guarantees, capital, or liquidity support) which, as demonstrated by the recent cases of Ireland and Iceland, can bring countries perilously close to a sovereign debt crisis (IMF, 2009c). Risk-shifting behaviour could, therefore, be particularly acute (and, by extension, particularly important for policymakers) when banks are large in systemic terms, but not necessarily when banks are large in absolute terms.

The analysis shows that, for a large panel of international banks, systemic size increases bank risk (based on the Merton (1974) distance-to-default model). The same finding holds for the subsample of European banks, albeit only in some specifications. Furthermore, upon closer examination, it is revealed that systemically larger banks have increased their risk-taking only during the recent crisis, though this effect is not confirmed in the case of Europe. More generally, the risk-increasing effect linked to systemic size does not extend to other systemic crises that occurred during the sampling period. Consequently, the link between systemic size and risk-taking only exists during the recent crisis and only when the analysis is conducted for the full sample.

Related Literature: Systemic Size and Risk in Banking

Empirical evidence on how risk-taking changes as banks grow in systemic size has remained scant to date and has not considered how the relationship between systemic size and risk changes during crisis periods. One view holds that banks take on more risk as they grow in systemic size. This is because the failure of a systemically large bank creates considerable negative externalities and these raise the expectation that a bank will be subject to a bailout (FSB, 2010; BCBS, 2011a)—with systemically large banks increasing their implicit claim on the financial safety net through higher risk-taking. Consistent with this view, Demirgüç-Kunt and Huizinga (2011) show that systemically large banks benefit from taking on more risk. The authors find that when systemically large banks increase their share price volatility, this will increase their market valuations and decrease their credit default swap (CDS) spreads relative to systemically smaller banks.[3]

In contrast to the risk-shifting argument, the opposite view holds that increases in systemic size cause banks to engage in less risk-taking. The fiscal costs of bailing out a systemically large bank can be prohibitive for countries, and thus raise questions over their long-term solvency. This exposes doubts over the ability of countries to bail out their systemically largest banks and raises the prospect of creditor losses should a systemically important bank default. In the absence of credible bank bailout guarantees, systemically larger banks may be subject to more, rather than less, market discipline and may display lower, rather than higher, risk as a result. Consistent with this, Demirgüç-Kunt and Huizinga (2010) find evidence of systemically larger banks being 'too big to save' by showing that systemically large banks are subject to greater levels of market discipline (as indicated by higher funding costs).

An important question addressed in this chapter is whether the risk-taking of systemically large banks is different during crisis periods. The relationship between systemic size and risk (be it positive or negative) could be time-contingent and more pronounced during a crisis period. For instance, systemically large banks may take less risk during a crisis if systemic risk considerations motivate regulators to engage in more aggressive interventions in failing banks (Allen and Gale, 2000) and, likewise, if 'too big to save' banks are subject to greater levels of market discipline (Demirgüç-Kunt and Huizinga, 2010).

By the same token, if there is a risk-increasing effect linked to systemic size, this effect may equally be larger during a crisis. During a systemic crisis, supervisors typically face fewer options of how to deal with bank failures (Barth, Caprio, and Levine, 2004). As a result, regulators may be reluctant to take over or close a failing bank if the banking sector is weak and the prospect of bank failures widespread (Acharya and Yorulmazer, 2007). Brown and Dinç (2011) show evidence of this 'too-many-to-fail effect' by demonstrating that a government's decision to intervene in problem banks depends on the financial health of other banks in that country. Critically for this chapter, Brown

[3] The current study can also be linked to a broader body of literature that examines the risk implications of bank growth in stand-alone size. Overall, the empirical evidence reported in this line of work is supportive of the notion that large banks tend to follow riskier strategies than smaller banks (Boyd and Runkle, 1993; Gropp, Gründl, and Güttler, 2010). Another separate but related stream of the literature looks into the effect of asset growth via mergers and acquisitions and finds some evidence consistent with the notion that bank growth leads to additional risk-taking. Benston, Hunter, and Wall (1995) show that US bank mergers and acquisitions are partly motivated by acquiring banks exploiting the financial safety net. Similarly, Penas and Unal (2004) find that a bank merger causes return increases for bondholders if the resulting bank becomes 'too big to fail'.

and Dinç (2011) also show that the prospect of regulatory forbearance during a systemic crisis is stronger for systemically larger banks.

While the 'too-many-to-fail' explanation relies on systemically large banks maximizing the value of the safety net via more aggressive risk-taking during a crisis, recent studies also emphasize that banks' performance during a crisis may result from bad luck (rather than bad behaviour). For instance, Fahlenbrach and Stulz (2011) and Beltratti and Stulz (2012) both show that the type of bank portfolio decisions which were value-creating before the crisis but caused banks to underperform during the crisis were unlikely to have been anticipated at the time they were made.

Sample

To build an international sample of banks, accounting and income statement data are extracted for all commercial banks and bank holding companies listed on Bureau van Dijk/IBCA's (International Bank Credit Analysis Ltd) Bankscope database between 1998 and 2010. The resulting list of banks is then matched with Datastream to obtain equity valuation data. International Securities Identification Number (ISIN) identifiers are used to match the databases and, where banks have previously been delisted and the ISIN identifiers are missing on Bankscope, banks are hand-matched across the two datasets. This yields an initial sample of 2,169 banks.

To increase the comparability of sample banks, banking firms traded on an over-the-counter (OTC) market are excluded. This criterion removes 516 firms from the sample, mostly very small US banks. Banks where the government (in)directly owns in excess of 50 per cent of the shares are excluded because the risk choices of government-owned banks are less likely to be driven by shareholder value considerations, and thus differ in important ways.

Banks with fewer than five years of financial data and banks based in countries with fewer than three sample banks are also excluded. This is to ensure that the methodological approach can reliably distinguish between country- and bank-specific factors behind bank risk-taking. Furthermore, a liquidity criterion on stock returns is stipulated. Since illiquid stocks will not accurately reflect information on the expected performance of a bank, they are unlikely to produce reliable default risk estimates. Therefore, bank stocks are excluded from the sample where more than 40 per cent of daily stock returns per year are zero or which have been listed for less than one hundred trading days in a given year.

The final sample, see Table 2.1, contains 823 unique banking firms, which are chartered in 45 different countries. As reported in Panel A of Table 2.1, the systemic size of banks varies widely across sample countries. Some small and

Table 2.1. Sample Distribution by Country and Year

	Banks		Observations		Average Systemic Size (%GDP)
	Number	Percentage	Number	Percentage	
Panel A: Sample Distribution by Country					
Argentina	3	0.365	34	0.414	2.767
Australia	11	1.337	118	1.438	16.539
Austria	3	0.365	24	0.292	52.454
Bangladesh	16	1.944	134	1.633	1.140
Belgium	3	0.365	36	0.439	142.744
Brazil	3	0.365	33	0.402	9.124
Canada	8	0.972	104	1.267	18.279
Chile	4	0.486	41	0.500	14.309
China	5	0.608	46	0.560	3.246
Denmark	11	1.337	102	1.243	21.495
Egypt	7	0.851	57	0.694	2.305
France	6	0.729	63	0.768	30.462
Germany	8	0.972	72	0.877	21.715
Greece	9	1.094	107	1.304	9.527
Hong Kong	9	1.094	108	1.316	11.393
India	19	2.309	164	1.998	1.264
Indonesia	3	0.365	26	0.317	2.921
Ireland	5	0.608	49	0.597	70.478
Israel	6	0.729	75	0.914	25.152
Italy	19	2.309	192	2.339	7.093
Japan	86	10.450	984	11.988	1.595
Jordan	3	0.365	15	0.183	58.139
Kenya	5	0.608	49	0.597	4.985
Korea	9	1.094	88	1.072	6.126
Malaysia	10	1.215	108	1.316	16.867
Mexico	3	0.365	29	0.353	3.068
Morocco	3	0.365	21	0.256	21.287
Pakistan	13	1.580	103	1.255	1.847
Philippines	5	0.608	45	0.548	8.314
Poland	10	1.215	107	1.304	3.803
Portugal	5	0.608	57	0.694	24.995
Qatar	4	0.486	26	0.317	17.829
Russia	3	0.365	16	0.195	0.983
Saudi Arabia	8	0.972	74	0.902	5.989
Singapore	3	0.365	39	0.475	70.317
South Africa	6	0.729	69	0.841	22.653
Spain	9	1.094	105	1.279	17.362
Sri Lanka	5	0.608	51	0.621	3.912
Sweden	3	0.365	38	0.463	74.209
Switzerland	7	0.851	67	0.816	112.810
Taiwan	20	2.430	166	2.022	6.938
Thailand	9	1.094	99	1.206	9.656
Turkey	12	1.458	99	1.206	5.534
United Kingdom	11	1.337	114	1.389	29.378
USA	413	50.182	4,054	49.391	0.199
Total	*823*	*100.000*	*8,208*	*100.000*	*7.187*
Panel B: Sample Distribution by Year					
1998			409	4.983	6.514
1999			534	6.506	5.354
2000			583	7.103	5.770

2001	561	6.835	6.912
2002	652	7.943	6.563
2003	689	8.394	6.563
2004	695	8.467	6.810
2005	723	8.808	6.830
2006	723	8.808	7.889
2007	700	8.528	8.880
2008	672	8.187	7.843
2009	650	7.919	8.350
2010	617	7.517	8.435
Total	*8,208*	*100.000*	

developed economies host banks that are large compared to GDP. For instance, the systemic size of the average bank in countries such as Belgium, Ireland, and Switzerland is 143 per cent, 70 per cent, and 113 per cent respectively. Conversely, average systemic size is lower in Japan (2 per cent), China (3 per cent), and the USA (0.2 per cent). US banks make up around half the sample. To ensure the results are not driven by US banks, each table reported in the analysis also includes regressions without US banks. Finally, Panel B of Table 2.1 shows a steady increase in systemic bank size during the sample period (as also depicted in Figure 2.1 for the subset of systemically largest banks).

Measuring Bank Default Risk

Bank risk is measured via the Merton distance-to-default (DD) model. This model boasts a wide range of empirical (e.g. Vassalou and Xing, 2004; Sundaram and Yermack, 2007) and commercial applications (including as a risk management tool in the banking industry; see Gropp, Vesala, and Vulpes, 2006). Default frequencies estimated using the DD model correlate approximately at the 80 per cent level, with default frequencies estimated using the commercially applied—and in many ways similar—Moody's KMV proprietary model (Bharath and Shumway, 2008). The DD model has been demonstrated to provide a suitable indicator of bank fragility, which outperforms other market-based indicators such as subordinated debt spreads in predicting bank default (Gropp, Vesala, and Vulpes, 2006). An additional advantage of using DD is that it may be calculated for all listed banks (while other market-based risk indicators, such as CDS spreads, are only available for a relatively small number of banks, especially outside the USA). Furthermore, recent analyses have also confirmed that risk metrics constructed in the spirit of the DD model are suitable indicators of bank distress during the recent crisis (Altunbaş, Manganelli, and Marquez-Ibanez, 2011).

The Merton model measures default risk as the number of standard deviations that the market value of bank assets are above the default point (the point where the market value of assets is less than the book value of total liabilities). Formally, DD at the end of year t is expressed as:

$$\mathrm{DD}_t = \frac{\ln\,(V_{A,t}/L_t) + (r_f - 0.5\sigma_{A,t}^2)T}{\sigma_{A,t}\sqrt{T}} \tag{1}$$

where $V_{A,t}$ is the market value of assets at the end of the fiscal year t, L_t is the book value of total liabilities, r_f is the risk-free rate (obtained for each country from the IMF International Financial Statistics (IFS) database), $\sigma_{A,t}$ is the annualized asset volatility at t (based on volatility of equity returns in a given year), and T is the time to maturity (conventionally set to one year).

The computation of DD_t requires estimates of $V_{A,t}$ and $\sigma_{A,t}$ neither of which are directly observable. Following Vassalou and Xing (2004), the values for $V_{A,t}$ and $\sigma_{A,t}$ are inferred through an iterative process based on the Black–Scholes–Merton pricing model. Specifically, the market value of a firm's equity ($V_{\mathrm{E,t}}$) is expressed as a function of the asset value by solving the following system of nonlinear equations:

$$V_{E,t} = V_{A,t}N(d_{1,t}) - X_t e^{-r_f T} N(d_{2,t}) \tag{2}$$

$$\sigma_{E,t} = \left(\frac{V_{A,t}}{V_{E,t}}\right) N(d_{1,t})\sigma_{A,t} \tag{3}$$

Equation (2) defines $V_{E,t}$ as a call option on the market value of the bidder's total assets, with $d_{1,t} = \frac{\ln\,(V_{A,t}/L_t)+(r_{f_t}+0.5\sigma_{A,t}^2)T}{\sigma_{A,t}\sqrt{T}}$ and $d_{2,t} = d_{1,t} - \sigma_{A,t}\sqrt{T}$. Equation (3) is the optimal hedge equation that relates the standard deviation of a bank's equity value to the standard deviation of a bank's total assets value (both on an annualized basis).

This system of equations is solved by employing, as starting values for $\sigma_{A,t}$, the historical volatility of equity (computed on a yearly basis using daily data) multiplied by the ratio of the market value of equity to the sum of the market value of equity and the book value of total liabilities, that is, $\sigma_{A,t} = \sigma_{E,t}V_{E,t}/(V_{E,t} + L_t)$. A Newton search algorithm then identifies the daily values for $V_{A,t}$ and $\sigma_{A,t}$ in an iterative process, which we then employ to compute DD_t as in Equation (1).

Methods and Control Variables

This section describes the econometric approach employed to investigate the impact of systemic size on bank default risk. This is followed by a discussion of the control variables and their expected impact on distance to default (DD).

The Econometric Model

The impact of bank systemic size on bank default risk is estimated by the following linear regression model:

$$DD_{i,t} = \alpha_i + \beta_i SYSTEMICSIZE_{t-1} + \gamma BC_{t-1} + \varphi CC_t + \text{YEAR DUMMIES} \quad (4)$$

SYSTEMICSIZE is the book value of total bank assets scaled by the GDP of the country in which a bank is chartered.[4] BC is a vector of bank-specific characteristics and CC is a vector of country-specific control variables. We employ the within estimator to control for unobserved bank heterogeneity caused by factors that remain constant across the sample period. This estimator, by computing a separate intercept for each bank, strips out cross-sectional variations before estimating the slope coefficients. This approach is, therefore, well-suited to capturing variations in risk-taking at the level of individual banks over time.

All variables, except for the country controls, are lagged by one year to reduce simultaneity and endogeneity bias, and are summarized in Table 2.2. Standard errors have been corrected for heteroscedasticity and are clustered at the bank level to remove any estimation bias resulting from within-group correlation in the sample.

Control Variables

The vector of bank controls contains the following variables. First, the models control for stand-alone size (SIZE) measured using the logarithmic transformation of bank total assets. Demirgüc-Kunt and Huizinga (2011) show that

[4] The measure of systemic size used in this study is the same as in Brown and Dinç (2011). However, the asset-to-GDP ratio is not the only way of capturing systemic size. For instance, Demirgüç-Kunt and Huizinga (2010, 2011) use total liabilities divided by GDP as a measure of systemic size. In the sample, liabilities/GDP and assets/GDP are correlated in excess of 99 per cent. The results reported here are, therefore, not sensitive to the employment of bank assets or liabilities to express the systemic importance of a bank. Furthermore, like other measures of bank size, the measure is skewed owing to the presence of some very large banks in the sample. However, in contrast to previous studies, this issue is addressed in two ways. First, the baseline specification is re-estimated after replacing systemic size with its log transformation. Second, sample banks that are larger than 100 per cent (50 per cent) of GDP are excluded. The main findings remain unchanged after these modifications.

Table 2.2. Variable Definitions and Descriptive Statistics

		N	Mean	Median	St.Dev.	1 Pctile	99 Pctile
DD	Distance to default	8,208	3.414	3.247	0.170	1.684	8.204
SYSTEMICSIZE	Book value of bank total assets over country GDP (%)	8,208	7.161	0.290	24.864	0.003	112.419
SIZE	Log transformation of bank total assets in US dollars	8,208	15.790	15.621	1.968	12.541	20.979
LOANS	Net loans over total assets (%)	8,208	62.902	64.472	24.071	13.122	87.490
DIVERSIFICATION	1 minus a Herfindahl index of income concentration based on four income categories: (i) net interest income; (ii) fees and commissions; (iii) trading income; (iv) other operating income (%).	8,208	29.194	27.089	15.380	0.000	64.525
EQUITY	Total equity over total assets (%)	8,208	8.488	8.028	2.530	4.849	22.930
ROA	Net income over total assets (%)	8,208	0.725	0.805	−3.896	1.273	3.397
TOBINQ	(Book value of liabilities + market value of equity)/book value of assets	8,208	1.053	1.032	0.933	0.112	1.447
ECONDEVELOP	Log of GDP per capita	8,208	3.096	3.574	1.170	−0.858	4.024
GDPVOL	The standard deviation of the logarithm of real yearly GDP growth based of five moving years of data	8,208	2.643	2.700	2.972	−6.300	10.000

the risk-return implications of a growth in absolute size are clearly different from those produced by an increase in systemic size. Similar to SYSTEMIC-SIZE, no a priori expectations are held regarding the sign of the effect of SIZE on default risk.

Bank asset structure is captured via the loan-to-asset ratio (LOANS). Baele, De Jonghe, and Vander Vennet (2007) show that European banks with larger loan-to-asset ratios are less exposed to market-wide volatility and, therefore, a positive sign is expected on LOANS. DIVERSIFICATION controls for the degree of income diversification, measured as 1 minus a Herfindahl index of bank income concentration based on (i) net interest income, (ii) fees and commissions, (iii) trading, and (iv) other operating income. Previous work has shown that diversification away from traditional interest-based activities will result in banks relying on more volatile income streams (DeYoung and Roland, 2001; Stiroh and Rumble, 2006) and that income diversification exposes banks to more systemic risk (De Jonghe, 2010; Brunnermeier, Dong, and Palia, 2012).

However, theoretical and empirical work has also demonstrated that it will become increasingly difficult for shareholders to monitor managers as the complexity of a firm increases (see Scharfstein and Stein, 2000; Goetz, Laeven, and Levine, 2011). Since Laeven and Levine (2009) have shown that bank risk-taking increases with the power of shareholders within the corporate governance structure of a bank, diversified banks may take on less risk than less diversified banks. No expectation is held regarding the impact of DIVERSIFICATION on bank risk-taking.

The payoff structure of bank equity, which combines unlimited upside with limited downside potential, is akin to that of a call option. When the share of loss-absorbing equity to total assets is low, shareholders will optimize the option value by taking on risk at the expense of debt holders and regulators (Bhattacharya and Thakor, 1993). The expectation is that the higher the amount of equity on a bank's balance sheet, the lower the incentives for banks to engage in risk-shifting behaviour in the interest of shareholders. EQUITY is measured via the equity-to-asset ratio and is expected to enter with a positive coefficient in the regression models.

Bank performance is controlled by using the ratio of net income to total assets (ROA). Bank profitability and default risk may be linked in two ways. On the one hand, higher profitability enables banks to retain earnings, build up capital, and lower risk (i.e. increase DD). On the other hand, higher profitability may be achieved on the basis of higher bank risk-taking (and, thus, be linked to lower DD).

TOBINQ, which is measured as the quasi-market value of assets (the sum of the book value of liabilities and the market value of equity divided by the book value of assets), controls for the future growth prospects of a bank. Growth prospects may act as a deterrent against risk-taking when banks seek to preserve their charter values through lower risk-taking (Keeley, 1990; Park and Peristiani, 2007). TOBINQ is expected to exercise a positive influence on DD.

Finally, and following Laeven and Levine (2009), the model also controls for the level of economic development (ECONDEVELOP; defined as the logarithmic transformation of GDP per capita) and the volatility of economic growth (GDPVOL; defined as the standard deviation of the logarithm of real yearly GDP growth computed over a five-year rolling interval). Banks operating in high-income countries are likely to operate under a stronger institutional and regulatory framework and such a framework may be more effective in monitoring, and potentially limiting, the risk-taking strategies of banks (Laeven and Levine, 2009). On the other hand, high-income countries, because they tend to be in a stronger position to finance bank bailouts, offer more credible bailout guarantees than low-income countries, and this could spur bank risk-taking. As far as GDPVOL is concerned, economic volatility may either increase banks' exposure to macro shocks or, alternatively, cause banks to implement more prudent risk-taking strategies in anticipation of macroeconomic risks. Therefore, no a priori expectations are held with regard to the effect of ECONDEVELOP and GDPVOL on distance to default.

Systemic Size and Bank Default Risk

This section analyses the impact of systemic size on bank default risk, with an initial focus on the full sample period (1998 to 2010) for all banks and for European banks, before an evaluation of the risk-taking behaviour of systemically large banks during systemic crises.

Systemic Size and Bank Default Risk during 1998–2010

We start the analysis by testing whether a bank-level increase in systemic size is associated with a change in bank default risk during the full sample period. The analysis is initially conducted using a parsimonious within-specification based on few control variables. The model is then extended by progressively adding more controls.

Table 2.3 shows that, as banks grow in systemic size, they lower their distance to default (that is, they increase their default risk). In all specifications in Table 2.3, systemic size enters with a negative and statistically significant coefficient. This result also holds when the log of systemic size is used to control for skewness in the distribution of systemic size, when the model includes stand-alone bank size, excludes US banks, or includes country-fixed effects (instead of bank-fixed effects) in an Ordinary Least Squares (OLS) specification.[5]

In terms of control variables, the results are generally in line with expectations. For instance, distance to default is higher in banks with lower leverage, higher profitability, and greater growth prospects (as measured by Tobin's Q). Overall, the models estimated in Table 2.3 perform well in explaining the determinants of bank risk-taking (with adjusted R-squared values of around 50 per cent).

Table 2.4 repeats the analysis presented in Table 2.3 based on European banks. The results are only partially consistent with what we present for the larger cross-country sample of banks. As indicated by a lower distance to default in some models, systemically larger banks engage in more risk-taking,

[5] The OLS specification has also been estimated without the inclusion of country controls. This modification leaves the major conclusions unaffected.

Table 2.3. Are Systemically Large Banks More Risky?

	(1)	(2)	(3)	(4)	(5)	(6)	(7)	(8)
		Log transf.	+ TOBINQ	+ Diversification	+ GDP volatility	+ Stand-alone size	Excl. US banks	OLS with country-fixed effects
SYSTEMICSIZE $_{t-1}$	−1.559***		−1.320***	−1.606***	−1.355***	−1.206***	−1.330**	−0.667**
	(3.44)		(2.98)	(3.49)	(2.97)	(2.68)	(2.57)	(1.98)
LN(SYSTEMICSIZE $_{t-1}$*)*		−0.205***						
		(2.65)						
SIZE $_{t-1}$						−0.119	−0.413***	
						(1.53)	(2.72)	
LOANS $_{t-1}$	−0.808**	−0.684**		−0.848***	−0.736**	−0.719**	−0.841*	−0.329
	(2.53)	(2.17)		(2.59)	(2.29)	(2.25)	(1.95)	(1.36)
DIVERSIFICATION $_{t-1}$				−0.301	−0.436*	−0.443*	0.002	0.049
				(1.23)	(1.81)	(1.85)	(0.01)	(0.26)
EQUITY $_{t-1}$	3.940***	4.003***	4.197***	3.962***	4.275***	4.194***	2.676*	4.363***
	(3.62)	(3.69)	(3.86)	(3.65)	(4.08)	(4.02)	(1.71)	(4.36)
ROA $_{t-1}$	26.920***	26.731***	24.773***	26.600***	22.422***	22.389***	7.985***	28.130***
	(11.64)	(11.60)	(10.61)	(11.42)	(9.54)	(9.52)	(2.99)	(11.03)
TOBINQ $_{t-1}$			1.186***		1.276***	1.193***	0.410	1.643***
			(2.83)		(3.25)	(3.00)	(0.82)	(4.53)
ECONDEVELOP $_t$	1.781***	1.705***	1.644***	1.783***	1.599***	1.716***	1.465***	1.482***
	(10.39)	(10.43)	(9.97)	(10.36)	(9.47)	(10.07)	(6.85)	(9.58)
GDPVOL $_t$					−10.217***	−10.062***	−10.815***	−9.688***
					(3.97)	(3.89)	(4.36)	(3.99)
Constant	−14.293***	−14.951***	−14.734***	−14.220***	−13.663***	−12.913***	−3.644*	−14.387***
	(8.64)	(9.26)	(8.90)	(8.55)	(8.12)	(7.06)	(1.81)	(8.83)
Observations	7,258	7,258	7,258	7,258	7,258	7,258	3,693	7,258
Bank-fixed Effects	Yes	Yes	Yes	Yes	Yes	Yes	Yes	Yes
Year-fixed Effects	Yes	Yes	Yes	Yes	Yes	Yes	Yes	Yes
Number of Banks	823	823	823	823	823	823	410	823
Adjusted R-squared	0.506	0.505	0.506	0.506	0.510	0.510	0.338	0.499

Table 2.3 shows the regression results on distance to default using the within estimator. t-statistics are reported in round brackets, standard errors have been corrected for heteroscedasticity and clustered at bank level. *SYSTEMICSIZE* is the ratio between bank total assets and country GDP; *SIZE* is the log of total assets; *LOANS* is the ratio between net loans and total assets; *DIVERSIFICATION* is equal to 1 minus a Herfindahl index of income concentration; *EQUITY* is the ratio between total equity and total assets; *ROA* is the ratio between net income and total assets; *TOBINQ* is the ratio between (book value of liabilities + market value of equity) divided by the book value of assets; *ECONDEVELOP* is the log of GDP per capita; *GDPVOL* is the five-year volatility of the real GDP growth rate.
* significant at 10%; ** significant at 5%; *** significant at 1%.

Table 2.4. Are Systemically Large Banks More Risky in Europe?

	(1)	(2)	(3)	(4)	(5)	(6)	(7)
		Log transf.	+ TOBINQ	+ Diversification	+ GDP volatility	+ Stand-alone size	OLS with country-fixed effects
SYSTEMICSIZE $_{t-1}$	−1.123*		−0.803	−1.104*	−1.103*	−0.420	−0.514
	(1.73)		(1.40)	(1.72)	(1.70)	(0.74)	(1.35)
LN(SYSTEMICSIZE $_{t-1}$*)*		−0.685**					
		(2.29)					
SIZE $_{t-1}$						−0.890***	
						(2.78)	
LOANS $_{t-1}$	−2.258*	−2.353**		−2.215*	−2.166*	−2.422**	1.557*
	(1.86)	(2.09)		(1.81)	(1.75)	(2.16)	(1.98)
DIVERSIFICATION $_{t-1}$				0.730	0.702	0.693	−0.524
				(0.91)	(0.89)	(0.92)	(0.89)
EQUITY $_{t-1}$	7.235*	5.223	6.031	7.218*	7.020*	4.783	4.106
	(1.78)	(1.31)	(1.53)	(1.78)	(1.74)	(1.30)	(1.34)
ROA $_{t-1}$	24.766**	26.536**	28.840**	24.358**	25.562**	30.205**	32.175***
	(2.40)	(2.48)	(2.20)	(2.40)	(2.09)	(2.51)	(3.16)
TOBINQ $_{t-1}$			−0.276		−0.423	−0.868	−1.175
			(0.27)		(0.40)	(0.76)	(1.30)
ECONDEVELOP $_{t}$	1.799	2.197**	0.523	1.839*	1.710	3.119**	−0.687
	(1.63)	(2.00)	(0.55)	(1.66)	(1.56)	(2.62)	(0.75)
GDPVOL $_{t}$					−5.210	−1.519	−10.495
					(0.44)	(0.13)	(0.88)
Constant	−13.583	−19.632*	−1.785	−14.337	−12.569	−10.885	10.833
	(1.27)	(1.79)	(0.18)	(1.33)	(1.14)	(1.09)	(1.22)
Observations	915	915	915	915	915	915	915
Bank-fixed Effects	Yes	Yes	Yes	Yes	Yes	Yes	Yes
Year-fixed Effects	Yes	Yes	Yes	Yes	Yes	Yes	Yes
Number of Banks	99	99	99	99	99	99	99
Adjusted R-squared	0.563	0.568	0.557	0.563	0.562	0.574	0.525

Table 2.4 shows the regression results on distance to default using the within estimator. t-statistics are reported in round brackets, standard errors have been corrected for heteroscedasticity and clustered at bank level. *SYSTEMICSIZE* is the ratio between bank total assets and country GDP; *SIZE* is the log of total assets; *LOANS* is the ratio between net loans and total assets; *DIVERSIFICATION* is equal to 1 minus a Herfindahl index of income concentration; *EQUITY* is the ratio between total equity and total assets; *ROA* is the ratio between net income and total assets; *TOBINQ* is the ratio between (book value of liabilities + market value of equity) divided by the book value of assets; *ECONDEVELOP* is the log of GDP per capita; *GDPVOL* is the five-year volatility of the real GDP growth rate.
* significant at 10%; ** significant at 5%; *** significant at 1%.

only in some specifications. Specifically, though the coefficient of SYSTEMICSIZE is negative under all regression models, it is significant at customary levels only in four out of seven specifications.

Prima Facie

The results discussed here show that banks become riskier as they grow in systemic importance. However, as demonstrated in the next section, this result is driven by the recent financial crisis.

Systemic Size, Bank Default Risk, and Systemic Crises

This section presents tests on whether systemic size causes European banks to be more risky during systemic banking crises. Based on stand-alone bank size, previous studies have established that larger banks are more exposed to systemic crises (De Jonghe, 2010; Beltratti and Stulz, 2012; Brunnermeier, Dong, and Palia, 2012).[6]

Systemically larger banks may be more exposed to a systemic crisis because of more aggressive risk-taking during the crisis. This could be the case if systemically large banks find it optimal to maximize the value of the safety net during periods of banking sector distress. The prospect of regulatory forbearance during a systemic crisis (see Acharya and Yorulmazer, 2007) permits banks to increase the value of their implicit claim on the financial safety net via more aggressive risk-taking. Since systemically larger banks will be the largest beneficiaries from regulatory forbearance (Brown and Dinç, 2011), systemically larger banks will be particularly prone to risk-shifting behaviour during the crisis. For this conjecture to hold in the context of the current study, systemically larger banks are expected to pursue more aggressive risk-taking during a crisis.

We test the conjecture that systemically larger banks maximize the value of the safety net during crisis periods by introducing interaction terms between a banking crisis indicator and the dependent variables in Tables 2.5 and 2.6. In Table 2.5, the models are estimated after adding a crisis indicator (GL_CRISIS), which equals one for all banks in 2008–9. Table 2.5 therefore examines the risk implications of the recent crisis, and the results show that systemically larger banks increased their risk-taking during 2008–9 (significant at 1 per cent). Table 2.6 examines the same conjecture (larger banks increased their risk-taking during the recent crisis) for European banks only.

[6] For instance, De Jonghe (2010) estimates the tail betas for European banks, and shows that shareholders in large banks are more likely to experience losses above those experienced by a European banking index during periods of adverse shocks to bank valuations.

Table 2.5. Are Systemically Large Banks More Risky during the Recent Crisis?

	(1)	(2)	(3)	(4)	(5)
Panel A: Regression Analysis					
SYSTEMICSIZE $_{t-1}$	−0.478	−0.394	−0.480	−0.263	0.235
	(1.05)	(0.82)	(0.94)	(0.56)	(0.46)
SYTEMICSIZE $_{t-1}$**GL_CRISIS*	−1.435***	−1.248***	−1.329***	−1.063***	−1.253***
	(7.85)	(6.55)	(6.47)	(4.74)	(5.18)
SIZE $_{t-1}$				−0.113	−0.461***
				(1.56)	(3.38)
SIZE $_{t-1}$* GL_CRISIS				−0.054*	−0.050
				(1.90)	(1.11)
LOANS $_{t-1}$	−0.356	−0.387	−0.965**	−0.391	−0.831**
	(1.14)	(1.23)	(2.30)	(1.26)	(2.01)
DIVERSIFICATION $_{t-1}$		−0.233	0.357	−0.267	0.329
		(0.89)	(1.05)	(1.02)	(0.99)
EQUITY $_{t-1}$	4.099***	5.287***	3.594**	5.422***	2.412
	(3.85)	(5.41)	(2.48)	(5.53)	(1.61)
ROA $_{t-1}$	29.005***	24.345***	10.325***	24.095***	10.336***
	(12.13)	(9.54)	(3.78)	(9.41)	(3.54)
TOBINQ $_{t-1}$		0.581	0.213	0.485	−0.058
		(1.40)	(0.40)	(1.16)	(0.11)
ECONDEVELOP $_{t}$	1.285***	1.326***	1.106***	1.453***	1.573***
	(7.40)	(7.35)	(5.87)	(7.93)	(7.19)
GDPVOL $_{t}$		−10.097***	−12.814***	−9.977***	−12.756***
		(3.98)	(5.27)	(3.92)	(5.18)
LOANS $_{t-1}$* GL_CRISIS	−0.795**	−0.866***	−0.522	−0.978***	−0.465
	(2.39)	(2.75)	(1.19)	(3.15)	(1.11)
DIVERSIFICATION $_{t-1}$* GL_CRISIS		−1.289***	−2.324***	−1.093***	−2.161***
		(4.35)	(5.62)	(3.60)	(5.40)
EQUITY $_{t-1}$* GL_CRISIS	−7.857***	−8.278***	−2.110	−9.110***	−3.117*
	(6.52)	(7.12)	(1.20)	(7.80)	(1.84)
ROA $_{t-1}$* GL_CRISIS	−11.685***	−8.721**	−7.788*	−7.810**	−4.407
	(3.29)	(2.52)	(1.65)	(2.25)	(0.90)
TOBINQ $_{t-1}$* GL_CRISIS		−0.396	−0.472	−0.434	−0.461
		(0.88)	(0.86)	(0.98)	(0.86)
ECONDEVELOP $_{t}$* GL_CRISIS	−0.468***	−0.550***	−0.356***	−0.539***	−0.333***
	(14.27)	(15.84)	(8.66)	(15.90)	(7.38)
GDPVOL $_{t}$* GL_CRISIS		49.514***	34.521***	51.115***	35.675***
		(12.62)	(8.78)	(12.69)	(9.04)
Constant	−9.791***	−10.667***	−6.995***	−10.088***	−3.580*
	(5.86)	(6.01)	(4.20)	(5.41)	(1.78)
Observations	7,258	7,258	3,693	7,258	3,693
Bank-fixed Effects	Yes	Yes	Yes	Yes	Yes
Year-fixed Effects	Yes	Yes	Yes	Yes	Yes
Incl. US Banks?	Yes	Yes	No	Yes	No
Number of Banks	823	823	410	823	410
Adjusted R-squared	0.536	0.550	0.393	0.551	0.398
Panel B: Impact of Systemic Size on Distance to Default during the Recent Crisis					
SYTEMICSIZE $_{t-1}$ + SYTEMICSIZE $_{t-1}$* GL_CRISIS	−1.914***	−1.642***	−1.808***	−1.326***	−1.019*
	(4.24)	(3.44)	(3.37)	(2.69)	(1.81)

Panel A shows the regression results on distance to default using the within estimator. t-statistics are reported in round brackets, standard errors have been corrected for heteroscedasticity and clustered at bank level. *SYSTEMICSIZE* is the ratio between bank total assets and country GDP; *SIZE* is the log of total assets; *LOANS* is the ratio between net loans and total assets; *DIVERSIFICATION* is equal to 1 minus the Herfindahl index of income concentration; *EQUITY* is the ratio between total equity and total assets; *ROA* is the ratio between net income and total assets; *TOBINQ* is the ratio between the quasi-market value of assets and the book value of assets; *ECONDEVELOP* is the log of GDP per capita; *GDPVOL* is the five-year volatility of the real GDP growth rate. Panel B shows the marginal effect of systemic size on distance to default during the recent crisis.

* significant at 10%; ** significant at 5%; *** significant at 1%.

Table 2.6. Are Systemically Large Banks More Risky in Europe during the Recent Crisis?

	(1)	(2)	(3)
Panel A: Regression Analysis			
SYSTEMICSIZE $_{t-1}$	−0.574	−0.353	0.594
	(0.89)	(0.55)	(1.06)
SYTEMICSIZE $_{t-1}$**GL_CRISIS*	−0.860**	−0.906**	−1.079**
	(2.18)	(2.42)	(2.12)
SIZE $_{t-1}$			−1.039***
			(3.29)
SIZE $_{t-1}$* GL_CRISIS			−0.028
			(0.23)
LOANS $_{t-1}$	−2.327**	−2.184*	−2.584**
	(2.02)	(1.88)	(2.46)
DIVERSIFICATION $_{t-1}$		1.225	1.231
		(1.14)	(1.22)
EQUITY $_{t-1}$	5.559	5.805	3.665
	(1.39)	(1.44)	(0.99)
ROA $_{t-1}$	32.424***	34.196**	36.433**
	(2.68)	(2.18)	(2.49)
TOBINQ $_{t-1}$		−0.925	−1.416
		(0.85)	(1.19)
ECONDEVELOP $_t$	1.494	1.315	2.884**
	(1.30)	(1.11)	(2.29)
GDPVOL $_t$		3.976	5.930
		(0.30)	(0.45)
LOANS $_{t-1}$* GL_CRISIS	0.077	−0.730	−0.523
	(0.09)	(0.77)	(0.68)
DIVERSIFICATION $_{t-1}$* GL_CRISIS		−3.796**	−3.824***
		(2.29)	(2.64)
EQUITY $_{t-1}$* GL_CRISIS	2.074	−1.061	−2.796
	(0.55)	(0.26)	(0.64)
ROA $_{t-1}$* GL_CRISIS	−19.857	−21.191	−15.636
	(1.55)	(1.50)	(1.15)
TOBINQ $_{t-1}$* GL_CRISIS		2.706***	2.929***
		(2.73)	(3.10)
ECONDEVELOP $_t$* GL_CRISIS	−0.333	−0.365	−0.339
	(0.80)	(0.87)	(0.85)
GDPVOL $_t$* GL_CRISIS		−26.253*	−20.863
		(1.78)	(1.49)
	−10.560	−8.501	−5.797
Constant	(0.94)	(0.70)	(0.53)
	915	915	915
Observations	99	99	99
Bank-fixed Effects	Yes	Yes	Yes
Year-fixed Effects	Yes	Yes	Yes
Number of Banks	99	99	99
Adjusted R-squared	0.569	0.574	0.590
Panel B: Impact of Systemic Size on Distance to Default during the Recent Crisis			
SYTEMICSIZE t-1 + SYTEMICSIZE t-1* GL_CRISIS	−1.434*	−1.259	−0.485
	(1.79)	(1.59)	(0.63)

Panel A shows the regression results on distance to default using the within estimator. t-statistics are reported in round brackets, standard errors have been corrected for heteroscedasticity and clustered at bank level. *SYSTEMICSIZE* is the ratio between bank total assets and country GDP; *SIZE* is the log of total assets; *LOANS* is the ratio between net loans and total assets; *DIVERSIFICATION* is equal to 1 minus the Herfindahl index of income concentration; *EQUITY* is the ratio between total equity and total assets; *ROA* is the ratio between net income and total assets; *TOBINQ* is the ratio between the quasi-market value of assets and the book value of assets; *ECONDEVELOP* is the log of GDP per capita; *GDPVOL* is the five-year volatility of the real GDP growth rate. Panel B shows the marginal effect of systemic size on distance to default during the recent crisis.

* significant at 10%; ** significant at 5%; *** significant at 1%.

In both Table 2.5 and Table 2.6 the coefficient on systemic size is no longer significant at customary levels once the interaction with GL_CRISIS is included in the analysis. However, only in the case of full sample analysis is there strong evidence of a risk-increasing effect of systemic size during the global crisis.

Next, a fairly conservative empirical strategy is used to rule out the idea that crises, other than the recent crisis, have caused systemically large banks to engage in additional risk-taking. Table 2.7 first examines the risk-taking implications linked to other domestic, and then to other regional, financial crises. To examine the effects of a domestic crisis, columns (1) and (2) are based on banks which are listed in countries that have experienced a financial crisis prior to 2008 (as identified in Laeven and Valencia, 2008). The binary variable D_CRISIS equals one for any country–year combination, which Laeven and Valencia (2008) identify as coinciding with a systemic crisis.[7] This approach is akin to focusing on domestic financial crises, since it involves computing the risk implications of a financial crisis only when banks are based in a country which has been affected by that crisis.

Columns (3) and (4) of Table 2.7 examine the risk implications of a regionally defined financial crisis (R_CRISIS). The results reported in these columns focus on South-East Asian economies, which Laeven and Valencia (2008) identify as having experienced six financial crises between 1998 and 2001.[8] This empirical approach is akin to analysing the effect of a regional crisis on bank risk-taking, since the analysis is conducted without stipulating that each of the countries contained in the subsample of Asian countries experienced a crisis during the sample period.

Table 2.7 shows that systemically larger banks did not take on additional risk during either domestic or regional banking crises. Jointly, the results show that systemic size is associated with increased bank risk-taking during the recent crisis, but not during other financial crises.

The additional risk-taking of systemically larger banks can also be detected in the subsample of European banks. The fact that additional risk-taking linked to systemic size can only be detected during the recent crisis is an important result. Evidently, the findings based on the recent crisis cannot be applied to financial crises more generally.

[7] The countries affected include Argentina (2001–3), Colombia (1998–2000), Czech Republic (1998–2000), Indonesia (1998–2001), Japan (1998–2001), Malaysia (1998–9), Philippines (1998–2001), Slovakia (1998–2002), Thailand (1998–2000), and Turkey (2000–1).

[8] The sample of Asian countries includes China, Hong Kong, Korea, Indonesia, Japan, Malaysia, the Philippines, Singapore, Taiwan, and Thailand.

Table 2.7. Systemic Bank Size and Risk during Domestic and Regional Banking Crises, 1998–2007

	'Domestic' Banking Crisis (CRISIS = D_CRISIS)		'Regional' Banking Crisis (CRISIS = R_CRISIS)	
	(1)	(2)	(3)	(4)
SYSTEMICSIZE $_{t-1}$	4.146	2.216	1.994	0.928
	(1.62)	(0.75)	(1.46)	(0.59)
SYTEMICSIZE $_{t-1}$* *CRISIS*	−0.187	−3.641	−0.675	−1.691
	(0.07)	(1.35)	(0.74)	(1.31)
SIZE $_{t-1}$		0.139		0.211
		(0.39)		(0.90)
SIZE $_{t-1}$* CRISIS		0.297*		0.175
		(1.82)		(1.56)
LOANS $_{t-1}$	−0.750	−1.040	−1.166	−1.287*
	(1.09)	(1.52)	(1.58)	(1.71)
DIVERSIFICATION $_{t-1}$	0.066	0.253	−0.283	−0.053
	(0.11)	(0.43)	(0.43)	(0.08)
EQUITY $_{t-1}$	8.481***	8.561***	7.195**	7.739**
	(3.29)	(3.23)	(2.37)	(2.50)
ROA $_{t-1}$	5.469	4.874	9.606	9.648
	(1.24)	(1.13)	(1.61)	(1.64)
TOBINQ $_{t-1}$	2.142**	2.251**	4.537***	4.838***
	(2.44)	(2.55)	(3.53)	(3.63)
ECONDEVELOP $_t$	1.646***	1.649***	1.261***	1.040**
	(5.74)	(3.71)	(3.14)	(2.43)
GDPVOL $_t$	0.705	1.483	−4.795	−5.753
	(0.20)	(0.47)	(1.21)	(1.45)
CRISIS	6.325**	3.878		
	(2.05)	(1.06)		
LOANS $_{t-1}$* CRISIS	2.327**	2.754***	1.212	1.369*
	(2.40)	(2.81)	(1.55)	(1.74)
DIVERSIFICATION $_{t-1}$* CRISIS	−1.694*	−2.357**	−0.949	−1.497*
	(1.79)	(2.52)	(1.22)	(1.87)
EQUITY $_{t-1}$* CRISIS	−5.159	−5.269	−8.172***	−6.213**
	(1.49)	(1.49)	(4.11)	(2.52)
ROA $_{t-1}$* CRISIS	4.302	4.738	−6.397	−6.992
	(0.63)	(0.70)	(0.92)	(1.01)
TOBINQ $_{t-1}$*CRISIS	−2.284	−2.767*	−3.032**	−3.117**
	(1.57)	(1.89)	(2.11)	(2.10)
ECONDEVELOP $_t$*CRISIS	−0.402**	−0.625***	−0.309***	−0.360***
	(2.17)	(2.78)	(3.99)	(4.24)
GDPVOL $_t$* CRISIS	−13.236*	−6.399	−6.475	−1.246
	(1.83)	(0.77)	(1.25)	(0.20)
Constant	−16.350***	−18.671***	−13.896***	−15.547***
	(5.37)	(5.02)	(3.59)	(3.45)
Observations	870	870	1069	1069
Bank-fixed Effects	Yes	Yes	Yes	Yes
Year-fixed Effects	Yes	Yes	Yes	Yes
Number of Banks	111	111	138	138
Adjusted R-squared	0.293	0.298	0.329	0.331

Table 2.7 shows the regression results on distance to default using the within estimator. t-statistics are reported in round brackets, standard errors have been corrected for heteroscedasticity and clustered at bank level. Columns (1) and (2) refer to countries which experienced a banking crisis before the recent crisis (2008–9) as identified by Laeven and Valencia (2008). CRISIS is defined as 1 if a country is facing a banking crisis in a given year (zero otherwise). Columns (3) and (4) are based on Asian banks and use data from 1998–2001, a period in which several Asian countries were affected by banking crises. *SYSTEMICSIZE* is the ratio between bank total assets and country GDP; *SIZE* is the log of total assets; *LOANS* is the ratio between net loans and total assets; *DIVERSIFICATION* is equal to 1 minus a Herfindahl index of income concentration; *EQUITY* is the ratio between total equity and total assets; *ROA* is the ratio between net income and total assets; *TOBINQ* is the ratio between the quasi-market value of assets and the book value of assets; *ECONDEVELOP* is the log of GDP per capita; *GDPVOL* is the five-year volatility of the real GDP growth rate; *CRISIS* is defined in columns (1) and (2) as D_CRISIS, that is, a dummy variable which is equal to 1 in a given country and year if a country experienced a banking crisis during the period between 1998 and 2007. The list of countries employed in the first two columns includes Argentina, Colombia, Czech Republic, Indonesia, Japan, Malaysia, Philippines, Slovakia, Thailand, Turkey. In columns (3) and (4), the sample is limited to Asian countries and CRISIS is R_CRISIS, defined as a regional variable equal to 1 for the period 1998–2001.
* significant at 10%; ** significant at 5%; *** significant at 1%.

Conclusions

Banks have rapidly grown in systemic size over recent decades. For an increasing number of banks, the book value of their assets now exceeds the GDP of the economy in which they are charted. The increase in systemic size raises a number of important issues with regard to the risk-taking behaviour of banks. It is a frequently raised concern that systemic size tempts banks to maximize the value of the financial safety net by taking on more risk. The performance of many of the systemically largest banks during the recent crisis has not dispelled such concerns. Many of the systemically largest banks were forced to turn to taxpayers to fund their recapitalization efforts to some extent during the crisis.

The results presented in this chapter demonstrate that during the recent crisis bank default risk has increased with systemic size. However, this result only holds when the analysis is conducted for the full sample, while no clear evidence emerges for the subsample of European banks. Furthermore, in the full sample systemic size has not increased bank default risk during previous crises, and there is no general risk-increasing effect linked to systemic size during non-crisis periods. Our main conclusion, therefore, is that with the exception of the recent crisis, banks do not take on additional risk as they grow in systemic size.

Our results give little justification for subjecting systemically large banks to stricter and time-invariant capital requirements than less systemically large banks (as, for instance, envisaged under Basel III via the higher capital requirements applied to GSIBs). While the results show that systemically large banks which were highly leveraged exploited the financial safety net through more aggressive risk-taking during the recent crisis, the results also show that the same is not true during earlier financial crises. Thus, there is no evidence, outside the recent crisis, that less leverage has mitigated against risk-shifting incentives for systemically large banks.

Therefore, subjecting systemically large banks to tougher leverage restrictions on a permanent basis, when additional equity is risk-relevant only under rare crisis events, does not appear warranted on the basis of the findings reported here. Instead, the results support the view that systemically large banks should issue hybrid securities such as contingent convertibles ('CoCos'), which convert into equity in the event of a systemic crisis. Flannery (2005) and Kashyap, Rajan, and Stein (2008) outline various proposals of how contingent capital can be employed in the banking industry to increase the resilience of banks during systemic crises. The current results contribute to this debate by demonstrating that contingent capital will be particularly effective in reducing bank risk-taking during a crisis when issued by systemically large banks.

3

Increases in Size and Bank Default Risk: Evidence from European Bank Mergers

Introduction and Literature Review

The purpose of this chapter is to analyse the default risk effects of mergers and acquisitions (M&A) on a sample of European bidding banks. In the past two decades, consecutive waves of consolidation have transformed the European banking industry. M&A has widened the scale and scope of banking firms and led to a sharp increase in concentration levels in most banking markets. Recently, this asset consolidation process has been given further impetus by the financial crisis, which emphasized the role of acquisitions as a means to prevent bank failures and costly bank bailouts by policymakers (see Group of Thirty, 2009). However, whether bank mergers are effective in reducing default risk and contribute to a more stable banking sector remains an open question.

Previous work on risk-taking and bank mergers does not analyse default risk, but relies instead on accounting (e.g. z-scores) or equity-based indicators of risk (which estimate a market model to decompose bank stock returns into systematic and idiosyncratic risk). However, equity-based measures of banking risk are unable to provide a direct assessment of default likelihood, and accounting measures of risk have little power to predict distress for US banks (Evanoff and Wall, 2001; IMF, 2009c). The analysis presented in this chapter, by contrast, estimates the changes in default risk around bank mergers based on a Merton distance-to-default (DD) model, which draws on both accounting and market data. The key advantage of this method is that it implicitly captures a bank's expected returns via the inclusion of the market value of assets. Gropp, Vesala, and Vulpes (2006) show that DD scores are an appropriate indicator of bank fragility for European banks that outperform pure market measures of risk, such as subordinated bond spreads, over most time horizons.

Risk considerations may be linked to merger strategies with different outcomes for the riskiness of the resulting institution. Two themes surface in the literature on the risk implications of bank M&A. Consolidation delivers diversification effects (and reduces risk) or, alternatively, the risk effects of consolidation are shaped by regulatory incentives (which may encourage increases in risk). As regards risk diversification strategies behind M&A, a number of simulation studies estimate the diversification potential of bank M&A. These studies report that bank M&A lowers the default probability of US institutions as a result of portfolio diversification (Emmons, Gilbert, and Yeager, 2004), geographic diversification (Hughes et al., 1999), and activity diversification (e.g. through mergers between banking and insurance firms (Boyd, Graham, and Hewitt, 1993; Estrella, 2001; Van Lelyveld and Knot, 2009). However, the results of simulation studies should be interpreted with care, because they disregard the organizational complexity, operational inefficiencies, and changes in bank strategy associated with acquisitions (Hughes et al., 1999; Knapp, Gart, and Becher, 2005). Akhavein, Berger, and Humphrey (1997) show that geographic diversification may leave the overall level of risk unaffected if banks—against the background of a more diversified loan portfolio—sharply increase lending in the post-merger period.[1]

Consistent with the argument that mergers are complex and their risk effects uncertain ex ante, studies that focus on the realized risk diversification effects of US bank mergers have produced mixed findings. While Mishra, Prakash, and Peterson (2005) find merger-related synergies reduce both total and idiosyncratic risk for US bank acquirers and Chionsini, Foglia, and Marullo-Reedtz (2003) show that bank M&A reduces the credit risk exposure of Italian banks, other studies question the relevance of risk diversification as a major force behind bank mergers. Amihud, DeLong, and Saunders (2002) find that cross-border bank mergers do not reduce the market risk of acquiring banks. Similar results are found by Craig and dos Santos (1997) for US bank mergers on the basis of accounting-based measures of risk. In a related study, Craig and dos Santos (1996) provide further evidence against risk

[1] The extent to which diversification in banking is associated with measurable risk-reduction benefits remains debated. It appears that, if they exist at all, risk-reduction benefits from diversification are small. For a sample of Italian banks, Acharya, Hasan, and Saunders (2006) find that only risky banks benefit from loan diversification and achieve lower risk. Other European studies show that more diversified banking activities do not lead to risk-reduction benefits (Baele, De Jonghe, and Vander Vennet, 2007; Mercieca, Schaeck, and Wolfe, 2007; Lepetit et al., 2008). At a macro level, Wagner (2008) suggests that diversification—by lowering banks' need for outside liquidity—encourages risk-taking and, because it exposes banks to similar type risks, discourages the provision of liquidity to other institutions. Diversification may, thus, increase the likelihood of a systemic crisis.

diversification as a motive for mergers by showing that acquired banks tend to be transformed post-M&A to resemble the strategic features of the acquiring institution.

Next to diversification effects, regulatory regimes may also give rise to a risk-related motive behind bank M&A. Elyasiani and Jia (2008) point out that banks with a high default risk face increased scrutiny by regulators and are more likely to be subjected to regulatory intervention. In cases where institutional failure appears imminent, regulators may even intervene and engineer deals (see Koetter et al., 2007). Further, stricter regulatory regimes may generally be more effective in containing risk-taking in the context of mergers. Buch and DeLong (2008) show, for a sample of cross-border mergers, that deals lead to a reduction in return variability (total risk) if the regulatory regime in the home market is stricter than the target bank regime.

The operation of bank bailout policies and deposit insurance schemes also give rise to well-defined moral hazard problems in the context of M&A and may lead to a merger-related increase in default risk. For instance, underpriced deposit insurance schemes may encourage banks to enhance their deposit subsidy through mergers that increase the risk and size of an institution, with the purpose of becoming too big to fail (John, John, and Senbet, 1991). However, the empirical evidence that banks use mergers for regulatory arbitrage or to extract deposit insurance benefits has hitherto been weak (Benston, Hunter, and Wall, 1995; Buch and DeLong, 2008).[2]

The Default Risk Implications of M&A—A New Empirical Analysis

In the rest of the chapter we analyse the default risk implications of M&A on acquiring banks from Europe. We start by showing that the average European bank merger does not affect the default risk of the acquirer. Next, we show this result also holds for merger types which offer the a priori largest scope for risk-related diversification benefits (i.e. cross-border and product-diversifying M&A). By contrast, relatively safe bidders increase their default risk in the post-merger period. Further, the possibility of merger-related increases in risk is particularly pronounced for relatively safe banks when deals are diversifying and/or completed under a bank regulatory regime, in the country of the biding bank, which is relatively weak.

[2] Benston, Hunter, and Wall (1995) examine takeover premiums in the US banking industry in the 1980s. The authors report that takeover premiums reflect a target's potential earning diversification over the ability of the merged institution to extract gains from deposit insurance.

Data and Methodology

Merger Sample

The sample of bank M&A is obtained from Thomson Financial (SDC Platinum). The selected mergers are announced and completed between 1992 and 2007 and involve bidders located in the European Union (EU-15), Norway, and Switzerland. Bidding firms are commercial banks, bank holding companies, and credit institutions, while targets may also be insurance companies (life and accident) and mortgage banks, as well as security brokers. Further, bidding banks are listed with equity returns available on Datastream and accounting data on Worldscope.

From an initial sample of 197 bank mergers, we drop deals due to one of the following reasons. In order to avoid confounding events, there need to be at least 180 trading days between separate merger announcements and not more than one deal pending until 180 days following completion of a deal by the same bank. As a result of this criterion, we lose fifty-four deals. We then verified the deal characteristics from SDC (announcement date, deal value) against news articles from various sources on LexisNexis. Inconsistencies between the data obtained from Thomson Financial and the press coverage of individual transactions were corrected or, if left unresolved, deals were omitted from our sample. Uncertainty over deal characteristics led to the omission of nine deals. Finally, while none of the remaining banks are failing banks, we ensured our sample did not contain mergers where the target was a failing bank, as indicated by either SDC or the press coverage surrounding a deal.

We do not stipulate a minimum size requirement. This is because we aim to examine the risk effects of the entire population of European bank mergers for which market and accounting data are available. Further, the vast majority of deals we include in our sample are sufficiently large to expect a measurable impact on the riskiness of the acquiring institution. In our sample, average relative size (measured as the ratio of deal value to the market value of the bidder) stands at 44 per cent. However, to ensure our results are not sensitive to the relative size of a merger, we also perform the analysis using minimum relative size requirements of 5 per cent (which reduces the sample size n by 33 to 101) and 10 per cent ($n = 87$). The results of our analysis are invariant to the imposition of these relative size requirements. Both the univariate tests and regression models yield qualitatively identical results to those reported below. We return to this in the robustness section.

The resulting dataset is described in Table 3.1. The sample consists of 134 acquisitions with bidders mainly operating in Italy (30), the UK (16), and Spain (14). In addition, the majority of the sampled deals (70) was announced over the period 1997–2001. It is worth emphasizing that the consolidation of bank

Table 3.1. Overview of M&A Sample

Panel A: Distribution of M&A by year

	Number of Mergers		Total Value		Average Value
	n	%	Mill USD	%	Mill USD
1992	3	2.24	417.33	0.08	139.11
1993	2	1.49	388.37	0.07	194.18
1994	4	2.99	6,780.94	1.22	1,695.23
1995	8	5.97	4,675.02	0.84	584.38
1996	8	5.97	8,123.31	1.47	1,015.41
1997	13	9.70	71,524.06	12.91	5,501.85
1998	13	9.70	63,687.18	11.50	4,899.01
1999	17	12.69	120,615.57	21.77	7,095.03
2000	16	11.94	61,570.94	11.12	3,848.18
2001	11	8.21	45,150.49	8.15	4,104.59
2002	5	3.73	2,912.14	0.53	582.43
2003	3	2.24	4,848.20	0.88	1,616.07
2004	4	2.99	24,473.13	4.42	6,118.28
2005	9	6.72	35,994.10	6.50	3,999.34
2006	12	8.96	62,154.68	11.22	5,179.56
2007	6	4.48	40,620.48	7.33	6,770.08
Total	134	100.00	553,935.94	100.00	

Panel B: Geographic Distribution

Acquirer Nation	Target Nation																	
	AU	BE	DE	FI	FR	GE	GR	IR	IT	NE	NO	PT	SP	SW	ST	UK	Others	Total
Austria (AU)	1																4	5
Belgium (BE)		2								2								4
Denmark (DE)			3								1							4
Finland (FI)				2														2
France (FR)					5				1								4	10
Germany (GE)	2	1			1	4											3	11
Greece (GR)							5										4	9
Ireland (IR)								1								1		2
Italy (IT)						1			28								1	30
Luxembourg													2					2
Netherlands (NE)		1							1	2							4	8
Norway (NO)											3							3
Portugal (PT)												5					1	6
Spain (SP)												1	6			1	6	14
Sweden (SW)				1										2			1	4
Switzerland (ST)															3		1	4
United Kingdom (UK)					1											7	8	16
Total	3	4	3	3	7	5	5	1	30	4	4	6	8	2	3	9	37	134

Deal values are in constant 2007-USD terms based on the Consumer Price Index (All Urban Consumers).

assets in a number of European economies has chiefly involved non-listed public sector and cooperative institutions (Hernando, Nieto, and Wall, 2009), which face increasing pressures to consolidate as a result of declines in government ownership or the phasing out of public guarantees of their liabilities.

Methodology: Merger-Related Changes in Default Risk

To estimate merger-related changes in the default risk of bidding banks, we apply the Merton distance-to-default (DD) model as in Akhigbe, Madura, and Martin (2007) and Gropp, Vesala, and Vulpes (2006). Default risk is measured as the number of standard deviations that the market value of bank assets are above the default point (the point where the market value of assets is less than the book value of total liabilities). Formally, DD on day *t* is expressed as:

$$DD_t = \frac{\ln\,(V_{A,t}/L_t) + (r_f - 0.5\sigma_{A,t}^2)T}{\sigma_{A,t}\sqrt{T}} \tag{1}$$

where $V_{A,t}$ is the market value of assets, L_t is the book value of total liabilities, r_f is the risk-free rate (proxied by the annualized yield on two-year government bonds in the bidding bank's country), $\sigma_{A,t}$ is the annualized asset volatility at *t*, and T is the time to maturity (conventionally set to one year).[3,4]

The computation of DD_t requires estimates of $V_{A,t}$ and $\sigma_{A,t}$ neither of which is directly observable. Following Akhigbe, Madura, and Martin (2007), Vassalou and Xing (2004), and Hillegeist and colleagues (2004), we infer the values of $V_{A,t}$ and $\sigma_{A,t}$ through an iterative process based on the Black–Scholes–Merton pricing model. Specifically, we express the market value of a firm's equity ($V_{E,t}$) as a function of the asset value by solving the following system of nonlinear equations:

$$V_{E,t} = V_{A,t}N(d_{1,t}) - X_t e^{-r_f T} N(d_{2,t}) \tag{2}$$

$$\sigma_{E,t} = \left(\frac{V_{A,t}}{V_{E,t}}\right) N(d_{1,t})\sigma_{A,t} \tag{3}$$

Equation (2) defines $V_{E,t}$ as a call option on the market value of the bidder's total assets, with $d_{1,t} = \frac{\ln\,(V_{A,t}/L_t)+(r_{f_t}+0.5\sigma_{A,t}^2)T}{\sigma_{A,t}\sqrt{T}}$ and $d_{2,t} = d_{1,t} - \sigma_{A,t}\sqrt{T}$.

[3] In the case of Greece, due to the lack of data on the yield of two-year government bonds during the earlier part of the sample period, we proxy the risk-free rate using the one-year Greek Treasury Bill rate.

[4] Our results are qualitatively identical if we employ the annualized yield on two-year German government bonds as the risk-free rate for all deals rather than annualized two-year rates in the bidding bank's country.

Equation (3) is the optimal hedge equation that relates the standard deviation of a bidder's equity value to the standard deviation of the value of total assets (both on an annualized basis).

To solve this system of equations, we employ, as starting values for $\sigma_{A,t}$, the historical volatility of equity (computed daily on the basis of a 90-trading-day rolling window) multiplied by the ratio of the market value of equity, and the sum of the market value of equity and the book value of total liabilities, that is, $\sigma_{A,t} = \sigma_{E,t}V_{E,t}/(V_{E,t} + L_t)$. A Newton search algorithm identifies the daily values of $V_{A,t}$ and $\sigma_{A,t}$ in an iterative process which we then employ to compute DD_t, as in (1).

The merger-related change in bidder distance to default is the difference in mean DD before the merger (over a-180 days to a-11 days relative to the merger announcement date a) and mean DD after completion (over c + 11 days to c + 180 days following the completion date c). We choose this time window to reduce the level of noise inherent in DD and to ensure that our default risk predictions are based on accounting data that relate to the post-merger period.

We eliminate general industry and time trends in risk by computing a daily default risk index for each banking sector. For every deal, we compute a DD market index as the value-weighted DD of all banks listed on Datastream in the bidder's country that are not involved in M&A during the merger announcement and effective window.[5] We then subtract changes between the pre-merger and post-merger value in the market default index from changes in DD that acquirers realize over the same time period. The industry-adjusted change in distance to default ($\Delta IADD$) for bidding banks that is due to M&A can, thus, be expressed as:

$$\begin{aligned}\Delta IADD &= \overline{DD}_{(c+11;c+180)} - \overline{DD}_{(a-180;a-11)} - \Big(\overline{DD}_{index,(c+11;c+180)} \\ &\quad - \overline{DD}_{index,(a-180;a-11)}\Big) \\ &= \Delta DD_{bidder} - \Delta DD_{index} \qquad (4)\end{aligned}$$

Bank Mergers and Bidder Default Risk

Default Risk Changes by Deal Type

Bank mergers offer opportunities to realize size-related diversification gains through risk pooling as long as the asset returns of the banks

[5] Following the application of these index criteria, the number of constituent banks in Finland, Austria, and Luxembourg declined substantially, raising concerns about the ability of our index to accurately capture banking sector risk in these countries. As a result, we aggregate some countries based on their geographic proximity. We create a Scandinavian banking sector default risk index (Finland, Norway, and Sweden), a Benelux index (Luxembourg, Belgium, and the Netherlands), and a German–Austrian index.

involved in M&A are less than perfectly correlated (Craig and dos Santos, 1997; Emmons, Gilbert, and Yeager, 2004). To the extent that European bank consolidation enhances profitability through increased market power in the post-merger period (see Coccorese, 2009) as well as changes in the management of the assets of the combined institution, M&A may lower the default risk of bidding banks even further. In this section, we examine the default risk implications of European bank M&A in general as well as for specific types of deals. Overall, the results we present below are not consistent with bank M&A generating measurable default risk effects.

Table 3.2 reports the pre- and post-merger values for industry-adjusted distance to default (IADD) based on our sample of 134 bank mergers. The results show that before M&A, European bidding banks are riskier than their industry peers. Mean (median) industry-adjusted DD in the pre-merger period is −0.112 (−0.289) and median IADD is statistically different from zero (at the 1 per cent level). To analyse whether mergers impact default risk, we test if the mean (median) merger-related change in IADD is equal to zero. Although around half of all sample deals generate an increase in industry-adjusted DD (i.e. lower default risk), Table 3.2 shows that mergers do not produce a statistically significant reduction in the riskiness of acquiring banks. Consequently, the distance to default, on average, neither increases nor decreases in the post-merger period.

Next, we test if the risk effects of bank mergers vary by the type of deal undertaken. The potential for merger-related risk reductions is particularly pronounced for either geographically or activity-diversifying mergers, because both deal types have the potential to substantially lower the volatility of bank profits (Boyd, Graham, and Hewitt, 1993; Estrella, 2001). On the other hand, diversifying mergers may lead to increased organizational complexity and/or significant changes in post-merger strategy, which may thwart bidders from realizing risk benefits as a result of M&A.

Table 3.3 reports the distance-to-default effects of deals that can be classified as either cross-border or cross-industry (defined as deals where acquirer and the target do not share the same two-digit standard industrial classification [SIC] code) compared with deals that are domestic or activity-focusing. Panel A of Table 3.3 focuses on geographic diversification, while Panel B analyses the effect of product diversification on IADD. The results offer further evidence that European bank mergers have no effect on the acquirer's distance to default. Regardless of the increased potential for risk diversification exhibited by cross-border and cross-industry bank mergers, the mean (median) change in IADD is not statistically different from zero for either diversifying or focusing deals.

Finally, we examine if supervisory regimes influence the risk effects of bank M&A. Under weaker supervisory regimes, banks may increase their risk-taking

Table 3.2. Bank Mergers and Industry-Adjusted Distance to Default (IADD)

	N	Mean (t-stat)	Median (z-stat)	ΔIADD > 0	
				N	%
IADD: Pre-Merger (a−180, a −11)	134	−0.112 (−0.772)	−0.289*** (−2.688)		
IADD: Post-Merger (c + 11, c + 180)	134	−0.197 (−1.288)	−0.341*** (−3.363)		
ΔIADD	134	−0.107 (−0.857)	−0.030 (−0.734)	66	49.3

***(**;*) denotes significance at 1% (5%; 10%).
Table 3.2 reports mean (median) industry-adjusted distance to default (IADD) for a sample of acquiring banks. Distance to default before the merger is computed as the average of the distance to default over the period from −180 days to −11 days relative to the announcement date (a), while the distance to default after the merger is computed as the average distance to default over the period from + 11 days to + 180 days after the effective date (c). The change in the industry-adjusted distance to default is the difference between the post-effective date and the pre-announcement period IADD, winsorized at the 1 per cent level. The *t*-test (rank-test) evaluates if the mean (median), IADD, and ΔIADD are equal to zero.

via M&A in order to shift the risk of default to regulators (Amihud, DeLong, and Saunders 2002). This way, bidding banks could manage to extract economic benefits from regulatory guarantees through implicit or explicit bank bailout policies (Benston, Hunter, and Wall, 1995). More stringent bank regulators, by contrast, will be able to contain risk-taking in the context of bank mergers. Consistent with this, Buch and DeLong (2008) show that bidding bank shareholders that operate under a strict bank regulatory regime experience a reduction in the variance of equity returns following cross-border bank mergers.

To test for the effect of bank regulation on default risk, we employ the index of supervisory strength from the Barth, Caprio, and Levine (2004) database.[6] Higher values indicate environments in which regulators possess more powers to take action against undesirable behaviour by banks. Panel C of Table 3.3

[6] The index measures bank supervisory strength as the equal-weighted sum (incl. sub-questions) of the following questions (yes = 1; no = 0): (1) Does the supervisory agency have the right to meet with external auditors to discuss reports without the approval of the bank? (2) Are the auditors required to communicate misconduct by managers/directors to the supervisory agency? (3) Can legal action against external auditors be taken by supervisors for negligence? (4) Can supervisors force banks to change internal organizational structure? (5) Are off-balance sheet items disclosed to supervisors? (6) Can the supervisory agency order directors/management to constitute provisions to cover actual/potential losses? (7) Can the supervisory agency suspend a director's decision to distribute: a) dividends? b) bonuses? c) management fees? (8) Can the supervisory agency supersede bank shareholder rights and declare a bank insolvent? (9) Does banking law allow a supervisory agency to suspend some or all ownership rights of a problem bank? (10) Regarding bank restructuring and reorganization, can the supervisory agency or any other government agency do the following: a) suspend shareholder rights? b) remove and replace management? c) remove and replace directors? We obtain updated values on regulatory variables from the Worldbank website (http://go.worldbank.org/SNUSW978P0) and construct the index such that we use the prevailing index value in the bidding bank country during the year of the acquisition.

Table 3.3. Bank M&A on the Industry-Adjusted Distance to Default, by Deal Type

	N	Mean(t-stat)	Median(z-stat)	ΔIADD > 0	N	Mean (t-stat)	Median (z-stat)	ΔIADD > 0
Panel A: Geographic Diversification	Domestic				Cross-Border			
IADD: Pre-Merger (a−180, a−11)	79	0.034 (0.168)	−0.202 (−1.564)		55	−0.321 (−1.650)	−0.433** (−2.321)	
IADD: Post-Merger (c + 11, c + 180)	79	0.011 (0.047)	−0.284* (−1.916)		55	−0.538*** (−2.958)	−0.495*** (−3.021)	
ΔIADD	79	−0.060 (−0.346)	−0.040 (−0.542)	47%	55	−0.174 (−1.002)	0.067 (−0.536)	53%
Panel B: Product Diversification	Focusing				Diversifying			
IADD: Pre-Merger (a−180, a −11)	101	0.009 (0.051)	−0.290** (−2.285)		33	−0.480* (−1.946)	−0.287 (−1.599)	
IADD: Post- Merger (c + 11, c + 180)	101	−0.086 (−0.457)	−0.320** (−2.559)		33	−0.535** (−2.431)	−0.419** (−2.242)	
ΔIADD	101	−0.106 (−0.732)	−0.040 (−0.777)	50%	33	−0.110 (−0.440)	−0.023 (−0.116)	49%
Panel C: Supervisory Power	High Supervisory Power				Low Supervisory Power			
IADD: Pre-Merger (a−180, a−11)	56	−0.065 (−0.322)	−0.038 (−0.889)		76	−0.151 (−0.728)	−0.494** (−2.423)	
IADD: Post- Merger (c + 11, c + 180)	56	0.046 (0.195)	−0.180 (−0.702)		76	−0.395* (−1.934)	−0.517*** (−4.064)	
ΔIADD	56	0.045 (0.223)	0.063 (0.155)	54%	76	−0.234 (−1.445)	−0.073 (−1.165)	46%

***(**;*) denotes significance at 1% (5%; 10%).

Panel A reports the sample mean (median) of the industry-adjusted distance to default (IADD) for domestic and cross-border deals. Panel B reports the sample mean (median) of the same risk measures computed for focusing and diversified mergers. A merger is defined as product diversifying if bidder and target do not share the same two-digit SIC code. Panel C summarizes the same statistics for mergers realized in high and low supervisory power regimes, identified on the basis of the Supervisory Power Index from Barth, Caprio, and Levine (2004). For each bank, distance to default before the merger is computed as the average of the distance to default over the period from −180 days to −11 days from the announcement (a), while the distance to default after the merger is computed as the average of the distance to default over the period from + 11 days to + 180 days after the effective date (c). Changes in the industry-adjusted distance to default is the difference between the post-effective date and pre-announcement period IADD, winsorized at the 1 per cent level. The *t*-test (rank-test) evaluates if the mean (median) IADD and ΔIADD are equal to zero.

classifies regulatory regimes as having high (low) supervisory power for index values above (below) the sample median. The results show that the strength of the acquirer's regulator does not impact the riskiness of bank acquisitions. Stricter regulatory regimes are, thus, unable to prevent risk-taking in M&A.[7] It is interesting to note, however, that bidding banks in the low supervisory power group exhibit above-industry levels of risk as indicated by negative IADD values in the pre-merger period (median highly significant), while the same is not true for the subset of banks in the high supervisory power group. This may be interpreted as an indication that the industry-adjusted risk profile of bidding banks varies with the ability of bank supervisors to curb risky behaviour.

Pre-Merger Risk and Merger-Related Changes in Default Risk

Next, we examine whether the default risk exhibited by bidding banks prior to a deal determines the risk implications of M&A. Our rationale for expecting that the default risk implications of bank M&A vary with the level of pre-merger risk is based on Acharya, Hasan, and Saunders (2006) and Brewer (1989), who report that high-risk banks benefit disproportionately from diversification.

Table 3.4 ranks bidding banks into quartile portfolios according to their pre-merger IADD. The percentage of bidding banks with a positive change in IADD (i.e. that experience a reduction in default risk via M&A) declines rapidly across risk quartiles from 62 per cent for high-risk banks (Q1) to 27 per cent for low-risk banks (Q4). Critically, changes in IADD are negative in Q4 (significantly below 5 per cent according to both the *t*-test and the z-test). This indicates that only relatively safe banks experience an increase in default risk as a result of M&A.

The result—that low-risk banks experience a deterioration in default risk—could be due to it being unlikely that low-risk institutions realize further diversification benefits through mergers. The complexity of deals and difficulties in achieving sustainable gains from M&A are well-documented (see Hughes et al., 1999). Also, changes in post-M&A strategy may cause a risk increase, for example if the acquiring bank expands its loan book (Akhavein, Berger, and Humphrey, 1997). However, the results on pre-merger risk and deal-induced changes in IADD could equally be consistent with explanations

[7] For each panel in Table 3.3, we also test for differences in the mean (median) changes in IADD associated with different types of deals (i.e. domestic versus cross-border, activity-diversifying versus focus, and deals completed under high versus low supervisory power). We are unable to find that merger-related changes in distance to default differ by the type of deal considered. In order to conserve space, we do not report the results of these tests in Table 3.3.

Table 3.4. Merger-Related Changes in Industry-Adjusted Distance to Default, by Default Risk Quartiles

Industry-Adjusted Distance-to-Default Quartiles		N	Mean (t-stat)	Median (z-stat)	ΔIADD>0
Q1 LOW distance default (High-risk)	IADD: Pre-Merger (a−180, a−11)	34	−1.720*** (−13.040)	−1.538*** (−5.086)	
	IADD: Post-Merger (c + 11, c + 180)	34	−1.448*** (−8.577)	−1.261*** (−5.018)	
	ΔIADD	34	0.217 (0.989)	0.290 (1.410)	62%
Q2	IADD: Pre-Merger (a−180, a−11)	33	−0.609*** (18.413)	−0.526*** (−5.012)	
	IADD: Post-Merger (c + 11, c + 180)	33	−0.420* (−2.021)	−0.379*** (3.332)	
	ΔIADD	33	0.162 (0.816)	0.190 (0.545)	59%
Q3	IADD: Pre-Merger (a−180, a−11)	34	0.045 (1.372)	0.072 (1.308)	
	IADD: Post- Merger (c + 11, c + 180)	34	0.025 (0.161)	0.060 (0.077)	
	ΔIADD	34	−0.020 (−0.129)	−0.030 (−0.368)	47%
Q4 HIGH distance to default (Low-risk)	IADD: Pre-Merger (a−180, a−11)	33	1.881*** (5.533)	1.066*** (5.012)	
	IADD: Post-Merger (c + 11, c + 180)	33	1.087** (2.500)	0.468** (2.135)	
	ΔIADD	33	−0.799** (−2.248)	−0.789*** (−2.671)	27%

***(***) denotes significance at 1% (5%; 10%).
Table 3.4 reports mean (median) of industry-adjusted distance to default (IADD) for a sample of acquiring banks by pre-merger distance-to-default quartiles. Distance to default before the merger is computed as the average of the distance to default over the period from −180 days to −11 days from the announcement (a), while distance to default after the merger is computed as the average of the distance to default over the period from + 11 days to + 180 days after the effective date (c). Changes in industry-adjusted distance to default is the difference between the post-effective date and pre-event period IADD, winsorized at the 1 per cent level. The *t*-test (rank-test) evaluates if the mean (median) IADD and ΔIADD are equal to zero.

that emphasize either the diversification benefits or the regulatory incentives inherent in M&A. Thus, diversification benefits should be particularly associated with cross-border and activity-diversifying mergers in the high-risk quartile (and less so in the low-risk group). By contrast, if regulatory strength across the EU has an impact on the risk effects of M&A, then the prospect of regulatory intervention is likely to be highest for the riskiest institutions (see Elyasiani and Jia, 2008), showing that regulators are particularly effective in curbing risk-taking through mergers for this group of banks (and less so for the low-risk group).

Table 3.5 examines both the diversification hypothesis and the regulatory influence hypothesis. Panel A of Table 3.5 focuses on the risk effects of domestic and cross-border bank mergers for the high- and low-risk quartile

Table 3.5. Risk Classes, Diversification, and Changes in Industry-Adjusted Distance to Default

		N	Mean (t-stat)	Median (z-stat)	IADD > 0	N	Mean (t-stat)	Median (z-stat)	IADD > 0
Panel A: Geographic Diversification		Domestic				Cross-Border			
High-risk banks (Q1)	IADD: Pre-Merger	18	−1.641***	−1.271***		16	−1.808***	−1.689***	
	(a−180, a−11)		(−8.583)	(−3.724)			(−9.847)	(−3.516)	
	IADD: Post-Merger	18	−1.406***	−1.168***		16	−1.500***	−1.350***	
	(c + 11, c + 180)		(−4.965)	(−3.550)			(−8.522)	(−3.516)	
	ΔIADD	18	0.133	0.152	56%	16	0.312	0.336	69%
			(0.365)	(0.588)			(1.323)	(1.344)	
Low-risk banks (Q4)	IADD: Pre-Merger	18	2.381***	1.334***		15	1.282***	0.789***	
	(a−180, a−11)		(4.536)	(3.724)			(3.519)	(3.408)	
	IADD: Post-Merger	18	1.766	0.664**		15	0.272	0.426	
	(c + 11, c + 180)		(2.465)	(2.025)			(0.800)	(0.795)	
	ΔIADD	18	−0.624	−0.774*	28%	15	−1.001**	−0.789*	27%
			(−1.150)	(−1.677)			(−2.255)	(−1.931)	
Panel B: Product Diversification		Focusing				Diversifying			
High-risk banks (Q1)	IADD: Pre-Merger	23	−1.540***	−1.363***		11	−2.095***	−1.804***	
	(a−180, a−11)		(−11.657)	(−4.197)			(−7.584)	(−2.934)	
	IADD: Post-Merger	23	−1.425***	−1.252***		11	−1.497***	−1.271***	
	(c + 11, + 180)		(−7.701)	(−4.136)			(−4.102)	(−2.847)	
	ΔIADD	23	0.115	0.015	52%	11	0.430	0.472*	82%
			(0.522)	(0.547)			(0.842)	(1.867)	
Low-risk banks (Q4)	IADD: Pre-Merger	24	2.164***	1.142***		9	1.125***	1.066***	
	(a−180, a−11)		(4.785)	(4.286)			(6.736)	(2.666)	
	IADD: Post-Merger	24	1.505**	0.906**		9	−0.027	0.134	
	(c + 11, c + 180)		(2.667)	(2.286)			(−0.078)	(0.415)	
	ΔIADD	24	−0.667	−0.788*	33%	9	−1.152**	−0.943**	11%
			(−1.438)	(−1.722)			(−2.684)	(−2.429)	

(continued)

Table 3.5. Continued

		N	Mean (t-stat)	Median (z-stat)	IADD > 0	N	Mean (t-stat)	Median (z-stat)	IADD > 0
Panel C: Supervisory Power		High Supervisory Power				Low Supervisory Power			
High-risk banks (Q1)	IADD: Pre-Merger (a−180, a−11)	9	−2.126*** (−7.504))	−1.975*** (−2.666)		25	−1.574*** (−11.260)	−1.286*** (−4.372)	
	IADD: Post-Merger (c + 11, + 180)	9	−1.784*** (−5.546)	−1.570*** (−2.666)		25	−1.328*** (−6.757)	−1.167*** (−4.265)	
	ΔIADD	9	0.032 (0.057)	0.712 (0.652)	67%	25	0.284 (1.245)	0.288 (1.224)	60%
Low-risk banks (Q4)	IADD: Pre-Merger (a−180, a−11)	14	1.547*** (3.287)	0.831*** (3.296)		18	2.198*** (4.373)	1.334*** (3.724)	
	IADD: Post-Merger (c + 11, c + 180)	14	1.302** (2.321)	1.168** (2.291))		18	0.944 (1.390)	0.223 (0.806)	
	ΔIADD	14	−0.245 (−0.441)	−0.609 (−0.847)	43%	18	−1.264** (−2.670)	−0.958*** (−2.766)	17%

(**;*) denotes significance at 1% (5%; 10%).

Panel A reports mean (median) of the industry-adjusted distance to default (IADD) for domestic and cross-border deals involving high- and low-risk banks on the basis of their pre-merger distance to default. High- (low-)risk banks are located in the first (fourth) DD quartile from −180 days to −11 days relative to the announcement date. Panel B reports the sample mean (median) of the same risk measures for activity-focusing and diversifying mergers. A merger is defined as diversified if the bidder and the target do not share the same two-digit SIC code. Panel C summarizes the same statistics for mergers realized in high and low supervisory power regimes, identified on the basis of the Supervisory Power Index from Barth, Caprio, and Levine (2004). Distance to default before the merger is computed as the average distance to default over the period −180 days to −11 days from the announcement (a), while distance to default after the merger is computed as the average of distance to default over the period from + 11 days to + 180 days after the effective date (c). Changes in the industry-adjusted distance to default is the difference in IADD between the post-effective date and pre-announcement period, winsorized at the 1 per cent level. The *t*-test (rank-test) evaluates if the mean (median) IADD and ΔIADD are equal to zero.

of banks.[8] The results show there is no statistically significant risk effect on bidding banks from cross-border mergers for the riskiest institutions. For low-risk institutions, we observe a statistically significant increase in default risk (i.e. a reduction in IADD) following cross-border deals. In Panel B, we observe very similar results for diversification on the basis of the activities in which merging firms engage. In the group of high-risk banks, we also find some evidence that product diversification lowers default risk (rank statistic significant at the 10 per cent level). Thus, we observe that diversification (in terms of both geography and activities) is risk neutral for risky banks, but generates an increase in default risk for the portfolio of the least risky institutions.

Our results are critical of the diversification potential of bank mergers. This is very much in the spirit of a wider literature, which does not report gains from US bank mergers (Shaffer, 1994; Akhavein, Berger, and Humphrey, 1997). Consistent with this, most studies which examine the risk effects of income diversification on European banks have not found any evidence that diversification lowers bank risk (Baele, De Jonghe, and Vander Vennet, 2007; Mercieca, Schaeck, and Wolfe, 2007; Lepetit et al., 2008). Wagner (2008) argues that by increasing homogeneity amongst financial institutions, diversification limits their ability to share risk, thereby increasing the likelihood of a systemic crisis.

Panel C of Table 3.5 reports IADD for high-risk and low-risk banks by supervisory strength in the bidder's country. The results confirm the regulatory hypothesis only for low-risk banks which increase their default risk when regulatory power is low. By contrast, the M&A risk effects for high-risk institutions are not affected by the power of the supervisory regime. This shows bank regulators are unable to contain risk-taking under regimes with fewer disciplinary powers (Buch and DeLong, 2008). However, since merger-related risk-taking under weak regimes is confined to the low-risk group, we do not interpret this finding as consistent with banks exploiting weaker regimes to shift risk onto regulators. Rather, it seems more likely that the least risky banks attract relatively less scrutiny under a weaker regulatory regime.

In summary, we find that the risk effects produced by mergers partly depend on pre-merger risk. We observe that the most risky banks do not benefit from M&A, while the relatively safe experience an increase in default risk following a deal. Further, the merger-related increase in risk for relatively safe banks is driven by cross-border and activity-diversifying mergers. Also, we show that risk-taking via M&A amongst the group of least risky banks is prevalent in weaker regulatory environments.

[8] While we examine the risk effects of diversification for each risk quartile, we only report the results for the lowest and highest risk quartile in order to conserve space. We do not find statistically significant differences between focusing and diversifying mergers other than those reported in Table 3.5.

So far, our analysis considers pre-merger risk, diversification, and the regulatory environment. However, it is conceivable that our main result above—the deterioration in default risk for relatively safe banks following M&A—is linked to specific strategies or pre-merger characteristics of the acquirer. For this reason, the following section examines changes in industry-adjusted distance to default (ΔIADD) for European bank mergers in a multivariate setting.

The Determinants of Changes in Default Risk

We assess how merger-related risk changes are affected by the deal characteristics and pre-merger fundamentals of the acquirer. Our model, estimated via OLS with robust standard errors, assumes the following specification:

$$\mathbf{\Delta IADD}_i = \alpha_0 + \gamma' \mathbf{DC}_i + \theta' \mathbf{AC}_{i,t-1} + \epsilon_i \tag{5}$$

where:

$\mathbf{\Delta IADD}_i$ is the merger-related change in industry-adjusted distance to default (see Section 2);

$\mathbf{DC}_i$ is a $(k \times 1)$ vector of merger characteristics, and

$\mathbf{AC}_{i,t-1}$ is a $(j \times 1)$ vector of acquiring bank characteristics at the end of the fiscal year before the announcement of the merger.

Among other variables, the vector of deal characteristics controls the method of payment, the status of the target bank, and deal size. The payment method is captured by a dummy variable which equals one if the deal is fully paid for in cash and zero otherwise (CASHONLY). Furfine and Rosen (2009) suggest that fully cash-financed mergers are likely to increase bidder risk, because bidders are substituting safe liquid assets for the (more risky) balance sheet of the target. Further, we consider the status of the target by distinguishing via a dummy variable between publicly listed and private target firms (LISTED). We hold no a priori expectations regarding the effect of the target status on the risk implications of a bank acquisition.

Deal size is measured by the logarithmic transformation of the US dollar value of acquisitions (LDEALV). Deal size can affect the risk profile of the acquirer in several ways. Larger deals may produce more diversification benefits and reduce the default risk of the acquiring bank. However, Hughes and colleagues (1999) argue that if larger deals bring about diversification benefits, they could encourage banks to take on more risk in the post-merger period. Further, larger mergers are also more complex and thus more difficult to integrate into the context of the bidding bank and may lead to institutions which are organizationally more complex (Knapp, Gart, and Becher, 2005). In the aftermath of a deal, large mergers may, therefore, cause an increase in default risk. Since deal values that are small in absolute terms may still yield similar type risk effects as large deals for small acquirers, we include a measure of relative size as the ratio of deal value to the market value of the acquirer's equity at the end of one year before the deal announcement (RELSIZE) in the regressions.

Echoing the univariate tests on the diversification effects of bank mergers—mentioned earlier in this chapter—we reveal whether deals entail geographic diversification (cross-border versus domestic mergers, CROSSB) or activity diversification (focusing versus diversifying mergers, CONGLOMERATE). Also, we test if highly specialized mergers, which are both geographically and activity-focusing, affect our default risk measure (DOMESTICFOCUS).

Moving on to the vector of acquiring bank characteristics, we consider measures of pre-merger performance and size. Some of these variables are related to agency explanations of M&A, which stress potential conflicts between managers and shareholders as regards the deployment of corporate resources and the riskiness of the institution (Jensen and Meckling, 1976). For example, declining market performance can be interpreted as an indicator that managers are entrenched and may act against the interests of shareholders. We measure pre-merger market performance (PREMERGERPERF) using industry-adjusted buy and hold returns on the bidding bank's equity over a period from −180 to −11 days relative to the deal announcement. Accounting performance is measured by ROA (pre-tax profits scaled by assets). Further, the market-to-book ratio (MTBV) can be used as a proxy for executive hubris, which we expect to be negatively associated with merger-related changes in distance to default. By contrast, Keeley (1990) argues that more valuable banks face fewer incentives to engage in risky projects, because valuable charters cannot be sold in the event of default.

Berger and Bonaccorsi di Patti (2006) show that leverage reduces agency cost in banking. Leverage increases the risk of liquidation (with the prospect of pay losses for executives) as well as pressures to generate cash flows sufficiently high to cover interest payments. Consequently, managers at banks with low leverage may be more likely to commit free cash flows to risky projects (mergers), which increase their pay as well as the likelihood of institutional default. We control for the level of bidder pre-merger leverage via the equity-to-assets ratio (LEVERAGE).[9]

[9] EQUITY correlates highly with total assets ($r = -.67$). To reduce the effects of multicollinearity between leverage and size in our regressions, we regress EQUITY on total assets and enter the residuals from this estimation as an explanatory variable into our regression. The estimated coefficient, therefore, measures the effect of leverage after controlling for size.

To capture the impact of management quality on the risk effects on mergers, we also include operating efficiency in the model (measured by the ratio of operating costs to total assets, OPCOSTS). Further, we expect a negative influence of acquirer size—measured by the log transformation of total bank assets (SIZE)—on merger-related changes in default risk. If the diversification benefits of mergers decline with bidder size, large banks face incentives to increase risk through M&A and to extract too-big-to-fail benefits from regulators (see John, John, and Senbet, 1991; Benston, Hunter, and Wall, 1995).

To assess the robustness of the univariate tests above, we control for the pre-merger risk profile of the acquiring bank. We construct a dummy that identifies low- (high-)risk bidders. This variable equals one if the bidder is located in the highest (lowest) pre-merger DD quartile. Further, to evaluate whether the risk implications of a deal explain the expected performance gains accruing from a bank merger, we include the cumulative abnormal returns (CAR) from −11 to + 1 days relative to the merger announcement date, as in Amihud, DeLong, and Saunders (2002) and Buch and DeLong (2008). Market model parameters are estimated using 110-day daily return observations starting from 120 days to 11 days before the acquisition announcement date supplied by Thomson Financial. We expect a CAR to exert a negative impact on merger-related changes in default risk. This is because increases in the risk of the acquiring bank should generate higher expected shareholder returns. Finally, we control for the influence of country characteristics on the risk effect of mergers by including in the regression model the real GDP growth rate (RGDPG) and an asset-based Herfindahl index (HH) of national banking market concentration. An overview of our variables and summary statistics are provided in Table 3.6.

The Influence of Deal and Acquirer Characteristics

Table 3.7 reports the results of the regressions on merger-related changes in industry-adjusted distance to default. The results show that various bidding bank characteristics drive merger-generated changes in distance to default. We also confirm two of our main results above: (i) low-risk banks increase their default risk after a merger, and (ii) diversification gains for European bidding banks do not appear to materialize.

Deal value exerts a negative impact on the risk effects of M&A (significant at the 5 per cent level). This shows that large bank mergers pose organizational and procedural hurdles in the post-merger integration process that may prevent merger benefits from materializing (Knapp, Gart, and Becher, 2005) or that as banks grow via M&A, they take on more risk (Hughes et al., 1999). This is also consistent with banks facing incentives to use mergers to become too

Table 3.6. Summary Statistics

		Definition	N	Mean	Median	Std.Dev.	5 Pctile	95 Pctile
Risk measures	IADD: Pre-Merger (−180, −11)	Pre-merger industry-adjusted distance to default	134	−0.112	−0.289	1.672	−2.262	2.824
	IADD: Post-Merger (+11, +180)	Post-merger industry-adjusted distance to default	134	−0.197	−0.341	1.768	−2.267	2.830
	ΔIADD	Merger-related change in industry-adjusted distance to default	134	−0.107	−0.030	1.444	−2.347	1.654
Deal characteristics	CASHONLY	Equals 1 if the deal is completely cash-financed (zero otherwise)	134	0.209	0.000	0.408	0.000	1.000
	LISTED	Equals 1 if the target is a listed company (zero otherwise)	134	0.515	1.000	0.502	0.000	1.000
	LDEALV	Log of the deal value (in million USD)	134	6.761	6.645	1.830	3.892	9.609
	RELSIZE	Ratio of the deal value to the acquirer's market value one year before announcement (%)	134	44.415	20.387	69.342	0.363	153.127
	CROSSB	Equals 1 for cross-border mergers (zero otherwise)	134	0.410	0.000	0.494	0.000	1.000
	CONGL	Equals 1 if the acquirer and the target do not share the same two-digit SIC code (zero otherwise)	134	0.246	0.000	0.432	0.000	1.000
	DOMESTICFOCUS	Equals 1 for mergers that are both domestic and focus (zero otherwise)	134	0.448	0.000	0.499	0.000	1.000
Acquirer characteristics	PREMERGERPERF	Buy and hold abnormal returns from −180 days to −11 days relative to the merger announcement (%)	134	−4.590	−4.140	20.590	−33.845	30.492
	ROA	Pre-tax profits over total assets (%)	131	1.027	0.971	0.751	0.048	2.048
	MTBV	Market-to-book ratio	132	2.214	2.072	1.143	0.791	4.841
	LEVERAGE	Book value of common equity to total assets, orthogonalized with respect to total assets (%)	134	0.000	−0.260	2.111	−2.959	3.863
	OPCOSTS	Total operating costs over total assets (%)	130	6.961	6.650	2.153	3.925	10.433
	SIZE	Log of bidder total assets (thousands of USD)	134	18.076	18.206	1.700	14.629	20.338
	TOTAL ASSETS	Bidder total assets (USD millions)	134	232,754.9	104,981.1	305,907.8	3,149.032	816,735.1
	LOWRISK		134	0.246	0.000	0.432	0.000	1.000

(*continued*)

Table 3.6. Continued

		Definition	N	Mean	Median	Std.Dev.	5 Pctile	95 Pctile
		Equals 1 if the bidder is located in the lowest pre-merger risk quartile (zero otherwise)						
	HIGHRISK	Equals 1 if the bank is in the highest pre-merger risk quartile (zero otherwise)	134	0.254	0.000	0.437	0.000	1.000
	CAR (-10, + 1)	Cumulative abnormal return between −10 days to + 1 day relative the merger announcement (%)	134	0.726	0.657	6.862	−9.677	13.721
Regulatory environment	SUPOWER	Measures the extent to which the supervisory environment is sensitive to bank risk-taking, the breadth of disciplinary powers available to regulators, and how well these powers are enforced. *Source*: Barth, Caprio, and Levine (2001)	132	8.985	9.000	2.389	6.000	13.000
Country controls	RGDPG	Real GDP growth rate (%)	134	2.754	2.795	1.399	0.715	4.746
	HH	Asset-based Herfindahl index	134	0.098	0.088	0.060	0.030	0.231

Table 3.8 reports summary statistics for the measures of default risk, deal characteristics, acquirer characteristics, the regulatory environment, and country control variables. The sample consists of 134 mergers announced over the period from 1992 to 2007, and involving bidders in the European Union, Norway, and Switzerland. All variables, apart from SUPOWER, are winsorized at the 1 per cent level.

Table 3.7. Changes in Industry-Adjusted Distance to Default: Deal and Acquirer Characteristics

Panel A	1	2	3	4	5	6	7	8	9
CASHONLY	−0.051	−0.050	0.054	0.074	0.050	0.071	0.040	0.137	0.057
	(0.16)	(0.15)	(0.15)	(0.21)	(0.13)	(0.20)	(0.11)	(0.40)	(0.16)
LISTED	0.532*	0.532*	0.445	0.452*	0.465*	0.475*	0.436	0.513*	0.458*
	(1.88)	(1.88)	(1.63)	(1.66)	(1.72)	(1.76)	(1.60)	(1.84)	(1.70)
LDEALV	−0.178**	−0.169**	−0.321***	−0.309***	−0.317**	−0.305***	−0.316***	−0.318***	−0.285***
	(2.19)	(2.14)	(2.64)	(2.85)	(2.61)	(2.81)	(2.74)	(2.62)	(2.86)
RELSIZE	0.004	−0.015	0.225	0.207	0.227	0.208	0.225	0.214	0.195
	(0.02)	(0.09)	(1.00)	(1.01)	(1.04)	(1.06)	(0.99)	(0.88)	(0.89)
CROSSB	−0.172		−0.479		−0.495		−0.432	−0.564	
	(0.60)		(1.06)		(1.10)		(1.01)	(1.25)	
CONGL	0.080		0.034		0.014		0.031	0.338	
	(0.30)		(0.11)		(0.05)		(0.10)	(1.01)	
DOMESTICFOCUS		0.253		0.583		0.607			0.352
		(0.91)		(1.51)		(1.59)			(0.97)
PREMERGERPERF			−0.343	−0.162	−0.377	−0.195	−0.343	−0.341	−0.154
			(0.43)	(0.21)	(0.47)	(0.25)	(0.43)	(0.44)	(0.20)
ROA			−33.276	−38.462	−30.398	−35.335	−32.770	−31.397	−34.226
			(1.33)	(1.46)	(1.18)	(1.31)	(1.30)	(1.28)	(1.29)
MTBV			0.204	0.203	0.176	0.171	0.203	0.199	0.182
			(0.93)	(0.93)	(0.79)	(0.78)	(0.93)	(0.95)	(0.91)
LEVERAGE			12.097	13.182*	11.582	12.553	11.576	13.906*	11.781
			(1.56)	(1.75)	(1.47)	(1.63)	(1.50)	(1.79)	(1.53)
OPCOSTS			−17.190**	−17.878**	−17.885**	−18.665**	−17.390**	−16.913**	−17.787**
			(2.27)	(2.33)	(2.32)	(2.38)	(2.21)	(2.27)	(2.40)
SIZE			−0.048	−0.051	−0.044	−0.047	−0.050	−0.037	−0.054
			(0.35)	(0.41)	(0.32)	(0.38)	(0.37)	(0.28)	(0.43)
LOWRISK	−1.016**	−0.988**	−1.018**	−0.943**	−0.936**	−0.851**	−0.954	−0.684	−1.281***
	(2.61)	(2.56)	(2.48)	(2.33)	(2.27)	(2.12)	(1.56)	(1.33)	(3.24)
HIGHRISK					0.283	0.311			
					(0.95)	(1.06)			
CAR (−10, + 1)			−0.918	−1.069	−0.642	−0.773	−0.887	−1.291	−1.256
			(0.50)	(0.62)	(0.36)	(0.45)	(0.48)	(0.67)	(0.71)

(continued)

Table 3.7. Continued

Panel A	1	2	3	4	5	6	7	8	9
RGDPG			22.424*	21.287*	24.900*	24.050*	22.190	23.729*	21.587*
			(1.70)	(1.73)	(1.82)	(1.89)	(1.66)	(1.86)	(1.77)
HH			−1.069	−0.205	−1.341	−0.515	−1.070	−1.204	−0.274
			(0.45)	(0.08)	(0.58)	(0.22)	(0.45)	(0.53)	(0.11)
LOWRISK CROSSB							−0.143		
							(0.19)		
LOWRISK CONGL								−1.179*	
								(1.67)	
LOWRISK								0.900	
DOMESTICFOCUS									(1.19)
Constant	1.133*	0.912*	3.601	3.174	3.449	2.992	3.615	3.251	3.174
	(1.97)	(1.75)	(1.39)	(1.21)	(1.32)	(1.14)	(1.38)	(1.31)	(1.21)
Obs.	134	134	130	130	130	130	130	130	130
Adjusted R^2	0.066	0.077	0.096	0.113	0.094	0.113	0.089	0.112	0.123
Panel B		Marginal Effects							
LOWRISK + LOWRISK CROSSB							−1.097**		
							(−2.32)		
LOWRISK + LOWRISK CONGL								−1.863***	
								(−3.69)	
LOWRISK + LOWRISK DOMESTICFOCUS									−0.381
									(−0.53)

big to fail in an attempt to extract benefits from regulators.[10] Further, the negative relationship between cost efficiency and merger-induced changes in IADD (at a 5 per cent level of significance) can be explained by the difficulties that inefficient banks face in successfully completing a merger. If we interpret cost efficiency as a proxy for managerial ability, this result implies that poorly managed banks are less likely to select acquisition targets that lower default risk.

In some of the model specifications, we observe a positive effect of the equity-to-asset ratio on changes in default risk. Thus, more highly capitalized banks tend to realize higher risk-reduction benefits from mergers. This result points to the importance of capital requirement regulations in promoting a sound banking industry. Further, bank mergers which are completed against the background of positive economic growth are linked to post-M&A risk reductions. While periods of economic growth may be accompanied by excessive risk-taking, GDP growth is also likely to increase the value of bidding bank assets, thereby reducing the probability of default.

The regression results in Table 3.7 confirm a number of findings in the univariate analysis. For instance, there are no risk diversification benefits from cross-border or activity-diversifying mergers (neither CROSSB nor CONGL enter the regressions at customary levels of significance). Also in line with the univariate analysis, low-risk banks experience a statistically significant increase in default risk following M&A. The dummy variable indicating low pre-merger risk enters all model specifications with a negative sign (significant at 5 per cent in all specifications without interaction effects). Consequently, the effect which the pre-merger risk of the acquiring bank has on merger-induced risk changes in the group of low-risk banks is not contingent on specific merger strategies or financial characteristics prevalent in this group of institutions.

We further investigate the interaction between pre-merger risk and diversification gains, and find additional confirmation of our univariate results. Specifically, we add interaction terms between the LOWRISK dummy and diversifying mergers (CROSSB and CONGL dummies) to the specifications, and we estimate the effect of the low-risk dummy on IADD for these diversifying deals (Panel B of Table 3.7). We reach the same conclusion as in the univariate analysis. When low-risk banks are involved in either geographically

[10] Rather unexpectedly, deal size and relative size are far from being perfectly correlated (r = .378). Therefore, both variables offer different information on deal characteristics. Furthermore, variance inflation factor (VIF) tests on the estimated models suggest that there is no evidence of multicollinearity in the regressions when the two variables are simultaneously included. However, as a further check, we re-estimate the main models by including each size variable separately. We continue to observe that the log of the deal size enters the regression with a negative and significant coefficient, while the low-risk dummy is significant in all specifications.

or product-diversifying mergers, changes in IADD are highly significant and negative. By contrast, mergers that are simultaneously domestic and focusing are risk neutral. This confirms that increases in default risk following bank mergers are particularly pronounced for the low-risk group of banks engaging in diversifying deals.

The Influence of Supervisory Power

We add the supervisory power index (SUPOWER) to the regressions to examine whether regulatory incentives motivate bank risk-taking in mergers in a multivariate framework. The results, reported in columns (1) to (4) of Table 3.8, show that the coefficient on SUPOWER is not significant at customary levels of significance. Consequently, supervisory power does not affect risk-taking in mergers for the general sample.

The results in the univariate tests in Table 3.5 indicate that deal-induced increases in risk are strongest under weak regulatory regimes. In columns (5) to (8), we consider the interaction between SUPOWER and LOWRISK as well as between a dummy variable, which takes the value of 1 if SUPOWER in the acquiring bank's country is above the sample median, and zero otherwise (DSUPOWER). In Panel B of Table 3.8, we compute the marginal effect of LOWRISK on changes in IADD for different supervisory strengths. The marginal effects can be interpreted as measuring the change in IADD for low-risk banks under a given supervisory regime. As SUPOWER increases, we expect the incentive for risk-taking should be reduced.

Our results confirm this expectation. When the supervisory power is high, the risk effect of mergers on low-risk bidders is not significantly different from the risk effect of M&A on the rest of the sample. Different risk effects of M&A are only observable under low and median supervisory powers where low-risk banks see an increase in their risk of default post-M&A. Therefore, we continue to observe that low-risk banks increase their default risk through M&A under relatively weak supervisory regimes.

Robustness

We conducted several tests to evaluate the robustness of our results. First, we assess the stability of our results when we impose a minimum value for RELSIZE. Although our sample includes many of the largest deals in Europe, it also contains a few deals where the target appears relatively small compared to the bidder. Therefore, we re-run the analysis after imposing minimum relative size requirements of 5 per cent (which reduces the sample size n to 101) and 10 per cent (n = 87). The results for these subsamples confirm our main findings and demonstrate that our findings are invariant to the

Table 3.8. Changes in Industry-Adjusted Distance to Default: The Regulatory Environment

Panel A	1	2	3	4	5	6	7	8
CASHONLY	0.032	0.060	0.088	0.115	0.049	0.077	0.141	0.158
	(0.09)	(0.18)	(0.25)	(0.34)	(0.14)	(0.23)	(0.40)	(0.46)
LISTED	0.460	0.447	0.441	0.426	0.462	0.450	0.414	0.401
	(1.64)	(1.60)	(1.53)	(1.50)	(1.65)	(1.62)	(1.42)	(1.40)
LDEALV	−0.322***	−0.308***	−0.312***	−0.294***	−0.320**	−0.306***	−0.286**	−0.268**
	(2.64)	(2.86)	(2.66)	(2.83)	(2.61)	(2.81)	(2.41)	(2.51)
RELSIZE	0.245	0.219	0.234	0.207	0.241	0.216	0.237	0.210
	(1.02)	(0.99)	(1.01)	(0.99)	(1.03)	(1.01)	(1.01)	(1.00)
CROSSB	−0.499		−0.563		−0.490		−0.541	
	(1.07)		(1.22)		(1.06)		(1.22)	
CONGL	0.040		0.066		0.038		0.119	
	(0.13)		(0.21)		(0.12)		(0.39)	
DOMESTICFOCUS		0.621		0.666*		0.606		0.610
		(1.53)		(1.66)		(1.50)		(1.54)
PREMERGERPERF	−0.374	−0.193	−0.402	−0.205	−0.341	−0.163	−0.436	−0.240
	(0.46)	(0.25)	(0.52)	(0.28)	(0.43)	(0.21)	(0.57)	(0.32)
ROA	−28.718	−34.839	−30.307	−36.794	−30.113	−36.196	−31.224	−37.559
	(1.14)	(1.32)	(1.20)	(1.38)	(1.20)	(1.37)	(1.26)	(1.43)
MTBV	0.165	0.166	0.159	0.160	0.172	0.174	0.156	0.160
	(0.73)	(0.74)	(0.77)	(0.76)	(0.73)	(0.74)	(0.72)	(0.72)
LEVERAGE	11.821	13.153*	15.402*	16.739**	11.481	12.740*	15.140*	16.304**
	(1.50)	(1.72)	(1.93)	(2.18)	(1.45)	(1.66)	(1.95)	(2.20)
OPCOSTS	−17.261**	−18.095**	−17.719**	−18.597**	−16.576**	−17.343**	−16.919**	−17.686**
	(2.24)	(2.31)	(2.25)	(2.32)	(2.12)	(2.17)	(2.11)	(2.15)
SIZE	−0.041	−0.043	−0.050	−0.056	−0.036	−0.039	−0.061	−0.067
	(0.30)	(0.35)	(0.39)	(0.46)	(0.26)	(0.30)	(0.48)	(0.55)
LOWRISK	−1.041**	−0.975**	−2.887*	−2.770*	−1.026**	−0.961**	−1.569***	−1.453***
	(2.52)	(2.42)	(1.98)	(1.95)	(2.45)	(2.35)	(3.26)	(3.11)
CAR (−10, + 1)	−0.843	−0.907	−0.779	−0.829	−0.851	−0.914	−0.477	−0.535
	(0.43)	(0.50)	(0.41)	(0.47)	(0.44)	(0.51)	(0.25)	(0.29)
RGDPG	22.523*	21.018*	21.864*	20.079*	22.710*	21.251*	23.417*	21.426*
	(1.70)	(1.71)	(1.70)	(1.72)	(1.73)	(1.74)	(1.91)	(1.90)
HH	−1.724	−0.825	−1.541	−0.557	−1.367	−0.463	−1.711	−0.659
	(0.71)	(0.32)	(0.65)	(0.22)	(0.57)	(0.19)	(0.74)	(0.27)

(continued)

Table 3.8. Continued

Panel A	1	2	3	4	5	6	7	8
SUPOWER	0.051	0.056	−0.008	−0.002				
	(0.65)	(0.74)	(0.09)	(0.03)				
			0.208	0.203				
SUPOWER × LOWIRSK								
			(1.29)	(1.29)				
DSUPOWER					0.186	0.197	−0.115	−0.081
					(0.62)	(0.67)	(0.37)	(0.26)
							1.318*	1.204*
DSUPOWER × LOWIRSK								
							(1.85)	(1.74)
Constant	3.121	2.626	3.835	3.336	3.306	2.849	3.739	3.307
	(1.17)	(0.95)	(1.47)	(1.22)	(1.26)	(1.06)	(1.50)	(1.26)
Obs.	128	128	128	128	128	128	128	128
Adjusted R^2	0.093	0.111	0.109	0.126	0.091	0.108	0.118	0.130
Panel B	**Marginal Effects**							
Low supervisory power			−1.847**	−1757**				
			(−2.58))	(−2.52))				
Median supervisory power			−1.016**	−0.946**				
			(−2.54)	(−2.42)				
High supervisory power			0.024	0.068			−0.251	−0.249
			(0.03)	(0.07)			(−0.43)	(−0.43)

***(**;*) denotes significance at 1% (5%; 10%).

The dependent variable is the change in the industry-adjusted distance to default. The model is estimated via OLS with robust standard errors; t-statistics are in parentheses. *Deal characteristics* include a dummy indicating if merger is fully paid by cash (CASHONLY), a dummy indicating the target is a listed company (LISTED), the log of the deal value (LDLV), the ratio of deal value to the bidder's market value of equity (RELSIZE), a dummy which is equal to 1 for cross-border mergers (CROSSB), a dummy which is equal to 1 if the bidder and the target do not share the same two-digit SIC code (CONGLOMERATE), and a dummy equal to 1 if the merger is both domestic and focus (DOMESTICFOCUS). *Acquirer characteristics* include the buy and hold return for the period from −180 to −11 before the net announcement of the same return computed for the market index (PREMERGERPERF), the ratio between pre-tax profit and total assets (ROA), the market-to-book ratio (MTBV), the equity-to-assets ratio before the merger, orthogonalized respect to size (LEVERAGE), the ratio of operating costs to total assets (OPCOSTS), the log of the bidder total assets at the end of the year before the announcement (SIZE), a dummy equal to 1 if the bidder is in the last quartile of the distribution of pre-merger industry-adjusted distance to default (LOWRISK), a dummy equal to 1 if the bidder is in the first quartile of the distribution of pre-merger industry-adjusted distance to default (HIGHRISK), the cumulative abnormal returns from −10 to + 1 day relative to the announcement date computed from a market model estimated over −120 to −11 days before the announcement (CAR (−10 + 1)). Other control variables include the real GDP growth rate (RGDPG) and an asset-based Herfindahl index of banking market concentration (HH). *The regulatory environment* is described through an index of the power of supervisory authorities in the bidder's country from the WorldBank database on bank regulation and supervision (SUPOWER). This index measures the degree to which the supervisory authority has the power to take specific actions against banks. DSUPOWER is a dummy which equals 1 if SUPOWER is above the sample median. *Panel B* shows the marginal effects of LOWRISK on IADD in three supervisory regimes: low (minimum value), median, and high (maximum value).

imposition of a minimum size criterion. We still observe a negative and significant risk effect of mergers for low-risk banks, especially when the supervisory regime is weak. We also continue to observe that diversifying deals increase default risk for the group of relatively safe acquirers. Further, the regression results are qualitatively unchanged.

Second, the risk effects of M&A may be partly determined by target bank characteristics beyond those that we have already controlled for in our analysis (e.g. via target status or the degree of activity diversification). We test whether target characteristics such as performance, size, capital adequacy, and operating efficiency explain the risk effects of M&A on bidding banks. None of these variables enter the regressions with coefficients that are statistically significant at customary levels. Furthermore, albeit not significant at conventional levels, the coefficients on a number of variables (size, ROA, operating efficiency) exhibit the expected sign. When we extend the model to control for acquiring bank characteristics, we continue to observe a significant negative coefficient for the low-risk dummy. Although we recognize the limitations of this analysis, given the decline in sample size ($n = 60$), we argue that these results show that our main conclusions are robust to the inclusion of target bank characteristics.

Third, the risk effects that mergers produce for low-risk banks compared with the rest of the sample may result from risk transfers between target and acquiring banks. We analyse whether low-risk banks select targets which have a different risk profile compared with the rest of the sample. For subsets of targets that were acquired by low-risk bidders and by other bidders, we compare several target accounting ratios which are likely to capture the risk profile (ROA, leverage, cost efficiency, and size). However, we do not find evidence that the targets acquired by low-risk banks differ with respect to their risk profile from the targets acquired by other bidders.

Finally, some studies have demonstrated the importance of the single currency on the European banking industry. For example, Ekkayokkaya, Holmes, and Paudyal (2009) show that the value effects of bidding bank shareholders have fallen since the establishment of European Monetary Union (EMU). Similarly, Haq and Heaney (2009) point out that the euro has caused a decline in banking risk in adopting countries and in countries neighbouring EMU members. Since our analysis covers a sample period which partly coincides with EMU, we test if the adoption of the euro impacts the risk effects produced by bank mergers. We introduce a dummy variable that takes the value of 1 for mergers announced after 1999 (and zero otherwise). The variable enters the regression model with a negative coefficient (not significant at conventional levels), while leaving the findings discussed in the previous section unaffected. Controlling for euro effects, therefore, does not modify our findings.

Conclusions

Sound financial intermediation relies on the ability of banks to manage risks effectively. The default of banking firms poses a difficult trade-off for policymakers between the negative externalities associated with institutional failures and costly government bailouts. Over past decades, repeated bank merger waves have raised concerns among bank stakeholders as regards the risk implications of financial consolidation on individual banks and on the banking system as a whole.

In this chapter, we have reviewed and analysed the default risk implications of M&A on acquiring banks from Europe. In terms of the new results presented here we started by showing that the average European bank merger does not affect the default risk of the acquirer. Next, we show this result also holds for merger types which offer the a priori largest scope for risk-related diversification benefits (i.e. cross-border and product-diversifying M&A). By contrast, relatively safe bidders increase their default risk in the post-merger period. Further, the possibility of merger-related increases in risk is particularly pronounced for relatively safe banks when deals are diversifying and/or completed under a bank regulatory regime in the country of the biding bank that is relatively weak.

Our results point to difficulties in achieving sustainable risk-reduction benefits from bank M&A, especially for banks which are already well-diversified. We also show that prudential regulation plays a role in preventing risk-increasing deals. Further, the regression analysis consistently identifies larger deals as causing an increase in bidder default risk. The overall results are critical of bank mergers exerting a risk-reducing and, thus, stabilizing effect on the safety and soundness of the banking sector in Europe.

Overall, our results convey a critical view of the risk-reduction potential of bank M&A. European bank mergers, at best, are risk neutral, yet offer substantial scope for increases in the likelihood of default. Our finding—that merger-related risk increases are particularly large for cross-border and activity-diversifying deals—is consistent with a host of theoretical and empirical studies which doubt that viable diversification gains and risk benefits can be realized through bank consolidation. Further, our finding that deal size exerts a negative influence on industry-adjusted distance to default raises concerns about the risk implications of banking mega-mergers on banking sector stability.

If risk reductions tend not to materialize, but there is a pronounced possibility that the acquiring bank exhibits a higher default probability post-M&A, European policymakers should consider the costs and benefits of bank consolidation carefully. While our study concentrates on acquiring bank risk, the risk implications of M&A for the wider banking sector and economy may be less negative than our results suggest. From a supervisory point of view, increases in risk following the completion of a merger might be justified if the deal involved a target which was substantially more risky than the acquirer (and which, in the absence of the deal, may well have failed). In this context, the effects of M&A on systemic stability, particularly of deals that lead to more complex banking organizations and deals which increase market concentration, remain unclear (e.g. Uhde and Heimeshoff, 2009).

While we point out a number of drivers of merger-related changes in default risk, future research should further understand the bank-specific drivers of risk-taking in the context of mergers. For instance, it would be valuable to assess the impact of executive pay on the risk implications of M&A. Outside the banking literature, Furfine and Rosen (2009) assess the effect of mergers on the acquirer's default risk. The authors identify executive remuneration (higher risk increases occur when CEOs have a higher share of option-based compensation) and the level of asymmetric information (expressed by the value of idiosyncratic volatility) as drivers of merger-related changes in default risk.

Part III
Risk in European Banking

4

The Trends and Composition of Banking Risk across Europe

Introduction and Literature

The large number of bank insolvencies observed across different countries during the financial crisis of 2007–9 has offered some support to the idea that the risks faced by the banking industry have changed over the past decades (Boot and Thakor, 2009). Banks seem to be more exposed to increasing sources of common shocks that raise the importance of the broad channel of systemic risk (De Bandt and Hartmann, 2000; Schuermann and Stiroh, 2006). Hence, the likelihood of a systemic crisis, due to shocks that hit multiple institutions simultaneously, appears to be greater than in the past. In accordance with this argument, the IMF has claimed that global bank linkages are at the root of the spread of the crisis across numerous countries, while the UK Financial Services Authority (FSA, 2009) and the Basel Committee on Banking Supervision (BCBS, 2011b) have pointed out the importance of interconnectedness in identifying systemically relevant banks.

In general, the long-term evolution of the risks in the banking industry has received limited and only US-focused analysis in the literature. For instance, Houston and Stiroh (2006) adopt the 'market adjusted return model' (as in Campbell et al., 2001; Ferreira and Gama, 2005; Kearney and Potì, 2008), to show an upward trend in the 'common sector component' of the volatility in the US financial sector. This result is consistent with the increasing trend in stock return correlation provided by De Nicolò and Kwast (2002) for a sample of large US financial institutions. In spite of these dynamics, Houston and Stiroh (2006) demonstrate that idiosyncratic risk still remains the dominant component of volatility within the financial industry, even though it has a declining weight. This contrasts with the increasing trend in idiosyncratic risk observed for the non-financial sector in the USA (Campbell et al., 2001). In a related study, Schuermann and Stiroh (2006) fail to detect any obvious trend in systematic risk for a sample of US banks.

This chapter extends these empirical studies by analysing two decades of data for seventeen European banking systems with the purpose of testing whether the banking industry over this time span has been characterized by a significant upward trend in the importance of common sources of variation, and, consequently, in the risk of cross-border crises, and whether this increase has been influenced by the adoption of the European Monetary Union (EMU) that is supposed to have accelerated the European integration process. Our focus on Europe is motivated by two reasons. First, in the last two decades the characteristics of European banking have been profoundly modified by the interactions between consolidation processes, financial innovation, and technological progress (Goddard et al., 2007; Molyneux and Wilson, 2007). These factors are deemed to have changed the nature of shocks faced by banks and enhanced the opportunities to spread those shocks among firms both within and outside the traditional banking system (Houston and Stiroh, 2006). Second, in the same time frame the European banking industry has been characterized by numerous changes in the regulatory framework aimed at removing restrictions on banking businesses and, more importantly, at favouring the integration and harmonization process across banking systems in different countries.

These regulatory changes also motivate our focus on banking systems rather than on financial systems. More precisely, since the early part of the sample period, the European context has adopted the universal banking model; as a consequence, non-bank financial institutions, rather than remaining independent entities, have been generally incorporated within banking groups. Banks, hence, play a key role in the stability/instability of the full European financial system. This role has clearly emerged during the financial crisis of 2007–9, where the propagation of shocks across Europe was generally produced by the difficulties faced by large banking groups.[1] Banking is, therefore, at the centre of the ongoing debate on how to regulate the financial industry in European countries.

To detect the trends in the sources of shocks that influence European banking systems, and their implications on the likelihood of cross-border crises, we use banking industry volatility as a good predictor of the probability of systemic crises.[2] Thus, we analyse the evolution of banking system

[1] Examples in this direction are the bailouts of HBOS in the UK and Fortis in Belgium, as well as the difficulties of other UK and Irish banking groups that have led to a broad nationalization process of the banking systems in the UK and Ireland.

[2] Moshirian and Wu (2009) show that banking industry volatility predicts banking crises in developed countries. Stiroh (2006b) also provides several arguments in favour of the choice of this measure as an indicator of bank risk. For instance, volatility is relevant to regulators, managers, and borrowers since they are concerned with the probability of the failure of banks and the related costs. This can be seen by the direct link between equity return volatility and asset volatility, usually employed to construct market measures of bank default risk, such as the distance to default.

volatility (computed at monthly intervals from 1988 to 2010) in the European context and, in particular, how this evolution has been affected by the changes in the sources of shocks.[3] To this end, we adopt an asset pricing framework to estimate the contributions of an 'international non-financial' component, a 'European non-financial' component, an 'international banking industry' component, a 'European banking industry' component, and a 'country' component in explaining the evolution of the volatility of bank stock returns over the sample period.[4] We argue that, as banking industry volatility is a reliable predictor of systemic crises, an increasing importance of non-domestic components would signal increasing cross-border commonalities in the banking industry and, then, a rise in the risk of cross-border crises.

This chapter extends two literatures on European banks. The first focuses on systemic risk and commonalities in bank stock returns, and generally concludes in favour of a growing degree of interdependency between banks in Europe. For instance, Schüler (2002) shows an increase in 'rolling window correlations' of adjusted bank stock returns from March 1980 to July 2001. Similar findings are offered in a later study by Vulpes and Brasili (2006) that shows an increase in commonalities in bank risk since 1999 for the EU-15 banking industry, and in an analysis conducted by De Nicolò and Tieman (2006) that looks at the convergence among measures of systemic risk across the European financial system. The importance of interdependencies between European banks is also pointed out by Gropp and Moerman (2004) in a study of contagion risk in EU banks. They conclude that there may be tight links among banks within countries, as well as links connecting the major banking systems in Europe, even though there appears to be no major difference between the strength of links among Euro area versus non-Euro area countries. In a related analysis, Gropp, Lo Duca, and Vesala (2009) find that cross-border contagion was significant and economically relevant in Europe during the period from January 1994 to January 2003. Moreover, Hartmann, Straetmans, and de Vries (2006) suggest that further banking integration in Europe could

[3] Publicly traded banks are broadly representative of a country's banking sector (Moshirian and Wu, 2009). In Europe listed banks represent at least 50 per cent of the banking system's total assets in the majority of the EU members (ECB, 2005) with the notable exceptions being Austria, Finland, Germany, and Portugal. However, in these countries listed banks still represent an average of 40 per cent of total banking system assets.

[4] We define as 'international non-financial' the component of banking system risk related to co-movements with the foreign stock markets consisting of non-financial firms; namely, all non-financial firms operating outside Europe. The 'European non-financial' component then captures the specific contribution of European non-financial stocks to banking volatility. Finally, the 'international banking industry' and 'European banking industry' components capture the additional contribution to banking volatility coming from, respectively, variations in the international and European banking industries, while the country component denotes the contribution from country stock market indices.

increase cross-border contagion risk in the future, though smaller countries appear to be more insulated from this type of risk.

We extend these studies by adopting a long-term perspective, based on robust trend tests, to analyse the evolution of the level and composition of banking volatility in European banking systems. Furthermore, we show how these trends differ according to the size of the banking system, measured via the average daily market capitalization over the full sample period, and we detect how this evolution has affected the degree of interdependency between European banking systems.[5] Our results suggest that, on average, banking volatility in Europe has not shown any upward trend over the sample period, even though the banking industry has suffered heavily from the short-term impact of common shocks, especially during the financial crisis of 2007–9. However, our analysis offers robust evidence of relevant changes in the composition of this volatility. We observe significant long-term trends in some of its components, with an increasing importance of the international and the European non-financial sources of shocks, especially for the largest banking systems. Notably, the increasing relative importance of these components is associated with an upward trend in the betas of European banking systems with respect to the international and European stock markets since the late eighties; namely, European banks have become progressively more exposed to non-domestic shocks. Furthermore, we show that the international banking industry component exhibits a sudden upward shift during the financial crisis of 2007–9 after a period of relative stability, while the relative share of the European banking industry component increases substantially only from 2005. Overall, the growing importance of common sources of variation in banking system volatility has led to an increase in the degree of interdependency between European banking systems in the order of 2.4 per cent per year.

This chapter also contributes to the literature on the impact of the euro on the banking industry (Francis and Hunter, 2004; Hartmann, Straetmans, and de Vries, 2006; Haq and Heaney, 2009). This literature offers conflicting evidence on how the euro has affected European banking over the past decades. Francis and Hunter (2004) show that this event has resulted in a significant decrease in the bank cost of equity (entirely produced by the decline in the currency risk premium) but a larger exposure of the European banking industry to market and currency risk. This is explained by an increasing integration that has led to increasing competitive pressures within the

[5] In the following analysis, and in line with previous studies on the volatility of stock returns, we employ market capitalization as the size variable as it is available at high frequency intervals. An alternative choice would be to employ the value of bank total assets. However, this would pose two major difficulties. First, this variable is not available for all countries from the same data source for the full sample period. Second, when available, its values usually refer to an annual frequency.

European banking system. Furthermore, the introduction of the euro seems to have generated a more widespread presence of bank contagion risk across European countries while the magnitude of the effects produced when contagion occurs has remained unchanged (Gropp, Lo Duca, and Vesala, 2009). In contrast, Haq and Heaney (2009) point to the benefits generated by the euro by showing that, after the introduction of the common currency, over 70 per cent of banking firms benefited from a decline in their volatility and 64 per cent of banks reduced their level of systematic risk. Notably, however, both Francis and Hunter (2004) and Haq and Heaney (2009) find that their results, ascribed to the adoption of the common currency, also applied outside the Euro area. It may be the case, therefore, that these changes in European banking since the late nineties reflect more general long-term dynamics in the banking industry. This would be consistent with the results proposed by Hartmann, Straetmans, and de Vries (2006), based on extreme value theory, which show that the introduction of the euro has had no impact on banking system risk in the Euro area. Our analysis complements the extant empirical evidence by examining whether the adoption of the euro has affected the long-term dynamics of volatility and its components in European banking systems. In contrast to Francis and Hunter (2004) and Haq and Heaney (2009), and similarly to Hartmann, Straetmans, and de Vries (2006), our tests do not offer evidence of any impact of the euro on European banking systems: the trends in the average banking volatility and in its components do not show any significant shift after the adoption of the euro. These trends appear, therefore, to be the effect of a long-term process started well in advance of the implementation of the EMU.

Research Approach

Measuring Banking System Volatility

For the period from 1 January 1988 to 31 December 2010, we estimate monthly historical volatilities for the banking system located in country *i* as the sum of the squared deviations of daily returns of a banking index from the realized mean in the month:[6]

$$\sigma_{it}^2 = \sum_{k=1}^{N_t} (R_{kt} - \bar{R}_t)^2 \qquad (1)$$

where there are N_t daily returns in month t.

[6] In line with this literature, in our analysis the term 'volatility' denotes the variance of stock returns and not their standard deviation.

Our choice to follow this approach is motivated by two reasons. First, as pointed out by Campbell and colleagues (2001), with sufficiently high frequency data, namely daily data according to this literature, volatility can be estimated accurately over an arbitrarily short time interval. Therefore, when the purpose of the empirical analysis is to provide a description of the historical movements in volatilities, multivariate variance models seem not to be necessary (Campbell et al., 2001). Schwert (2002) confirms this conjecture by showing that this simple approach, when based on daily data, approximates particularly well the forecast of volatility from Generalized AutoRegressive Conditional Heteroskedasticity (GARCH) models. In line with this argument several empirical studies have employed daily data with the purpose of analysing the evolution of stock return volatility computed at monthly intervals (see, for example, French, Schwert, and Stambaugh, 1987; Schwert, 1989; Campbell et al., 2001; Ferreira and Gama, 2005; Houston and Stiroh, 2006; Wei and Zhang, 2006).

Second, the use of monthly measures of banking system return volatility allows us to construct sufficiently long time series of its components (identified through simple variance decomposition) that can be used to conduct our trend analysis.

Decomposing Banking System Volatility

Next, we decompose our measure of volatility separately for each European country via a return-generating model, with the purpose of distinguishing how an 'international non-financial' component, a 'European non-financial' component, an 'international banking industry' component, a 'European banking industry' component, and a 'country' component contribute to the evolution of banking system volatility at the country level. To construct the proxies for each component, we adopt the following criteria. First, the 'international non-financial' and the 'international banking industry' components are expressed by indices that exclude European countries in order to highlight the distinction between international and European sources of variation. Second, the 'European non-financial' and the 'European banking industry' components are proxied by constructing European indices that are 'country-specific', namely, they exclude the country where the banking system is located to reduce spurious correlations and the double counting of the country effect. Third, the country indices exclude financial firms in an attempt to emphasize the distinction between non-financial components and banking components in influencing the risk of the banking systems.

More precisely, the return-generating model is specified as follows:

$$R_{it} = \alpha_i + b_i^I R_I + b_i^E \varepsilon_{it}^E + b_i^{I\_IND} \varepsilon_{it}^{I\_IND} + b_i^{E\_IND} \varepsilon_{it}^{E\_IND} + b_i^C \varepsilon_{it}^C + \varepsilon_{it} \quad (2)$$

where R_{it} is the return of a banking system in country i at time t, $R_{I_{it}}$ is the return from the 'international non-financial' index, while ε_{it}^E, $\varepsilon_{it}^{I\_IND}$, $\varepsilon_{it}^{E\_IND}$, and ε_{it}^C are components uncorrelated with respect to R_{it} and to each other, derived according to the methodology discussed in the Appendix. These series of uncorrelated components refer, respectively, to the 'European non-financial', 'international banking industry', 'European banking industry', and 'country' components of the return-generating model.

This model leads, therefore, to the following decomposition of banking system volatility:

$$\sigma_i^2 = (b_i^I)^2 \sigma_I^2 + (b_i^E)^2 \sigma_{\varepsilon^E}^2 + (b_i^{I\_IND})^2 \sigma_{\varepsilon^{I\_IND}}^2 + (b_i^{E\_IND})^2 \sigma_{\varepsilon^{E\_IND}}^2 + (b_i^C)^2 \sigma_{\varepsilon^C}^2 + \sigma_\varepsilon^2 \quad (3)$$

In other words, the volatility of a banking system is the sum of: 1) an 'international non-financial' component; 2) a 'European non-financial' component; 3) an 'international banking industry' component; 4) a 'European banking industry' component; 5) a 'country' component; and 6) an idiosyncratic component. The relative share of each component can then be expressed in the following way:

$$1 = \frac{(b_i^I)^2 \sigma_I^2}{\sigma_i^2} + \frac{(b_i^E)^2 \sigma_{\varepsilon^E}^2}{\sigma_i^2} + \frac{(b_i^{I\_IND})^2 \sigma_{\varepsilon^{I\_IND}}^2}{\sigma_i^2} + \frac{(b_i^{E\_IND})^2 \sigma_{\varepsilon^{E\_IND}}^2}{\sigma_i^2} + \frac{(b_i^C)^2 \sigma_{\varepsilon^C}^2}{\sigma_i^2} + \frac{\sigma_\varepsilon^2}{\sigma_i^2}$$

$$= w_I + w_E + w_{I\_IND} + w_{E\_IND} + w_C + w_\varepsilon \quad (4)$$

In the spirit of Eiling and Gerard (2007) we interpret the first ratio as a measure of international integration and the second ratio as an indicator of European integration conditioning on the international integration.

These proportions depend on the banking system sensitivity to a specific component and on the volatility of the same component. Specifically, the variance explained by a component j can increase due to an increase in the banking system sensitivity (b_i^j) or an increase in the component volatility (σ_j^2). Since we are interested in the historical movements of banking system volatility on a monthly basis, we should quantify both determinants of the relative importance of each component over this short period. Nevertheless, while the historical volatility of each component can be estimated for a short time interval according to the approach outlined earlier, the estimation of the betas would require the fitting of our model on a small number of daily observations such as the number of trading days in a specific month. Instead we assume that the betas are constant over a longer six-month time period, where we require a minimum of eighty daily returns.[7] As a result, though the betas are assumed to remain constant over that period, the contribution of each component in explaining the variance of a banking system can change on the basis of its volatility. The error that we introduce through this assumption is thus proportional to the beta volatility over six months. However, though simplified, this approach does not require an even stronger assumption of a unit and constant beta for all the banking systems with respect to a component, as in the case of the implementation of the 'market adjusted return model'.[8]

Finally, from the volatility measures and their components, computed at country level, we derive monthly value-weighted average indicators, where each country's weight is measured in terms of its contribution to the banking industry market capitalization at the end of the previous month. Hence, similar to Kearney and Potì (2008), who employ value-weighted volatility indicators as proxies for the level and composition of volatility in a 'typical' stock listed in the Euro area, we use these average indicators as proxies for the level and composition of volatility in a 'typical' banking system located in Europe.[9]

Data

Our analysis is based on daily, continuously compounded dividend-adjusted returns from banking and country value-weighted indices over the time period from 1 January 1988 to 31 December 2010, for the EU-15 countries, plus Norway and Switzerland. All these indices are provided by Datastream International.[10] From the same data source we obtain an international market index for non-financial firms and an international banking index; namely, world indices that exclude European countries, which we employ to control

[7] Later in this chapter we show that our results are qualitatively unchanged if we relax this assumption.

[8] Notably, Bekaert, Hodrick, and Zhang (2008) show that the unit beta restrictions, as adopted by Campbell and colleagues (2001), limit substantially the ability of a factor model to describe stock return co-movements.

[9] Therefore, our indicators are not measuring total banking volatility in Europe. Specifically, according to a portfolio approach, total volatility requires computing not only variance components but the covariance terms between each couple of banking systems. We elaborate on this later in this chapter when we discuss the implications of our results for the interdependencies of banking systems across Europe.

[10] Datastream banking indices include all types of publicly traded banks in a country, with the exclusion of investment banks. These indices are a subset of the more general financial service indices that also include consumer finance, other specialized financial institutions, and insurance companies.

for the international components in our return-generating model.[11] In the following analysis all returns are denominated in local currency. Thus, the broader market indices are converted into the relevant currency before implementing the variance decomposition through our linear model. In other words, we assume the perspective of the local investor in each country (see Beckers et al., 1992; Drummen and Zimmerman, 1992).

Table 4.1 shows summary statistics of the daily returns of the seventeen countries included in our sample. During the full sample period the annualized average daily return is positive for all the banking indices, even though there are notable differences across countries. For example, the annualized daily average return ranges from a minimum of 2.02 per cent for Portugal to a maximum of 13.48 per cent for Norway. Similarly, European banking indices differ substantially in terms of average annualized daily volatility over the full sample period. Scandinavian countries and Ireland exhibit the highest level of volatilities while the remaining small banking systems (Austria, Denmark, Luxembourg, and Portugal) show the lowest level of volatility. Table 4.1 also reports the relative importance of each country in terms of average market weight over the full sample period. Only six countries (UK, Germany, Spain, Italy, Switzerland, and France) show an (average) individual share greater than 7 per cent. Furthermore, overall, these countries represent about 80 per cent of the total average daily market capitalization of the full sample, with the UK exhibiting the largest share (around 28 per cent).[12] In the following sections we evaluate how the high degree of concentration of our sample impacts on the empirical results by repeating the analysis separately for these six banking systems ('large' banking systems) and for the rest of our sample ('small' banking systems).

The Evolution of Banking System Volatility in Europe

Evolution of the Average Volatility of the European Banking Systems

Figure 4.1 shows the evolution of the value-weighted average of monthly return volatilities computed at the level of the country and of its twelve-month moving average, expressed in annualized terms over the period from 1988 to 2010.

[11] We employ this set of indices instead of indices provided by the local stock exchanges in order to eliminate the distortions that can be generated by differences in terms of construction of the index. Furthermore, we do not employ alternative sources of provider (for example, Morgan Stanley Capital International (MSCI)—Barra) since they are not available at a daily frequency for the whole period under consideration. The sector classifications adopted by Datastream are based on the Financial Times Stock Exchange categories (FTSE Actuaries).

[12] At the end of 2009, according to the European Banking Federation (EBF, 2009), the same group of countries held 77 per cent of the total assets of the 17 European banking systems included in this study; namely, a value similar to that obtained in terms of average market capitalization over the sample period.

Table 4.1. Statistics of Daily Banking Returns

1	2	3	4	5	6	7	8
Country	DSMnemonic	Start date	Mean p.a.	S.Dev. p.a.	Min. daily	Max daily	w_{av}
Austria	BANKSOE	01.01.1988	8.30%	25.60%	−13.52%	14.33%	1.08%
Belgium	BANKSBG	01.01.1988	5.13%	29.73%	−25.41%	18.60%	3.38%
Denmark	BANKSDK	01.01.1988	10.14%	22.92%	−14.64%	15.32%	1.74%
Finland	BANKSFN	01.04.1988	8.01%	42.50%	−55.37%	26.64%	0.36%
France	BANKSFR	01.01.1988	9.78%	30.46%	−11.29%	18.33%	8.14%
Germany	BANKSBD	01.01.1988	4.36%	26.68%	−16.46%	15.87%	14.02%
Greece	BANKSGR	02.01.1990	9.07%	33.95%	−11.07%	16.69%	2.11%
Ireland	BANKSIR	01.01.1988	2.82%	48.20%	−74.77%	29.93%	1.84%
Italy	BANKSIT	01.01.1988	5.91%	23.57%	−9.86%	15.80%	10.42%
Luxembourg	BANKSLX	03.01.1992	11.98%	17.10%	−10.00%	15.93%	0.46%
Netherlands	BANKSNL	01.01.1988	2.51%	39.99%	−129.59%	15.18%	4.02%
Norway	BANKSNW	11.01.1990	13.48%	36.15%	−37.82%	25.53%	0.71%
Portugal	BANKSPT	03.01.1990	2.02%	19.47%	−10.08%	12.79%	1.44%
Spain	BANKSES	01.01.1988	8.20%	24.91%	−11.49%	19.08%	11.51%
Sweden	BANKSSD	01.01.1988	12.43%	33.60%	−20.44%	20.73%	3.51%
Switzerland	BANKSSW	01.01.1988	5.81%	26.56%	−11.43%	17.78%	7.76%
UK	BANKSUK	01.01.1988	11.04%	27.51%	−19.43%	18.83%	27.97%

Table 4.1 reports the summary statistics of daily returns for our sample of seventeen European banking systems. For the majority of the banking indices, the sample period runs from 1 January 1988 to 31 December 2010. The first column reports the initial date that a banking index becomes available, while the second column refers to the Datastream mnemonic. The mean and standard deviation, reported in columns 4 and 5, are expressed in annualized terms by assuming 260 trading days in a year. Column 8 reports the average weight of a country with respect to the full sample of European banking systems.

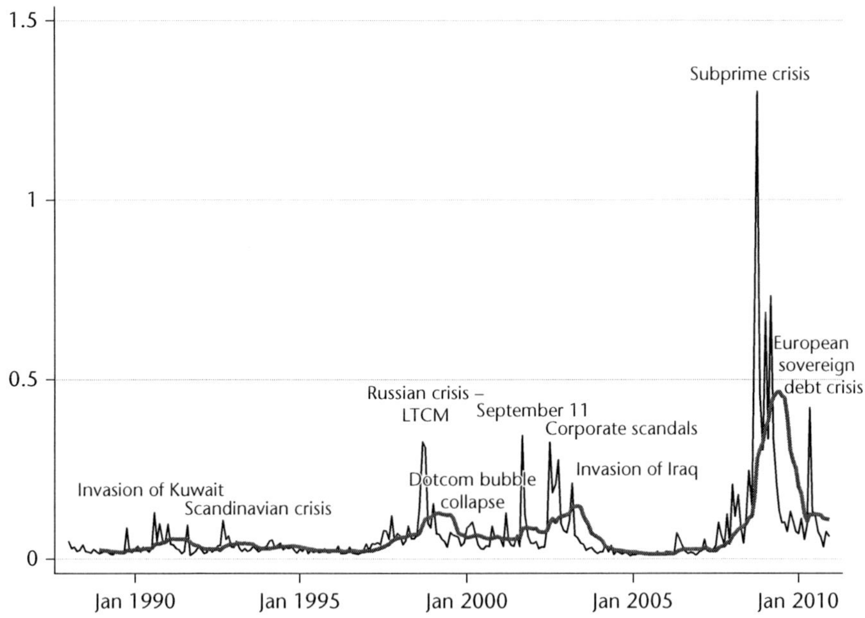

Figure 4.1. Evolution of Value-Weighted Volatility in the European Banking Systems

Figure 4.1 plots the value-weighted average total volatility estimated at monthly intervals for a sample of seventeen countries. We consider countries with different sample lengths. The sample starts in January 1988 and ends in December 2010. The bold line represents the twelve-month moving average.

Figure 4.1 provides evidence consistent with recent empirical analyses based on the volatility in the US banking system before the financial crisis of 2007–9 (Houston and Stiroh, 2006; Stiroh, 2006b) and outlines the large impact of this crisis on banking systems. As in Houston and Stiroh (2006), Figure 4.1 shows that, before the recent financial crisis, the banking industry suffered heavily from the impact of common shocks, which were mainly concentrated in the period from mid-1997 to mid-2003. In particular, high levels of banking system volatility have been associated with the Russian bond default and the collapse of Long-Term Capital Management (LTCM) in the second half of 1998, September 11 in 2001, and the corporate scandals in 2002. The impact of these events is, however, far from that of the global financial crisis that started in the second half of 2007: during this crisis the average banking system volatility has achieved a value more than three times larger than in the case of the LTCM default and September 11. Furthermore, a remarkable increase in banking system volatility has been also produced by the European sovereign debt crisis in the first half of 2010. Overall, there does not appear to be any clear long-term trend in banking system volatility since the late eighties, but only several sudden increases in its level (with a peak during the global financial crisis of 2007–9) due to shocks whose effects disappear after a short period.

A clearer picture of the changes in the average volatility of European banking systems is, however, offered by Figure 4.2, which plots the evolution of the relative share of the value-weighted average volatility explained by the components defined earlier in the chapter. Figure 4.2 clearly highlights a remarkable change in the average composition of banking system volatility across Europe in the last two decades, due to the increasing contribution of international and European non-financial sources of variation that lead to a decline in the additional contribution of the country and idiosyncratic components. In other words, in the spirit of Eiling and Gerard (2007), banking systems are becoming more and more integrated within the international and European context, and this seems to be a long-term process that started at the beginning of our sample period.[13]

Furthermore, it is worth noting that the reduction in the relative importance of the idiosyncratic component, especially in the second part of the sample period, is in line with the conclusions of Houston and Stiroh (2006) for the USA. This reduction can be generally linked with worldwide changes in the banking industry such as deregulation and consolidation processes (Demsetz and Strahan, 1997; Houston and Stiroh, 2006). These changes have led to larger and more (internally and externally) diversified financial institutions that are likely to show a lower degree of specific/idiosyncratic risk. In line with this interpretation, Baele, De Jonghe, and Vander Vennet (2007) show that more diversified European banks benefit from a lower degree of idiosyncratic risk but exhibit a larger exposure to systematic shocks.

Interestingly, the relative importance of the international banking industry component exhibits a sudden upward shift during the financial crisis of 2007–9, after a period of relative stability. This shift underlines the pivotal role played by international financial shocks during the crisis, which has also led to a decline in the international non-financial component of banking system volatility. Furthermore, the European banking industry component does not show any clear trend until the last five years of the sample period where, by contrast, we observe a clear, increasing pattern of its contribution to the value-weighted average volatility. We conjecture that this growing importance of the European banking industry component in the most recent years might be linked to the increasing participation of EU banks in the European money market, with a consequent increase in their exposure to common liquidity shocks. Similarly, common exposures to shocks might be

[13] These same figures show that the relative importance of the international and European non-financial components drop substantially in the years 1999–2000. Since this result has been generally found also for non-financial firms, it is not probably due to the impact of some specific bank effects, but can be ascribed to the temporarily deviating behaviour that stocks of some specific industrial sectors (i.e. telecoms and technology) exhibit in those years (Brooks and Del Negro, 2004).

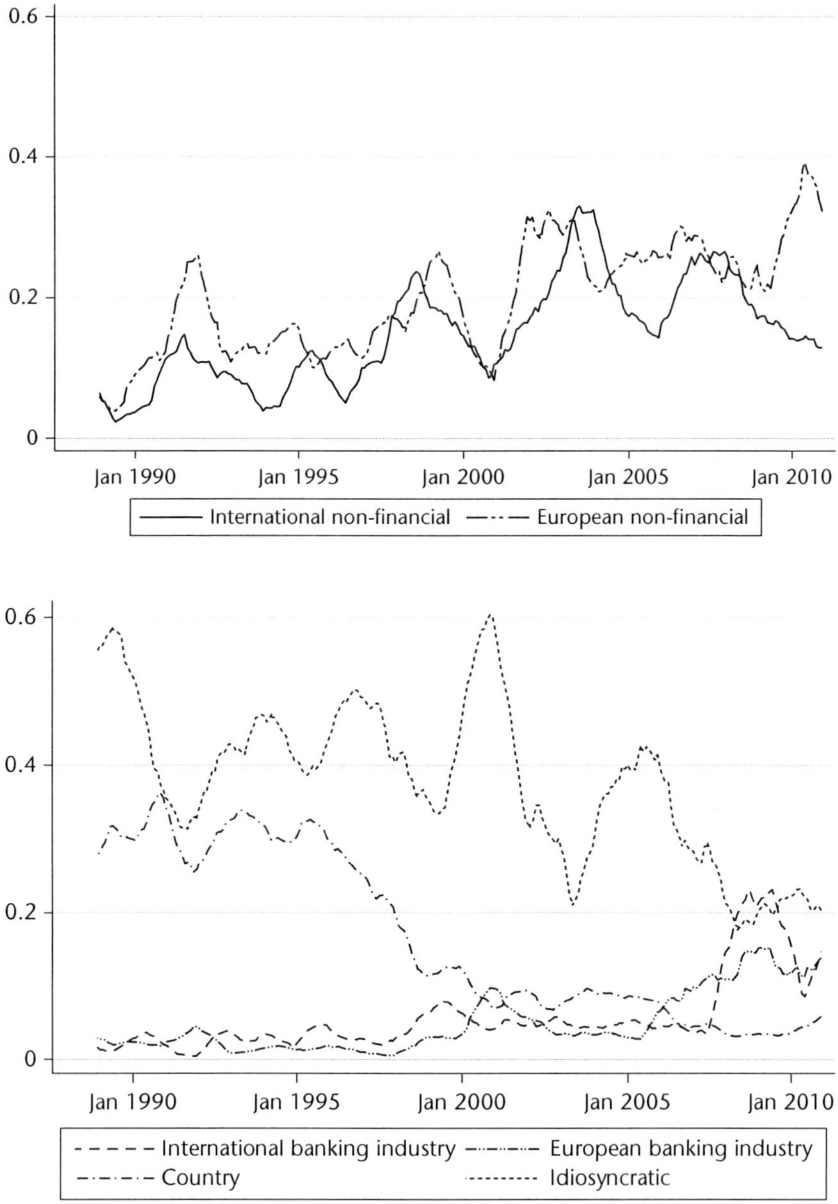

Figure 4.2. Value-Weighted Shares of Volatility Components in the European Banking Systems

Figure 4.2 plots the value-weighted shares of the components of banking system volatility. Series are backwards twelve-month moving averages.

Table 4.2. Summary Statistics of Value-Weighted Average Volatility and Volatility Components in European Banking Systems

	Full sample period						1988–98						1999–2010					
	Mean	Median	Stdev.	Min.	Max	N	Mean	Median	Stdev.	Min.	Max	N	Mean	Median	Stdev.	Min.	Max	N
Panel A: Total Banking Systems																		
Average Volatility	0.071	0.036	0.122	0.009	1.303	276	0.041	0.028	0.043	0.010	0.327	132	0.099	0.054	0.159	0.009	1.303	144
International Non-financial Component	0.147	0.129	0.093	0.005	0.419	276	0.101	0.079	0.079	0.005	0.419	132	0.189	0.178	0.086	0.021	0.410	144
European Non-financial Component	0.199	0.178	0.112	0.017	0.557	276	0.142	0.124	0.084	0.017	0.508	132	0.251	0.236	0.108	0.047	0.557	144
International Banking Industry Component	0.060	0.039	0.065	0.002	0.394	276	0.029	0.023	0.025	0.002	0.117	132	0.087	0.055	0.078	0.010	0.394	144
European Industry Component	0.051	0.032	0.051	0.002	0.243	276	0.020	0.016	0.015	0.002	0.073	132	0.080	0.064	0.055	0.014	0.243	144
Country Component	0.167	0.117	0.118	0.021	0.420	276	0.274	0.287	0.079	0.073	0.420	132	0.069	0.066	0.034	0.021	0.195	144
Idiosyncratic Component	0.376	0.383	0.137	0.098	0.764	276	0.434	0.442	0.107	0.155	0.671	132	0.324	0.300	0.140	0.098	0.764	144
Panel B: Large Banking Systems																		
Average Volatility	0.067	0.035	0.110	0.007	1.015	276	0.039	0.025	0.045	0.007	0.360	132	0.093	0.047	0.141	0.008	1.015	144
International Non-financial Component	0.158	0.143	0.099	0.004	0.441	276	0.109	0.086	0.085	0.004	0.441	132	0.204	0.190	0.090	0.020	0.434	144
European Non-financial Component	0.206	0.189	0.116	0.013	0.591	276	0.147	0.126	0.090	0.013	0.550	132	0.261	0.240	0.112	0.048	0.591	144
International Banking Industry Component	0.062	0.040	0.071	0.001	0.397	276	0.029	0.020	0.028	0.001	0.134	132	0.093	0.057	0.084	0.008	0.397	144
European Banking Industry Component	0.053	0.034	0.054	0.001	0.258	276	0.020	0.015	0.017	0.001	0.080	132	0.084	0.066	0.059	0.012	0.258	144
Country Component	0.178	0.119	0.138	0.015	0.469	276	0.303	0.322	0.093	0.062	0.469	132	0.064	0.056	0.039	0.015	0.202	144
Idiosyncratic Component	0.342	0.340	0.142	0.082	0.807	276	0.393	0.400	0.117	0.119	0.654	132	0.295	0.260	0.147	0.082	0.807	144
Panel C: Small Banking Systems																		
Average Volatility	0.088	0.046	0.180	0.013	2.434	276	0.051	0.036	0.042	0.013	0.326	132	0.122	0.056	0.241	0.013	2.434	144
International Non-financial Component	0.103	0.077	0.078	0.005	0.359	276	0.071	0.053	0.060	0.005	0.325	132	0.132	0.113	0.081	0.009	0.359	144
European Non-financial Component	0.169	0.153	0.101	0.023	0.540	276	0.120	0.102	0.071	0.030	0.359	132	0.214	0.204	0.105	0.023	0.540	144
International Banking Industry Component	0.050	0.032	0.053	0.003	0.383	276	0.032	0.025	0.027	0.003	0.181	132	0.067	0.044	0.064	0.003	0.383	144
European Banking Industry Component	0.043	0.030	0.039	0.003	0.195	276	0.019	0.015	0.016	0.003	0.102	132	0.066	0.053	0.041	0.010	0.195	144
Country Component	0.116	0.112	0.048	0.023	0.243	276	0.143	0.141	0.039	0.057	0.243	132	0.091	0.081	0.041	0.023	0.229	144
Idiosyncratic Component	0.517	0.545	0.155	0.136	0.834	276	0.612	0.622	0.116	0.241	0.834	132	0.430	0.414	0.133	0.136	0.699	144

Table 4.2 reports the summary statistics of monthly average volatility and volatility components for the value-weighted average of seventeen European banking systems. The sample period runs from 1 January 1988 to 31 December 2010, for a total number of 276 monthly observations. Volatility components are expressed in relative terms with respect to bank average volatility.

also associated to similarities in European banks' investment strategies as outlined by the European sovereign debt crisis, which has seen numerous European banks highly exposed because of their investments in European government bonds. Furthermore, the rise in the importance of the European banking industry component might reflect the interconnections produced via the network of branches and subsidiaries of European banks across European countries.[14]

The evidence offered by Figures 4.1 and 4.2 is confirmed by the results reported in Table 4.2. Panel A shows descriptive statistics for the average volatility and the relative share of each component for the full sample period and for two sub-periods, conventionally identified by the introduction of the euro. This Panel suggests two major conclusions. First, the level of banking system volatility becomes higher in the second part of our sample period, as a consequence of the effect of a series of common shocks, as shown by Figure 4.1. Second, the composition of banking system volatility has changed dramatically since the late eighties with an increase in the contribution of international and European non-financial components and with a substantial decline in the relative importance of the country component, as suggested by Figure 4.2.

Panels B and C report the results of the same analysis, conducted by distinguishing between large and small banking systems. As discussed previously, to this end we consider as 'large' the top six banking systems in terms of average daily market capitalization (UK, Germany, Italy, Spain, Switzerland, and France) that represent about 80 per cent of the average total market value of our sample. It seems to be clear that the importance of international and European non-financial components is substantially higher in the large banking systems than in the small banking systems where the idiosyncratic component remains dominant. Notably, the greater importance of the idiosyncratic component in small banking systems as compared to large banking systems might be influenced by the smaller average bank size and by the lower number of banks included in the portfolio that comprises the small banking indices.[15] Nevertheless, over the sample period, the small banking systems show, on average, a greater decline in this component (−18.2 p.p.: from 61.2 per cent to 43.0 per cent) than large banking systems (−8.8 p.p.: from 39.3 per

[14] For instance, according to the ECB (2010), the total assets of branches and subsidiaries coming from one of the EU-15 countries and located in the others EU-15 countries are equal to 18.6 per cent of the EU-15 banking system total assets.

[15] Banks operating in small banking systems generally show a smaller size than banks in large banking systems and this, as suggested by Baele, De Jonghe, and Vander Vennet (2007), might be associated to a lower degree of functional diversification, with the effect of increasing their exposure to idiosyncratic shocks. Furthermore, according to a portfolio view, a larger number of banks in the index is likely to indicate a more diversified portfolio of banks with a consequent decline in idiosyncratic risk.

cent to 29.5 per cent); namely, in these banking systems common sources of shocks are also increasing in their importance.

Trend Analysis

We initially test for the presence of stochastic trends in the volatility series, via the augmented Dickey Fuller (ADF) test, estimated with a constant and a time trend. The number of lagged differences to be included is determined by the standard *t*-test of significance of the last lagged difference term.

The results of these tests, reported in Table 4.3, show that we are able to reject the null hypothesis of a unit root in the volatility series in all specifications of the ADF test, suggesting, therefore, that shocks have only a temporary impact on these series. By contrast, we generally reject the null hypothesis of a unit root for the volatility components only when a trend variable is introduced in the ADF test. Thus, these components tend to be trend stationary. An exception to this general conclusion is observed for the international non-financial and the international banking industry components that do not appear to be stationary in spite of the specification of the ADF test. Notably, when we split the sample between large and small banking systems, we observe that this result is common to both groups of banking systems. The non-stationarity of these two series is likely to be due to the impact of the financial crisis of 2007–9 that, as shown by Figure 4.2, has been associated with a declining trend in the international non-financial component and to a sudden upward shift of the international banking industry component. As a consequence, the financial crisis is likely to have modified the mean and the variance of these two time series.

To test for the presence of a linear time trend in volatility and in each component we employ the Vogelsang approach (1998). This is based on the following two regressions that are estimated via OLS:[16]

$$y_t = \mu + \beta t + \varepsilon_t \tag{5}$$

$$z_t = \mu t + \beta \times ST_t + S_t \tag{6}$$

where

[16] This approach is characterized by several advantages as compared to the traditional OLS regression. Specifically, estimates of serial correlation parameters are not needed and the adjusted t-statistic is robust to I(0) and I(1) errors; namely, in the case of both stationary errors (I(0)) and when the errors are stationary after one differentiation (I(1)).

Table 4.3. Unit Root Tests—Value-Weighted Average Volatility and Volatility Components in European Banking Systems

	Average Volatility	International Non-financial Component	European Non-financial Component	International Banking Industry Component	European Banking Industry Component	Country Component	Idiosyncratic Component
Panel A: Total Banking Systems							
Intercept	−3.766***	−2.520	−3.103**	−1.408	−1.403	−1.536	−4.220***
	(0.003)	(0.111)	(0.026)	(0.578)	(0.581)	(0.515)	(0.000)
Lag order	4	7	6	7	5	2	1
Intercept and trend	−4.092***	−2.860	−4.290***	−2.664	−3.729**	−3.559**	−5.472***
	(0.006)	(0.176)	(0.003)	(0.251)	(0.021)	(0.034)	(0.000)
Lag order	4	7	6	7	4	2	1
Panel B: Large Banking Systems							
Intercept	−4.480***	−2.526	−3.096**	−1.640	−1.392	−1.492	−2.934**
	(0.000)	(0.109)	(0.027)	(0.462)	(0.586)	(0.537)	(0.042)
Lag order	2	7	6	7	5	2	5
Intercept and trend	−4.847***	−2.898	−4.201***	−2.961	−3.674**	−3.361*	−5.393***
	(0.000)	(0.163)	(0.005)	(0.143)	(0.024)	(0.057)	(0.000)
Lag order	2	7	6	7	4	2	1
Panel C: Small Banking Systems							
Intercept	−4.011***	−2.181	−4.147***	−1.810	−2.217	−2.187	−1.771
	(0.001)	(0.213)	(0.000)	(0.375)	(0.200)	(0.211)	(0.395)
Lag order	4	8	2	7	5	7	8
Intercept and trend	−4.309***	−2.645	−6.103***	−2.491	−5.360***	−3.156*	−3.744**
	(0.003)	(0.260)	(0.000)	(0.332)	(0.000)	(0.093)	(0.020)
Lag order	4	8	2	7	2	7	8

Table 4.3 shows the results of the Augmented Dickey Fuller (ADF) test for series of average volatility and for its components as defined in Decomposing Banking System Volatility. All the series are estimated at monthly intervals for the period from January 1988 to December 2010. Volatility components are expressed in relative terms with respect to bank average volatility. The ADF test is estimated both with an intercept and an intercept and a time trend. P values, reported in brackets, are based on Mackinnon (1994). The number of lags is determined by 'the general to specific' method recommended by Campbell and Perron (1991).

***(**;*) Denotes significance at 1% (5%;10%) level.

$$z_t = \sum_{j=1}^{t} y_j, ST_t = \sum_{j=1}^{t} t_j = (t + t^2)/2, S_t = \sum_{j=1}^{t} \varepsilon_j$$

The z_t regression is obtained as partial sums of the y_t regression while the statistics for determining the significance level of β and μ are modifications of the *t*-statistics computed by OLS. Specifically, the *t*-statistic is adjusted according to the following formula:

$$t - PS^1 = T^{-1/2} t_z \exp\left(-bJ_T^1\right) \quad (7)$$

where T is the length of the sample period, b is a constant while J_T^1 requires the estimation of the following regression:

$$y_t = \mu + \beta t + \sum_{t=2}^{9} c_i t^i + \varepsilon_t \quad (8)$$

Then J_T^1 can be calculated as follows:

$$J_T^1 = \frac{(RSS_y - RSS_J)}{RSS_J} \quad (9)$$

where RSS_y is the residual sum of squares from Equation (5) and RSS_J is the residual sum of squares from Equation (8).[17]

The results of this test, reported in Table 4.4, are consistent with the description provided by Figures 4.1 and 4.2. Panel A of Table 4.4 confirms that over the full sample period there is no evidence of a significant upward trend in the average banking volatility, while we observe a radical change in its composition. We find a highly significant positive trend both in the international and European non-financial components, which seem to have progressively replaced the country component. In annual terms, the international and European non-financial components have increased by about 1 per cent per year over the sample period, while the country component has decreased by 1.75 per cent per annum across the same time horizon. Therefore, these positive trends imply that banking systems are becoming more and more integrated into the international market, even though the European dimension still plays an increasing and significant independent role.

In Panels B and C, we repeat the analysis by distinguishing between large and small banking systems. These tests suggest that banking system size exercises a strong impact on our results. For instance, while large banking

[17] This statistic is used to smooth discontinuities in the limiting distribution of the statistics as the errors go from I(0) and I(1) in the case where b is greater than zero. For a given significance level of the test, b can be chosen to ensure that the critical values of $t-PS^1$ are the same when the residuals are I(0) and I(1). As a consequence, J_T^1 ensures that the t-tests from the Z_t regression are robust for I(1) errors; namely, in the case of errors that are stationary after one differentiation. The critical values of these tests and the optimal values of b are provided by Vogelsang (1998).

Table 4.4. Deterministic Trends—Value-Weighted Average Volatility, Volatility Components, and Betas in European Banking Systems

	(1)	(2)	(3)	(4)	(5)	(6)	(7)	(8)	(9)
	Average Volatility	International Non-financial Component	European Non-financial Component	International Banking Industry Component	European Banking Industry Component	Country Component	Idiosyncratic Component	International Beta	European Beta
Panel A: Total Banking Systems									
Trend	3.500	7.893**	7.868**	3.385	3.149	−14.579*	−7.679*	139.160**	154.798**
	(1.117)	(3.447)	(4.929)	(1.189)	(1.042)	(−2.616)	(−2.078)	(3.808)	(2.555)
Annualized trend (%)	0.420	0.947	0.944	0.406	0.378	−1.749	−0.921	2.783	3.096
Panel B: Large Banking Systems									
Trend	3.343	8.565**	8.128**	3.743	3.316	−16.820*	−6.932	142.987**	147.756**
	(1.158)	(3.473)	(4.450)	(1.343)	(0.926)	(−2.102)	(−1.670)	(3.745)	(2.276)
Annualized trend (%)	0.401	1.028	0.975	0.449	0.398	−2.018	−0.832	2.860	2.952
Panel C: Small Banking Systems									
Trend	3.949	5.687**	7.042**	2.223	2.709**	−4.091**	−13.307**	121.372*	179.800**
	(0.913)	(2.490)	(5.556)	(0.754)	(2.392)	(−2.898)	(−5.546)	(2.348)	(2.304)
Annualized trend (%)	0.474	0.682	0.845	0.267	0.325	−0.491	−1.597	2.427	3.596

Table 4.4 shows the estimated deterministic linear trends in the time series of value-weighted volatility and volatility components, and in the value-weighted series of international and European betas computed for seventeen European banking systems. Value-weighted volatility and volatility components are estimated at monthly intervals for the period from January 1988 to December 2010. Risk components are expressed in relative terms with respect to bank average volatility. The time series of international and European betas are estimated at six-month intervals for the period from January 1988 to December 2010 for a total number of observations equal to 46. The Vogelsang (1998) $t\text{–}PS^1$ statistics are reported in round brackets. The trend coefficient is multiplied by 10^4. The 5 per cent (10%) critical value (two-sided) is 2.152 (1.720) while the appropriate value of constant b is 0.995 (0.716) (see Table II in Vogelsang (1998)). These statistics are robust to various forms of serial correlation.

** (*) Denotes significance at 5% (10%) level. The annual trend is obtained by multiplying the trend coefficient for 12. t- statistics are reported for the 10% level when trends are not significant at the 5% level.

systems show a much larger positive time trend in the international component and a much faster decline in the country share of the average volatility, small banking systems exhibit a significant positive time trend in the European banking industry component and a significant negative time trend in the idiosyncratic component. These latter findings are likely to reflect the rising importance of cross-border banking groups in Belgium and Netherlands and in the Scandinavian banking systems.

To summarize, we find robust evidence of an increasing trend in the international and European non-financial components of banking system volatility. On average, however, these trends are greater for large banking systems, while the most remarkable result for small banking systems is the substantial decline in the idiosyncratic component. Hence, this latter finding also implies that the smallest banking systems are moving towards a volatility composition where commonalities play a much larger role than in the past. Therefore, in contrast to Schuermann and Stiroh (2006) for the USA, our results show a gradual increase in the importance of the broad channel of systemic risk over the past two decades.

Finally, to show that the increasing relevance of international and European non-financial components is not merely due to a rise in the volatility of the international and European markets over time, without any change in the exposure to non-domestic shocks by banking systems, in Figure 4.3 we plot the value-weighted average of the six-month betas that we have employed to

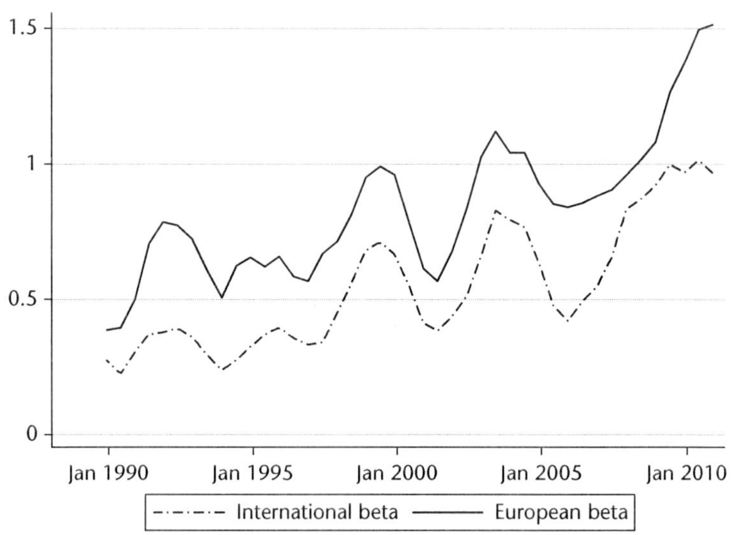

Figure 4.3. International and European Betas of European Banking Systems

Figure 4.3 plots the four-semester moving average of the value-weighted international and European betas for the sample of seventeen European banking systems.

decompose banking system volatility. Figure 4.3 shows that there has been a substantial rise in the international and European betas of banking systems over the sample period. In addition, the exposure is larger for European shocks than for international shocks.

Formal time trend tests, reported in the last two columns of Table 4.4, confirm this visual impression. Focusing initially on the full sample, we observe a significant positive time trend for both the international and European betas that, in annualized terms, have increased, respectively, by 2.8 per cent and 3.1 per cent per year. When we split the sample between large and small banking systems, we observe that in large banking systems international and European betas have grown at similar pace while small banking systems show a much faster increase in their exposure to European shocks. In other words, regional factors still play a pivotal role in Europe especially in the case of small banking systems.

The Composition of Banking System Volatility and Banking Systems' Interdependencies

Next, we assess how the evolution in the composition of banking system volatility discerned earlier in this chapter has affected the degree of interdependency between European banking systems. The results reported imply that the banking systems across Europe have become more exposed to sources of common shocks; thus, they should be characterized by an increasing degree of interconnectedness over the sample period.

We quantify the growth in banking interdependencies in Europe by analysing the trend in banking system co-movements over the sample period. To this end, we adopt a portfolio approach; namely, we start by measuring the *total* banking system volatility in Europe by treating each banking system in our sample as part of a portfolio identifying the European system. Next, we compute, at a monthly frequency, the *total* volatility, that is, the variance, of this portfolio. Finally, we derive an indicator of banking system co-movement in Europe as the relative contribution of the covariance component to the *total* volatility of this portfolio. In line with the analysis presented in the previous sections, we should observe an increasing importance of the covariance component over the sample period.

This is confirmed by Figure 4.4, where we plot the relative contribution of the covariance component. Figure 4.4 shows clearly that our proxy of bank interdependencies has exhibited a remarkable upward trend since the beginning of the sample period.

Further evidence is offered by Table 4.5, which reports the results of the trend analysis conducted on *total* volatility and its covariance component. These tests show that there is no evidence of a significant upward trend in our

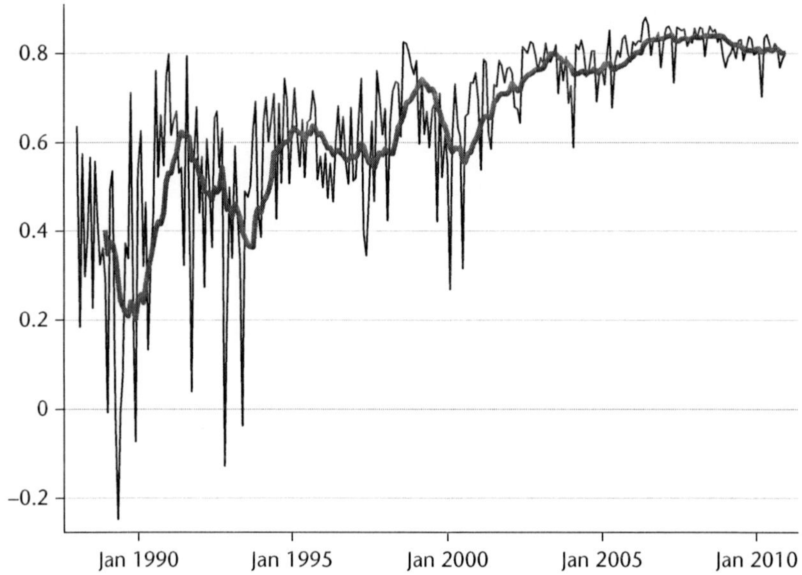

Figure 4.4. Evolution of Banking Interdependencies in Europe

Figure 4.4 plots the banking interdependencies across Europe measured by the covariance component of total banking system volatility. The bold line represents the twelve-month moving average.

Table 4.5. Total Banking Volatility and its Covariance Component in Europe

	Total Banking Systems		Large Banking Systems		Small Banking Systems	
	Total Banking System Volatility	Covariance Component	Total Banking System Volatility	Covariance Component	Total Banking System Volatility	Covariance Component
Trend	3.134 (1.496)	20.145** (9.346)	3.197 (1.517)	19.507** (11.030)	2.948 (1.363)	24.405** (8.390)
Annualized trend (%)	0.376	2.417	0.384	2.341	0.354%	2.929

Table 4.5 shows the tests for a deterministic trend for total banking volatility and for its covariance component. The tests have been conducted for the full sample and separately for the set of large and small banking systems. These indicators have been computed at monthly intervals according to a portfolio approach, as described in The Composition of Banking System Volatility and Banking Systems' Interdependencies. The sample period spans the period from January 1988 to December 2010. The presence of determinist trends is tested via the Vogelsang (1998) t–PS^1 statistics, reported in round brackets. The trend coefficient is multiplied by 10^4. The 5 per cent (10%) critical value (two-sided) is 2.152 (1.720) while the appropriate value of constant b is 0.995 (0.716) (see Table II in Vogelsang (1998)). This statistic is robust to various forms of serial correlation.

** (*) Denotes significance at 5% (10%) level. t- statistics are reported for the 10% level when trends (trend shifts) are not significant at 5% level.

indicator of *total* volatility. More importantly, they highlight the influence played by the interdependencies between banking systems on *total* volatility: the trend coefficients assigned to banking system co-movements (i.e. the share of the covariance component) are systematically positive and highly significant. Specifically, in the full sample, the relative share of the covariance component has increased by around 2.4 per cent per year in the last two decades, while for the set of large (small) banking systems it has a value of 2.3 per cent (2.9 per cent).

Hence, the changing composition of banking system volatility has determined an increasing degree of interdependency across European banking systems. These interdependencies are, therefore, becoming a major threat to the stability of the banking systems in the European context as they increase the risk of cross-border crises. Overall, our results suggest that, although banking systems across Europe have not become *individually* riskier, they have become more interconnected, with the effect of increasing the potential for systemic risk in Europe (De Nicolò and Kwast, 2002; Acharya, 2009).

The Impact of the Euro

Several studies suggest that the introduction of the euro since 1999 has led to relevant changes in European banking risk (Francis and Hunter, 2004; Haq and Heaney, 2009) with spill-over effects also occurring for countries outside the Euro zone (Haq and Heaney, 2009). More generally, the level of integration in Europe is supposed to have increased, due especially to a rise in cross-border activities since the formation of the EMU. For instance, Allen and Song (2005) provide evidence of an increase in regional financial integration for EMU countries after the adoption of the euro via mergers and acquisitions in the financial industry. In a similar vein, outside the banking literature Bartram, Taylor, and Wang (2006) show that financial market dependence increases for large equity markets after the introduction of the common currency. In the context of our analysis, these findings should imply the presence of significant shifts in the dynamics of banking system volatility and in its composition, as pointed out previously in this chapter. For instance, after the introduction of the euro we should observe an acceleration in the rising importance of non-domestic components of banking system volatility and in the decline of the country component, as an indication of increasing integration.

We test for the influence of the introduction of the euro on our results by adopting the Vogelsang (2001) test for shifts in time trends. This test is robust to any form of serial correlation and is based on the estimation by OLS of the two following equations:

$$y_t = \mu + \beta t + \gamma DT_t + \varepsilon_t \tag{10}$$

$$z_t = \mu t + \beta \times ST_t + \gamma SDT + S_t \tag{11}$$

where
$DT = t - T_b$ if $t > T_b$ and 0 otherwise; T_b is the break date; $z_t = \sum_{j=1}^{t} y_t$,

$ST_t = \sum_{j=1}^{t} t_j = (t + t^2)/2, SDT_t = (DT_t^2 + DT_t)/2; S\sum_{j=1}^{t} \varepsilon_j$

The corrected t-statistic is then computed in a similar manner as in the case of the trend test discussed earlier in this chapter.

The results of this test estimated for the full sample, reported in Panel A of Table 4.6, show that, on average, the introduction of the euro has not generated any significant shift in the trends observed in the banking industry since the late eighties. Thus, the changing nature of banking system volatility has been a long-term process not significantly affected by the introduction of the euro.

When we split the sample between large and small banking systems, we achieve largely similar conclusions. For the set of large banking systems, the results show only a significant (at the 10 per cent level) acceleration in the growth of the European industry component, but this acceleration appears driven by the financial crisis in the latest part of the sample period.[18] For the group of small banking systems, our analysis does not offer any evidence of significant shifts in the trends in volatility after the adoption of the common currency.

The last two columns of Table 4.6 report the results of the same tests repeated for international and European betas. Once again, we do not find evidence of a significant shift in trends after the introduction of the common currency.[19] Putting together these results with the evidence offered by Figure 4.3 of larger international and European betas in the second half of our sample period, we achieve substantially different conclusions from Haq and Heaney (2009). Through a dummy variable model, they show that 64 per cent of European banks have reduced their level of systematic risk after the introduction of the euro. By contrast, we do not find any significant impact of the euro on the long-term dynamics of banking systematic risk. Furthermore, the (average) international and European betas of the European banking industry are higher in the latter part of the sample period; namely, after the

[18] When we limit the analysis to the pre-crisis, we do not find any significant shift in the European banking industry component.

[19] We obtain similar results when we test for a shift in trend in total volatility and its covariance components as described in Table 4.5.

Table 4.6. Test for Shifts in the Deterministic Trend in Value-Weighted Average Volatility, Volatility Components and Betas in European Banking Systems after the Introduction of the Euro

	Average Volatility	International Non-financial Component	European Non-financial Component	International Banking Industry Component	European Banking Industry Component	Country Component	Idiosyncratic Component	International Beta	European Beta
Panel A: Total Banking Systems									
Trend shift	4.387	−3.670	1.604	6.087	7.982	3.079	−15.208	57.418	57.159
	(0.252)	(−0.299)	(0.167)	(0.556)	(1.237)	(0.091)	(−1.074)	(0.266)	(0.165)
Annualized trend shift (%)	0.526	−0.440	0.192	0.730	0.958	0.369	−1.825	6.890	6.859
Panel B: Large Banking Systems									
Trend shift	2.807	−4.808	0.991	6.357	9.138*	4.213	−15.892	24.741	24.875
	(0.171)	(−0.378)	(0.089)	(0.573)	(1.314)	(0.086)	(−0.927)	(0.102)	(0.066)
Annualized trend shift (%)	0.337	−0.577	0.119	0.763	1.097	0.506	−1.907	2.969	2.985
Panel C: Small Banking Systems									
Trend shift	10.933	1.282	4.012	5.164	3.543	−5.054	−7.968	182.308	188.046
	(0.507)	(0.099)	(0.611)	(0.438)	(0.796)	(−0.720)	(−0.933)	(0.740)	(0.597)
Annualized trend shift (%)	1.312	0.154	0.481	0.620	0.425	−0.606	−1.907	21.877	22.566

Table 4.6 shows the estimated shift in deterministic linear trends in the time series of value-weighted volatility and volatility components and in the value-weighted international and European betas computed for a sample of seventeen European banking systems. Value-weighted volatility and volatility components are estimated at monthly intervals for the period from January 1988 to December 2010. Risk components are expressed in relative terms with respect to bank average volatility. The time series of international and European betas are estimated at six-month intervals. The Vogelsang (2001) $t\text{–}PS_t$ statistics are reported in round brackets. The shift in the trend coefficient is multiplied by 10^4. The appropriate critical values are taken from Table II in Vogelsang (2001). These statistics are robust to various forms of serial correlation.

** (*) Denotes significance at 5% (10%) level. The annualized shift in the deterministic trend is obtained by multiplying the coefficient for 12. t- statistics are reported for the 10% level when trend shifts are not significant at the 5% level.

adoption of the euro, as suggested by Francis and Hunter (2004). However, in contrast to Francis and Hunter (2004), we show that this increase is the consequence of the long-term dynamics observed within the European banking systems since the late eighties. In sum, our findings are in line with the conclusion proposed by Hartmann, Straetmans, and de Vries (2006) on the lack of any significant influence of the euro on banking risk.

Possible Determinants of the Changing Composition of Banking System Volatility

The Role of Cross-Border Banking

While our findings so far demonstrate that the introduction of a common currency did not play a significant role with regard to the trends of the volatility series, they may also imply that the growing internationalization of the European banking systems observed over the sample period has contributed to a change in the composition of banking system volatility in the last two decades.

The extensive deregulation process implemented in the last twenty years in the banking industry has reduced the entry barriers for cross-border activities, increasing the opportunities for geographic diversification. However, although international geographic diversification may reduce the level of the idiosyncratic risk of banks according to a portfolio view of the banking business, it may also raise their exposure to non-domestic shocks. More recently, Outreville (2010) shows that the expected risk benefits related to geographic diversification vanish when banks achieve a very high degree of internationalization, which is likely to expose them to new sources of shocks. This could be the case both when European banks operate in foreign countries via branches and subsidiaries and when they provide direct cross-border lending to non-financial corporations. The consequent exposure to non-domestic shocks may also amplify systemic risk across countries whenever banks behave in a coordinated manner by holding similar portfolios under the expectation of being bailed out by the monetary authorities (Buch and Neugebauer, 2009; Farhi and Tirole, 2009). Furthermore, Cetorelli and Goldberg (2008) show that large global banks in the USA smooth domestic liquidity shocks by means of internal capital markets with their foreign affiliates. However, this contributes to the transmission of domestic shocks more broadly to foreign markets. Similarly, Morgan, Rime, and Strahan (2004) observe that US bank integration, finalized by the introduction of the Riegle-Neal Act in 1994 that has removed restrictions on geographic diversification across states, has led to a smoother state-level business cycle but has increased the synchronization of state-level fluctuations. This might have the effect of increasing the exposure of banks to similar macroeconomic risks.

To analyse how the cross-border activities in European countries since the late eighties might have impacted on the evolution of banking system volatility, we rely on the locational statistics from the Bank for International Settlement, that offer evidence on the international position of banks.[20] This position represents a comprehensive indicator of the channels through which shocks might be transmitted across countries, as it includes both the value of interbank assets with related and unrelated banks and the value of cross-border lending to non-financial corporations.

The evolution of the cross-border activities in European countries over the sample period provides support to the possibility of an influence played by the internationalization of the banking industry on the composition of banking system volatility. More precisely, during the sample period, the GDP-weighted average of the ratio between the international position of European banks (classified according to the country of ownership) and GPD have grown substantially, increasing from 35.1 per cent in the first quarter of 1988 to 149 per cent in the last quarter of 2010;[21] this in spite of the decline observed in the latest part of the sample period due to the global financial crisis.[22] Notably, as reported by Allen and Song (2005), the growth has been faster from 2002, probably due to the implementation of several large cross-border mergers and acquisitions. However, we also observe that cross-border banking shows a tendency to increase in Europe in the earlier part of our sample period and well before the introduction of the common currency; therefore, the growth in cross-border activities is clearly not entirely driven by monetary integration.

Table 4.7 summarizes some simple tests aimed at detecting the implications of the growth of cross-border activities on the composition of banking system volatility in European countries.[23] Panel A, which focuses on aggregate data at the European level, shows parametric and non-parametric correlations between the (value-weighted average) international and European

[20] More precisely, the information on cross-border banking are drawn from Table 8A of BIS Locational Statistics.

[21] A different proxy of the degree of internationalization of a banking system may be represented by the share of total assets produced by foreign branches and subsidiaries in a given banking system. However, this indicator is only available over the period from 1997 to 2009 and only for the subset of EU-15 countries. Although, for a smaller sample and for a shorter time horizon, we still observe evidence of an increasing importance of cross-border banking in Europe: this ratio has increased from 20.7 per cent to 25.0 per cent.

[22] The GDP-weighted average of the ratio between the international position of European banks and country GDP achieved its maximum value (203 per cent) in March 2008, then has declined steadily in the latest part of the sample period.

[23] Since the cross-border data are available at a quarterly frequency, we conduct the analysis by considering the average value of our monthly risk components in a given quarter.

Table 4.7. International and European Non-Financial Components and Cross-Border Banking

	(1)	(2)	(3)	(4)	(5)	(6)
	International non-financial component			European non-financial component		
Panel A: Correlation Analysis						
	Pearson correlation	Spearman correlation			Pearson correlation	Spearman correlation
Cross-border	0.500***	0.630***			0.576***	0.631***
	(0.000)	(0.000)			(0.000)	(0.000)

P-values in parentheses; * significant at 10%; ** significant at 5%; *** significant at 1%

Panel B: Country-Level Regression	(1)	(2)	(3)	(4)	(5)	(6)
			Excluding the Financial Crisis			Excluding the Financial Crisis
Log (Cross-border)	0.013***	0.008***	0.010***	0.006*	−0.000	0.011***
	(5.15)	(4.01)	(4.71)	(1.91)	(0.06)	(3.92)
Log (Size)		0.032***	0.034***		0.041***	0.040***
		(25.50)	(24.04)		(23.62)	(21.16)
Constant	0.101***	−0.170***	−0.184***	0.080***	−0.231***	−0.212***
	(5.18)	(9.78)	(9.93)	(4.02)	(6.83)	(6.35)
Observations	1429	1429	1191	1429	1429	1191
Ad. R-squared	0.404	0.604	0.616	0.313	0.536	0.503
Quarterly dummies	Yes	Yes	Yes	Yes	Yes	Yes

Robust t statistics in parentheses;* significant at 10%;** significant at 5%;*** significant at 1%.

Panel A shows parametric and non-parametric correlation coefficients between the value-weighted average international and European components of banking volatility and the GDP-weighted average ratio between banks' international position and GDP (cross-border) computed at the country level. *Panel B* presents the OLS regression results on the relationship between the international and European components and cross-border banking at the country level. Initially, the models have been estimated by controlling for quarterly dummies and then for the size of the banking system (log of market capitalization). T statistics refer to standard errors that are robust to heteroscedasticity.

components of banking system volatility and our (GDP-weighted average) measure of cross-border banking. These results offer indications of a positive and significant relationship between the two volatility components and cross-border banking as all correlation coefficients are positive and significant at the customary levels. However, we acknowledge that these preliminary findings might reflect the fact the two series only share the same deterministic trend over the sample period; namely, these results do not imply any causal relationship.

Thus, we provide further tests in Panel B, where we extend the analysis down to the country level through a multivariate approach. Specifically, we regress the two volatility components, measured at the country level, on the (log) of our cross-border measure controlling for quarterly dummies; we then extend the model controlling for the size of the banking systems (measured in terms of market value) and limit the analysis to the pre-crisis period, spanning from January 1988 to June 2007, to remove the influence produced by the sharp decline of cross-border banking observed during the financial crisis. We suppose that if cross-border banking contributes to the changing composition of bank volatility, we should observe a larger share of the international and European non-financial components in banking systems where the relevance of cross-border activities is greater. In general, we find indications in line with this argument, especially for the international non-financial component and when we focus on the pre-crisis period. Hence, although based on a simplified approach and affected by data limitations, these tests seem to point to the importance of the growing degree of internationalization as a key driver of the changing composition of banking system volatility in Europe.

Nonetheless, untabulated tests also show that the contribution provided by our proxy of cross-border banking to the explanatory power of the models reported in Table 4.7 is much lower with respect to the importance played by the size factor. In other words, other determinants related to the size of the banking business appear to exercise a relevant role with regard to the changing composition of banking system volatility.

The Role of Bank Size and Diversification

The banking indices employed in our analysis generally include very large financial institutions. This is especially true for the group of six countries that we have qualified as 'large banking systems' and that show, on average, the largest exposure to international and European shocks. The banking indices in these countries are dominated by a handful of very large and complex banks that have substantially increased their size and market share over the sample period and have been characterized by an increasing degree of functional diversification.[24]

Several analyses have demonstrated the positive link between size, diversification, and bank exposure to common shocks (Schuerman and Stiroh, 2006; Baele, De Jonghe, and Vander Vennet, 2007; Stiroh, 2009; De Jonghe, 2010). More importantly, from a systemic stability perspective, Wagner (2010a) shows theoretically how diversification increases similarities between financial institutions, leading to an increase in the correlation of their asset risk. This effect is more pronounced for higher degrees of diversification that are typically achieved by large banks, as those driving our results. In addition, diversification—by lowering banks' need for outside liquidity—encourages risk-taking and, as it exposes banks to similar types of risk, discourages the provision of liquidity to other institutions (Wagner, 2008). As a result, diversification may increase the likelihood of a systemic crisis.

Overall, we conjecture that the size effect observed in our analysis might be capturing the importance of diversification strategies on the composition of banking system volatility.[25]

Robustness Tests

Several tests have been conducted to assess the robustness of our major findings. First, we evaluate whether our conclusions vary with changes in the sample composition. Initially, we test how our main findings are affected by the unbalanced structure of our sample, which is determined by the fact that data for a few banking systems are available only since the beginning of the nineties. Thus, we repeat the trend analysis by focusing on the subsample of banking systems with complete market data for the full sample period. Our major conclusions remain largely unaffected; namely, while we still do not observe any trend in banking volatility, we confirm significant changes in its composition. Next, we consider whether the introduction of the euro has affected only the subset of Euro countries. Hence, we rerun the test on shifts in trends only on this subsample of countries. Once again, our results remain qualitatively unchanged: there is no evidence of any significant shift in volatility and volatility components with the adoption of the euro.

[24] For instance, this is the case of Deutsche Bank and Commerzbank in Germany, UniCredit and Intesa in Italy, Banco Santander and BBVA in Spain, Royal Bank of Scotland, Lloyd, and Barclays in the UK.

[25] Ideally, we would have liked to provide a direct test on the importance of diversification on the composition of banking system volatility. However, we are not aware of any proxy of the degree of diversification at level of the banking system that might be available at monthly (quarterly) frequency, which is the frequency of our volatility components.

While the analysis discussed in earlier in the chapter has focused on absolute size, it could be the case that the relative size of the banking systems, with respect to the size of the real economy (measured in terms of GDP), matters more for the exposure to international and European shocks. Accordingly, we repeat the analysis separately for relatively large and small banking systems, identified on the basis of the ratio between banking system market capitalization and GDP.[26] The results suggest that both relatively large and small banking systems show significant long-term trends in the international and European non-financial components of banking system volatility. Furthermore, the group consisting of small banking systems in relative terms shows a significant long-term trend in the European industry component as was the case for small banking systems in absolute terms. The only major difference compared to the analysis conducted in terms of absolute size refers to the evolution of the idiosyncratic component. This component shows a significant declining long-term trend only in the group of 'relatively large' banking systems. In the other group of banking systems, however, the idiosyncratic component is still lower in the second half of the sample period.[27] In general, we conclude that the changes in the composition of banking system volatility are not limited to 'relatively large' banking systems.

Finally, we test the robustness of our conclusion of an increasing exposure (beta) of banking systems to international and European shocks. Since our main findings are based on a limited number of observations (46), we re-estimate European banking systems' international and European (region) betas in two alternative ways to increase the number of observations. First, we estimate rolling window international and European betas by means of a 130-day window.[28] The results of the trend tests conducted on this measure of beta risk confirm the increasing exposure of banking systems to international

[26] We classify the banking systems as 'relatively large' if the ratio between market capitalization and GDP is, on average, above 10 per cent over the sample period, and the remaining banking systems as 'relatively small'. The first group consists of eight banking systems including UK, Switzerland, Ireland, Luxembourg, Belgium, Sweden, Spain, and Greece.

[27] As an alternative criterion, we classify banking systems on the basis of the ratio between banking system total assets and country GDP at the end of 2009. More precisely, we classify as relatively large banking systems those with a ratio of total assets over GDP larger than 350 per cent and as small the remaining banking systems. While this approach produces some differences in the way we group the banking systems, with the UK, Switzerland, Ireland, Luxembourg, Belgium, Austria, France, Denmark, and the Netherlands identified as relatively large, we still observe in both groups an increasing trend in the international and European non-financial components. However, while the results for relatively large banking systems are similar to when the analysis has been conducted by grouping banking systems on the basis of absolute size (market capitalization), in the group of relatively small banking systems we observe a lack of any significant long-term trend in the country and idiosyncratic components. Nonetheless, in these banking systems also, the country and idiosyncratic components decline substantially over the sample period.

[28] We compute a value-weighted average for each daily beta estimated at the country level and then we use the simple average in a given month in our trend analysis.

and European non-financial shocks and the differences between large and small banking systems. Second, we re-estimate the model at monthly intervals for each banking system and then we derive a market-weighted average of international and European betas. Trend tests on these measures largely confirm our major conclusions of a significant upward trend in the international and European betas.

Conclusions

Overall, our analysis provides robust evidence of significant changes in the composition of banking system volatility over the sample period, as a consequence of a positive long-term trend in the relative importance of international and European non-financial components and a reduction in the contribution of country and idiosyncratic components. This growth in the relative importance of international and European non-financial components of banking system volatility has been associated with a significant upward trend in the (value-weighted average) international and European betas of the European banking systems. Furthermore, while there was a sudden upward shift in the international banking industry component during the global financial crisis of 2007–9, we show that an upward long-term trend in the relative importance of the European banking industry component characterizes the set of small banking systems. For the full sample of banking systems, the increasing contribution of this component to banking volatility is restricted to the period from 2005 to 2010. In general, this evolution in the composition of banking system volatility has led to a substantial increase in the degree of interdependency between banking systems that we estimate to be in the order of 2.4 per cent per year.

This chapter also adds to the literature dealing with the impact of the euro on European banks. We show that, on average, the move towards a common currency has not produced significant shifts in the long-term dynamics of banking volatility and its components (see Hartmann, Straetmans, and de Vries, 2006). Although we observe a higher exposure of banking systems to non-domestic shocks in the latter part of the sample period, in line with the evidence provided by Francis and Hunter (2004), we show that this increasing exposure is the result of long-term trends in the European banking industry since the late eighties. We conjecture that this evolution may reflect the growing importance of cross-border activities in the European banking systems, and we provide evidence that points towards a positive relationship between the degree of internationalization of a banking system and the relative size of non-domestic components of banking volatility. We also suggest that the increasing degree of functional diversification might have played a role in the increase of commonalities across banking systems.

Ultimately, this chapter shows the growing relevance of the broad channel of systemic risk (De Bandt and Hartmann, 2000); namely, our results imply a rise in the likelihood that shocks can simultaneously affect a large number of institutions. Therefore, in light of these findings, regulatory reforms aimed at effective crisis management and resolution, or the orderly winding up of a failing cross-border bank, are essential to safeguarding systemic stability in Europe (see Eisenbeis and Kaufman, 2008; Krimminger, 2008; EC, 2009, 2010). The development of a European resolution framework may contribute to reducing the systemic implications of cross-border failures and may remove the need to resort to exceptional national regulatory measures in times of crisis, as those implemented during the subprime crisis.

Appendix

Equation (2) is derived by assuming that the return of a European index of non-financial firms ($R_{E_{it}}$), the return of an international banking industry index ($R_{I\_IND_{it}}$), the return of a European banking index ($R_{E\_IND_{it}}$), and the return of a country index ($R_{C_{it}}$) are generated as follows:

$$R_{E_{it}} = \delta_i + \eta_i R_{I_{it}} + \varepsilon_{it}^{E} \tag{1A}$$

$$R_{I\_IND_{it}} = \theta_i + \omega_i R_{I_{it}} + \kappa_i R_{E_{it}} + \varepsilon_{it}^{I\_IND} \tag{2A}$$

$$R_{E\_IND_{it}} = \gamma_i + \lambda_i R_{I_{it}} + \phi_i R_{E_{it}} + \varsigma_i R_{I\_IND_{it}} + \varepsilon_{it}^{E\_IND} \tag{3A}$$

$$R_{C_{it}} = \varphi_i + \tau_i R_{I_{it}} + \omega_i R_{E_{it}} + \chi_i R_{I\_IND_{it}} + \psi_i R_{E\_IND_{it}} + \varepsilon_{it}^{C} \tag{4A}$$

where $R_{I_{it}}$ is the return on an international index of non-financial firms and ε_{it}^{E}, $\varepsilon_{it}^{I\_IND}$, $\varepsilon_{it}^{E\_IND}$, and ε_{it}^{C} are mean zero error terms that are orthogonal to the right-hand-side variable in their respective regression and refer to country *i* and time *t*.

By replacing $R_{E_{it}}$ in Equation (2A) with (1A), $R_{E_{it}}$ and $R_{I\_IND_{it}}$ in Equation (3A) with (2A) and (1A), and $R_{E_{it}}$, $R_{I\_IND_{it}}$, $R_{E\_IND_{it}}$ in Equation (4A) with (3A), (2A), and (1A) we can also write that:

$$R_{I\_IND_{it}} = \theta_i^{I\_IND} + \bar{\omega}_i^{I\_IND} R_{I_{it}} + \kappa_i \varepsilon_{it}^{E} + \varepsilon_{it}^{I\_IND} \tag{5A}$$

$$R_{E\_IND_{it}} = \delta_i^{E\_IND} + \eta_i^{E\_IND} R_{I_{it}} + \phi_E^{I\_IND} \varepsilon_{it}^{E} + \varsigma_i \varepsilon_{it}^{I\_IND} + \varepsilon_{it}^{E\_IND} \tag{6A}$$

$$R_{C_{it}} = \varphi_i^C + \eta_i^C R_{I_{it}} + \phi_i^C \varepsilon_{it}^E + \chi_i^C \varepsilon_{it}^{I\_IND} + \psi_i \varepsilon_{it}^{E\_IND} + \varepsilon_{it}^C \qquad (7A)$$

where

- $\theta_i^{I\_IND} = (\theta_i + \kappa_i \delta_i)$
- $\bar{\omega}_i^{I\_IND} = (\bar{\omega}_i + \kappa_i \eta_i)$
- $\delta_i^{E\_IND} = (\gamma_i + \phi_i \delta_i + \varsigma_i \theta_i^{I\_IND})$,
- $\eta_i^{E\_IND} = (\lambda_i + \phi_i \eta_i + \varsigma_i \bar{\omega}_i^{I\_IND})$,
- $\phi_i^{E\_IND} = (\phi_i + \varsigma_i \kappa_i)$
- $\varphi_i^C = (\varphi_i + \omega_i \delta_i + \chi_i \theta_i^{I\_IND} + \psi_i \delta_i^{E\_IND})$,
- $\eta_i^C = (\omega_i + \omega_i \eta_i + \chi_i \bar{\omega}_i^{I\_IND} + \psi_i \eta_i^{E\_IND})$
- $\phi_i^C = (\chi_i \kappa_i + \omega_i + \psi_i \phi_i + \psi_i \varsigma_i \kappa_i)$,
- $\chi_i^C = (\chi_i + \psi_i \varsigma_i)$.

The residuals series are, therefore, uncorrelated with our proxy for the 'international' market and are uncorrelated to each other.

Thus, if we denote as R_{it} the return on a banking index that refers to country i, and we assume that this return depends on the international non-financial, European non-financial, international banking industry, European banking industry, and country components as follows

$$R_{it} = \alpha_i + \beta_i^I R_{I_{it}} + \beta_i^E R_E + \beta_i^{I\_IND} R_{I\_IND_{it}} + \beta_i^{E\_IND} R_{E\_IND_{it}} + \beta_i^C R_{C_{it}} + \varepsilon_{it} \qquad (8A)$$

where β_i^I β_i^E, $\beta_i^{I\_IND}$, $\beta_i^{E\_IND}$, and β_i^C express the sensitivity of the banking system in country i to these components, and ε_{it} represents the unexplained residual, under the assumption that Equations 1A, 2A, 3A, and 4A are correctly specified, we can postulate that the 'true' return-generating model is based on the following equation:[29]

$$R_{it} = \alpha_i + b_i^I R_{I_{it}} + b_i^E \varepsilon_{it}^E + b_i^{I\_IND} \varepsilon_{it}^{I\_IND} + b_i^{E\_IND} \varepsilon_{it}^{E\_IND} + b_i^C \varepsilon_{it}^C + \varepsilon_{it} \qquad (9A)$$

where

- $b_i^I = \beta_i^I + \beta_i^E \eta_i + \beta_i^{I\_IND} \bar{\omega}_i^{I\_IND} + \beta_i^{E\_IND} + \eta_i^{E\_IND} + \beta_i^C \eta_i^C$;
- $b_i^I = \beta_i^E + \beta_i^{I\_IND} \kappa_i + \beta_i^{I\_IND} \phi_i^{E\_IND} + \beta_i^C \phi_i^C$;
- $b_i^{I\_IND} = \beta_i^{I\_IND} + \beta_i^{E\_IND} \varsigma_i + \beta_i^C \chi_i^C$;
- $b_i^{E\_IND} = \beta_i^{E\_IND} + \beta_i^C \psi_i$;
- $b_i^C = \beta_i^C$.

[29] As this approach leads to uncorrelated factors in the return-generating model, it resembles the empirical strategy applied by Drummen and Zimmermann (1992) to investigate the structure of European stock returns, and by Clayton and Mackinnon (2003) to investigate the link between real estate and investment trust (REIT) returns and stock, bond, and real estate factors. Specifically, they obtain uncorrelated components in a multifactor model by orthogonalization. However, the major difference in our approach is the assumption regarding the 'true' returns-generating process. As suggested by Akella and Chen (1990), under the assumption that Equation (9A) is the 'true' generating process, our estimates are unbiased. Furthermore, the returns-generating process assumed in the arbitrage pricing theory (APT) is similar to Equation (9A) (see Wei, 1988).

5

The Determinants of European Bank Exposure to Systemic Shocks

Introduction

The global financial crisis, which erupted in the middle of 2007, has highlighted the inadequacy of existing banking regulations with regards to safeguarding systemic stability. The regulatory framework is deemed to have been insufficient to limit excessive risk-taking by banks and, consequently, to contain the number of bank defaults over the crisis period. As a result, a general consensus among academics and regulators has emerged on the need to modify the regulatory framework with the purpose of introducing new rules that aim to enhance the resilience of individual banks, and of the full financial system, to shocks (Keys et al., 2009). Overall, in spite of the growing importance of the macroprudential view of regulation (Morris and Shin, 2008; Brunnermeier et al., 2009; Acharya et al., 2010; Adrian and Brunnermeier, 2010) that focuses on the stability of the system as a whole and where the cost of regulation for an institution depends on the negative systemic externalities that it may cause, the microprudential approach to regulation remains a key component of the prospective new rules. In other words, the assessment of the riskiness of each institution and how to enhance the ability of each institution to resist shocks are still major regulatory objectives.

This microprudential perspective of regulation is clearly stated in the new accord on capital regulation, known as Basel III, that was published by the Basel Committee on Banking Supervision in December 2010 and contains the key elements of the new regulatory framework. The Basel III Accord states that: 'The reforms strengthen bank-level, or microprudential regulation, which will help raise the resilience of individual banking institutions to periods of stress' (BCBS, 2010: 2). To this end, the new rules, while aimed at increasing the overall capital requirements for banks above the conventional threshold of

8 per cent by January 2019 and the quality of equity components as cushions against losses, introduce restrictions on bank characteristics in terms of leverage ratios and liquidity provisions.

However, whether the regulatory restrictions on these two bank characteristics may indeed be effective in strengthening the resilience of banks to systemic shocks, and whether they need to be accompanied by the adoption of other prudential rules, remains a matter of discussion (see Hellwig, 2010; Ibragimov, Jaffee, and Walden, 2011). For instance, several policy initiatives focus on the importance of imposing restrictions on bank business models. The Dodd–Frank Wall Street Reform and Consumer Protection Act, adopted in the USA in July 2010, goes beyond the framework proposed by the Basel III Accord to introduce restrictions on the diversification of business models via the adoption of the 'Volcker rule'.[1] Similarly, in the UK the Independent Commission on Banking, established in June 2010, suggests the creation of ring-fence banks, which have to focus exclusively on retail banking, and have to be legally separated from other entities when they belong to a financial group. These banks, and all institutions deemed to be systemically relevant, are required to respect stricter prudential requirements than in the Basel III Accord.

Several other proposals have instead advocated the introduction of rules based on bank size (Dermine and Schoenmaker, 2010). These proposals span from the adoption of a size cap, which limit the size of banks to formal recommendations, to the implementation of higher capital surcharges for large and complex banks. While these policy interventions are generally motivated by the difficulties faced by the largest financial institutions during the recent turmoil, they are in sharp contrast with the strategy followed by the regulatory authorities during the crisis, which have favoured the creation of even larger and more complex financial institutions by encouraging mergers between large banks in an attempt to limit the impact of bank failures.[2]

This chapter examines whether an increase in bank size is indeed detrimental for bank resilience to systemic shocks by looking at an extensive sample of listed banks across seventeen European countries. The contribution of the current analysis is threefold. First, the chapter utilizes a novel empirical approach, based on contingent claim analysis and the Merton (1974) distance-to-default model (see Gropp and Moerman, 2004; Gropp,

[1] This rule, originally proposed by the former Chairman of the Federal Reserve, Paul Volcker, limits the ability of banks to engage in proprietary trading and to invest in hedge and private equity funds.

[2] For instance, the US regulators have favoured the mergers of Bank of America with Merrill Lynch and Countrywide and J.P. Morgan Chase with Bear Stearns. In the UK, in September 2008 Lloyd TSB acquired the failing HBOS and achieved a final size equal to one-third of the UK's savings and mortgage market. Subsequently, the Lloyd group benefitted from the UK bailout package implemented in October 2008.

Vesala, and Vulpes, 2006) to estimate how the risk of failure of a bank changes following systemic shocks. The approach proposed here is consistent with a conventional definition of systemic risk, namely, the risk of default of the banking system considered as a whole (see Acharya and Yorulmazer, 2007, 2008). Second, the analysis contributes to the debate on the re-regulation of the banking industry by showing that the prudential rules prospected by the Basel III Accord, though useful, need to be accompanied by additional restrictions on banks. In particular, we show that imposing regulatory constraints on bank size appears the most effective tool, *ceteris paribus*, to reduce the default risk of a bank given systemic events. Third, we exploit the cross-country dimension of the European banking industry to derive regulatory implications on how to design a size cap on banks. More precisely, by jointly analysing the influence played by bank absolute and systemic size, measured via the ratio between bank total assets and country GDP (Brown and Dinç, 2011), we conclude that such a regulatory intervention should focus on bank absolute size and be country-specific, with smaller European countries requiring smaller banks.

Literature and Related Research

This chapter is related to the literature on systemic risk and its regulatory implications (see the surveys in Kaufman, 1994, and De Band and Hartmann, 2000; Acharya and Yorulmazer, 2007, 2008; Acharya, 2009). In this literature, systemic risk is conventionally identified as the risk of joint failures in the financial system (Acharya and Yorulmazer, 2007, 2008) associated to correlated investments across banks (Acharya, 2009) or to forms of contagion (De Band and Hartmann, 2000).

The recent global financial crisis has stimulated a growing debate among academics and regulators on how to re-regulate the banking industry with the purpose of containing the effects posed by systemic shocks. In this respect, a first group of studies has adopted a macroprudential view of banking regulation to focus on the contribution that each individual institution provides to the overall systemic risk and on its determinants (Adrian and Brunnermeier, 2010; Huang, Zhou, and Zhu, 2010; Brunnermeier et al., 2012). The conclusion emerging from these analyses is that the systemic relevance of a financial institution increases with increasing size, leverage, maturity mismatch, and non-interest income. Acharya and colleagues (2010) extend the macroprudential analyses by showing that the contribution to systemic risk of a financial institution can be measured by its propensity to be undercapitalized when the system as a whole is undercapitalized, and by demonstrating the ability of this measure to predict the risks emerging during the crisis of 2007–9.

A second strand of the literature has instead focused on the measurement of a bank's exposure to shocks and on the identification of its determinants while adopting a microprudential perspective of banking regulation. For example, Knaup and Wagner (2012) propose a forward-looking approach based on changes in the perceived tail risk, measured via changes in put option prices, to capture the exposure of a bank to a large prolonged decline in the market. They show that the tail-risk exposure increases when banks are involved in non-traditional activities and with the amount of uninsured debt, while bank size does not exercise any significant influence. The approach adopted by Knaup and Wagner (2012), however, does not focus on a bank's risk exposure with respect to systemic shocks as suggested by the theoretical literature on systemic risk. Furthermore, their analysis is based on a short time period, partly covering the recent financial crisis, and limited to a sample of US bank holding companies (BHCs); as a consequence, it may be difficult to generalize the conclusions emerging from this study.

The only empirical evidence on Europe is provided by De Jonghe (2010), who employs a measure of tail risk (based on extreme value theory) that captures the probability of a sharp decline in a bank's stock price, conditional on a crash in a banking stock index, to analyse how individual banks react to systemic shocks. The implementation of this approach, however, requires a long time series of stock returns, and this leads to the unrealistic assumption of a constant bank risk exposure over this time span (see Adams, Füss, and Gropp, 2010). In contrast to Knaup and Wagner (2012), De Jonghe reveals that bank size seems to play a pivotal role in determining a bank's exposure to shocks, with smaller banks appearing to be in a better position to withstand extremely adverse systemic conditions. This finding is consistent with the evidence—based on extreme value theory—of a higher contagion risk across large banks at the country level offered by Pais and Stork (2011).

The analysis of the current chapter is related to the 'microprudential' group of studies and has several distinguishing features. First, this chapter adopts a new approach to measuring a bank's exposure to systemic shocks that is coherent with the idea that systemic risk reflects the risk of default of the banking system considered as a whole (see Acharya and Yorulmazer, 2007, 2008). Specifically, as explained later in this chapter, the empirical design proposed here focuses on the sensitivity of the default risk of individual banks to changes in the health of the banking system in both normal and extreme systemic conditions. To this end, the present analysis builds upon a set of empirical studies that employs the Merton (1974) distance-to-default model with the purpose of investigating the time series properties of the default risk in the financial industry (Gropp and Moerman, 2004; Akhigbe, Madura, and Martin, 2007; Bartram, Brown, and Hund, 2007; Bernoth and Pick, 2010).

Second, the current analysis assesses the implications of regulatory interventions on bank size on bank exposure to systemic shocks, and compares their economic impact with that exercised by regulatory interventions similar to those contained in the Basel III Accord and in the Dodd–Frank Wall Street Reform and Consumer Protection Act in the USA.

Third, the present study exploits the cross-country dimension of the European banking system to analyse whether the optimal bank size is related to the size of the economy and how this might influence the design of a size cap in the banking industry. Recently, Demirgüç-Kunt and Huizinga (2011) have shown that banks that are large in relative terms with respect to the size of the economy exhibit clear specificities. More precisely, they show that while there is a trade-off between risk and return in banks that are large in absolute terms, in 'relatively large' banks more risk-taking is not associated with higher returns. Furthermore, they demonstrate that 'relatively large' banks have higher funding costs as they are perceived to be too big to save. While this latter result indicates that these banks are also subject to market discipline, Brown and Dinç (2011) show that 'relatively large' banks are more likely to benefit from regulatory forbearance and this might create incentives to invest in risky activities. This chapter extends the analysis of bank absolute and relative size to the exposure to systemic shocks, and derives regulatory implications on the optimal design of a size restriction in banks.

Sampling Criteria and Sample Size

The analysis is based on a sample of banks selected from seventeen European countries (the fifteen EU countries, and Norway and Switzerland) that have been listed over the period 1992–2008.[3] The European banking industry offers a fruitful ground for investigating the relationship between systemic risk exposure and bank characteristics (Baele, De Jonghe, and Vander Vennet, 2007). For example, while the rescue of a bank remains under the responsibility of the domestic country, the integration process favours the growth of banks beyond the national borders. Thus, the European context favours the development of systemically relevant banks, compared to the size of the domestic economy, without any appropriate cross-border resolution regime. Furthermore, in contrast to the US industry, a consistent deregulation process starting with the Second Banking Coordination Directive (adopted in 1989

[3] To reduce the survivorship bias within the dataset that could be particularly acute because of the waves of mergers and acquisitions involving European banks during the period under consideration, the sampling process has also involved delisted institutions as identified by Datastream International. The online version of BankScope, that maintains information on dead institutions, is the source for the accounting data.

and further enforced in the following years) has increased the scope for diversification in Europe, allowing banks to engage in a wide range of activities. As a result, compared to their US counterparts European banks may be involved in a larger set of activities, which they have been able to undertake for a longer time period. Consequently, banks with completely different business structures and lines of business are more likely to be observed within the European context. The focus on listed banks is motivated by two main reasons. First, although numerically limited, listed banks tend to be representative of a country's banking system (Moshirian and Wu, 2009).[4] Second, market information offers the opportunity to compute high frequency indicators of banking risk, at the individual bank and aggregate levels, to monitor the soundness and stability of the financial system (ECB, 2005).

The sampling process has been conducted with the purpose of identifying institutions with an interest in commercial banking, though they may be engaged in multiple business lines as is typical of modern banks. To this end, data have been drawn on the business focus of banks by jointly considering the specialization criteria provided by BankScope and the primary SIC code, as reported for each bank by Thomson Financial. Thus, via these two sources of data, investment banks, banks focusing on medium- and long-term credit lending, and non-banking credit institutions have been excluded from the sample, due to their specificities in terms of core business and asset and liability structure. Bank holding companies (BHCs) with an interest in commercial banking, namely with a primary SIC code equal to 602 (commercial banks), are included in the sample.

These selection criteria led to an initial sample of more than 4,000 firms' year-observations, on which further selection criteria were imposed. First, thin trading heavily affects banking stocks in some European countries (such as Denmark, Portugal, and Austria) and this might affect the validity of the risk indicators (influenced by the volatility of daily stock returns). Thus, a minimum liquidity criterion is imposed by maintaining in the sample only those banks with at least 70 per cent of non-zero daily returns in each year, computed from market data extracted from Datastream. Second, given the purpose of computing risk measures at yearly intervals, a bank needs to have at least 100 daily observations in a year to remain in the sample for that year. Finally, the sample only includes banks with at least five consecutive years of accounting data available on the BankScope database. This requirement ensures a minimum level of consistency in the measure of systemic risk. More importantly, it allows us to exploit the panel data structure of the sample when the analysis focuses on the determinants of bank exposure to systemic shocks.

4 According to the ECB (2005), listed banks represent at least 50 per cent of the banking system's total assets in the majority of the EU members.

Tables 5.1 shows the distribution of the final sample by year and across countries. The sample comprises 153 banks (including 57 that have been delisted over the sample period) with a total number of 1,677 yearly observations and shows a high degree of concentration (approximately 37 per cent of the sample) in two countries (Italy and France) that reflect the structural differences across European banking systems.[5]

The Exposure of Banks to Systemic Shocks and Its Determinants

This section first describes the methodology employed to compute the default risk for the banking system, then introduces the key risk variables employed in the empirical analysis. The last part is devoted to the description of the determinants of a bank's exposure to systemic shocks.

A Proxy of the Default Risk of the Banking System

The approach to measuring the sensitivity of a bank's default risk to systemic shocks is based on the idea that systemic risk reflects the risk of default of the banking system considered as a whole (see Acharya and Yorulmazer, 2007, 2008). Hence, this sensitivity can be measured by looking at how the risk of default of a bank reacts to changes in the default risk of the system. The implementation of this approach requires two preliminary steps: (i) the identification of the boundaries of the system; (ii) the computation of a proxy for the distress risk of this system.

The boundaries of the system are identified following previous studies on European banking that focus on the European level rather than on the country level. Baele, De Jonghe, and Vander Vennet (2007) claim that European factors provide a better description of the risk factors embedded in bank stocks in Europe than country factors. This is likely to be related to the evolution of the banking regulatory landscape in Europe over the last two decades, as it has removed barriers to operate across countries and business lines and has stimulated a sharp increase in the competitive pressures within and, especially, across European banking systems (Goddard et al., 2007). Furthermore, Gropp and Kashyap (2010) point out that while the hypothesis of banking integration, measured in terms of convergence in banks' profitability, is not

[5] Banking systems in France and Italy are characterized by a large number of medium-sized banks that are listed on the stock markets. In contrast, in several other countries the number of listed banks is generally limited to the largest firms within the industry (e.g. Belgium, Ireland, Finland, and Sweden). As shown in the robustness section, the results are generally unchanged when Italian or French banks are excluded from the sample.

Table 5.1. Sample

Panel A: Sample distribution by year

	Number	Percentage
1992	63	3.76
1993	77	4.59
1994	83	4.95
1995	83	4.95
1996	88	5.25
1997	91	5.43
1998	96	5.72
1999	100	5.96
2000	111	6.62
2001	113	6.74
2002	113	6.74
2003	108	6.44
2004	118	7.04
2005	113	6.74
2006	113	6.74
2007	106	6.32
2008	101	6.02
Total	*1,677*	*100*

Panel B: Sample distribution by country

	Number of banks	Number of obs.	Percentage of banks	Percentage of obs.
Austria	2	16	1.31	0.95
Belgium	4	36	2.61	2.15
Denmark	8	82	5.23	4.89
Finland	2	18	1.31	1.07
France	25	219	16.34	13.06
Germany	8	93	5.23	5.55
Greece	12	152	7.84	9.06
Ireland	3	50	1.96	2.98
Italy	36	403	23.53	24.03
Luxembourg	1	8	0.65	0.48
Netherlands	3	29	1.96	1.73
Norway	4	32	2.61	1.91
Portugal	5	66	3.27	3.94
Spain	12	160	7.84	9.54
Sweden	4	56	2.61	3.34
Switzerland	10	99	6.54	5.90
UK	14	158	9.15	9.42
Total	*153*	*1,677*	*100*	*100*

Panel A shows the yearly distribution of the sample of banks extracted from BankScope. Panel B shows the distribution by country. The sample consists of 153 unique listed banks selected from 17 European countries.

confirmed for unlisted European banks, listed banks show a tendency to revert to the average profit rates in the area.

A contingent claim approach (CCA) is employed to estimate the default risk for the full system. This approach combines accounting and market information to obtain indicators of default risk via the application of option pricing theory (Zambrana, 2010). More precisely, CCA is initially used to estimate daily values of the distance to default at the bank level according to the methodology summarized in the Appendix. The distance to default (DD) expresses the number of standard deviations that the market value of bank assets are above the default point (the point where the market value of assets is less than the book value of total liabilities) by modelling bank equity as a call option on the market value of assets. At the bank level, Gropp, Vesala, and Vulpes (2006) show that DD is a direct indicator of bank fragility that outperforms other indicators of risk in predicting bank defaults in Europe. More recently, the Financial Stability Board (FSB, 2009) has invoked the use of these types of distress risk indicators to enhance systemic risk analysis, as they might contribute to identifying systemically relevant banks.

Next, the default risk of the banking system (IDD) is derived by aggregating individual bank DD. The European Central Bank (ECB, 2005) suggests that aggregate measures of individual bank distance to default can be employed as indicators of the stability of the full system, and when 'assessed against historical episodes of financial instability, tend to give easily identifiable signals well in advance' (p. 62). Accordingly, following Bernoth and Pick (2010), the default risk of the system is defined as the value-weighted average of DD computed at a daily frequency and at the level of the bank. This index is constructed as 'bank specific': for each bank it is defined as the weighted average of the default risk of the remaining banks in the sample and this eliminates the influence of spurious correlation when the sensitivity measures are estimated.

Notably, aggregated series of DD are commonly used in policy reports on financial stability as indicators of systemic risk. For instance, the IMF employs aggregate DD series in country reports for the Euro area and the United States (Zambrana, 2010). Recently, Carlson, King, and Lewis (2008) employed a similar indicator to assess the health of the US banking system, reaching the conclusion that their DD index properly captures the evolution of systemic risk over a period of three decades. As is the case for the results proposed by Carlson, King, and Lewis (2008), IDD shows a high level of systemic risk in Europe in the periods of the LTCM and the Russian bond defaults, as well as in years of negative stock market conditions, such as the period 2000–2 with the WorldCom bubble collapse and September 11. Furthermore, the value of IDD declines rapidly during the latest part of the sample period; that is, since the beginning of the sub-prime crisis. In line with expectations, the highest level of systemic risk is observed in 2008 as a consequence of the worsening of the international financial crisis.

Measuring the Sensitivity of a Bank's Default Risk to Systemic Shocks

The proxy of banking system risk is employed to compute two new indicators of the exposure of banks to systemic shocks. The first, named as distance-to-default beta (β_{DD}), is the slope coefficient of the following regression model:

$$\left(\frac{DD_t^i - DD_{t-1}^i}{|DD_{t-1}^i|}\right) = \alpha_0 + \beta_{DD_{i,t}}\left(\frac{IDD_t^i - IDD_{t-1}^i}{|IDD_{t-1}^i|}\right) + \varepsilon_{i,t} \quad (1)$$

where $\frac{DD_t^i - DD_{t-1}^i}{|DD_{t-1}^i|}$ is the daily relative change in the distance to default for bank i, $\frac{IDD_t^i - IDD_{t-1}^i}{|IDD_{t-1}^i|}$ is the daily relative change in the distance-to-default index computed for bank i and $\varepsilon_{i,t}$ is the unexplained residual. Thus, $\beta_{DD_{i,t}}$ measures how the default risk of a bank reacts to changes in banking system risk, with higher values denoting larger exposure to systemic shocks. To reduce the impact of outliers, which can be especially severe for banks with low values of DD, and to remove the distributional assumptions of conventional estimations methods, $\beta_{DD_{i,t}}$ is estimated via median regression. Therefore, Equation (1) models the median relative change in bank DD at yearly intervals conditional on changes in banking system risk proxied by the DD index.[6]

The recent crisis has, however, emphasized the importance of considering the resilience of banks to shocks when the system is in extreme stress conditions. In accordance with this, the Basel III Accord introduces liquidity provisions based on stress scenarios. Furthermore, De Jonghe (2010) shows that risk indicators of 'tail dependence' and 'central dependence' may have substantially different information content. Thus, the second risk measure employed in the analysis emphasizes the tail profile of systemic risk. More precisely, the focus is on extreme increases in systemic risk (defined as a value of the (relative) daily change in IDD in the lower 2.5 percentile of the yearly distribution) and the number of times the (relative) daily changes in an *individual bank DD* is in the lower 2.5 percentile of the yearly distribution when there are

[6] As pointed out by Gropp and Moerman (2004), in banks with low DD it might be more likely to observe outliers in the form of larger relative changes of default risk due to a scale effect. As a consequence, OLS regression can substantially bias the estimation of the sensitivity measure. Median regressions belong to the family of quantile regressions that aim to estimate the quantiles of the conditional distribution of the response variable as functions of the observed covariates. Koenker and Hallock (2001) show that quantile regression is equivalent to minimizing a sum of asymmetrically weighted absolute residuals by means of a linear programming method.

such extreme systemic conditions.[7,8] Hence, this second measure, that, following Bae, Karoly, and Stulz (2003), is named henceforth as 'coexceedances', counts how many times the system and an individual bank are *jointly* in the left tail of the distribution of the relative change in DD, with values that range from 0 to 3 when the number of coexceedances is, respectively, equal to 0, 1, 2, or at least 3.

Panel A of Table 5.2 presents descriptive statistics for the two risk metrics. This Panel shows that the mean and median values of the risk measures based on the DD are, respectively, equal to 0.198 and 0.11, and highlight the presence of a large variability in the sample in terms of bank exposure to shocks. This is also confirmed by the second measure: on average, the selected banks show a number of coexceedances equal to 1, although there seem to be clear differences across banks.[9]

Panel B of Table 5.2 clarifies to what extent more conventional risk measures are close to the DD-based indicators. To this end, the Panel reports the correlation coefficients between the risk measures described above and two alternative risk metrics computed on the basis of the distribution of stock returns: the (OLS) industry beta (β_R) and the number of coexceedances defined as the number of yearly extreme negative stock returns at the bank level observed when there are extreme negative returns in a banking index.[10] Not surprisingly, as the distance to default is influenced by the volatility of a bank's stock return distribution, the DD-based indicators are positively and significantly correlated with these alternative risk measures. However, as reported in the same Panel, the correlation coefficients are also significantly different from one; namely, the results are far from suggesting a perfect linear association between the DD-based indicators and more conventional risk metrics. Furthermore, when the analysis focuses on megabanks, those that are deemed to be more relevant for financial stability, the values of the

[7] This extreme measure of the sensitivity of bank default risk to systemic risk is computed by retaining in the sample only banks continuously listed in a given year, to ensure a perfect match between the annual distribution of the daily change in DD at the bank level and the same distribution at the system level. Furthermore, the 2.5 percentile is defined as a threshold since it allows the identification of a sufficient number of extreme events to run the multivariate analysis and, at the same time, gives a very stringent definition of extreme events. The results shown in the robustness section are generally unchanged when the 5 percentile is used to construct the measure of extreme risk.

[8] Notably, Bae, Karoly, and Stulz (2003), Gropp and Moerman (2004), and Gropp, Lo Duca, and Vesala (2009) use a similar measure to test for the presence of contagion across equity markets and across banks, respectively.

[9] The two measures seem to properly capture the exposure of banks to systemic shocks. For instance, in 2008, that is, at the peak of the crisis, both measures include four UK banks in the list of top ten risky institutions. Notably, the UK banking system has been particularly hard hit by the crisis, with £37 billion being devoted to bailing out banks.

[10] For this latter measure of risk, a banking index specific for each bank is constructed and, once again, the 2.5 percentile is employed as a threshold.

Table 5.2. Risk Measures

Panel A: Descriptive statistics

	Definition	N	Mean	Median	St.Dev	p1	p99
β_{DD}	Distance-to-default beta	1,677	0.198	0.110	0.230	−0.032	0.983
Coexceedances	Number of DD coexceedances	1,640	0.926	1.000	1.004	0.000	3.000

Panel B: Correlation with conventional measures of risk

		Full Sample (Median Total Assets: 25.326 BLN €)			*Megabanks* (Median Total Assets: 141.273 BLN €)		
		β_{DD}	Coexceedances	β_R	β_{DD}	Coexceedances	β_R
Coexceedances	N: 1,640	0.559			0.514		
	$H_0:\rho = 0$	(0.000)			(0.000)		
	$H_0:\rho = 1$	(0.000)			(0.000)		
OLS industry beta: β_R	N: 1,677	0.672	0.486		0.493	0.353	
	$H_0:\rho = 0$	(0.000)	(0.000)		(0.000)	(0.000)	
	$H_0:\rho = 1$	(0.000)	(0.000)		(0.000)	(0.000)	
Coexceedances_return	N: 1,640	0.537	0.63	0.539	0.471	0.554	0.376
	$H_0:\rho = 0$	(0.000)	(0.000)	(0.000)	(0.000)	(0.000)	(0.000)
	$H_0:\rho = 1$	(0.000)	(0.000)	(0.000)	(0.000)	(0.000)	(0.000)

Panel A summarizes the descriptive statistics for the risk variables. Panel B reports pairwise correlation coefficients computed for the measures of banking risk, p-values are shown in round brackets. β_{DD} is the distance-to-default beta, Coexceedances is the number of coexceedances based on extreme increases in the risk of default, β_R is the OLS market beta, Coexceedances_return is the number of coexceedances based on extreme negative stock returns.

correlation coefficients decline remarkably.[11] More precisely, the correlation between β_{DD} and β_R is equal to 0.493 for these banks while it increases to 0.672 in the full sample. Similarly, the correlation coefficients between the two measures of coexceedances is 0.554 for megabanks and 0.63 for the full sample.[12] Overall, therefore, conventional risk metrics provide only a partial picture on how the default risk of a bank changes with systemic shocks, especially in the group of megabanks: the DD indicators, in effect, do not simply reflect the properties of a bank stock return distribution as is the case of more conventional risk parameters.

Determinants of Bank Exposure to Systemic Shocks

Table 5.3 shows the definition of the variables employed as determinants of a bank's risk exposure in the empirical analysis and the main descriptive statistics.

A first set of variables refer to bank size. In the aftermath of the recent global crisis, several policymakers and regulators have evoked the break-up of financial institutions as a necessary regulatory intervention to reduce the risks of financial instability (Dermine and Schoenmaker, 2010). While this intervention has been generally motivated by recalling the negative externalities posed by the failure of a large banking firm on the whole system, the empirical evidence normally suggests that the larger banks are also more exposed to market-wide events (Baele, De Jonghe, and Vander Vennet, 2007; De Jonghe, 2010) and to contagion risk (Pais and Stork, 2011), and are more likely to fail (Demirgüç-Kunt and Huizinga, 2011). In the context of the current analysis, therefore, this would imply a positive relationship between bank absolute size (*SIZE*), measured via the log of bank total assets (in thousands of euro), and the chosen measures of risk.

However, the focus on absolute size, as in previous studies, is not sufficient if the purpose is to inform the debate on how to design size restrictions in the banking industry. This is due to the fact that the relevance of a bank for the stability of the system is likely to vary with the size of the economy: banks that appear relatively small in absolute terms may be systemically important as they are operating in relatively small economies. Similarly, large banks in absolute terms tend to be less important when they operate in a large domestic economy. Furthermore, relatively large banks benefit from a more pronounced implicit bailout guarantee and this should favour more risky

[11] Banks with an average of log of total assets above the sample median are defined as 'megabanks'.

[12] These differences in the magnitude of the correlation coefficients computed for the full sample and for megabanks are also highly statistically significant according to a z-statistic. In the interest of brevity, the results of these tests are not reported.

Table 5.3. Descriptive Statistics of the Determinants of Bank Exposure to Systemic Shocks

		N	Mean	Median	Sd	p1	p99
Panel A: Microprudential variables							
SIZE	Log of total assets	1,677	17.19	17.05	1.91	13.12	21.07
SYSTEMIC (%)	Bank total assets over country GDP	1,677	23.40	5.80	46.66	0.08	246.94
SH_{NON} (%)	Ratio of non-interest income over operating income	1,677	40.04	38.63	15.77	6.41	89.16
GROWTH (%)	Three-year average of the log growth in total assets $(Ln(TEA_t) - Ln(TEA_{t-1}))$	1,597	12.48	10.64	13.31	-9.78	55.21
LIQUIDITY (%)	Primary liquidity over total assets	1,677	8.06	4.45	10.03	0.16	46.94
DEPOSITS (%)	Retail deposits over total debts	1,677	53.37	53.96	19.07	5.84	97.29
LEVERAGE	Assets over book equity	1,677	18.83	17.09	9.12	5.60	48.96
Panel B: Control variables							
CHARTER	Market value of equity over book value of equity	1,669	1.60	1.36	1.51	0.06	7.71
CONCENTRATION	Herfindahl index of bank asset concentration	1,677	0.11	0.09	0.08	0.03	0.35
RGDPG (%)	Real GDP growth rate (World Economic Development Indicators)	1,677	2.76	2.41	2.09	0.45	10.92
INFLATION (%)	Inflation rate (World Economic Development Indicators)	1,677	2.26	2.16	1.70	−1.18	8.05

Table 5.3 shows the descriptive statistics for variables employed as determinants of the sensitivity of bank default risk to systemic shocks. The accounting data are drawn from BankScope for the sample period 1992–2008.

investments that reduce their resilience to shocks under systemic events. In addition, these banks might reduce the risk to be perceived as too big to save by investing in correlated exposures with respect to the rest of the industry to exploit the too-many-to-fail effect in times of crisis (Acharya and Yorulmazer, 2007); namely, so as to increase the risk of joint failures in the industry and the chances of regulatory forbearance. Accordingly, we extend the analysis to look at whether a bank's risk exposure is influenced by its systemic size (*SYSTEMIC*), expressed by the ratio between bank total asset and country size as measured by total GDP (Brown and Dinç, 2011).[13]

Nonetheless, SIZE and SYSTEMIC are not directly introduced into the regression model for two reasons. First, they are highly correlated with some of the explanatory variables that describe other features of the banking business and that might be subject to regulatory prescriptions. Second, and more importantly, the chapter aims at testing whether size per se is a key driver of bank exposure to systemic shocks, while SIZE and SYSTEMIC may reflect the

[13] The results presented in the following sections remain unchanged if systemic size is measured by the ratio of total liabilities and GDP as in Demirgüç-Kunt and Huizinga (2011).

impact of other factors that are typically associated with a larger production scale in Europe (i.e. a higher leverage ratio, a higher share of non-interest income, etc.). Thus, the two size variables are regressed with respect to the remaining microprudential variables employed in the analysis and the residual is then the size factor (respectively *R_SIZE* and *R_SYSTEMIC*) used in the regression models (see De Jonghe, 2010). Hence, the coefficients assigned to these adjusted size variables express the pure effect of bank absolute and relative size on the exposure to systemic shocks; namely, they represent the consequences on the exposure to shocks produced by being a large institution, in absolute and/or relative terms, independently from the business focus and from any other structural characteristic of the firm.[14]

The analysis also controls for other bank-specific characteristics that might be subject to regulatory restrictions such as bank business focus, growth, liquidity, the liability composition, and leverage.

The influence of a bank's business focus on the measures of risk is captured via the ratio between non-interest income to total operating income ($\mathbf{SH}_{\mathrm{NON}}$). From a systemic perspective, several theoretical studies argue that the development of diversified financial institutions may be detrimental for financial stability. For instance, Wagner (2010) shows that while diversification may reduce the default risk of an individual institution, it may increase the risk of joint failures in the banking system by raising bank exposure to common sources of risks. Similarly, Ibragimov, Jaffee, and Walden (2011) show that there is a threshold above which the individual benefits related to diversification strategies are lower than the costs due to an increasing risk of joint bank failures in the banking system. In terms of benefits at the bank level, the majority of the empirical analyses, limited to the US banking system, show that the move towards fee-based business lines does not lead to any decline in banking risk (DeYoung and Roland, 2001; Stiroh, 2004; Stiroh and Rumble, 2006). This is usually explained by the low switching costs of non-interest income activities as compared to the lending business, higher operating leverage due to the greater reliance on fixed inputs, like labour, and higher financial leverage generated by lower levels of capital requirements (DeYoung and Roland, 2001). This critical view of diversification benefits in US banks is also confirmed by analyses based on a long time period, including more recent years, and on the comparison of market-based risk measures in universal and traditional banks (Geyfman and Yeager, 2009). The few studies available for the European banking industry achieve similar conclusions (see Baele, De Jonghe, and Vander Vennet, 2007; Mercieca, Schaeck, and Wolfe, 2007;

[14] It is worth noting that the two size variables are far from being perfectly correlated. More precisely, the correlation coefficients between the raw values is 58 per cent, while for the adjusted values it is around 44 per cent.

Lepetit et al., 2008). In sum, the departure from traditional core activities is likely to increase the exposure of banks to systemic shocks.

Banking growth (*GROWTH*) is measured as the three-year moving average of the log difference in the volume of total earning assets ($\text{Ln}(\text{TEA}_t) - \text{Ln}(\text{TEA}_{t-1})$). The implications of banking growth at the individual bank level has been substantially overlooked in the literature. While Knaup and Wagner (2010) show the importance of loan growth in determining a bank's tail-risk exposure in the USA over a short time period, and Foos, Norden, and Weber (2010) point out the negative implications of abnormal loan growth on risk-taking in a cross-country sample, the evidence on how the exposure to systemic shocks is affected by the growth in earning assets in Europe is lacking. As banking growth is generally associated with riskier and more opaque investments, it is also likely to increase the risk that banks fail under systemic events.

The remaining microprudential variables focus on determinants of bank exposure to risk that are related to conventional tools of prudential regulation such as liquidity and capital requirements. The ratio between 'primary' liquidity (central banks' credits, government securities, and cash) and total assets (*LIQUIDITY*) is used to assess the importance of liquid assets in enforcing the ability of banks to withstand shocks. Notably, a larger share of liquid assets may reduce the cost of liquidating assets in the case of a systemic shock, in response to the reduction of the overall amount of liquidity in the market. Next, the analysis controls for the funding mix via the ratio between retail deposits and total debts (*DEPOSITS*). In recent years, banks have shifted away from deposits to finance their growth via other types of liabilities (Gropp and Heider, 2010). The implications of this shift for bank risk exposure are, however, unclear. Conventional banking theory emphasizes the liquidity risk associated with deposit funding especially under a bank run or panic (Bhattacharya and Takor, 1993) while more recent theoretical models show that the ability of a bank to provide liquidity services on both sides of the balance sheet can improve its liquidity management (Kashyap, Rajan, and Stein, 2002). In line with this latter argument, Gatev, Schuermann, and Strahan (2009) show that transaction deposits contribute to hedging bank liquidity risk from unused loan commitments, especially in times of tight market liquidity. Furthermore, non-deposit funding may also generate liquidity risk, as wholesale financiers may have incentives to withdraw funding based on imperfect public information (Huang and Ratnoviski, 2010).

Finally, the set of microprudential variables includes the leverage ratio measured, as in Adrian and Brunnermeier (2010), via the ratio between total assets and book value of equity (*LEVERAGE*). As equity capital is likely to act as a protective buffer against systemic shocks and give banks a shelter against unexpected losses, higher leverage should denote an increasing exposure to systemic shocks. Furthermore, under a systemic shock, highly leveraged banks might be forced to de-leverage by liquidating assets at fire-sale prices in response to the increasing credit rationing by creditors facing liquidity constraints (Shleifer and Vishny, 2010; Acharya and Viswanathan, 2011). This would suggest that higher leverage banks are more prone to failure in the case of a systemic event (Acharya and Thakor, 2011) as shown by Berger and Bouwman on a sample of US banks (2012).[15] However, Boyson, Helwege, and Jindra (2010) show that this result is unlikely to be ascribed to fire sales of assets, as commercial banks do not shrink in asset size or reduce security holdings during crises but manage their liquidity risk exposure by relying on debt and equity issues and cutting dividends.

A second group of variables includes bank characteristics that are not under the direct control of regulators, namely, bank charter value (*CHARTER*) expressed by the ratio between market and book value of equity, the degree of concentration in the domestic banking market, measured by the Herfindahl index of bank total assets (*CONCENTRATION*), and macroeconomic factors such as the country real GDP growth rate (*RGDP*) and the inflation rate (*INFLATION*). Notably, starting from Keeley (1990) there is an extensive literature pointing out the disciplining role of CHARTER on bank risk-taking, but the implications of this variable on bank exposure to systemic risk are less clear. For instance, Acharya (2009) suggests that banks with higher charter values should have less incentives to undertake correlated investments with the rest of the industry. By contrast, Saunders and Wilson (2001) argue that, to the extent that banks build up their charter value via risky investments, they are more subject to common shocks.

To conclude, the descriptive statistics reported in Table 5.3 indicate the presence of large differences across banks in the sample. More precisely, the sample is characterized by the presence of banks with different business models and business structures in terms of revenue composition, leverage, and funding mix.

Is Size Important for a Bank's Exposure to Systemic Shocks?

This section first discusses the empirical results on impact of size and other determinants on the distance-to-default beta ($\hat{\beta}_{DD}$), then focuses on the relationship between banks' coexceedances and bank characteristics. The last part of this section analyses how the results differ in the case of megabanks.

[15] Data limitations exclude the possibility of employing any capital adequacy ratio (regulatory capital over risk-weighted assets) as a control variable. Furthermore, the loan-to-asset ratio is not included in the analysis as it is highly correlated with the share of non-interest income.

Table 5.4. Bank Characteristics and Exposure to Systemic Risk

	(1)	(2)	(3)	(4)	(5)	(6)	(7)	(8)
Panel A: Regression Analysis								
	OLS				Fixed effect			
				Economic Impact (3) p.p.				Economic Impact (7) p.p.
R_SIZE	0.070***	0.072***	0.074***	13.98	0.060***	0.049**	0.061***	11.52
	(9.67)	(9.87)	(10.21)		(3.29)	(2.47)	(3.00)	
SH_{NON}	0.400***	0.394***	0.333***	5.11	0.239***	0.190***	0.189***	2.90
	(5.95)	(5.62)	(5.84)		(3.92)	(2.98)	(2.99)	
GROWTH		0.148**	0.119**	1.34		0.107*	0.078	
		(2.38)	(2.02)			(1.96)	(1.44)	
LIQUIDITY	−0.127	−0.137	−0.172		0.159	0.140	0.108	
	(1.17)	(1.25)	(1.55)		(1.55)	(1.36)	(1.09)	
DEPOSITS	−0.070	−0.062	−0.090		−0.010	0.003	−0.029	
	(1.04)	(0.90)	(1.37)		(0.12)	(0.03)	(0.34)	
LEVERAGE	0.008***	0.008***	0.008***	7.56	0.008***	0.007**	0.007***	6.61
	(4.65)	(4.76)	(5.08)		(3.08)	(2.42)	(2.65)	
CHARTER			0.034***	3.74			0.019**	2.09
			(4.49)				(2.37)	
CONCENTRATION			−0.134				−0.228	
			(0.74)				(1.17)	
RGDP			0.670				0.926*	
			(1.25)				(1.81)	
INFLATION			2.396***				2.536***	
			(4.37)				(4.26)	
Constant	−0.075	−0.077	−0.194*		−0.165***	−0.118*	−0.214***	
	(0.83)	(0.82)	(1.92)		(2.69)	(1.80)	(2.66)	

Observations	1483	1406	1406		1483	1406	1406	
Ad. R-squared	0.545	0.550	0.573		0.343	0.317	0.338	
Year dummies	Yes	Yes	Yes		Yes	Yes	Yes	
Country dummies	Yes	Yes	Yes					
Fixed Effect	No	No	No		Yes	Yes	Yes	
Robust t-statistics in parentheses								
Panel B: Wald test on the equality of economic impact played by bank characteristics on distance-to-default beta								
H0: Economic impact R_SIZE = Economic impact SH_{NON}				36.09***				6.78**
				(0.000)				(0.010)
H0: Economic impact R_SIZE = Economic impact GROWTH				73.00***				6.73**
				(0.000)				(0.010)
H0: Economic impact R_SIZE = Economic impact LEVERAGE				10.62***				3.67*
				(0.001)				(0.057)

Panel A shows the regression results of the determinants of the distance-to-default beta. In the first three columns the model has been estimated via OLS while in columns 5, 6, and 7 the results refer to the within estimator; t-statistics are reported in round brackets, standard errors have been corrected for heteroscedasticity and clustered at the level of the bank. *R_SIZE* is the residual from a regression of the log of total assets on the remaining 'microprudential variables';SH_{NON} is the ratio between non-interest income and total operating income; *GROWTH* is the three-year moving average of the log change in earning assets; *LIQUIDITY* is the ratio between central bank deposits, government securities, and cash over total assets; *DEPOSITS* is computed as customer deposits over total debts; *LEVERAGE* is the ratio between total assets and total book value of equity; *CHARTER* is the ratio between market and book value of equity; *CONCENTRATION* is the Herfindahl index of bank asset concentration computed at the country level; *RGDP* is the annual real GDP growth rate; and *INFLATION* is the inflation rate. Panel B reports the Wald test on the equality of the economic impact produced on the distance-to-default beta by changes in bank characteristics.

* significant at 10%; ** significant at 5%; *** significant at 1%.

Determinants of Bank Exposure to Systemic Shocks in Normal Times

Panel A of Table 5.4 reports the estimation results for the relationship between a bank's exposure to systemic risk ($\hat{\beta}_{DD}$) and bank characteristics. Following Stiroh (2004), the models have been estimated first via OLS and then by controlling for bank fixed effects that capture the impact of unobserved heterogeneity across banks.[16] As in Baele, De Jonghe, and Vander Vennet (2007), with the exclusion of macroeconomic variables, all variables have been lagged one year to reduce simultaneity and endogeneity bias. Furthermore, as in Gatev, Schuermann, and Strahan (2009), in both the OLS and the within-estimator regressions, standard errors have been corrected for heteroscedasticity and clustered at the level of the bank. Finally, as GROWTH is available for a smaller number of observations, Table 5.4 presents the regression results with and without the inclusion of this variable in the models.

The findings suggest that bank size is pivotal in determining a bank exposure to shocks. However, the non-interest income share, the leverage ratio, and, to a minor extent, the growth in earning assets are also significant determinants of $\hat{\beta}_{DD}$. By contrast, liquidity and the share of retail deposits over total debts do not seem to influence the risk measure.[17] These empirical findings are robust to changes in the model specification and to changes in the econometric approach.

More specifically, R_SIZE enters all specification with a positive and highly significant coefficient; namely, larger banks are more prone to fail under systemic shocks. This result is supportive of the arguments that the risk of failure generally increases with bank size (Boyd and Runkle, 1993; De Nicoló et al., 2004; Demirgüç-Kunt and Huizinga, 2011) and larger banks are more exposed to common sources of shocks (Baele, De Jonghe, and Vander Vennet, 2007; De Jonghe, 2010). However, it contrasts with the recent finding of Knaup and Wagner (2012): of a negative relationship between bank size and the exposure to tail risks.

Furthermore, the current analysis confirms the rationale of recent regulatory calls to refocus the banking business on traditional lending activities: SH_{NON} is positively related to $\hat{\beta}_{DD}$, showing that the departure from traditional commercial banking practices offer a lower protection against systemic shocks. Overall, this result confirms that non-interest income activities are more volatile business lines and this higher volatility tends to outweigh the

[16] The within estimator allows the influence of bank unobserved heterogeneity due to factors that remain constant over the sample period to be controlled. This estimator allows each bank to have its own intercept in the regression; therefore, the results are simply driven by within-bank variation over time as the bank-specific intercept strips out all the cross-sectional variation before estimating the slope coefficients. Under this specification, country dummies cannot be included.

[17] The conclusions remain similar if the data for the year 2008 are excluded from the sample with the purpose to remove the influence of the sub-prime crisis from the analysis.

potential gains from diversification (Stiroh, 2006). From a systemic perspective, this finding implies that the departure of banks from traditional business lines increases the exposure of bank to common shocks by increasing their similarities (Wagner, 2010; Ibragimov, Jaffee, and Walden, 2011).

In terms of other variables, Panel A outlines the importance of LEVERAGE in determining the exposure of banks to systemic shocks: more leveraged banks exhibit a higher sensitivity to changes in systemic risk and, thus, are more prone to fail, as suggested by Acharya and Thakor (2011) and Berger and Bouwman (2012). Finally, GROWTH enters the models with a significant coefficient in five out of six specifications, implying that a faster increase in the size of earning assets normally weakens the resilience of banks to shocks as suggested by Knaup and Wagner (2012) for a sample of US BHCs.

The introduction of the set of control variables in columns 3 and 7 does not modify the major conclusions, but offers further insights into the determinants of a bank's risk exposure. For example, this exposure increases with the market-to-book ratio, with the inflation rate, and, in part, with the real GDP growth.[18] Notably, the results for the charter value complement the evidence for the USA on its impact on systemic risk contribution (Brunnermeier et al., 2011): 'glamour banks' not only provide the largest contribution to systemic risk, being thus more relevant from a macroprudential perspective, but are more exposed to systemic shocks. It seems that banks may build up their charter values by risky investments that lead to an increase in their exposure to common shocks (Saunders and Wilson, 2001).

Next, column 4 (8) simulates the impact of alternative regulatory restrictions on a bank's risk exposure by providing some comparative figures on how $\hat{\beta}_{DD}$ changes with similar increases in the microprudential variables that show a significant coefficient. More precisely, following Hutton, Marcus, and Tehranian (2009), column 4 (8) reports the changes in $\hat{\beta}_{DD}$ produced by a shift in the value of an explanatory variable from the 25th to 75th percentile of the distribution for the OLS (fixed effect) regression. This approach shows that changes in factor R_SIZE produces the major impact on$\hat{\beta}_{DD}$, followed by changes in the leverage ratio and in SH_{NON}. Panel B offers indications as to whether these differences are also statistically significant by reporting the results of a Wald test on the equality between the economic impact played by R_SIZE and by other bank characteristics on $\hat{\beta}_{DD}$. In general, this test demonstrates that the effect of R_SIZE tends to be statistically higher than the economic impact of other variables especially in the OLS specification.

[18] The positive influence of inflation is consistent with the evidence offered by Heffernan (2003) on a higher probability of bank failures in the case of higher inflation rates, as they prompt fears of future recession, and hence a rise in problematic banks.

In summary, the analysis presented here suggests that, while one of the key bank characteristics at the centre of the new regulatory framework (leverage) proposed by Basel III contributes to determining a bank's exposure to systemic shocks, other bank characteristics (only marginally considered by the new regulations) influence the exposure of banks to systemic events: this exposure being positively related to size, the non-interest income share, and growth. Hence, bank stability may benefit from imposing limits on the leverage ratio but other regulatory restrictions on bank characteristics would also be justified. In particular, the comparison of the impact produced by changes in bank characteristics on $\hat{\beta}_{DD}$ shows that the establishment of constraints on bank size appears to be particularly effective in reducing the risk that a bank fails from systemic shocks.

The Impact of Bank Size on Bank Exposure to Systemic Shocks When the System is Under Stress

Panel A of Table 5.5 reports the estimation results of the relationship between the yearly coexceedances measured at the level of a bank and bank size, and controlling for other potential determinants. Since this risk indicator is a count variable the analysis is conducted via an ordered logit model.[19] This model assumes that the ordinal variable, in the current case the number of coexceedances (Y), taking up to m values, is the discretized version of an underlying continuous variable (Y^*), which depends linearly on a set of covariates:

$$Y^*_{i,t} = \boldsymbol{\theta}'\chi + \varepsilon_{i,t} \tag{2}$$

where $\boldsymbol{\theta}'$ is a vector of explanatory variables including the microprudential variables, the set of control variables discussed earlier in this chapter, time dummies, and country dummies. Furthermore, Y is determined by Y* and by a set of additional threshold parameters $\gamma_1, \gamma_{2 \ldots\ldots}, \gamma_{m-1}$ as follows:

$$Y \leq j \Leftrightarrow Y^* \gamma_j (j = 1, \ldots\ldots, m-1) \tag{3}$$

With the additional assumption that the residual term (ε) has a cumulative logistic distribution, the probability of observing a value of Y not larger than j, conditional on the set of covariates, can be expressed as follows:[20]

[19] A count variable is a categorical variable measured according to an ordinal scale. It is worth noting that a similar empirical approach has been used in the literature to model and predict the changes in supervisory bank ratings (Curry, Fissel, and Hanweck, 2008).

[20] A Wald test is employed to assess whether each threshold parameter is significantly different from its adjacent threshold. This seems to be indeed the case, hence the distinction between the four types of coexceedances (i.e. 0, 1, 2, and at least 3) is appropriate for the current sample.

Table 5.5. Bank Characteristics and Exposure to Extreme Systemic Risk: Ordered Logistic Regression

	(1)	(2)	(3)	(4)	(5)	(6)
Panel A: Regression analysis						
						Economic Impact (5)
R_SIZE	0.519***	0.578***	0.517***	0.581***	0.600***	1.133
	(10.37)	(10.31)	(10.49)	(10.45)	(11.12)	
SH_{NON}	2.549***	2.973***	2.358***	2.927***	2.538***	0.390
	(5.90)	(5.79)	(5.37)	(5.65)	(5.31)	
GROWTH			2.267***	1.159**	1.015**	0.115
			(5.22)	(2.44)	(2.15)	
LIQUIDITY	−1.540**	−2.495**	−1.659***	−2.485**	−2.636***	−0.235
	(2.45)	(2.51)	(2.71)	(2.55)	(2.75)	
DEPOSITS	0.117	−0.527	0.025	−0.520	−0.818	
	(0.29)	(0.77)	(0.06)	(0.77)	(1.27)	
LEVERAGE	0.040***	0.035**	0.040***	0.036**	0.037***	0.350
	(4.20)	(2.43)	(4.41)	(2.53)	(2.64)	
CHARTER					0.245***	0.270
					(3.92)	
CONCENTRATION					1.329	
					(0.82)	
RGDP					15.857**	
					(2.52)	
INFLATION					4.463	
					(0.50)	
Observations	1470	1470	1393	1393	1393	
Log likelihood	−1750.26	−1541.61	−1621.91	−1472.90	−1460.45	
Pseudo-R2	0.083	0.173	0.089	0.173	0.180	
Year dummies	No	Yes	No	Yes	Yes	
Country dummies	No	Yes	No	Yes	Yes	

Robust z-statistics in parentheses

Panel B: Wald test on the equality of economic impact played by bank characteristics on the log odds	
H0: Economic impact R_SIZE = Economic impact SH_{NON}	39.91***
	(0.000)
H0: Economic impact R_SIZE = Economic impact GROWTH	95.65***
	(0.000)
H0: Economic impact R_SIZE = Economic impact LEVERAGE	32.38***
	(0.000)
H0: Economic impact R_SIZE = Economic impact LIQUIDITY	109.28***
	(0.000)

Panel A shows the results of ordered logistic regression where the dependent variable is the number of coexceedances computed on the basis of the number of extreme increases in the default risk. z-statistics are reported in round brackets, standard errors have been corrected for heteroscedasticity and clustered at the level of the bank. *R_SIZE* is the residual from a regression of the log of total assets on the remaining 'microprudential variables'; SH_{NON} is the ratio between non-interest income and total operating income; *GROWTH* is the three-year moving average of the log change in earning assets; *LIQUIDITY* is the ratio between central bank deposits, government securities, and cash over total assets; *DEPOSITS* is computed as customer deposits over total debts; *LEVERAGE* is the ratio between total assets and total book value of equity; *CHARTER* is the ratio between market and book value of equity; *CONCENTRATION* is the Herfindahl index of bank asset concentration computed at the country level; *RGDP* is the annual real GDP growth rate; and *INFLATION* is the inflation rate. *Panel B* reports the Wald test on the equality of the economic impact produced on log odds by changes in bank characteristics.
* significant at 10%; ** significant at 5%; *** significant at 1%.

$$P(Y \leq j|\boldsymbol{\theta}) = \frac{\exp\,(\gamma_j - \boldsymbol{\theta}'\chi)}{1 + \exp\,(\gamma_j - \boldsymbol{\theta}'\chi)} \tag{4}$$

This implies a linear relationship between the logit of Y and the explanatory variables, as reported below:

$$\log\left[\frac{P(Y>j|\boldsymbol{\theta})}{P(Y \leq j|\boldsymbol{\theta})}\right] = \boldsymbol{\theta}'\chi - \gamma_j \tag{5}$$

Hence, the model predicts the probability associated with each event and how this probability changes as a consequence of a change in bank-specific characteristics.[21]

The results in Table 5.5 appear in line with the conclusions achieved in the previous section: the likelihood of coexceedances at the bank level is higher when banks become larger. However, this likelihood also increases when banks show a higher share of non-interest income, are more highly leveraged, and indulge in aggressive growth strategies (as expressed by a larger increase in the volume of earning assets). In general, bank characteristics that weaken a bank's shelter from systemic shocks in normal conditions play a similar role when the banking system is under stress. Nonetheless, in contrast to the results presented for the determinants of a bank's risk exposure in normal times, these new tests provide evidence of the importance of bank liquidity, as banks that benefit from a larger share of liquid assets are less likely to suffer from coexceedances. The fact that the importance of liquidity emerges only in such extreme systemic conditions suggests the need to design liquidity requirements on the basis of stress scenarios, as in the Basel III Accord.

The results are robust to the inclusion of country and time dummies and of other control variables.[22] Notably, outside the set of microprudential variables, and in line with the findings discussed earlier in this chapter, the results presented here confirm the fact that 'glamour' banks are subject to larger declines in their distance to default under extreme stress conditions.

Column 6 offers some comparative figures on the relative importance of the explanatory variables by reporting the changes in the log odds when one variable moves from the 25th percentile to the 75th percentile of the distribution while the others remain unchanged. Similar to the results presented in Table 5.4, this analysis identifies that the three most important factors in

[21] As in the case of the linear model, with the exclusion of macroeconomic factors, all variables have been lagged one year, and standard errors have been corrected to control for heteroscedasticity and have been clustered at the level of the bank to relax the assumption of independence over time between each bank.

[22] Notably, country and time dummies increase substantially the explanatory power of the model: these two groups of variables raise the pseudo-R2 by 9 percentage points. This can be interpreted as an indication of the influence of general market conditions on the risk that banks fail.

determining bank exposure to shocks when the banking system is under stress is the pure size factor, the leverage ratio, and the share of non-interest income—with the size effect still playing the most important role. This is confirmed by Panel B, which shows that the economic impact of the size effect is significantly larger than the economic impact played by the other variables, according to a Wald test.

Finally, Table 5.6 reports the value of the predicted probabilities of the number of coexceedances and how these probabilities are affected by changes in the explanatory variables. The evidence offered by Table 5.6 eases the interpretation of the results since the coefficients of the ordered logit model are not linearly related to the probability of occurrence of each event. Hence, the influence of bank characteristics on these probabilities cannot be inferred simply from the coefficients reported in Table 5.6.[23]

Panel A of Table 5.6 shows descriptive statistics for the predicted probabilities of each event computed at the level of the bank. These statistics point out

Table 5.6. Predicted Probabilities of Coexceedances in Risk

	Pr (Coexceedances = 0)	Pr (Coexceedances = 1)	Pr (Coexceedances = 2)	Pr (Coexceedances = 3)
Panel A: Predicted probabilities of coexceedances				
Mean	40.7	29.5	17.9	11.9
Median	38.1	32.5	16.2	5.5
Standard deviation	26.4	10.6	11.7	15.3
Panel B: Relative changes in probabilities (%)				
R_SIZE	−40.48	59.64	158.77	200.59
SH_{NON}	−15.64	18.71	39.51	46.29
GROWTH	−4.99	5.05	10.24	11.94
LIQUIDITY	4.00	−3.58	−7.04	−7.87
LEVERAGE	−14.50	15.75	34.06	39.84
CHARTER	−11.19	12.37	25.72	29.84

Panel A reports descriptive statistics of the predicted probabilities of 0, 1, 2, and 3 or more extreme increases in bank default risk in a given year. These probabilities have been computed on the basis of the model in column 5 of Table 5.5. Panel B reports the relative change in the probabilities when an explanatory variable moves from the 25th to the 75th percentile while the remaining variables are at the sample median. *R_SIZE* is the residual from a regression of the log of total assets on the remaining 'microprudential variables'; $\mathbf{SH_{NON}}$ is the ratio between non-interest income and total operating income; *GROWTH* is the three-year moving average of the log change in earning assets; *LIQUIDITY* is the ratio between central bank deposits, government securities, and cash over total assets; *LEVERAGE* is the ratio between total assets and total book value of equity; *CHARTER* is the ratio between market value of equity and book value of equity.

[23] For the sake of simplicity and brevity, Table 5.6 does not show the results of these analyses for the full set of models presented in Table 5.5 but focuses on the model estimated for the full sample period and that controls for the impact of time and country dummies. In other words, Table 5.6 summarizes the predicted probabilities of each event and the marginal effects derived from the model reported in column 5 of Table 5.5.

that the most likely event for the banks in the present sample is to show a number of coexceedances equal to zero: the median probability of zero coexceedances is equal to about 38 per cent, while, as the number of coexceedances increases, the probability of each event becomes substantially smaller. Panel B highlights the economic impact of each bank characteristic by showing how the predicted probabilities change when an explanatory variable, that enters in the regression model with a significant coefficient, moves from the 25th to the 75th percentile of the distribution while the remaining variables are fixed at the median values. This exercise confirms the evidence offered by column 7 of Table 5.5: the three most important determinants of bank exposure to shocks in extreme systemic conditions are the (pure) size effect, the share of non-interest income, and the leverage ratio, with the size effect still playing the major role. In sum, the results discussed in this section point out that several bank characteristics contribute to explaining the risk that a bank suffers from coexceedances. Although the majority of these variables exercise a similar effect on $\hat{\beta}_{DD}$, liquidity is only relevant for bank exposure when the banking system suffers from extreme negative shocks.

Does Systemic Size Matter to the Design of a Size Cap?

The major policy implication emerging from our analysis is that a cap on bank absolute size, *ceteris paribus*, is likely to be the most effective microprudential tool if the purpose is to improve the resilience of banks to shocks. However, the design of such a cap may need to take into account the interaction between bank size and the dimension of the domestic economy. In other words, the relevance of a bank's absolute size for financial stability is likely to vary with the size of the economy, as banks that appear relatively small in absolute terms may be systemically important if they are operating in relatively small economies. By contrast, the negative externalities posed by banks that appear large in absolute terms are likely to be less severe in the case of institutions operating in a large domestic economy.

Table 5.7 offers indications as to whether any regulatory restrictions on bank size needs to be tailor-made on the basis of the dimension of the domestic economy by replacing bank absolute size with bank systemic size, defined as bank total assets scaled by the country GDP, in the regression analysis.

This analysis indicates that R_SYSTEMIC shows consistently a positive and highly significant coefficient; namely, large banks with respect to the size of the economy in which they are located are more likely to show an increase in their default risk under systemic shocks. This conclusion holds in spite of changes in the regression models, and both in the case of the exposure of banks in normal conditions and in extreme stress conditions. This result has

Table 5.7. Systemic Size and Bank Exposure to Systemic Risk—Megabanks

	(1)	(2)	(3)	(4)	(5)	(6)	(7)	(8)	(9)
Panel A: Regression Analysis									
	Dependent Variable: Distance-to-Default Beta						Dependent Variable: Number of Coexceedances		
	OLS			Fixed Effect			Ordered Logit		
			Economic Impact (2)			Economic Impact (5)			Economic Impact (8)
R_SYSTEMIC	0.267***	0.258***	5.39	0.229***	0.237***	4.95	1.551***	1.545***	0.323
	(7.58)	(7.29)		(4.71)	(5.66)		(6.43)	(6.32)	
SH_{NON}	0.448***	0.403***	6.19	0.234***	0.231***	3.55	2.953***	2.697***	0.414
	(7.27)	(7.36)		(4.50)	(4.60)		(6.93)	(6.66)	
GROWTH	0.107*	0.089	1.01	0.124**	0.104**	1.18	0.737	0.680	
	(1.91)	(1.61)		(2.54)	(2.18)		(1.50)	(1.37)	
LIQUIDITY	−0.067	−0.038		0.065	0.086		−1.923*	−1.774	
	(0.57)	(0.30)		(0.68)	(0.89)		(1.87)	(1.53)	
DEPOSITS	−0.071	−0.098		0.071	0.052		−0.874	−1.094	
	(0.94)	(1.37)		(1.00)	(0.79)		(1.22)	(1.61)	
LEVERAGE	0.008***	0.008***	7.56	0.003**	0.003*	2.83	0.029*	0.030*	0.283
	(4.05)	(4.10)		(1.98)	(1.89)		(1.67)	(1.74)	
CHARTER		0.026***	2.86		0.018**	1.98		0.174***	0.192
		(3.42)			(2.38)			(3.22)	
CONCENTRATION		−0.408***			−0.542***			0.255	
		(2.65)			(3.73)			(0.11)	
RGDP		0.917*			0.821*			15.328**	
		(1.83)			(1.71)			(1.97)	
INFLATION		1.344***			2.069***			−4.403	
		(3.03)			(3.97)			(0.44)	
Constant	0.016	−0.037		−0.120**	−0.165***				
	(0.16)	(0.36)		(2.07)	(2.68)				
Observations	1406	1406		1406	1406		1393	1393	
Adjusted R-squared	0.514	0.527		0.340	0.359				
Pseudo-R2							0.144	0.149	

(*continued*)

Table 5.7. Continued

	(1)	(2)	(3)	(4)	(5)	(6)	(7)	(8)	(9)
Panel A: Regression Analysis									
	Dependent Variable: Distance-to-Default Beta						Dependent Variable: Number of Coexceedances		
	OLS			Fixed Effect			Ordered Logit		
			Economic Impact (2)			Economic Impact (5)			Economic Impact (8)
Year dummies	Yes	Yes		Yes	Yes		Yes	Yes	
Country dummies							Yes	Yes	
Fixed effect	Yes	Yes		Yes	Yes				
Robust t (z)-statistics in parentheses									
Number of banks	153	153		153	153		153	153	
Panel B: Wald test on the equality of economic impact played by bank characteristics									
H0: Economic impact R_SYSTEMIC = Economic impact SH_{NON}			0.50 (0.479)			2.16 (0.144)			1.52 (0.218)
H0: Economic impact R_SYSTEMIC = Economic impact GROWTH			–			14.97*** (0.000)			
H0: Economic impact R_SYSTEMIC = Economic impact LEVERAGE			1.01 (0.317)			1.87 (0.174)			0.07 (0.794)
H0: Economic impact R_SYSTEMIC = Economic impact LIQUIDITY									

Panel A shows the regression results of the determinants of the distance-to-default beta and of the number of coexceedances. In the first two columns the models has been estimated via OLS while in columns 4 and 5 the results refer to the within estimator and columns 7 and 8 refer to the ordered logit model; t (z)-statistics are reported in round brackets, standard errors have been corrected for heteroscedasticity and clustered at the level of the bank. *R_SYSTEMIC* is the residual from a regression of the ratio of bank total assets and country GDP on the remaining 'microprudential variables'; SH_{NON} is the ratio between non-interest income and total operating income; *GROWTH* is the three-year moving average of the log change in earning assets; *LIQUIDITY* is the ratio between central bank deposits, government securities, and cash over total assets; *DEPOSITS* is computed as customer deposits over total debts; *LEVERAGE* is the ratio between total assets and total book value of equity; *CHARTER* is the ratio between market and book value of equity; *CONCENTRATION* is the Herfindahl index of bank asset concentration computed at the country level; *RGDP* is the annual real GDP growth rate; and *INFLATION* is the inflation rate. Panel B reports the Wald test on the equality of the economic impact produced on the distance-to-default beta (log odds) by changes in bank characteristics.

* significant at 10%; ** significant at 5%; *** significant at 1%.

two possible interpretations related to regulatory distortions. First, it might be the case that the externalities created by the implicit bailout guarantee associated with the too-big-to-fail status are more pronounced in large banks operating in small countries. As a consequence, large banks operating in these countries are likely to show more aggressive risk-taking strategies that weaken their resilience during crisis periods. Second, in small economies the spillover effects generated by the failure of a large institution might be stronger, raising the importance of the too-many-to-fail effect and the risk of regulatory forbearance (Brown and Dinç, 2011). In other words, the failure of a large institution in a small country might generate a high risk of simultaneous crashes in other components of the financial system, and this induces regulatory interventions to support the failing institutions.

In order to elaborate on the optimal design of a size cap in banks, Panel B reports a Wald test on the equality between the magnitude of the economic impacts produced by an increase in systemic size and by increases in other microprudential variables. These tests show that the effect produced by an increase in systemic size on bank exposure to shocks is similar to those determined by an increase in the interest income share and in the leverage ratio. As absolute size outperforms all the other microprudential variables in similar tests discussed earlier in this chapter, we interpret this finding as an indication that the impact of relative size on the exposure of banks to shocks, though significant, is weaker than the impact played by an increase in absolute size.[24]

Putting together the results discussed earlier in this chapter with the evidence offered by Table 5.7, it is possible to argue that larger banks located in small countries are more likely to fail from systemic shocks; namely, the optimal bank size is smaller in smaller countries (Demirgüç-Kunt and Huizinga, 2011). Furthermore, the design of any regulatory restrictions in terms of bank size requires a focus on absolute size and needs to be country-specific, with smaller European countries requiring smaller banks.

Robustness Tests

The stability of the above results has been assessed via a broad set of robustness tests. First, the impact of the concentration of the sample in two countries (Italy and France) is examined by re-estimating the linear and ordered logistic models after excluding one of these countries from the sample: this exercise

[24] In line with this interpretation, unreported tests show that, especially in the case of the exposure to extreme systemic shocks, when R_SIZE is introduced as a further control variable the coefficient and the significant levels of R_SYSTEMIC declines substantially. To save space, we do not report the results of these tests.

leaves the conclusions substantially unaffected. Second, while care has been exercised to select banks with an interest in commercial banking, a few banks show a very low share of retail deposits in their liability structure. Thus, the analysis is re-estimated by imposing a minimum value of this ratio of 15 per cent, and the major conclusions are confirmed. Third, though the analysis employed lagged explanatory variables, the results may still be influenced by endogeneity. Thus, the analysis reported in Tables 5.4 and 5.7 is run by using a two-step generalized method-of-moments (GMM) system estimator for panel data, where contemporaneous values of the explanatory variables are used and where all bank characteristics are treated as endogenous, with their lags at time t-2 used as instruments (see Blundell and Bond, 1998). This test confirmed that absolute and relative size, the non-interest income share, leverage, and growth are key determinants of a bank's exposure to systemic shocks.

Two further final tests focus on the robustness of the results suggested by the ordered logit models. Specifically, an alternative definition of coexceedances is considered by adopting the 5 percentile as a new threshold and the ordered logistic model is re-estimated with this new measure as the dependent variable.[25] This test provides further evidence in favour of the major results but also suggests the presence of one relevant difference as compared to the preferred model; namely, a negative and significant coefficient is observed for the ratio between retail deposits and total debts. Finally, untabulated tests found that a large number of extreme events is concentrated in the year 2001. Nonetheless, re-estimating the models without this year did not change the findings.

The Possible Negative Effects of a Cap on Bank Size

The results presented here are clearly supportive of recent regulatory calls to break up the largest banking firms operating in the financial system. However, it needs to be noted that the benefits that a size cap may produce for bank stability, as identified by the analysis of this chapter, have not been contrasted with the negative effects that may emerge after the introduction of such a regulatory restriction because of changes in bank behaviour (Stern and Feldman, 2009). For instance, Dermine and Schoenmaker (2010) argue that size limits may increase the domestic focus of banks, whose effects on the default risk of an individual institution and for the stability of the system are difficult to predict. More precisely, the authors conjecture that there could be an

[25] This alternative indicator ranges from 0 to 4, assuming a value equal to 4 only when the number of coexceedances is larger than 3.

unexpected increase in risk due to the lack of credit risk diversification at the bank level.

Furthermore, Wheelock and Wilson (2011) suggest that size restrictions may increase intermediation costs by reducing economies of scale. For a sample of US banks, they show that over the period from 1984 to 2006, most US banks benefitted from increasing returns to scale, suggesting that scale economies are a possible reason for the growth in average bank size. However, while these results are in line with more recent studies on economies of scale in banking (Hughes, Mester, and Moon, 2001), they contradict earlier evidence, which appears quite sceptical on the cost benefits associated to an increasing production scale (McAllister and McManus, 1993; Mester, 2005). Essentially, the earlier literature concludes that banks exhaust scale economies at \$100–\$200 million of total assets; namely, the cost savings are normally very limited.

Other negative ex post effects generated by a size cap may be related to forms of regulatory arbitrage: to the extent that the regulatory framework does not extend the boundaries well beyond the banking system, banks might be tempted to shift some activities to the less regulated shadow financial system. Finally, unexpected consequences could be related to the lending function and the regulatory limits imposed on the degree of concentration of the loan portfolio. The need to shift a large share of the lending activity for large corporates to the market for syndicated loans might determine problems of information sharing among lenders and reduce the effectiveness of their monitoring function.

Conclusions

This chapter has analysed, within the European context, the determinants of the risk that banks fail under systemic shocks, utilizing a novel empirical approach based on contingent claim analysis and the Merton (1974) distance-to-default model. Overall, while the results support the introduction of leverage and liquidity requirements, as stipulated in the Basel III Accord, they also show that several bank characteristics that are not at the centre of the new regulatory landscape are key determinants of the risk that a bank fails from systemic shocks. The risk exposure of banks, both in normal and extreme systemic conditions, increases with size, the share of non-interest income activities, and the growth of earning assets.

Furthermore, the comparative analysis of the impact of different bank characteristics on bank exposure to shocks shows that, *ceteris paribus*, the Basel III interventions are likely to be less effective than imposing a cap on bank absolute size. The design of size restrictions appears, however, to be related to the size of the economy in which a bank is operating. More precisely, as the risk exposure of a bank increases with both absolute and systemic size (defined in relative terms with respect to the size of the economy), and in spite of the integration process of the financial industry in Europe, any regulatory intervention on size needs to be country-specific, with smaller European economies needing smaller banks. This result has relevant implications for the literature on the determinants of optimal bank size that has generally assumed the perspective of the individual institution without any consideration for the systemic context. By contrast, the current chapter highlights the importance of incorporating, in any decision model of optimal bank size, the costs that size produces in terms of exposure to systemic shocks and the linkages with the overall size of the economy.

In summary, how to design regulatory restrictions on bank size does not appear an easy task for regulators, although the benefits in terms of bank resilience to shocks that, *ceteris paribus*, are associated with such a regulatory restriction seem particularly pronounced. The difficulties posed by such a regulatory intervention, and the importance of bank size for banks' exposure to systemic shocks, speak in favour of the adoption of prudential rules designed for large and complex financial institutions.

Appendix: Estimates of Distance to Default at the Bank Level

Bank distance to default (DD) on day t, based on the Merton credit risk model, is computed as follows:

$$DD_t = [\ln (V_{A,t}/X_t) + (r_f - 0.5\sigma^2_{A,t})T]/\sigma_{A,t}\sqrt{T} \tag{1A}$$

where $V_{A,t}$ is the market value of assets, X_t is the book value of total liabilities, r_{f_t} is the risk-free rate (proxied by the twelve-month German interbank rate), $\sigma_{A,t}$ is the annualized asset volatility at t, and T is the time to maturity (conventionally set to one year). The computation of DD_t requires estimates of $V_{A,t}$ and $\sigma_{A,t}$ (neither of which are directly observable) that we infer through an iterative process based on the Black–Scholes–Merton pricing model (Vassalou and Xing, 2004; Akhigbe, Madura, and Martin, 2007). Thus, the market value of a firm's equity ($V_{E,t}$) is expressed as a function of the asset value by solving the following system of nonlinear equations:

$$V_{E,t} = V_{A,t}N(d_{1,t}) - X_t e^{-r_f T}N(d_{2,t}) \tag{2A}$$

$$\sigma_{E,t} = \left(\frac{V_{A,t}}{V_{E,t}}\right)N(d_{1,t})\sigma_{A,t} \tag{3A}$$

Equation (2A) defines $V_{E,t}$ as a call option on the market value of the bank's total assets, with $d_{1,t} = [\ln(V_{A,t}/X_t) + (r_{f_t} + 0.5\sigma^2_{A,t})T]/\sigma_{A,t}\sqrt{T}$ and $d_{2,t} = d_{1,t} - \sigma_{A,t}\sqrt{T}$. Equation (3A) is the optimal hedge equation that relates the volatility of a bank's equity value to the volatility of the value of total assets (both on an annualized basis). We solve this system by employing, as starting values for $\sigma_{A,t}$, the values of $\sigma_{E,t}$ (computed daily on the basis of a one-year rolling window) multiplied by the ratio between $V_{E,t}$ and the sum of $V_{E,t}$ and X_t. A Newton search algorithm identifies the daily values for $V_{A,t}$ and $\sigma_{A,t}$ in an iterative process, which we then employ to compute DD as in (1A). Following Gropp, Vesala, and Vulpes (2006), infrannual (daily) observations of X_t are obtained by cubic spline interpolation.

Part IV

Corporate Governance in European Banking

6

Board Monitoring, Regulation, and Performance in the European Banking Industry

Introduction

It is a widely held view that banks and other closely regulated firms are not subject to the same contracting costs between managers and shareholders as less tightly regulated companies (Kole and Lehn, 1999; Booth, Cornett, and Tehranian, 2002; Mallin, Mullineux, and Wihlborg, 2005). If regulation restricts managerial discretion and its scope to adversely affect shareholder wealth, the requirement on shareholders to put in place board mechanisms to monitor managers is somewhat reduced (Baysinger and Zardkoohi, 1986; Shleifer and Vishny, 1997). Thus, regulation may act as a substitute for monitoring by boards. Alternatively, if strict regulatory environments promote firm-level governance that is effective in controlling for agency cost, a complementary relationship exists between governance and regulation. The purpose of this chapter is to analyse the monitoring effects of boards of directors versus bank regulators in preventing value-destroying acquisition strategies in an international sample of banks. The bank regulatory regimes of many countries continue to vary in terms of their sensitivity to bank risk-taking, disciplinary powers, and enforcement mechanisms.

Mergers and acquisitions (M&A) provide a suitable setting in which to examine the effectiveness of management monitoring. This is because M&A are important managerial initiatives that are subject to board scrutiny and have observable performance effects. Further, Jensen (1986) argues that acquisitions intensify the conflicts of interest between managers and shareholders in public corporations. Agency explanations of M&A emphasize that the market for corporate control may yield sizable personal gains to managers at the expense of shareholder wealth (Morck, Shleifer, and Vishny, 1990;

Masulis, Wang, and Xie, 2007). In the case of banking, a large merger performance literature reports that, while bidding bank shareholders tend to realize wealth losses as a result of M&A (Pilloff, 1996; DeLong and DeYoung, 2007; Van Hoose, 2009: 90–4), managers at the bidding bank benefit from higher prestige and increased remuneration packages in the post-merger period (Bliss and Rosen, 2001; Anderson, Becher, and Campbell, 2004).

Few studies on bank governance that focus on European banks exist to date. One of the reasons for this is the limited availability of reliable data on the corporate governance of European banks. For instance, data on individual directors as well as their professional background is not available in some countries or has only recently been made available in others. That means a meaningful quantitative analysis of governance issues in banking is difficult if we were to focus on European banks only. For this reason, this chapter adds data on US banks to a sample of European banks. Therefore, this chapter analyses a cross-country sample of European and US banks in order to understand the relationship between governance and regulation in banking.

In this chapter, we employ three board-monitoring mechanisms (board independence, CEO–chair duality, and board diversity) and develop hypotheses which compare the substitution versus complementarity perspectives. We analyse the interaction of board monitoring with bank regulatory regimes to impact the bidder announcement effect. We find that two board-monitoring mechanisms improve acquisition performance in strict regulatory regimes. Thus, board independence and diversity are linked to higher bidder announcement returns in strict regulatory regimes. In less strict regulatory environments, board monitoring is virtually irrelevant in improving the performance outcomes of merger activities.

The chapter adds to the growing literature that examines whether corporate governance impacts on performance, and makes several important contributions. First, we contrast the *effectiveness* of banks' internal monitoring capabilities across (country) regulatory regimes. In a recent paper related to our chapter, Becher and Frye (2011) also examine the relationship between governance and regulation. While Becher and Frye (2011) consider multiple industry regulatory regimes within a single nation, we compare governance arrangements within a single industry spread across multiple national regulatory regimes. Second, previous studies contrast the governance arrangements of regulated and unregulated industries without examining the performance effects of such arrangements. Our analysis, by contrast, gauges the realized performance changes linked to governance in the market for corporate control.

Theory and Hypotheses Development

Outside shareholders are incentivized to put in place monitoring devices, which are effective in mitigating against agency costs (Jensen and Meckling, 1976; Shleifer and Vishny, 1997). However, for tightly regulated firms, it has been suggested that regulators can perform subsidized monitoring and disciplinary services that lead to outcomes similar to those achieved by board monitoring (Demsetz and Lehn, 1985; Baysinger and Zardkoohi, 1986). Below, we develop three hypotheses that address the effectiveness of the following board-monitoring variables within the bank regulatory environments of the USA and Europe: board independence, CEO/chairman duality, and board diversity.

More independent boards are believed to exert greater vigilance. Fama and Jensen (1983) argue that independent directors are incentivized to scrutinize diligently, because such directors seek to protect their reputation as effective monitors of managerial discretion. As a result, more independent boards will exert greater disciplinary powers, for instance, by dismissing underperforming CEOs (Weisbach, 1988; Byrd and Hickman, 1992). Board independence will, therefore, increase general bank performance (Cornett, McNutt, and Tehranian, 2009) as well the performance of complex decision-making tasks such as bank merger strategies (Subrahmanyam, Rangan, and Rosenstein, 1997; Cornett et al., 2003).

To the extent that regulators monitor bank management, the need for independent boards to monitor diligently and effectively is reduced. Admittedly, the interests of regulators are different from those of shareholders. In the banking industry, regulatory efforts are aimed at maintaining the safety and soundness of the financial system. Nonetheless, bank regulation restricts some of the strategic options available to managers which otherwise could have adverse effects on bank performance (see Demsetz and Lehn, 1985). In most countries, regulators have the authority to restrict the type of activities that banking firms may engage in, require increases in regulatory capital, enforce reversals of high-risk policies, and veto takeover proposals. Further, regulators have disciplinary powers which help create an environment of accountability for managers (Hadlock, Lee, and Parrino, 2002). In strict regulatory environments, regulators may fine or dismiss bank directors without trial or hearing and require new board elections to be held. It could, therefore, be argued that if regulators effectively provide subsidized monitoring and discipline, independent boards are not required to monitor diligently and effectively. Therefore,

> *Hypothesis 1a: If board monitoring and bank regulation are substitutes, board independence will not improve the bidder announcement returns under strict regulatory regimes.*

On the other hand, if a complementary relationship exists between corporate governance and regulation, more independent boards will be more effective under a stricter regulatory environment. Stricter bank regulation may exist along with more effective board independence due to the signalling effect embedded in strict regulation. Roe (2003) notes that it is the political will behind regulation (and not the design) that acts as the primary determinant of its effectiveness. Mahoney (2001) argues that regulation should not be understood as a narrow set of rules. Instead, governments employ regulation as a mechanism to signal intent about good practice and a commitment to enforce this practice. Therefore, it could be argued that even when regulators do not stipulate levels of board independence (or other governance arrangements), their presence will still coerce regulated firms into adopting effective governance structures (Becher and Frye, 2011). This is because directors of regulated firms wish to be perceived by regulators as managing their firm well, and are mindful of the legal and reputational consequences which would result if regulators lost trust in them (Baxter, 2003). The stronger the powers that regulators have been equipped with to intervene and discipline, the greater the 'threat of action' (Booth, Cornett, and Tehranian, 2002) that regulators pose to independent directors. Strict bank regulation, therefore, provides incentives to independent directors to monitor soundly and effectively. Consequently,

Hypothesis 1b: If board monitoring and bank regulation are complements, board independence will improve the bidder announcement returns under strict regulatory regimes.

Next to board independence, the leadership structure of a board may impact the quality of board decision-making. Fama and Jensen (1983) argue that separating the positions of chairman and CEO (such as to charge the latter with the running of the company and the former with the running of the board) prevents boards from being unduly influenced by a single person. The underlying rationale is that CEO–chairman duality is likely to lead to a concentration of power which impairs effective board monitoring. When the board leadership structure is separated, by contrast, managerial initiatives will be subject to greater scrutiny, resulting in a higher likelihood of disciplinary action against underperforming CEOs (Goyal and Park, 2002) and improved firm performance (Rechner and Dalton, 1991; Baliga, Moyer, and Rao, 1996). Consistent with this, Masulis, Wang, and Xie (2007) note that bidding boards are in a better position to scrutinize complex merger proposals when the positions of CEO and chairman of the board are separated.

Similar to the arguments presented for Hypothesis 1, we propose two contrasting hypotheses regarding the interaction between board size and bank regulation. If strict regulation can be understood as providing monitoring and disciplinary services not unlike those provided by board monitoring, strict regulation will act as a disincentive for effective monitoring under a separated board leadership structure. Therefore, we would not expect to see increases in merger performance if the roles of CEO and chairman are separated under a strict bank regulatory regime. By contrast, stricter regulation may help lower agency costs when powerful regulators signal intent to intervene and enforce. If this is the case, stricter bank regulation will increase the monitoring productivity of a separated board leadership structure.

Hypothesis 2a: If board monitoring and regulation are substitutes, separating the roles of CEO and chairman will not improve the bidder announcement returns under strict regulatory regimes.

Hypothesis 2b: If board monitoring and regulation are complements, separating the roles of CEO and chairman will improve the bidder announcement returns under strict regulatory regimes.

Finally, the diversity of the board of directors may also improve its monitoring effectiveness. Organizational scholars argue that diverse groups, through interaction between the various group members, produce a variety of different perspectives that will ultimately improve the quality of decision-making (Richard, 2000). Consequently, diversity will stimulate board activism and more diligent monitoring (Ely and Thomas, 2001). The ability of diverse boards to reduce agency costs should, therefore, create value for shareholders (Carter et al., 2007) and lead to general improvements in corporate performance (Shrader, Blackburn, and Iles, 1997; Erhardt, Werbel, and Shrader, 2003; Farrell and Hersch, 2005). The enhanced cognitive abilities and activist nature of diverse boards suggests that diverse boards are also associated with improved M&A performance (see Hagendorff, Collins, and Keasey, 2007).

As previously stated, we argue that if bank regulators offer subsidized monitoring services, diverse boards are not pressured to monitor diligently under strict regulatory regimes. By contrast, if stricter bank regulation can be understood as a signal which conveys a threat of action in the event of managerial or monitoring failures, this will encourage effective monitoring by diverse boards under strict bank regulatory regimes. Our final set of hypotheses, thus, is:

Hypothesis 3a: If board monitoring and regulation are substitutes, board diversity will not improve the bidder announcement returns under strict regulatory regimes.

Hypothesis 3b: If board monitoring and regulation are complements, board diversity will improve the bidder announcement returns under strict regulatory regimes.

Data and Variables

M&A Sample

The sample of bank M&A on which we base our analysis was obtained from the Securities Data Corporation's (SDC) Mergers and Acquisitions Database.

Sampled mergers were announced and completed between 1996 and 2004 and involved acquirers and targets that are both listed in the USA or Europe (i.e. Belgium, Denmark, France, Germany, Greece, Italy, the Netherlands, Portugal, Spain, Sweden, Switzerland, and the UK).

Further, we imposed the sampling criteria that deals are majority bank acquisitions (that led to acquirers owning at least 50 per cent of the target's equity) which are valued at more than $100 million (expressed in inflation-adjusted 2004 US$ terms), and that there are more than one hundred trading days between separate merger announcements by the same bidder. Further, sample banks are commercial banks and BHCs with share price data on Datastream. Finally, target banks are not a failing institution as indicated by the SDC database (a failing institution as a target could mean that the deal is involuntary).

The resulting dataset of bank M&A is described in Table 6.1. With 151 out of 204 sample transactions, US banks make the largest contribution to our sample. This is an accurate reflection of the relative pace of bank merger activity in Europe and the USA. It is important to bear in mind that a number of European economies have less developed capital markets than the USA and, consequently, fewer listed banks which engage in M&A. As a result, the consolidation of bank assets in countries such as Germany, France, and Italy over the period of study has largely involved non-listed public sector and cooperative institutions (see Berglöf et al., 2005) for which market data are not available. We test whether the results we report in this chapter are sensitive to the inclusion of US data in the robustness section and find that the overall results are invariant to the exclusion of the USA from our sample.

Table 6.1. Sample Overview

By Bidder Country			By Announcement Year		
Country	N	Percentage	Year	N	Percentage
Belgium	6	2.94	1996	11	5.39
Denmark	2	0.98	1997	30	14.71
France	6	2.94	1998	32	15.69
Germany	2	0.98	1999	27	13.24
Greece	7	3.43	2000	29	14.22
Italy	6	2.94	2001	28	13.73
Netherlands	5	2.45	2002	14	6.86
Portugal	2	0.98	2003	17	8.33
Spain	4	1.96	2004	16	7.84
Sweden	1	0.49			
Switzerland	3	1.47			
United Kingdom	9	4.41			
United States	151	74.02			
Total	204	100.00	Total	204	100.00

Dependent Variable

Our main dependent variable is the bidder announcement effect. In an efficient capital market where assets are priced rationally, changes in the bidder's market valuation around acquisition announcements provide an accurate assessment of the net benefits accruing to bidders following the completion of a deal. We calculate the bidder announcement effect by adding cumulative abnormal returns over an event window of (t-2, $t+2$) with 0 as the announcement date supplied by SDC Platinum. We estimate market model parameters using 100-day daily return observations starting from 121 days to 21 days before the acquisition announcement. Share price data and national bank sector indices are from Datastream. We follow Dodd and Warner (1983) and standardize abnormal returns by their estimation period variance:

$$SAR_{it} = AR_{it} \Bigg/ \left[\hat{\sigma}_i \sqrt{1 + \frac{1}{T_i} + \frac{(R_{mt} - \overline{R}_m)^2}{\sum_{t=1}^{T_i} (R_{mt} - \overline{R}_m)^2}} \right], \quad (1)$$

where:

SAR	= standardized abnormal returns (AR)
$\hat{\sigma}_i$	= estimation period variance of AR
T	= number of days (100) in the estimation period
R_{mt}	= return of the bidding bank
$\overline{R}_m$	= average return on the market index

We then use the abnormal return statistics as reported in Boehmer, Musumeci, and Poulsen (1991) to correct for increases in the variance of abnormal returns around merger announcements.

Board-Monitoring Variables

In order to test our three hypotheses relating to how board monitoring interacts with the regulatory regime, we collect data on board independence, CEO/chairman duality, and different measures of board diversity. Board data for US banks are from proxy statements filed with the Securities and Exchange Commission (SEC). For European bidders, governance data were extracted from annual reports and other company publications such as corporate governance reports and press releases. We obtain the last filing or publication before a deal was announced.

Board independence (Hypothesis 1) is the number of independent board directors divided by board size. Directors are classified as independent if they are not employees, former employees, or relatives of employees (see Hermalin and Weisbach, 2003).[1] *CEO/chair duality* (Hypothesis 2) is a dummy variable which takes the value of one if the CEO of the bidding bank is also the chairman of the board (and zero otherwise).

We use different variables to capture the diversity of the acquiring bank's board (Hypothesis 3). We measure *occupational diversity* as in Hillman, Cannella, and Paetzold (2000) by classifying directors as insiders, outside business experts, support specialists (e.g. law and accounting experts), or community leaders (e.g. politicians, clergy, academics). We then use these classifications to compute a Herfindahl-type index (which increases with the level of diversity across a board) as 1- Σp_i^2, where p is the proportion of group members in i different categories. *Age, tenure,* and *expertise diversity* are calculated by dividing the mean by the standard deviation of director characteristics. We measure age and tenure in years and expertise as the number of outside directorships held by directors.

Regulatory Strictness

We measure the overall *strictness of regulatory environments* using a database compiled by Barth, Caprio, and Levine (2001). The regulatory data refer to the time period 1998–2000 and have been widely used in empirical research (see Laeven and Levine, 2007; Buch and DeLong, 2008). We employ the data to build an index as suggested in Buch and DeLong (2008), which focuses on three regulatory aspects that are relevant to our investigation: the extent to which the regulatory environment is sensitive to bank risk-taking, the breadth of disciplinary powers available to regulators, and how well these powers are enforced. The index ranges between 0 and 12 to reflect the inclusion of 12 indicators (see Table 6.3 for a complete list). Higher scores are assigned to banking sectors with stricter regulatory environments. Table 6.2 shows that the strength of regulatory regimes in Europe varies greatly between the UK and Belgium (both with scores of 9) and countries such as Sweden, which scores as low as 3.[2]

[1] In the banking industry, director independence may be impaired by the presence of loan relationships between outside directors and banks. Due to the unavailability of such data for most countries, our measure of independence does not take loan relationships between banks and insiders into account. In the USA, Regulation O of the Federal Reserve Board stipulates that credit extensions to insiders must be disclosed if they, in aggregate, equal, or exceed $500,000 or 5 per cent of bank's capital, whichever is less.

[2] While financial supervision in Sweden scores highly as regards transparency rules, Sweden exhibits the least strictest regulatory environment in the sample due to the absence of a rule-based framework for intervention (e.g. following a decline in capital adequacy) as well as the inability of regulators to supersede shareholder rights (e.g. by ordering dividend cuts).

Table 6.2. Bank Regulatory Index

Panel A: Composition

(1) Must banks disclose risk management procedures to the public?
(2) Are risk-weights in line with Basel guidelines?
(3) Does the capital–asset ratio vary with a bank's credit risk?
(4) Does the capital–asset ratio vary with market risk?
(5) Is there a formal definition of 'non-performing loan'?
(6) Are there any mechanisms whose infraction leads to automatic imposition of sanctions on banks' directors and managers?
(7) Can the regulatory agency order directors/management to constitute provisions to cover actual/potential losses?
(8) Can the regulatory agency suspend a director's decision to distribute dividends, bonuses, or management fees?
(9) Have any such actions been taken in the past five years?
(10) Can the regulatory agency supersede bank shareholder rights and declare a bank insolvent?
(11) Does banking law allow the regulatory agency to suspend some or all ownership rights of a problem bank?
(12) Can the regulatory agency or any other government agency take measures aimed at bank restructuring and reorganization?

Panel B: Country Scores

Country	Regulation
Belgium	9
Denmark	6
France	4
Germany	4
Greece	4
Italy	5
Netherlands	5
Portugal	6
Spain	7
Sweden	3
Switzerland	7
United Kingdom	9
average	*5.75*
United States	9

The country index is computed to reflect the inclusion of twelve indicators (yes = 1; 0 = no). Source: Buch and Delong (2008).

The variation in the level of regulatory strictness shows that despite recent efforts to harmonize regulatory practices—most notably in the European Union, but also to a lesser degree at an international level—differences in the regulation of banking systems across developed countries persist. With regards to merger activities, such differences have meant, for example, that banks in the USA have not been permitted to diversify into non-depository activities. While most of these restrictions were repealed by the Gramm–Leach–Bliley Act (GLBA) in 1999, US banks still face some restrictions over their potential acquisition targets. For example, banks are not allowed to take stakes in non-financial firms, and acquisitions of more than 25 per cent of a target's equity require regulatory approval. Banks in Europe, on the other hand, have enjoyed a more lenient regime as reflected in the prevalence of the universal banking model in many European economies.

Control Variables

We collect additional board and director data to ensure our results are robust to other factors which may impact the quality of decision-making on bank boards in the context of M&A. *Board size* is the number of directors elected to the board. Jensen (1993) argues that larger boards hinder communication, coordination, and, ultimately, the decision-making capabilities of the board. Further, larger boards create environments in which CEOs are less likely to face challenges to their initiatives and in which they can exert greater managerial power (Yermack, 1996). We expect smaller boards to be associated with better performing M&A, because smaller boards are less likely to be driven by a non-value maximizing agenda (Eisenberg, Sundgren, and Wells, 1998) and are more effective when scrutinizing the performance effects of bank mergers (Cornett et al., 2003).

Both *CEO age* and *CEO tenure* capture the level of expertise accumulated by the top executive regarding the organizational as well as the wider economic environment of a bank. Kosnik (1990) finds that older CEOs engage less frequently in greenmail transactions (where CEOs privately repurchase equity from dissident shareholders at a premium). For the US banking industry, Cornett and colleagues (2003) show that CEO age is positively and significantly related to the announcement period returns that bidding banks realize. We, therefore, expect that longer-tenured and older CEOs (both measured in years) are less likely to harm shareholders' interests.

Are busy boards more effective monitors? If boards meet more frequently, and directors interact more often, board vigilance is likely to increase, which may lead to fewer value-destroying acquisitions as a result. Vafeas (1999) and Fich and Shivdasani (2006) find a negative association between the number of board meetings and corporate valuations for non-financial firms in the USA. However, the results do not permit conclusions regarding the direction of causality. Adams and Mehran (2005) examine whether active boards increase the market valuations of banks, but cannot find any evidence consistent with this. We measure *board activity* as the number of board meetings (including extraordinary meetings) in the fiscal year before the deal announcement.

Previous research has also indicated a number of factors unrelated to governance or regulation which have an impact on the performance of bank acquisitions. Among the deal characteristics shaping merger performance are *merger finance* (a binary variable which equals to one if a deal is completely cash-financed, and zero otherwise), *product diversification* (a binary variable which is equal to one if first two digits of the four-digit SIC code are not identical, and zero otherwise),[3] *deal value* (million US dollars in 2004 terms), and *target profitability* (measured by earnings per share). Both smaller and more profitable targets may make it easier for an acquirer to create value via M&A. We control for merger finance and diversification because both non-cash finance and financial diversification may be driven by non-value maximizing agendas and may, hence, be associated with underperformance (DeLong, 2001; Beitel, Schiereck, and Wahrenburg, 2004). This is because a high share of non-cash finance may signal lower levels of commitment to a deal by a bidder (Shleifer and Vishny, 2003) and diversification may be motivated by a managerial desire to smooth company earnings over time (Morck, Shleifer, and Vishny, 1990).

We also include a variable called *investor protection*, which is an index of shareholder rights multiplied by an index of the rule of law (both taken from La Porta et al. (1998)) to capture a range of institutional differences across countries. More sophisticated investor protection regimes have been linked to improved stock market development (La Porta et al., 2000), lower private benefits of control (Dyck and Zingales, 2004), and more active takeover markets (Rossi and Volpin, 2004). In short, the investor protection variable proxies for the extent to which market-based forms of corporate governance prevail in an economy which may impact upon the market reaction to M&A in these environments.

Table 6.3 presents correlations between the various variables. Generally, the correlations between the variables are low. There is a negative relationship between board size and board independence ($p < .05$). This is consistent with explanations of excess managerial power, which stress that larger boards tend to be less independent as they are more likely to be under the control of the CEO (Yermack, 1996; Eisenberg, Sundgren, and Wells, 1998). Also, the correlation table shows that smaller boards meet more often ($p < .05$).

[3] We follow Campa and Hernando (2004) and classify deals as diversifying if the first two digits of the SIC code of the main industry of the institutions involved in a deal are not identical. Admittedly, SIC codes may not always convey an accurate picture of the activities of financial firms (see DeLong, 2001). Hence, we used a second measure of diversification that may be more suitable to account for the nature of some of the banks as integrated financial firms with more than one SIC code. We follow Sirower (1997) and examine the number of industry classification codes shared between bidders and targets. The results based on this diversification measure, which only classifies deals as diversifying if bidders and targets do not share any SIC codes, are virtually identical to the results reported in this section.

Table 6.3. Correlations and Summary Statistics

	Mean	S.D.	(1)	(2)	(3)	(4)	(5)	(6)	(7)	(8)	(9)	(10)	(11)	(12)	(13)	(14)
(1) CAR[−2; + 2] (%)	−0.47	1.01														
(2) Board independence	0.78	0.22	*0.11*													
(3) Log(board size)[a]	15.53	0.31	−0.01	*−0.16*												
(4) Chair/CEO duality	0.42	0.49	0.09	*−0.20*	0.09											
(5) Occupational diversity	0.53	0.12	*0.15*	0.08	−0.08	−0.03										
(6) Age diversity	8.42	2.16	0.13	0.07	0.01	−0.08	−0.18									
(7) Expertise diversity	0.83	1.14	0.04	−0.07	0.18	0.02	−0.15	0.18								
(8) Log(CEO age)[a]	55.13	0.09	0.16	0.00	0.00	−0.15	−0.05	*0.33*	0.06							
(9) Log(CEO tenure)[a]	10.23	0.85	−0.10	0.17	−0.09	−0.30	0.14	0.11	−0.11	0.18						
(10) Log(board activity)[a]	9.04	3.18	−0.06	0.12	*−0.18*	0.07	0.09	−0.01	−0.19	−0.21	0.02					
(11) Cash finance	0.22	0.42	*0.21*	−0.07	0.05	0.15	−0.08	−0.06	0.27	0.02	−0.13	−0.05				
(12) Product focus dummy	0.80	0.40	−0.14	0.02	−0.11	−0.16	−0.10	0.01	−0.22	0.02	0.12	0.10	*−0.21*			
(13) Log(deal value)[a]	3,359.68	9,575.49	0.03	−0.14	0.15	0.16	−0.20	0.06	0.12	−0.03	−0.23	0.02	−0.09	−0.11		
(14) Target profitability	2.25	4.74	−0.06	−0.03	0.18	0.11	0.01	−0.09	0.22	−0.11	−0.22	−0.18	−0.03	−0.21	0.20	
(15) Investor protection	43.22	14.23	*−0.22*	0.27	−0.19	*−0.23*	0.11	0.11	−0.16	0.17	0.28	−0.10	−0.23	0.18	−0.24	*−0.24*

[a] Summary statistics are not based on logarithmic transformations.

Table 6.3 presents pairwise correlation coefficients between variables. Bold coefficients indicate statistical significance at 5 per cent. Definitions of board variables are in Table 6.2. The cash finance dummy equals one if the transaction is completely cash-financed (and zero otherwise) and the product focus dummy equals one if the first two digits of the four-digit SIC code between bidder and target are identical (zero otherwise). Deal values are in millions of 2004-USD and the profitability of the target is measured as earnings per share (EPS) in the year before a deal was announced. Investor protection is an index of anti-director rights multiplied by an index of the quality of law enforcement (both from La Porta et al., 1998).

Empirical Analysis

Market Reaction to Merger Announcements

Table 6.4 reports economically and statistically significant wealth losses for bidding bank shareholders around the announcement of M&A. For US deals, mean CAR[−2, 2] is −0.47 per cent (t = −10.17, p<.001). Announcement returns remain negative and statistically significant for each subset of deals. For the European subsample, there is no evidence consistent with bidding banks benefitting from M&A. Average announcement returns are not statistically different from zero. The only subsample to create value is the all-cash subsample of deals which do not involve the bidder's equity as a transaction currency. Shleifer and Vishny (2003) argue that cash insulates bidding bank shareholders from managerial opportunism by signalling greater commitment to an acquisition target than deals funded by acquirers' potentially overvalued equity.

The wealth losses that bidding bank shareholders realize in the market for corporate control are in line with what previous studies report (see, for example, Pilloff, 1996; DeLong and DeYoung, 2007). Shareholder wealth losses in the context of M&A point to conflicting interests between managers and shareholders which, at least in part, could be resolved by effective monitoring provided by the board of directors (Masulis, Wang, and Xie, 2007).

Board Monitoring in Europe and the USA

Table 6.5 reports the characteristics of bank boards in Europe and the USA. The data presented show that the boards of European and US banking firms differ in a number of ways. For instance, European bank boards are relatively larger, less independent, and less diverse in terms of the occupational background of its members (all statistically significant). Also, CEO–chair duality, where CEOs also act as chairman of the board, is much more widespread in Europe than in the USA. In our sample, 28 per cent of US bank boards have CEOs which are also chairmen, while the same ratio is 81 per cent in Europe.

Given that most European bank regulatory regimes are less strict that the US regime, the findings presented in Table 6.5 are not consistent with the view that board-level monitoring and regulation act as substitutes. Rather, the results suggest that the relationship between regulation and monitoring should be understood as a relationship of complements. The next section, *Regression Results: Board Monitoring and Regulation*, analyses this in more detail by examining the implications of bank-level governance on the realized bidder announcement effect of M&A.

Table 6.4. Bidder Announcement Returns, CAR[−2, 2]

	Whole Sample		All-cash		Some Stock		Domestic M&A		Cross-border M&A	
	Mean	*t*-Stat	Mean	*t*-Stat	Mean	*t*-Stat	Mean	*t*-Stat	Mean	*t*-Stat
Panel A: US deals										
	−0.47%	(−10.17)***	−0.27%	(−5.28)***	−0.49%	(−12.65)***	−0.47%	(−10.17)***	n.a.	
N	*151*		*19*		*132*		*151*			
Panel B: European deals										
	−0.08%	(−3.12)***	0.32%	(6.23)***	−0.15%	(−8.67)***	−0.08%	(3.17)***	−0.08%	(6.22)***
N	*53*		*26*		*27*		*29*		*24*	

The sample consists of completed bank mergers between 1996 and 2004 in Europe and the USA. Cumulative announcement returns (CAR) are based on standardized market model abnormal returns and are calculated against value-weighted bank sector indexes available on Datastream. Deals are classified all-cash if financed by 100 per cent cash. Cross-border deals involve bidders and targets in different countries. The statistical significance of mean abnormal returns is determined using a one-sample *t*-test.
* significant at 10%; ** significant at 5%; *** significant at 1%.

Table 6.5. Background Statistics: Bank Governance in Europe and the USA

	USA							Europe							(EUR—USA)	
	N	Mean	P25	P50	P75	Min	Max	N	Mean	P25	P50	P75	Min	Max	t-stat	z-stat
Board size	151	14.93	12.00	14.00	18.00	6.00	31.00	53	17.25	15.00	18.00	20.00	8.00	27.00	(3.07)***	(3.06)***
Board independence	151	0.81	0.75	0.82	0.88	0.55	0.94	53	0.70	0.61	0.67	0.75	0.45	0.93	(−7.52)***	(−6.06)***
Board activeness	151	9.01	6.00	8.00	12.00	4.00	18.00	53	9.26	7.00	8.00	12.00	4.00	15.00	(0.40)	(0.55)
CEO/chair duality (1 = yes)	151	0.28	0.00	0.00	1.00	0.00	1.00	53	0.81	1.00	1.00	1.00	0.00	1.00	(7.66)***	(6.76)***
CEO age	151	55.54	52.00	56.00	59.00	41.00	68.00	53	53.98	48.00	54.00	59.00	40.00	65.00	(−1.75)*	(−1.27)
CEO tenure	151	12.11	7.00	12.00	16.00	1.00	31.00	53	4.87	2.00	5.00	6.00	1.00	13.00	(−6.95)***	(−6.85)***
Occupational diversity	151	0.54	0.45	0.57	0.66	0.13	0.76	53	0.50	0.42	0.49	0.58	0.00	0.69	(−2.23)***	(−2.62)***
Age diversity	151	8.54	6.73	8.08	10.29	3.71	16.09	53	8.08	7.03	8.16	8.84	4.63	14.94	(−1.00)	(−0.81)
Tenure diversity	151	1.40	1.10	1.28	1.48	0.79	4.69	53	1.44	1.22	1.40	1.63	0.73	3.00	(0.38)	(1.35)
Expertise diversity	151	0.75	0.43	0.70	0.92	0.20	2.27	53	1.05	0.84	1.08	1.27	0.47	1.83	(3.71)***	(4.11)***

Table 6.5 provides descriptive statistics for the sample of 137 completed bank mergers between 1996 and 2004 in Europe and the USA. Data are for bidding banks and presented by the bidder's country. Variable definitions are in Table 6.4. *t*-statistics test for differences in means and *z*-statistics for differences in medians using a Wilcoxon two-sample test.

* significant at 10%; ** significant at 5%; *** significant at 1%.

Regression Results: Board Monitoring and Regulation

To assess the productivity of board monitoring in Europe and the USA and its implications for the relationship between governance and regulation, we estimate the effects of board governance on the bidder announcement effect of M&A (CAR[−2; + 2]) in different regulatory environments. Table 6.6 regresses board governance data as well as control variables on the stock market reaction (CAR[−2, 2]) around bank merger announcements. We distinguish between bidding banks domiciled in countries with a Buch and DeLong (2008) score below 9 (less strict regulatory environment; Regressions 1 to 3) and banks domiciled in environments with a score of 9 (strict environment; Regressions 4 to 6).[4]

Table 6.6 shows systematic differences in the effectiveness of board monitoring under stricter and less strict bank regulatory regimes. Regression 1 reports that under less strict bank regulatory regimes board monitoring is irrelevant in affecting merger announcement returns. None of the coefficients on the board variables enter the regression specification with a statistically significant sign. This is inconsistent with board monitoring and regulation acting as substitutes. We, therefore, reject Hypotheses 1a, 2a, and 3a. To preserve degrees of freedom, we add control variables sequentially in Regressions 2 and 3. Amongst the controls, the cash finance variable enters the regressions with a positive sign ($p < .05$). Also, deal value enters the model with a negative sign ($p < .05$) indicating that smaller deals, presumably because their integration into the context of the acquiring firm will be less costly, receive a more positive market reaction. Despite the small number of observations for the low regulatory strictness subsample, there is a very high degree of overlap between the signs and magnitude of the estimated variables across regression specifications. This lends support to the robustness of our finding that board monitoring has only a negligible role to play in preventing value-destroying acquisition strategies in less strict regulatory environments.

The results for high-strength regulators (Regressions 3 to 6), by contrast, show that a number of board characteristics are related to bidding bank returns. For instance, the coefficient on board independence has a positive and significant sign (Model 4, coefficient = .63, $p < .05$; Model 5, coefficient = .65, $p < .05$; Model 6, coefficient = .57, $p < .05$). This offers support for Hypothesis 1b—that board independence is a complement to bank regulation when

[4] In the regression analysis, we compare strict ($r = 10$) with less strict ($r < 9$) environments. This is motivated by a desire to retain a sufficiently large subsample of deals completed in less strict regulatory environments in order to perform meaningful regression analyses. When we define 'less strict regulation' as $r \leq 4$, the results for Regression (1) (which are based on a subsample of 16 observations) are qualitatively identical to those reported in Table 6.6. We, therefore, conclude that the results in Table 6.6 are invariant to changes in the cut-off point, to distinguish between strict and less strict regulatory environments.

Table 6.6. CAR[−2, 2] and Board Governance around M&A Announcements

	LESS STRICT Regulatory Regime (r < 9)						STRICT Regulatory Regime (r = 9)					
	(1)		(2)		(3)		(4)		(5)		(6)	
	Coeff	Std.err	Coeff	Std.err	Coeff	Std.err	Coeff	Std.err	Coeff	Std.err	Coeff	Std.err
Board independence	0.15	(0.42)	0.07	(0.42)	0.19	(0.44)	0.63**	(0.25)	0.65*	(0.26)	0.57**	(0.27)
Chair/CEO duality	−0.02	(0.20)	−0.10	(0.20)	−0.05	(0.20)	0.04	(0.17)	0.02	(0.17)	0.08	(0.18)
Occupational diversity	0.61	(0.76)	0.50	(0.77)	0.34	(0.80)	1.37**	(0.59)	1.25**	(0.57)	1.19**	(0.60)
Age diversity	0.00	(0.04)	0.02	(0.04)	0.01	(0.05)	0.00	(0.03)	0.01	(0.03)	0.02	(0.03)
Expertise diversity	−0.01	(0.08)	−0.07	(0.09)	−0.02	(0.10)	0.03	(0.07)	0.01	(0.07)	0.02	(0.07)
Log(board size)	−0.35	(0.30)	−0.35	(0.29)	−0.31	(0.31)	−0.09	(0.24)	−0.09	(0.24)	−0.07	(0.25)
Log(CEO age)	2.02	(2.06)	1.84	(2.05)	1.99	(2.12)	1.64**	(0.75)	1.57**	(0.76)	1.34**	(0.61)
Log(CEO tenure)	0.01	(0.11)	0.00	(0.11)	−0.04	(0.12)	−0.02	(0.09)	−0.04	(0.09)	−0.06	(0.09)
Log(board activity)	−0.34	(0.25)	−0.35	(0.25)	−0.19	(0.27)	−0.07	(0.19)	−0.10	(0.19)	−0.02	(0.21)
Cash finance			0.41**	(0.20)	0.37**	(0.15)			0.24**	(0.12)	0.13**	(0.07)
Product focus dummy			−0.22	(0.24)	−0.18	(0.26)			−0.13	(0.22)	−0.08	(0.24)
Log(deal value)					−0.07**	(0.04)					−0.06	(0.08)
Target profitability					0.04	(0.03)					0.04	(0.04)
Investor protection					0.02	(0.01)					0.02	(0.02)
Constant	−7.32*	(4.38)	−6.50	(4.35)	−7.92*	(4.67)	−6.73*	(3.55)	−6.23*	(3.54)	−6.62	(4.08)
Observations	38		38		38		166		166		166	
Adj. R-squared (%)	3.24		3.62		9.05		8.60		13.50		16.10	

Table 6.6 reports least squares regressions for a sample of completed bank mergers between 1996 and 2004 in Europe and the USA on cumulative announcement returns (CAR). CAR are based on standardized market model abnormal returns computed against a value-weighted bank sector index available on Datastream. Regulatory strictness (*r*) is an index of regulatory strictness prevailing in the bidding bank's country from Buch and DeLong (2008). The cash-only dummy equals one if the transaction is completely cash-financed (and zero otherwise) and the product focus dummy equals one if the first two digits of the four-digit SIC code between bidder and target are identical (zero otherwise). Deal values are in millions of 2004-USD and the profitability of the target is measured as EPS in the year before a deal was announced. Investor protection is an index of anti-director rights multiplied by an index of the quality of law enforcement (both from La Porta et al., 1998). Heteroscedasticity-robust standard errors are reported in parentheses.

* significant at 10%; ** significant at 5%; *** significant at 1%.

improving the performance of M&A. Consequently, boards with a higher share of independent directors inspire investor confidence in the value-creating potential of a deal under a strict regulatory regime, but not under less strict regulatory environments.

Further, occupational diversity improves the expected gains from acquisitions under a strict regulatory environment which is consistent with Hypothesis 3b (Model 4, coefficient = 1.37, $p < .05$; Model 5, coefficient = 1.25, $p < .05$; Model 6, coefficient = 1.19, $p < .05$). Consequently, board diversity and bank regulation act as complements. Apparently, boards whose members come from a wider range of occupational backgrounds are, therefore, likely to be more critical of managerial initiatives under a strict regulatory regime.

Among the control variables which are significant is the log transformation of CEO age, which has a positive and significant sign ($p < .05$). Consequently, expectations about merger-related gains following a deal are greater if directors are older, and, presumably, more experienced. Finally, the cash finance variable exerts a statistically significant impact on announcement returns ($p < .05$), while the investor protection variable has the conjectured positive sign (though it is not significant at customary levels).

The results offer support for two out of the three hypotheses we developed above. The fact that board independence and occupational diversity are effective in improving the expected returns of bank mergers under strict regulatory regimes is consistent with Hypotheses 1b and 3b. By contrast, we do not find that CEO–chair duality (Hypothesis 2) affects the expected returns from M&A. One explanation for this could be that because our model examines the simultaneous effectiveness of various governance mechanisms, we are unable to analyse possible trade-offs in the effectiveness of individual governance devices. For example, more independent boards may be less likely to require CEO–chair duality to bring about better performing M&A than less independent boards. While a detailed analysis of the relationships between individual governance devices goes beyond the scope of this chapter, it may be possible that individual governance devices act as substitutes for each other.

We argue that, collectively and in general, our results back the notion that governance acts as a complement to stricter regulation. This is because, under less strict regulatory regimes, not a single one of the board-monitoring mechanisms examined in Table 6.7 enters the regression with a coefficient that is statistically significant at customary levels. By contrast, board governance affects the expected outcomes from bank mergers in strict regulatory environments.

We also test whether similar empirical relationships between bidding bank boards and performance exist in the market for corporate control when we examine long-term operating performance (rather than acquirer returns at the time of the bank merger announcement). Following Healy, Palepu, and Ruback (1992) and Cornett, McNutt, and Tehranian (2006), we measure performance changes as pre-tax operating cash flows (measured as income before taxes and extraordinary items plus interest expenses on debt) divided by the book value of assets. We refer to this measure as OPCFROA.[5] We compute performance changes between one year before and three years after the completion of a deal and adjust performance data using an asset-weighted index of all listed banks available on Datastream in the bidding bank's country. Consequently, OPCFROA gauges changes in recorded performance net of industry or economy-wide phenomena.

Table 6.7 reports regressions of our board characteristics on market-adjusted changes in OPCFROA between years −1 and + 3 relative to the completion of a merger. As previously, we distinguish between strict ($r = 9$) and less strict ($r < 9$) regulatory regimes. While the results show some small differences to the regressions in Table 6.6 (for instance, the results support Hypothesis 3b, but not Hypothesis 1b), it is important to bear in mind that, owing to the unavailability of some accounting items over the longer examination period, these regression are based on a much smaller subsample. Overall, the findings in Table 6.7 are broadly in line with the results we report regarding the market reaction to bank merger announcements in Table 6.6. Thus, board monitoring is practically irrelevant in determining the long-term performance of bank mergers in lenient regulatory environments (Regressions 1 to 3), while a number of board characteristics (notably, board diversity) impact post-merger performance changes under a more strict bank regulatory regime. Thus, the regressions on long-term performance confirm the complementarity view by showing that board governance is associated with measurable performance improvements only under a strict bank regulatory regime.

[5] Long-run performance changes may also be measured on the basis of market returns. However, there are a number of methodological difficulties associated with this method (Barber and Lyon, 1997; Fama, 1998) which are especially severe in multi-country settings when equity markets differ in terms of their sensitivity to news. Further, the use of OPCFROA has three distinct advantages. First, it captures realized gains from M&A rather than expected gains as evident in market returns. Second, unlike standard profitability measures, OPCFROA is not sensitive to the method of debt finance (debt finance means lower post-merger profitability), while controlling for interest payments to depositors. Third, OPCFROA is a more precise measure of performance changes than Tobin's q, which is routinely used in corporate governance research. Since Tobin's q controls for market valuation, it partly reflects a company's growth opportunities. This could be problematic, since poorly performing firms may deliver above-market returns to shareholders if, for example, there is market speculation of an imminent takeover approach (see Cornett, McNutt, and Tehranian, 2006).

Table 6.7. Board Characteristics and Industry-Adjusted Operating Performance

	LESS STRICT Regulatory Regime (r < 9)						STRICT Regulatory Regime (r = 9)					
	(1)		(2)		(3)		(4)		(5)		(6)	
	Coeff	Std.err	Coeff	Std.err	Coeff	Std.err	Coeff	Std.err	Coeff	Std.err	Coeff	Std.err
Board independence	−0.20	(0.40)	−0.19	(0.40)	−0.14	(0.41)	0.09	(0.35)	0.08	(0.36)	0.04	(0.35)
Chair/CEO duality	−0.03	(0.17)	−0.07	(0.17)	−0.15	(0.18)	−0.07	(0.13)	−0.10	(0.12)	−0.18	(0.13)
Occupational diversity	1.12	(0.83)	1.39	(0.86)	1.25	(0.87)	0.89	(0.64)	1.05	(0.74)	0.84	(0.82)
Age diversity	0.71	(0.76)	1.08	(0.83)	1.19	(0.86)	0.67	(0.84)	0.83	(0.89)	0.75	(0.85)
Expertise diversity	0.75	(0.46)	0.76	(0.46)	0.53	(0.40)	0.10**	(0.28)	0.10**	(0.29)	0.83*	(0.32)
Log(board size)	−0.20	(0.38)	−0.40	(0.41)	−0.24	(0.42)	0.10	(0.36)	0.00	(0.38)	0.01	(0.43)
Log(CEO age)	1.04	(0.96)	1.26	(0.98)	1.22	(0.98)	1.81**	(0.85)	1.87**	(0.85)	1.87**	(0.85)
Log(CEO tenure)	−0.06	(0.12)	−0.07	(0.12)	−0.09	(0.13)	−0.10	(0.16)	−0.11	(0.16)	−0.05	(0.15)
Log(board activity)	0.08	(0.23)	0.09	(0.23)	0.15	(0.24)	0.36*	(0.15)	0.35**	(0.17)	0.25**	(0.11)
Cash finance			0.06	(0.22)	0.19	(0.23)			0.03	(0.21)	0.07	(0.22)
Product focus dummy			−0.26	(0.22)	−0.43	(0.23)			−0.16	(0.18)	−0.23	(0.13)
Log(deal value)					0.07	(0.08)					0.05	(0.09)
Target profitability					−0.04	(0.09)					0.00	(0.12)
Investor protection					0.02	(0.01)					0.02	(0.04)
Constant	4.81	(4.08)	5.53	(4.29)	6.88	(4.45)	6.36	(3.38)	7.07	(3.53)	9.57	(5.37)
Observations	29		29		29		108		108		108	
Adj. R-squared (%)	3.41		4.63		6.84		14.51		16.63		26.42	

Table 6.7 reports least squares regressions for a sample of completed bank mergers between 1996 and 2004 in Europe and the USA on bidders' industry-adjusted OPCFROA (operating cash flows divided by the book value of assets) from years −1 to year 3 following the completion of a bank merger. Regulatory strictness (*r*) is an index of regulatory strictness in the bidding bank's country from Buch and DeLong (2008). The cash-only dummy equals one if the transaction is completely cash-financed (and zero otherwise) and the product focus dummy equals one if the first two digits of the four-digit SIC code between bidder and target are identical (zero otherwise). Deal values are in millions of 2004-USD and the profitability of the target is measured as EPS in the year before a deal was announced. Investor protection is an index of anti-director rights multiplied by an index of the quality of law enforcement (both from La Porta et al., 1998). Heteroscedasticity-robust standard errors are reported in parentheses.

* significant at 10%; ** significant at 5%; *** significant at 1%.

Robustness

The virtual absence of any effects of board characteristics on M&A performance in less strict regulatory environments raises the question of whether alternative governance mechanisms that we have not controlled for in our analysis drive the reported results. For example, product market competition is an important monitoring mechanism (Shleifer and Vishny, 1997; Roe, 2003; Masulis, Wang, and Xie, 2007). With the exception of Germany and, perhaps, Italy, less strict bank regulatory environments have very concentrated markets for banking services. Consequently, it is conceivable that, in the face of increased competitive forces, banks domiciled in these environments choose their governance optimally, such that more vigilant boards have no marginal effect on merger outcomes. To test this, we calculate a Herfindahl index (sum of squares of banks' market shares available on Worldscope, based on total assets) for each country and run the regressions—separately for the high and low market concentration terciles—in Tables 6.6 and 6.7. We are unable to detect statistically meaningful differences in the monitoring effectiveness of board variables between the resulting portfolios. Consequently, it would seem that the results we report are not driven by cross-country differences in market concentration levels.

Do the reported results hold over time? Following the passing of the GLBA in 1999, one of the differences in bank regulation between Europe and the USA—the activities that banking firms are permitted to engage in—has become less pronounced. Consequently, it may be the case that results are weaker for the period that follows the deregulation of banking activities in the USA and so the regressions in Table 6.6 and 6.7 are run separately for US bank mergers completed before 2000 (pre-GLB) and afterwards (post-GLB). However, there are only marginal differences between the regression results in separate time periods and results for the complete sample period.

Serial acquisitions form a sizable share of M&A activities in the banking industry. For transactions that are part of a merger programme, there may be an anticipation effect that potentially depresses the announcement returns that serial acquirers earn vis-à-vis first-time bidders (see Song and Walkling, 2006). Further, the long-term performance effects of frequent acquirers may also be different from single acquirers. To try to account for this, we add a binary variable (zero for first bids and one for second or higher order bids) to the regressions on CAR[−2,2] and industry-adjusted OPCFROA. However, the merger programme dummy does not enter the regressions at customary significance levels, indicating that serial acquirers do not have different performance implications.

Concluding Remarks

In this chapter, we analyse the interaction between monitoring by bank boards and regulatory regimes in the takeover market. Using a sample of 204 US and European bidding banks, we test the effectiveness of three board-monitoring mechanisms (board independence, CEO–chair duality, and board diversity) in affecting the announcement returns of bank M&A across bank regulatory environments of varying strictness. We find that in strict regulatory regimes board independence and board diversity are effective in improving the returns of bidding banks. Given that strict bank regulators provide monitoring and disciplinary services which are similar to those provided by board monitoring, our finding that strict regulation facilitates effective board monitoring is not consistent with the notion that regulation and firm governance are substitutes. Instead, our results point to a complementary relationship between regulation and some governance mechanisms.

Our work supports earlier studies that view board monitoring and industry regulation as complements (Baxter, 2003; Becher and Frye, 2011), and have implications for theoretical work in this area in two ways. First, previous empirical work has interpreted the existence of enhanced monitoring arrangements (e.g. more independent boards) in stricter regulatory regimes as support for the complementarity hypothesis. However, the extant work makes no reference to the realized performance implications of these arrangements. By contrast, we show that interactions between regulation and board monitoring lead to more *effective* governance arrangements in regulated firms. We, therefore, advance existing theory in this area by showing that board-monitoring arrangements are associated with measurable shareholder wealth gains in strict regulatory regimes (rather than the presence of indicators of better monitoring). Second, theoretical arguments have so far stressed that regulation per se could exert strong signalling effects (Booth, Cornett, and Tehranian, 2002; Baxter, 2003). Since our study compares the effectiveness of regulation across multiple regulatory regimes, we are able to show that regulation improves the effectiveness of board monitoring only for the strictest regulatory regimes in our sample.

Further, this study enhances our understanding of differences in the effectiveness of governance systems across countries. Extant research is heavily skewed towards the USA. In particular, previous work which has established a link between board monitoring and bank performance in the market for corporate control (e.g. Subrahmanyam, Rangan, and Rosenstein, 1997; Cornett et al., 2003; Becher and Campbell, 2004) is based on a US market and regulatory context. Our findings suggest that, for banking studies at least, the results of these studies may have been partly shaped by strict US bank regulation and may, therefore, not be applicable to institutional contexts with less strict regulators. In that sense, our findings emphasize the need for future research to examine the effectiveness of governance devices outside the USA.

Our chapter is not without shortcomings. First, we infer the intensity of board monitoring from the composition of the board. For instance, we assume that monitoring intensity increases with the share of independent directors on the board. While this assumption is a cornerstone of the corporate governance literature in economics and finance, it is important to point out that our approach does not directly study board monitoring or the processes which underlie it. Future research should, therefore, go beyond linking board structure to performance and consider process variables which explain the dynamics that lead to board characteristics having a beneficial effect on corporate performance under different regulatory regimes. Second, board characteristics are examined at the BHC-level and not at the level of individual subsidiaries, for which governance data tend to be less readily available. Therefore, it is possible that variables such as board activity understate the true level of interaction between bank directors.

Finally, this study is a single-industry study. It could be argued that banking firms enjoy a special, if not unique, position due to the large negative externalities associated with their failure and the access to public funds which results from this. The degree to which regulatory practices affect and complement board monitoring could, therefore, be particularly large for banking firms and our results may not be generalizable to other tightly regulated industries (such as some utilities, as well as gas and oil extracting companies). However, given that regulators in other regulated industries also provide monitoring services and exert disciplinary powers on management, we expect our results to hold for other regulated firms as well. However, this is an empirical question for future research to examine.

A further avenue for future research is to revisit the question of substitution versus complementarity while also considering the relationships among individual governance devices in the presence of regulatory regimes of varying strictness. As well as the interaction between governance and regulation, the interactions among individual governance variables should be examined further. For example, boards which are more independent may not rely on other governance mechanisms such as CEO–chair duality in order to improve merger performance. Clearly, interactions between governance mechanisms are likely to exist.

This chapter has been written against the background of the failure of financial institutions in the USA, Europe, and elsewhere, and debates among policymakers as regards the future of both bank regulation and bank governance. For example, a number of countries are contemplating restricting the activities that banks may engage in or introducing formal qualifications for the members of bank boards. However, an important practical implication of our work is that regulation and governance should not be viewed in isolation. Attempts to raise a board's ability to critically assess managerial risk-taking are more likely to be successful if effective bank-level governance is accompanied by strict industry regulation. Any role of government (via bank regulation) in reducing agency costs is only likely to be successful when governments signal their intent to interfere and enforce by giving powerful mandates to bank regulators. Half-measured attempts to increase the strictness of bank regulation are, thus, unlikely to improve the effectiveness of bank-level monitoring. In the same vein, for investors and practitioners our results highlight the fact that legislation which increases board power will equally be unlikely to be effective in bringing about performance gains if corporate governance arrangements at the firm level are not supported by a strict regulatory framework.

7

Executive Pay and Risk-taking in the European Banking Industry

Introduction

Compensation practices in the banking industry are widely believed to have induced excessive risk-taking and, thus, to have played an important role in causing the recent financial crisis (e.g. Bebchuk and Spamann, 2009; Board of Governors et al., 2010; IMF, 2010). This chapter analyses the effects of CEO cash bonuses on the level of bank default risk for a sample of European banking firms—as a means comparison we also include results for the USA.

By way of preview, our analysis, in general, shows that increases in CEO cash bonuses lower the default risk of banks. We explain this finding by arguing that, because bonus payments are contingent on bank solvency, they lower the risk preferences of CEOs. We also demonstrate that the risk-reducing effect of cash bonuses disappears as banks move closer to the point of default. At the most risky banks, our results show bonus payments promote rather than mitigate bank risk-taking. This finding is consistent with the view that financially distressed banks seek to maximize the value of the financial safety net.

Our investigation is undertaken against the background of an emerging policy consensus in the USA and Europe that compensation practices and bonus payments in particular have promoted excessive risk-taking at financial firms. For instance, the Financial Stability Board (FSB, 2009) concludes in a report for the Group of Twenty that 'high short-term profits led to generous bonus payments to employees [which] amplified the excessive risk-taking that severely threatened the global financial system' (p. 3). In response, US compensation guidelines for CEOs and other senior executives at large banks come close to dictating that bonuses be paid in equity-based instruments, that the payment be deferred, and that vesting be performance-contingent (Board of

Governors et al., 2010: 33). Similarly, the Committee of European Banking Supervisors (CEBS, 2010) proposes in its draft guidelines on remuneration policies that at least 50 per cent of variable compensation (including bonus payments) should be non-cash.[1] Crucially, our finding that CEO bonuses are linked to lower default risk challenges the view underlying these regulatory guidelines: that cash-based executive compensation is linked to high risk-taking in the banking industry.

Given the attention which CEO compensation has recently attracted, it is important to gain a better understanding of how the structure of CEO compensation contracts relates to the riskiness of banks. However, most of the extant literature focuses on the risk incentives exerted by executives holding stock options (e.g. Hubbard and Palia, 1995; DeYoung, Peng, and Yan, 2010; Hagendorff and Vallascas, 2011), while largely overlooking the role of CEO cash bonuses as a risk-taking incentive. Exceptions to this are studies by Harjoto and Mullineaux (2003) and Fahlenbrach and Stulz (2011). However, Harjoto and Mullineaux restrict their analysis to showing that CEO bonuses and stock volatility are positively linked and Fahlenbrach and Stulz study the effects of CEO bonuses on bank performance (rather than bank risk) during the recent financial crisis.

The lack of empirical work on CEO bonus plans on bank risk is unfortunate for two reasons. First, CEO cash bonuses are an important component of executive pay. In our sample of European and US banks, CEO bonus payments make up a third of total CEO compensation. Second, the effect of bonus payments on managerial risk preferences is likely to differ from that exerted by option grants. Figure 7.1 illustrates the shape of a typical bonus function. CEO cash bonuses generally become payable once an earnings-based target over a one-year period has been met (Murphy, 2000). After exceeding this threshold, the CEO payoffs from bonus plans increase in performance until capped at a maximum payout. Therefore, for earnings performance exceeding the threshold at which bonus payments become payable, CEO bonus plans do not provide convex payoffs (Smith and Stulz, 1985) and should not promote excessive risk-taking (see Noe, Rebello, and Wall, 1996; Duru, Mansi, and Reeb 2005). This is in sharp contrast to CEO holdings of stock options. Since the payoffs from option holdings are convex functions of the volatility of stock returns, options incentivize CEOs to increase the volatility of share prices by

[1] Previously, the Financial Services Authority (FSA) introduced a new remuneration code for UK financial firms which effectively limited basic compensation and bonus payments to 50 per cent of CEO compensation (with the rest paid in equity and equity-like instruments). Also, both the UK and France have introduced a 50 per cent tax on bonuses paid during 2009 (see IMF, 2010: Appendix 2; pp. 32–9), 'FSA Unveils Tough New Pay and Bonus Code', *Financial Times*, 30 July 2010; 'Big Bonuses Face Curbs', *Financial Times*, 17 May 2010).

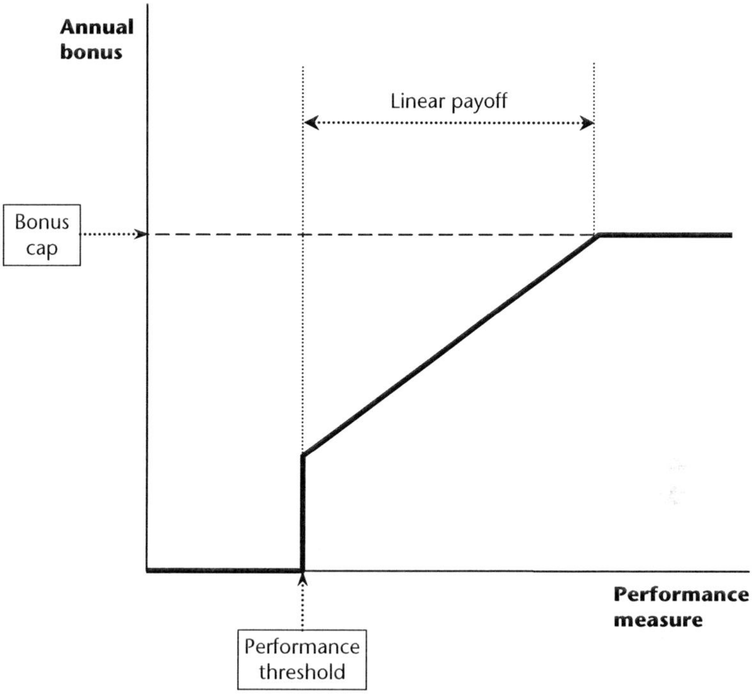

Figure 7.1. A 'Typical' Bonus Function
Adapted from Murphy (2000)

engaging in riskier activities (Guay, 1999; Rajgopal and Shevlin, 2002; Coles, Daniel, and Naveen, 2006).

This chapter extends the literature on the link between executive compensation in banking and risk-taking (e.g. Mehran and Rosenberg, 2007; DeYoung, Peng, and Yan, 2010) by providing cross-country evidence on the bonus–risk relationship in the banking industry. Existing studies have limited their focus on a US market context to analyse the link between bonus payments and bank performance (Fahlenbrach and Stulz, 2011), stock volatility (Harjoto and Mullineaux, 2003), and bank default risk relative to non-cash compensation (Balachandran, Kogut, and Harnal, 2010).

Next to the international dimension, the present analysis augments the results of previous studies in two ways. First, we explore how the managerial risk-taking preferences related to cash bonus payments differ at distressed banks. In these banks, shareholder-designed compensation contracts are likely to promote risk-shifting to bondholders and regulators because shareholders gain more from high-risk activities which maximize the value of the financial safety net than from attempts to increase low levels of charter value (Keeley, 1990; Park and Peristiani, 2007).

Second, our analysis is also able to shed some light on the debate of whether bonuses exert undesirable short-term effects on banks. A popular criticism of bonuses in banking is that they fuel a culture of short-termism where excessive risks are taken to meet short-term performance goals (e.g. FSB, 2009: 13). Our results show that changes in cash bonuses have measurable long-term effects which are of even higher magnitude than their short-term effects. Therefore, our findings are at odds with the view that the effect of bonuses is short-term and add to a growing literature which shows that bonus compensation is an essential part of the long-term compensation policy of a firm (Gibbons and Murphy, 1992; Indjejikian et al., 2011).

While the vast majority of previous work on CEO compensation and risk-taking has analysed risk on the basis of either market indicators (Fahlenbrach and Stulz, 2011) or accounting indicators (Coles, Daniel, and Naveen, 2002; Rajgopal and Shivaram, 2002; Mehran and Rosenberg, 2007), our study examines the effect of cash bonuses on bank risk-taking using the Merton distance-to-default (DD) model. As shown by Gropp, Vesala, and Vulpes (2006), DD scores that draw on both accounting and market data are an appropriate indicator of bank fragility which outperforms pure market measures of risk, such as subordinated bond spreads, over most time horizons. Further, DD is a measure with relevant behavioural implications for bank CEOs, because sharp increases in bank default risk are likely to trigger government recapitalizations, which have negative implications for the reputation and career paths of bank CEOs (Mehran and Rosenberg, 2007).

We analyse the bonus–relationship by means of a partial adjustment model and by using a dynamic panel GMM estimator. Essentially, our results are based on an instrumental variable approach, which uses lagged values of pay variables as instruments (which we demonstrate to be valid) for pay variables. This approach controls for unobservable heterogeneity, simultaneity issues (e.g. when CEO pay incentives are jointly determined with a firm's investment and other financial policies; see Coles, Daniel, and Naveen, 2006) as well as for dynamic endogeneity (e.g. when current risk affects future CEO pay, which, in turn, affects future risk-taking). Wintoki, Linck, and Netter (2011) demonstrate the importance of controlling for dynamic endogeneity in corporate governance research. The authors find that few of the previously identified relationships between corporate governance and firm performance are confirmed after controlling for a firm's history through a dynamic panel GMM estimator.

Theoretical Background and Hypotheses Development

Theoretical Background

Executive compensation policy may serve as a mechanism to reduce conflicts between managers and shareholders over the deployment of corporate resources and the riskiness of the firm. Over the past two decades, performance-related pay has increased markedly in and outside the banking industry. Generally, the increasing use of performance-sensitive compensation is consistent with agency theory, which suggests that optimal executive compensation needs to align the interests of risk-averse managers with those of risk-neutral shareholders by motivating managers to commit to risk-increasing but positive net present value (NPV) projects (Jensen and Meckling, 1976; Smith and Stulz, 1985).

In the banking industry, the monitoring of managerial risk-taking is subject to a theoretically well-defined moral hazard problem. Banks are highly leveraged institutions. Given the call option properties of equity, bank shareholders face limited downside risk but stand to benefit more from high-risk strategies that increase the volatility of bank assets than shareholders in less leveraged firms (Jensen and Meckling, 1976; John and John, 1993; Noe, Rebello, and Wall, 1996). Shareholder incentives to increase risk are further aggravated by deposit insurance and the operation of implicit bailout policies, which insulate many bank creditors from losses in the event of institutional failure and which reduce their propensity to limit excessive risk-taking by executives (see John, Saunders, and Senbet, 2000; John, Mehran, and Qian, 2010).[2] As a result, shareholders are likely to use their control over CEO pay to encourage managerial risk-taking and the shifting of risk to regulators and bondholders (Benston, Hunter, and Wall, 1995; Hubbard and Palia, 1995; Bolton, Mehran, and Shapiro, 2010).

Therefore, the effect that different components of CEO incentive compensation have on bank risk depends on the degree to which these components mitigate or aggravate risk-shifting incentives. In the next subsection, *CEO Bonuses and Bank Risk-taking*, we develop expectations about how CEO bonus plans affect bank risk-taking.

CEO Bonuses and Bank Risk-taking

Theoretical work posits that CEO cash bonuses can play an important role in mitigating managerial incentives to engage in risk-shifting. In a theoretical

[2] While many European countries either did not have explicit deposit insurance during our sampling period or had insurance schemes which were less generous than the US scheme, the operation of implicit or explicit bailout policies in many European countries may not cause regulatory moral hazard on a scale comparable to that caused by the blanket guarantees of the Federal Deposit Insurance Corporation in the USA.

model, Smith and Stulz (1985) show that as long as cash bonuses increase linearly with corporate performance, the payoffs from a bonus plan are non-convex and, therefore, not inherently risk-rewarding. Only when performance is below the earnings-based threshold at which bonuses become payable, do bonus plans resemble a call option on the performance measure. Put differently, when corporate performance is below this threshold, bonus plan payoffs will be convex and offset the concavity of the CEO's risk-averse utility function. However, when performance is above the threshold (and below the bonus cap), the CEO payoff function is linear with performance and will not incentivize risk-averse CEOs to increase bank risk to secure higher bonus payments.[3]

Other work suggests that, rather than having no effect on risk-taking, bonuses lower the risk preferences of the CEO. One such argument goes that, because bonus payments can only be received in a state of solvency, they incentivize CEOs to avoid bankruptcy (Brander and Poitevin, 1992; John and John, 1993). Consistent with this, Duru, Mansi, and Reeb (2005) find that earnings-based cash bonuses make managers seek stable cash flows to meet contractual debt obligations. The authors show that the costs of debt financing decrease for firms which pay higher CEO cash bonuses, and contend that this reflects the lower agency costs of debt and reduced risk-shifting incentives in these firms.

In spite of the above, claims that cash bonuses encourage banks to engage in 'excessive' risk-taking continue to be made (for instance, in FSB, 2009). However, the case for bonuses increasing risk rests on two assumptions, both of which have recently been challenged by empirical evidence. The first assumption is that cash bonus contracts do not sufficiently expose managers to downside risk and, therefore, reward managers for taking on more risk to achieve the performance goals underlying bonus contracts. In contrast to this, empirical studies have shown that bonus contracts tend to punish underperformance more than they reward strong performance (Leone, Wu, and Zimmerman, 2006; Indjejikian et al., 2011). If bonus contracts leave CEOs with more downside risk than upside risk, it seems improbable that risk-averse CEOs would commit to risky asset choices to increase their cash compensation.[4]

[3] Kim, Nam, and Thornton (2008) confirm the theoretical predictions made by Smith and Stulz (1985) using estimates of the performance thresholds underlying individual CEO bonus plans. However, it is important to bear in mind that, because the conditions under which managerial option plans are granted are seldom disclosed, estimates of the position of a CEO on the bonus payoff function will be imprecise. This is why our analysis is unable to empirically examine this aspect of risk-taking on bonus payments directly.

[4] One explanation advanced for bonus contracts producing asymmetric payoffs is that CEOs' bonus payments are partly based on performance gains which have yet to materialize at the time the bonus becomes payable. Should the anticipated performance not materialize, it will be difficult

The second assumption is that, by making bonus payments contingent on annual performance targets, shareholders design bonuses to affect short-term behaviour and managers pursue higher risk-taking strategies to achieve these short-term goals. While some evidence exists that managers may ration productive effort in order to maximize bonus payments (Holthausen, Larcker, and Sloan, 1995; Bouwens and Kroos, 2011),[5] this does not rule out the fact that bonuses can be designed as long-term compensation tools. In fact, Gibbons and Murphy (1992) and Indjejikian et al. (2011) show that bonus plans provide managers with long-term incentives to exert effort. These studies document the fact that companies consider a trade-off between bonuses and career incentives over time horizons of multiple years when devising managerial compensation packages.

The narrow empirical evidence available for the US banking industry reaches conflicting conclusions on the role of CEO bonus payments and bank risk. Harjoto and Mullineaux (2003) report a positive association between bonus payments and return volatility (risk). In a recent working paper, Balachandran, Kogut, and Harnal (2010) proffer some evidence that the sum of bonus and other cash incentives reduces the probability of bank default. Based on the theoretical arguments above, and in line with the findings of this latter study, we expect to find that higher CEO bonus payments lower the default risk of a bank.

While the banking literature recognizes that CEO cash bonuses do not increase managerial risk preferences in general, previous studies have identified two factors which may moderate the bonus–risk relationship. First, cash bonuses may promote managerial risk-shifting at financially distressed banks (Noe, Rebello, and Wall, 1996; Benston and Evan, 2006). At distressed banks with poor growth prospects, higher risk-taking maximizes the value of the safety net to a bank (e.g. Keeley, 1990; Park and Peristiani, 2007). This is because when the value attributed to the growth prospects of a bank (the so-called charter value) is low, the prospect of losing charter value in the event of institutional failure is not a sufficient deterrent against risk-shifting behaviour. Consistent with this, Akerlof and Romer (1993) propose the 'looting

for companies to claw back overpaid funds from the CEO. However, this so-called 'settling up problem' has been questioned recently. For instance, Shaw and Zhang (2010) are only able to replicate Leone, Wu, and Zimmerman's (2006) finding that cash compensation is more sensitive to downside than to upside risk when underperformance is measured in terms of stock returns, not when using other measures of performance.

[5] The notion that bonuses impact short-term CEO behaviour has been advanced in Weizman's (1980) 'ratcheting' argument. Accordingly, managers faced with earnings-based bonus contracts may intentionally withhold productive effort to avoid future losses which would result if favourable performance at present led to higher performance targets in the immediate future. Holthausen, Larcker, and Sloan (1995) and Bouwens and Kroos (2011) have found evidence consistent with ratcheting by management.

hypothesis'. When senior management knows that there is a high likelihood a bank could fail, they are likely to undertake riskier strategies in an effort to boost short-term performance. While such behaviour may increase the probability of bank default, managers expect to benefit in terms of continuous employment and future pay should their gamble pay off. Similarly, Edmans and Liu (2011) argue that since CEO cash bonuses are only paid in states of solvency, CEOs at distressed firms may engage in risk-shifting to 'gamble for solvency' with little regard for the liquidation value of a firm.[6]

The second factor that may moderate the bonus–risk relationship is the overall strength of the bank regulatory regime. When the prospect of regulatory intervention is low, cash bonuses may lose their risk-reducing effect (Noe, Rebello, and Wall, 1996). Webb (2008) suggests that as regulatory monitoring weakens, bank executives become less risk averse. Consequently, it could be argued that when regulatory environments are less strict and the probability of regulatory intervention is low, CEOs may be become more responsive to incentives to shift risk to regulators.

We sum up our expected findings as follows. We expect to find that CEO bonus payments mitigate risk-shifting incentives. However, when banks are financially distressed (we do not consider the strength of the regulatory regime in the current research), we do not expect to find that CEO bonus payments lower the default risk of a bank.

Sample and Remuneration Data

The Sample of Banks

Our analysis is based on 117 listed banks (41 European banks and 76 US banks) in the period 2000–8. To build the subsample of European banks, we start with the universe of listed banks which are listed on Bankscope and chartered in Europe (EU-15 plus Norway and Switzerland). After excluding institutions with SIC codes 6211 and 6199, we identified 200 banks. Next, we stipulate that sample banks have at least five years of accounting data and equity return data subject to the same liquidity criterion we applied to the US sample. Applying these criteria halved the number of banks in our sample.

[6] Similarly, if CEOs believe that previously paid bonuses will not have to be returned in the event of institutional failure in a future year, it could also be argued that bonus payments at distressed banks will insulate CEOs from the longer-term negative effects of high-risk, negative NPV projects and provide incentives to shift earnings over time (Duru, Mansi, and Reeb, 2005). However, there are two exceptions to this—although, admittedly, both of these have been difficult to enforce in the past. In the USA, the Federal Deposit Insurance Corporation (FDIC) may sue bank managers for gross negligence if the case can be made that a CEO contributed to the failure of bank. Also, some CEOs may have agreed to clawback provisions, which stipulate repayment of cash bonuses in the event of subsequent underperformance.

We also stipulate that sample banks need to have CEO remuneration data available for at least five consecutive years. We hand collect compensation data from annual reports and governance reports. The levels of CEO pay disclosure vary widely across European countries. In a first group of countries (Belgium, France, Ireland, Italy, the Netherlands, and the UK), pay disclosure requirements are very high and comparable to those applicable to listed US firms. In a second group of countries (Austria, Germany, and Spain), detailed disclosure of CEO pay is not required, but a small number of banks still disclose CEO pay data. Finally, a third group of countries (Switzerland, Greece, Portugal, Norway, Finland, Sweden, and Luxembourg) does not disclose CEO pay data for most of the sample period and typically reports pay data aggregated at the level of the board. In order to be sampled, European banks have to be based in the first and second group of countries. Since we require five years of CEO pay data for our dynamic panel, we are unable to include banks in the third group, which have only recently started to publish CEO pay data. Our final sample contains forty-one European banks.

For the US subsample, we collect compensation data from Standard & Poor's ExecuComp database. Since ExecuComp's coverage is restricted to firms currently or previously included in the S&P 500, S&P MidCap 400, and S&P SmallCap 600, we eliminate many banks at this point. We extract compensation data for firms with SIC codes between 6000 and 6300. We require at least five years of compensation data to implement the dynamic panel model. We then exclude firms with SIC 6282 (investment advice) and SIC 6111 (federal credit agency). Out of firms with SIC codes 6211 (security brokers and dealers) and 6199 (finance services) we only retain Citigroup in the sample, as we classify the remaining banks in this group as pure investment banks. We do so, because the subsample of European banks consists of commercial banks only and we seek to build a sample of institutions which engage in similar types of activities. Based on these criteria, our search yielded an initial sample of 103 US banks.

Since we wish to use identical data sources for all sample banks, we further stipulate that banks need to have five years of accounting data on Fitch's IBCA's Bankscope database and equity return data on Datastream over the same time period. We lose five banks as a result of this criterion. Further, since our default risk calculations require daily market data, we ensure that the calculations are reliable and stipulate that sample banks have at least 70 per cent of non-zero daily returns on Datastream each year. We lose a further twenty-two banks as a result of this liquidity criterion. Our final sample contains seventy-six US banks.

The distribution of the final sample by year and country is reported in Table 7.1. European sample banks are mostly located in the UK and in Italy, which reflects the concentration of listed banks in both of these countries.

Table 7.1. Sample Overview

Panel A: Sample Distribution by Year

	No.	*%*
2000	82	9.16
2001	90	10.06
2002	98	10.95
2003	109	12.18
2004	117	13.07
2005	111	12.40
2006	108	12.07
2007	95	10.61
2008	85	9.50
Total	895	100.00

Panel B: Sample Distribution by Country

	No. of banks	*No. of obs.*	*% of banks*	*% of obs.*	*Average assets (min. US$)*
Austria	1	5	0.85	0.56	
Belgium	1	8	0.85	0.89	
France	4	34	3.42	3.80	
Germany	3	17	2.56	1.90	
Ireland	3	26	2.56	2.91	
Italy	11	88	9.40	9.83	
Netherlands	4	27	3.42	3.02	
Spain	4	29	3.42	3.24	
UK	10	83	8.55	9.27	
Europe	*41*	*317*	*35.03*	*35.42*	*498,070.6*
USA	76	578	64.96	64.58	103,651.1
Total	117	895	100.00	100.00	601,721.7

Further, in spite of having selected the largest listed US banks, the average size of US banks in our sample is smaller than that of the European banks.[7]

Bonus Data

For US banks, we extract compensation data from ExecuComp. We obtain the variables SALARY, BONUS, and OTHCOMP to construct measures of CEO cash compensation.[8] While ExecuComp offers a much broader range of remuneration data than we extract, the range of compensation data we examine in this study is determined by the availability of similar data for European banks. For

[7] We assess the implications of size differences between the US and European banks for our results in the robustness section where we re-estimate our main models after excluding smaller banks. Our main results are not affected if we exclude the smallest banks from the sample.

[8] We do not use the data field TDC1 as a measure of total compensation, because it includes a valuation of new stock option grants and no comparable data on CEO stock options grants are available for most European banks.

the latter group of banks, we use annual reports and governance reports to hand collect CEO data on basic salary, cash bonuses, and other forms of cash compensation.

Using the information collected, we construct two remuneration variables. *LGBONUS* is the logarithmic transformation of 1 plus the total cash bonus received by the CEO (in $thousands; for European banks, currency conversions are based on IMF exchange rates at the date of the annual report). The relative importance of bonus payments is captured by *RELBONUS*, which is the ratio of CEO cash bonuses to total cash compensation.[9]

Table 7.2 reports descriptive statistics on the bonus variables and demonstrates that cash bonuses are key components of CEO pay in the banking industry. Panel A of Table 7.2 shows that the average (median) bonus paid over the sample period is $1.234 ($0.461) million. On a bank-year basis, cash bonuses on average contribute one-third to total CEO compensation.[10]

Next, Panel B of Table 7.2 reports basic descriptive statistics for European and US banks. The analysis of the two subsamples shows that the value of bonuses and total compensation appears to be larger in Europe. Nonetheless, the ten largest bonus payments are all made to US bank CEOs. For instance, the CEO of Citigroup, Sanford Weill, received a bonus of $29 million in 2003, while the CEO of Countrywide Financial Corporation, Angelo Mozilo, received a bonus of around $20 million in the same year. In Europe, Josef Ackermann, the CEO of Deutsche Bank, received a cash bonus of $12 million in 2007, while the CEO of Unicredit, Alessandro Profumo, received a bonus of $8.8 million during the same year.

Since bank size is a major determinant of executive compensation policies, Panel C of Table 7.2 reports summary statistics for the sample after excluding banks located in the lowest quartile of the distribution of average total assets during the sample period. After excluding these smaller (mainly US) banks, the summary statistics provide few indications that European and US compensation practices are different.[11]

[9] Obviously, cash bonuses are not the only type of CEO compensation that could affect bank risk-taking. However, data availability issues prevent us from controlling for the complete suite of equity- and debt-like forms of compensation which CEOs may receive next to bonus payments.

[10] Interestingly, the share of bonus payments declined to 10 per cent of total CEO pay in 2008. While the declining share of bonus payments denotes a sharp change in the remuneration practices at banks in the aftermath of the recent financial crisis, our results are not affected by this since our regression models employ lagged explanatory variables. The last year of compensation data employed in our models is 2007.

[11] In untabulated tests, we evaluate whether there are statistically significant differences between the compensation practices of European and US banks. We employ the Wilcoxon rank-sum test to examine if differences between US and European banks in Panel C of Table 7.2 are statistically significant. We do not find significant differences between US and European banks. For the sake of brevity these results are not reported.

Table 7.2. Descriptive Statistics: CEO Bonus Pay

		N	Mean	Median	St.Dev.	1 Pctile	99 Pctile
Panel A: Full Sample							
	Total bonus	895	1,234.45	460.47	2,468.79	0.00	13,000.00
	Total compensation	895	2,512.62	1,435.96	3,060.79	314.88	16,097.19
	LGBONUS	895	4.85	6.13	3.18	0.00	9.47
	RELBONUS (%)	895	32.73	35.40	25.97	0.00	90.04
Panel B: For Europe and the USA							
	Total bonus	317	1,278.66	631.83	1,756.77	0.00	8,533.69
	Total compensation	317	2,842.79	1,920.09	2,817.37	185.25	14,038.48
Europe	LGBONUS	317	5.47	6.45	2.89	0.00	9.05
	RELBONUS (%)	317	33.62	34.77	22.54	0.00	75.00
	Total bonus	578	1,210.20	396.15	2,784.16	0.00	16,986.75
	Total compensation	578	2,331.54	1,274.06	3,174.20	359.03	18,677.29
USA	LGBONUS	578	4.52	5.98	3.18	0.00	9.74
	RELBONUS (%)	578	32.24	36.03	27.68	0.00	91.30
Panel C: Europe and the USA (excl. Small Banks)							
	Total bonus	312	1,294.71	661.59	1,766.14	0.00	8,533.69
	Total compensation	312	2,876.25	1,937.10	2,827.27	185.25	14,038.48
Europe	LGBONUS	312	5.47	6.50	2.91	0.00	9.05
	RELBONUS (%)	312	33.55	34.76	22.61	0.00	75.00
	Total bonus	380	1,659.90	610.99	3,331.67	0.00	18,484.41
	Total compensation	380	2,961.92	1,706.10	3,674.60	611.60	20,361.20
USA	LGBONUS	380	4.85	6.42	3.43	0.00	9.824
	RELBONUS (%)	380	35.37	40.82	29.08	0.00	91.45

Table 7.2 reports summary statistics for remuneration variables based on a sample of 117 European and US banks for the period 2000–8. Total bonus are total bonus payments during the reporting year. Total compensation is the sum of basic salary, bonus payments, and other income. LGBONUS is the log transformation of 1 + total bonus. RELBONUS are CEO bonus payments over total compensation (%). Small banks are banks located in the lowest quartile of the sample distribution of total assets.
Sources: ExecuComp (USA) and bank annual reports (Europe).

Measuring Bank Default Risk

We measure bank risk via the Merton distance-to-default (DD) model. This model boasts a wide range of empirical (e.g. Vassalou and Xing, 2004; Sundaram and Yermack, 2007) and commercial applications. Generally, DD values provide a suitable indicator of bank fragility which outperforms other market-based indicators such as subordinated debt spreads in predicting bank default (Gropp, Vesala, and Vulpes, 2006) and which is available for all listed banks (while other market-based risk indicators such as CDS spreads are only available for a limited number of banks, especially in Europe).

The Merton model measures default risk as the number of standard deviations that the market value of bank assets are above default point (the point where the market value of assets is less than the book value of total liabilities). Formally, DD at the end of year t is expressed as:

$$\mathrm{DD}_t = \frac{\ln\,(V_{A,t}/L_t) + (r_f - 0.5\sigma_{A,t}^2)T}{\sigma_{A,t}\sqrt{T}}, \tag{1}$$

where $V_{A,t}$ is the market value of assets at the end of the fiscal year t, L_t is the book value of total liabilities, r_f is the risk-free rate (proxied by the yield on one-year US treasury bills for US banks and by the one-year interbank (EURIBOR) rate for European banks), $\sigma_{A,t}$ is the annualized asset volatility at t (based on volatility of equity returns in a given year), and T is the time to maturity (conventionally set to one year). The computation of DD_t requires estimates of $V_{A,t}$ and $\sigma_{A,t}$ neither of which are directly observable. Following Akhigbe, Madura, and Martin (2007), Vassalou and Xing (2004), and Hillegeist and colleagues (2004), we infer the values for $\sigma_{A,t}$ and $\sigma_{A,t}$ through an iterative process based on the Black–Scholes–Merton pricing model. Specifically, we express the market value of a firm's equity ($V_{\mathrm{E,t}}$) as a function of the asset value by solving the following system of nonlinear equations:

$$V_{E,t} = V_{A,t}N(d_{1,t}) - X_t e^{-r_f T} N(d_{2,t}) \tag{2}$$

$$\sigma_{E,t} = \left(\frac{V_{A,t}}{V_{E,t}}\right) N(d_{1,t})\sigma_{A,t} \tag{3}$$

Equation (2) defines $V_{E,t}$ as a call option on the market value of the bidder's total assets, with $d_{1,t} = \frac{\ln\,(V_{A,t}/L_t) + (r_{f_t} + 0.5\sigma_{A,t}^2)T}{\sigma_{A,t}\sqrt{T}}$ and $d_{2,t} = d_{1,t} - \sigma_{A,t}\sqrt{T}$. Equation (3) is the optimal hedge equation that relates the standard deviation of a bank's equity value to the standard deviation of a bank's total assets value (both on an annualized basis).

To solve this system of equations, we employ as starting values for $\sigma_{A,t}$ the historical volatility of equity (computed on a yearly basis using daily data) multiplied by the ratio of the market value of equity to the sum of the market value of equity and the book value of total liabilities, i.e. $\sigma_{A,t} = \sigma_{E,t}V_{E,t}/(V_{E,t} + L_t)$. A Newton search algorithm then identifies the daily values for $\sigma_{A,t}$ and $\sigma_{A,t}$ in an iterative process which we then employ to compute DD_t as in Equation (1).[12]

In Table 7.3 we offer some preliminary evidence on the relationship between DD and CEO bonus pay. More precisely, Table 7.3 reports the mean and median values of our risk measure for banks that show low and high values of LGBONUS and RELBONUS. The results show that the mean and

[12] The distance to default of the banks in our sample assumes particularly low values in 2008—the peak of the recent financial crisis. More precisely, the mean (median) DD in 2008 is equal to 1.27 (1.27) against a value of 4.41 (4.14) for the rest of the sample period. DD, therefore, seems to be particularly effective in tracking the evolution of bank default risk.

Table 7.3. Distance to Default in Banks with High and Low CEO Bonus Pay

Panel A: DD in banks with low and high values of LGBONUS

	LOW LGBONUS (1)	HIGH LGBONUS (2)	(2) minus (1) (3)
Mean DD	3.754	4.417	0.663*** (5.183)
Median DD	3.614	4.175	0.561*** (5.084)
N	895	895	

Panel B: DD in banks with low and high values of RELBONUS

	LOW RELBONUS (1)	HIGH RELBONUS (2)	(2) minus (1) (3)
Mean DD	3.719	4.452	0.733*** (5.760)
Median DD	3.563	4.178	0.615*** (5.677)
N	895	895	

Panel A reports the mean and median of DD for banks that with low and high values of LGBONUS (based on the median of the sampling distribution). Panel B reports mean (median) DD for banks that show low and high values of RELBONUS (relative to the median of the sampling distribution). Column 3 shows the results of a *t*-(z-)test of equality in the mean (median) DD between the two groups.
* significant at 10%; ** significant at 5%; *** significant at 1%.

median values of DD are higher in banks where CEOs receive larger bonus payments. In addition, as reported in column 3, the differences between the two groups of banks are statistically significant at customary levels. The results of this simple univariate test support theoretical arguments in favour of a risk-reducing effect of cash bonuses.

Empirical Design

The Model

In this chapter, we build on previous work and model the relationship between CEO remuneration and bank risk-taking in a dynamic framework.[13] We assume that banks have an internally optimal, unobservable target distance to default to which they revert over time. We also assume that reversion to this target level of risk will not be instantaneous, but will take place via observable changes in distance to default over time. Therefore, observable

[13] Among others, Shrieves and Dahl (1992), Rime (2001), and Jokipii and Milne (2011) use a dynamic framework to model the capital buffers held by banks.

adjustments in risk over time ($DD_{i,t} - DD_{i,t-1}$) will be a fraction of the differences between the target level of risk ($DD^*_{i,t}$) and levels of risk existing at t-1.

$$DD_{i,t} - DD_{i,t-1} = \lambda(DD^*_{i,t} - DD_{i,t-1}) + \varepsilon_{i,t}, \tag{4}$$

In this framework, λ is the adjustment speed towards the long-term distance to default targeted by a bank. The adjustment speed will lie between the [0, 1] interval. If $\lambda = 0$, no observable risk adjustment between risk in a given time period t and the risk observed in the previous period occurs, whereas $\lambda = 1$ indicates that adjustment to the target distance of default is instantaneous.

Since the target level of risk is unobservable, we express $DD^*_{i,t}$ as a function of bonus payments, $BONUS_{t-1}$, a vector of bank characteristics $X_{i,t-1}$, and unobservable bank attributes (B_i):

$$DD^*_{i,t} = \gamma\, BONUS_{i,t-1} + \beta X_{i,t-1} + B_i \tag{5}$$

Therefore, substituting Equation (5) into Equation (4), distance to default at a given time period t and its determinants will be driven by the following process:

$$DD_{i,t} = (1-\lambda)DD_{i,t-1} + \lambda(\gamma BONUS_{i,t-1} + \beta X_{i,t-1} + B_i) + \varepsilon_{i,t} \tag{6}$$

Here, $\lambda \times \beta$measures the short-term effect of a variable on distance to default in a given period, while β captures the long-term effect of a variable by measuring its effect on the unobservable target level of default risk. Consequently, the impact of each explanatory variable on the target level of risk $DD^*_{i,t}$ can be derived by scaling the coefficients in Equation (6) by the speed of adjustment λ.

Estimation Method and Control Variables

To account for the impact of unobservable bank heterogeneity on default risk, we estimate Equation (6) by using a dynamic panel data method. Specifically, we use the generalized method of moments (GMM) estimator, which is an instrumental variable estimator proposed by Blundell and Bond (1998). This system GMM estimator uses both the lags of the explanatory variables and the data from the original level specification as instrumental variables.

A critical advantage of any GMM estimator is that it controls for endogeneity in the relationship between risk and managerial incentives. This is because the specification allows variables to be treated as strictly exogenous regressors, endogenous regressors, and predetermined regressors.[14] Thus, our method examines the effect of CEO pay on bank risk while ruling out reverse causality arguments, according to which bank CEOs who wish to pursue more risky

[14] Commonly, in the difference equation, first differences in endogenous variables are instrumented with lags of the specific variables. In the level equation, endogenous variables in levels are instrumented with lags of their first differences.

strategies encourage their boards to offer risk-inducing packages. Further, our approach controls for dynamic endogeneity (when past compensation structures affect future bank risk-taking, which, in turn, affects future CEO compensation structures; see Wintoki, Linck, and Netter, 2011).

Additionally, the specific system estimator we employ in this study has two key advantages over other dynamic panel data methods (most notably, the difference in-difference estimator proposed by Arellano and Bond (1991)). First, as long as the instruments are valid, the GMM estimator exhibits higher levels of both consistency and efficiency. Second, unlike the difference estimator, the system GMM estimator permits the use of time-invariant (or highly persistent) variables in our specifications.

System GMM specifications may be estimated either via a one-step or a two-step approach. While the one-step estimation produces unbiased standard errors, it is not asymptotically efficient in the estimation of the coefficients. The asymptotically more efficient two-step estimator, on the other hand, tends to bias the estimated standard errors downwards (Blundell and Bond, 1998). We follow studies such as Goddard and colleagues (2011) and Florackis and Ozkan (2009) and employ the asymptotically efficient two-step GMM system as well as the Windmeijer (2005) procedure to lower the bias and correct the standard errors.

Finally, the validity of our approach rests on two assumptions (which we confirm to be valid for each of our estimations). First, for the instruments to be valid, they need to be uncorrelated with the error term. We use the Hansen *J*-statistic of over-identifying restrictions to test this assumption (where statistically insignificant values confirm the validity of the instruments). Second, the system GMM estimator requires stationarity in the post-instrumentation error terms. This implies the absence of second-order serial correlation in the first difference residual. We employ the m_2 statistic developed by Arellano and Bond (1991) to test for the lack of second-order serial correlation in the first-difference residual. An insignificant m_2 statistic indicates that the model is correctly specified.

Our models control for several bank characteristics that may affect the level of bank default risk. First, we control for bank leverage defined as 1 minus the ratio of the book value of equity to total assets (*LEVERAGE*). Given the call option properties of equity (which combine unlimited upside with limited downside potential), the benefits to shareholders associated with risk-shifting increase with firm leverage (Jensen and Meckling, 1976). Therefore, higher levels of bank leverage will induce CEOs to shift risk to regulators and debt holders (John and John, 1993). We expect LEVERAGE to increase the target levels of default risk and, hence, a negative relationship between LEVERAGE and DD.

We control for bank performance measured by the ratio of pre-tax profits to total assets (*ROA*). We introduce this variable to the baseline specification because earnings are the most frequent performance measure on which bonus payments are based (Murphy, 2000; BCBS, 2011).[15] Also, we wish to control for any possible link between bank profitability and default risk. For instance, higher profitability may make it easier for banks to retain earnings, build up capital, and increase DD. On the other hand, higher profitability may equally be due to higher risk-taking (and therefore be linked to lower DD). We also control for the future growth prospects of a bank because growth prospects may constrain risk-taking. Commonly, a bank's future growth prospects are captured by charter value. Keeley (1990) and Park and Peristiani (2007) show that managements' desire to preserve charter value will help mitigate against managerial risk-shifting incentives. We proxy charter value (*CHARTER*) by the market to book ratio. We expect CHARTER to enter our model with a positive coefficient.

We measure the importance of fee-based and trading activities in a bank's business model via the ratio of non-interest income to total operating income (*NONINTSHARE*). Previous studies generally conclude that the revenue streams associated with non-conventional business lines tend to be more volatile than interest-based activities (Stiroh, 2006). We, therefore, expect NONINTSHARE to exert a negative influence on distance to default.

The impact of bank *SIZE* (measured by the log transformation of total assets) on managerial risk-taking is ambiguous ex ante. On the one hand, large banks may benefit from a broader investment opportunity set, including improved access to funding and capital markets. On the other hand, large banks enjoy greater protection under the financial safety net. Therefore, implicit and explicit too-big-to-fail policies may exacerbate existing risk-shifting incentives and increase the level of risk (see Benston, Hunter, and Wall, 1995).

The final vector of control variables includes corporate governance and CEO characteristics. Agency theory postulates that conflicts over the riskiness of a firm ensue because managers are risk averse and shareholders are risk neutral. When the board's interests are aligned with those of shareholders, this should be associated with increased risk-taking, while banks with less shareholder-oriented boards should be associated with less risk-taking (Pathan, 2009). We measure the degree to which the board's interests are aligned with those of shareholders through a measure of board independence (*INDEP*). INDEP is the share of directors who are not executives, former executives, or related to (former) executives to board size. Further, as a proxy for CEO power, we use a dummy variable which is equal to one if the CEO also acts as chairman of the

[15] A recent report by the Basel Committee (BCBS, 2011) into remuneration in the banking industry states that 'measures of financial performance, such as targets based on revenue, profit or income, cash flow or return on equity, are still frequently used for performance measurement. Measures used are often accounting-based and retrospective' (p. 3).

board (*DUALITY*). We expect INDEP to exert a risk-increasing effect and DUALITY to exert a risk-reducing effect. Finally, we also include *AGE* as the log transformation of CEO age in our model. Webb (2008) argues that older CEOs with longer tenure and an established track record are subject to less regulatory scrutiny than younger CEOs and should, therefore, display more risk-taking behaviour.

Finally, when estimating Equation (6), we make the assumption that the bonus variables, LEVERAGE and ROA are endogenous with respect to bank risk. This assumption is strongly supported by previous work. First, Coles, Daniel, and Naveen (2006) point out that managerial incentives, investment, and financial policies are likely to be jointly determined. Thus, treating the bonus variables as strictly exogenous would bias inferences about any causal relationship between firm risk and managerial incentives. Second, banks adjust their equity ratio (through changes in their capital buffers) and their risk simultaneously (e.g. Shrieves and Dahl, 1992; Altunbaş, et al., 2007; Jokipii and Milne, 2011). In our empirical design, this implies a mutual causal relationship between DD and LEVERAGE.[16] Finally, the endogeneity of ROA could be explained by either a trade-off between risk and return (i.e. higher profitability is achieved through increased bank risk-taking) or, alternatively, the notion that the default risk of a bank affects the investment strategies which managers pursue in search of maximizing future returns (e.g. poor performance could lead banks to engage in a 'gamble for solvency').

Panel A of Table 7.4 presents descriptive statistics of the default risk scores, the CEO bonus variables, and the control variables described earlier in this chapter. For ease of exposure, we replicate the summary statistics on the compensation data which we have presented in Table 7.2. Panel B of Table 7.4 reports pairwise correlations between the variables.

Bonus Compensation and Bank Default Risk

Multivariate Results

In this section, we analyse the impact of CEO cash bonuses on the target level of default risk. We expect bonus payments to exert a positive (i.e. risk-reducing) influence on the distance to default of a bank. Since cash bonuses can only be received in states of bank solvency, larger cash bonus payments should incentivize CEOs to avoid default. Further, the payoffs from cash

[16] The number of instruments may affect the validity of the specification tests. To limit the number of instruments as well as for simplicity's sake, we assume that the lagged values of the remaining bank characteristics are exogenous with respect to bank risk. However, our results are confirmed when we model all bank characteristics as endogenous and use their lag values (from time *t-2*) as instruments.

Table 7.4. Summary Statistics and Correlations

Panel A: Descriptive Statistics

	Description	N	Mean	Median	St.Dev.	1 Pctile	99 Pctile
DD	Distance to default	895	4.085	3.920	1.939	−0.060	8.814
LGBONUS	Log (1 + total bonus)	895	4.854	6.134	3.179	0.000	9.473
RELBONUS	Bonus over total compensation (%)	895	32.732	35.397	25.967	0.000	90.036
LEVERAGE	1−(Equity over total assets) (%)	895	92.062	92.269	3.730	79.405	97.854
ROA	Pre-tax profits over total assets (%)	895	1.352	1.386	1.214	−3.039	4.690
CHARTER	Market value of equity scaled by book value of equity	895	1.908	1.736	1.050	0.250	5.687
NONINTSHARE	Non-interest income over total operating income	895	37.805	37.150	19.266	2.224	86.698
ASSETS	Total assets ($million)	895	243,351	42,927	484,413	1,524	2,459,149
SIZE	Log of total assets ($million)	895	17.744	17.575	1.854	14.237	21.623
INDEP	Number of independent directors over board size (%)	805	73.186	75.000	14.732	33.333	100.00
DUALITY	Binary variable, which is equal to 1 if the CEO also acts as chairman of the board	895	0.521	1.000	0.500	0.000	1.000
AGE	Log of CEO age (years)	876	4.021	4.043	0.126	3.664	4.277

Panel B: Correlation Matrix

	(1)	(2)	(3)	(4)	(5)	(6)	(7)	(8)	(9)	(10)	(11)
(1) DD	1										
(2) LGBONUS	0.190***	1									
(3) RELBONUS	0.189***	0.912***	1								
(4) LEVERAGE	−0.122***	0.181***	0.149***	1							
(5) ROA	0.355***	0.270***	0.270***	−0.360***	1						
(6) CHARTER	0.195***	0.287***	0.326***	−0.031	0.525***						
(7) NONINTSHARE	0.067*	0.275***	0.319***	0.164***	0.149***	0.203***	1				
(8) SIZE	0.076*	0.223***	0.215***	0.490***	−0.210***	−0.221***	0.382***	1			
(9) INDEP	0.006	−0.078*	−0.036	0.125***	−0.172***	−0.179***	0.104**	0.189***	1		
(10) DUALITY	0.043	−0.012	0.081*	−0.251***	0.148***	0.162***	0.069*	−0.186***	−0.128***	1	
(11) AGE	0.070*	−0.044	0.005	−0.231***	0.056	−0.028	0.056	−0.042	0.048	0.291***	1

Panel A of Table 7.4 reports summary statistics for the variables employed in the analysis. Panel B shows pairwise correlation coefficients and the related significant values. The data refer to a sample of 117 European and US banks during the period 2000–8. In European countries where two-tier board structures exist, DUALITY is defined as the CEO acting as chairman of the supervisory board.

* significant at 10%; ** significant at 5%; *** significant at 1%.

bonuses tend to be linear functions of performance which do not reward increased risk-taking (provided that current bank performance does not place CEOs below the threshold at which a bonus is payable; see Smith and Stulz, 1985).

The results reported in Table 7.5 confirm our expectations. Panel A reports the results of the two-step system GMM estimations on bank default risk. The estimated coefficients can be interpreted as the short-term determinants of bank default risk. Both LGBONUS (which measures the absolute dollar contribution of bonus payments to CEO wealth) and RELBONUS (which captures the importance of cash bonuses relative to total cash compensation) enter the models with a positive sign (both highly statistically significant). Accordingly, higher bonus payments lower default risk. This result is robust to the inclusion of bank control variables and country dummies.[17]

In all models reported in Table 7.5, specification tests confirm the validity of our empirical approach. First, there is no second-order serial correlation in the first difference residual, as indicated by an insignificant m_2 statistic. Second, the validity of our instruments is confirmed by an insignificant Hansen *J*-statistic of over-identifying restrictions. The latter confirms the absence of correlation between the instruments and the error term. While this test offers support for the validity of the instruments *as a group*, Table 7.5 also reports the results of a difference in *J*-test to assess the validity of the specific instruments we employ for the bonus variables, EQUITY and ROA. The results show that these instruments are valid as we cannot reject the null hypothesis of exogeneity of the instruments. Third, as required by the partial adjustment framework, the coefficients on the lagged dependent variables (DD_{t-1}) are positive, statistically significant at customary levels and lie within the [0;1] interval. Next to confirming the validity of adopting a dynamic framework, the observed coefficients of previous DD on current DD also indicate the speed at which banks adjust towards their long-run level of risk. Our estimations show that sample banks close between 47 per cent and 46 per cent (i.e. 1 minus the coefficient on DD_{t-1}) of the gap between desired and actual risk in one year.[18]

[17] To avoid perfect collinearity between any bank-specific effects and the country fixed effects, we only introduce country dummies into the model specifications if we have at least three banks for a country.

[18] The adjustment speed in our sample of US and European banks is higher than the adjustment speed which Jokipii and Milne (2011) estimate for a sample of US banks. This could be explained by several reasons. First, Jokipii and Milne (2011) employ accounting data, while the inclusion of market data in the DD calculations makes our risk measure more forward-looking. Second, the banks in our sample are larger and may, hence, have more opportunities to alter their risk level more rapidly than smaller banks (e.g. via easier access to funding and capital markets). Third, while we employ annual data over a recent and relatively short time period, Jokipii and Milne (2011) examine bank risk using quarterly data during 1986–2008.

Table 7.5. Distance to Default and CEO Bonus Pay

	(1)	(2)	(3)	(4)	(5)	(6)
Panel A: Regression Results						
DD_{t-1}	*0.535****	*0.531****	*0.543****	*0.546****	*0.538****	*0.539****
	(9.06)	*(10.54)*	*(9.34)*	*(10.67)*	*(10.15)*	*(10.27)*
LGBONUS $_{t-1}$	*0.073****	*0.058****			*0.055****	
	(3.47)	*(2.83)*			*(2.71)*	
RELBONUS $_{t-1}$			*0.721****	*0.527***		*0.568***
			(2.89)	*(2.22)*		*(2.15)*
LEVERAGE $_{t-1}$	*−8.897****	*−10.246***	*−7.524***	*−10.278****	−2.289	−2.559
	(2.68)	*(2.31)*	*(2.35)*	*(2.72)*	(0.37)	(0.55)
ROA $_{t-1}$	21.032	*26.161**	23.544	*27.375**	19.085	28.603
	(1.27)	*(1.82)*	(1.37)	*(1.75)*	(0.73)	(1.10)
CHARTER $_{t-1}$	*−0.150**	−0.123	*−0.175***	−0.133	−0.126	−0.158
	(1.70)	(1.49)	*(1.98)*	(1.64)	(1.07)	(1.44)
NONINTSHARE $_{t-1}$	*−0.754****	*−0.802***	*−0.828****	*−0.814***	*−0.782***	*−0.878***
	(2.64)	*(2.47)*	*(2.81)*	*(2.52)*	*(2.40)*	*(2.41)*
SIZE $_{t-1}$	*0.131****	*0.134****	*0.131****	*0.138****	*0.112****	*0.112****
	(3.23)	*(3.79)*	*(3.14)*	*(4.26)*	*(2.78)*	*(3.20)*
INDEP $_{t-1}$					−0.122	−0.106
					(0.85)	(0.68)
DUALITY $_{t-1}$					0.332	0.365
					(0.84)	(0.95)
AGE $_{t-1}$					0.207	0.227
					(0.66)	(0.79)
Constant	*4.892**	6.223	3.690	*6.185**	−2.062	−1.798
	(1.88)	(1.61)	(1.46)	*(1.86)*	(0.34)	(0.40)
Observations	778	778	778	778	684	684
Number of banks	117	117	117	117	114	114
Year dummies	Yes	Yes	Yes	Yes	Yes	Yes
Country dummies	No	Yes	No	Yes	Yes	Yes
m_2- p-values	0.976	0.916	0.981	0.907	0.968	0.907
J-test p-values	0.437	0.426	0.317	0.485	0.526	0.572
Difference in *J*-test p-values	0.427	0.392	0.297	0.453	0.575	1.000
Panel B: Long-term Marginal Effects						
LGBONUS $_{t-1}$	*0.157****	*0.124****			*0.119***	
	(12.66)	*(7.88)*			*(6,63)*	
RELBONUS $_{t-1}$			*1.578****	*1.161***		*1.232***
			(8.13)	*(4.87)*		*(4.46)*
Panel C: H_0 Long-term Marginal Effects = Short-term Marginal Effects						
LGBONUS $_{t-1}$	*9.83****	*6.74****			*5.42***	
	(0.000)	*(0.009)*			*(0.020)*	
RELBONUS $_{t-1}$			*6.63***	*4.42***		*3.98***
			(0.010)	*(0.036)*		*(0.046)*

* significant at 10%; ** significant at 5%; *** significant at 1%.

Panel A reports regression results, obtained via the two-step system GMM estimator proposed by Blundell and Bond (1998) of the impact of cash bonuses on distance to default (DD), with Windmeijer (2005) corrected standard errors in parentheses. The model controls for bank characteristics, time dummies, and country dummies. LGBONUS measures log (1 + cash bonus). RELBONUS is the ratio of cash bonuses to total cash compensation. LEVERAGE is equal to total liabilities over total assets, ROA is pre-tax profits scaled by total assets, CHARTER is the ratio between the market value of equity and the book value of equity. NONINTSHARE is the ratio of non-interest income over total operating income. SIZE is the log of bank total assets. INDEP is the ratio of independent directors to board size. DUALITY is a dummy which is equal to 1 if a top executive is also the chairman of the board at the end of the fiscal year. AGE is the log of CEO age. When country dummies are included, there need to be a minimum of three banks in a country. The difference in *J*-test assesses the validity of the specific instruments we employ for the bonus variables, EQUITY and ROA. Panel B shows the long-term marginal effects computed for the compensation variables. The level of significance has been derived using a non-linear Wald test with χ^2-statistics reported in parentheses. Panel C shows the results of a Wald test of equality between the long-term and the short-term effect. χ^2-statistics are reported with the associated p-values in parentheses.

Interesting results also emerge when we examine the coefficients on the control variables. First, we observe a negative relationship between LEVERAGE and distance to default. This is consistent with the argument that risk-taking incentives increase with bank leverage as leverage improves the expected payoff from risky investment strategies (Jensen and Meckling, 1976; John and John, 1993). Second, banks that engage in non-interest income activities exhibit a lower distance to default, as suggested by previous studies on the impact of diversification strategies on banking risk. Third, larger banks are associated with lower risk-taking. While this result runs contrary to too-big-to-fail arguments (i.e. large banks face incentives to increase risk-taking in an effort to maximize the value of safety net guarantees), the positive coefficient on SIZE is consistent with larger banks having access to more diversified and liquid sources of funding as well as perhaps more advanced risk management techniques.

In columns (5) and (6), we re-estimate the models after including corporate governance variables. Due to missing board data for some banks, the sample size for these models is reduced by around 10 per cent compared with previous specifications. However, in spite of the reduction in the sample size, we can confirm the main finding of a positive association between CEO cash bonus compensation and distance to default.

The coefficients reported in Panel A of Table 7.5 measure the short-term impact of bank characteristics on bank default risk. Our empirical strategy also allows us to explore the long-term marginal effects of bonus payments on the target level of default risk which we report in Panel B (computed as the coefficients reported in Panel A divided by 1 minus the coefficients on lagged DD). For ease of exposition, we only present the long-term marginal effects on the bonus variables, and RELBONUS are both positive and highly significant showing that CEO cash bonuses also exert a risk-reducing effect on the level of risk which banks target in the long-term. Further, as shown in Panel C, the magnitude of effect of bonus compensation on the long-term effects are higher than the short-term effects (significant at below 5 per cent). This finding is particularly interesting, because it demonstrates that the risk effects of bonuses are higher in the long- than in the short-term. Evidently, bonuses are not a short-term compensation tool.

Additional Analysis: Dealing with Omitted Pay Variables

Cash compensation is not the only type of incentive compensation which could affect the risk preferences of bank CEOs. Both equity-like compensation such as options and stock grants (Smith and Stulz, 1985; Guay, 1999) as well as debt-based compensation such as pension arrangements (Sundaram and Yermack, 2007; Edmans and Liu, 2011) may equally affect managerial risk-taking.

However, data availability issues make it difficult to directly control for the various non-cash related components of CEO compensation. These data issues not only apply to some European banks (which seldom disclose information such as strike prices and expiry dates, which are essential to value CEO stock options), but to US banks. For instance, SEC rules only mandated the disclosure of CEO pensions and other forms of deferred compensation from spring 2007 (before that, the pension values of US CEOs have to be approximated using elaborate actuarial methods, as in Sundaram and Yermack, 2007).

Given these data issues, it is important that we can demonstrate that the positive relationship between distance to default and bonus payments we report is not driven by omitted pay variables. For instance, if bonus payments were a substitute for other forms of pay, CEOs with higher bonus compensation may receive fewer options grants. Given CEO options are associated with higher bank risk-taking (Mehran and Rosenberg, 2007; Hagendorff and Vallascas, 2011), options acting as substitutes for bonuses could provide an explanation for our results.

We use a variety of tests to exclude this and similar explanations for our main finding that bonuses lower bank risk. Using ExecuComp (for US banks) and annual reports (for European banks), we are able to determine for all banks if and when CEOs are given option grants. As a preliminary test for whether options and bonus payments are substitutes, we examine whether bonus compensation is lower when options are granted more frequently. We compare the values of the bonus variables in banks below and above the median of the sample distribution of the frequency at which CEOs are granted options. The results of this simple comparison show that bonuses and option grants act as complements rather than substitutes. In the group of banks above the median of the option distribution, bonuses make up 37 per cent of total CEO cash compensation while this share drops to 29 per cent in the group of banks below the median (difference is significant at 1 per cent).

To further rule out any remaining concerns that our results are driven by omitted pay variables, we run several additional tests and report the results in Table 7.6.[19] First, we exclude banks that grant cash bonuses but no stock options to CEOs during the sample period. At a minimum, this exclusion should eliminate any effects stemming from banks employing cash bonuses as a substitute for stock options. Second, we exclude CEOs who do not hold options during the sample period. It is conceivable that these CEOs will attribute more value to cash bonuses than CEOs with more varied pay incentive structures. The results of these additional tests are reported in the first four

[19] In the interest of brevity, Table 7.6 estimates models without controlling for country dummies. The addition of these dummies, however, does not modify our conclusions. For the sake of brevity these further results are not reported.

Table 7.6. Additional Analysis: Dealing with Omitted Pay Variables

	Excl.banks		Excl. CEOs					
	without CEO options		without options		Controlling for CEO options		Controlling for CEO fixed effects	
	(1)	(2)	(3)	(4)	(5)	(6)	(7)	(8)
Panel A : Regression Results								
DD_{t-1}	*0.490****	*0.483****	*0.499****	*0.487****	*0.491****	*0.505****	*0.444****	*0.432****
	(8.03)	*(8.27)*	*(8.37)*	*(8.81)*	*(8.2)*	*(9.36)*	*(6.57)*	*(6.25)*
$LGBONUS_{t-1}$	*0.065****		*0.069****		*0.095****		*0.060***	
	(3.18)		*(2.90)*		*(4.23)*		*(2.55)*	
$RELBONUS_{t-1}$		*0.715***		*0.704***		*1.080****		*0.602***
		(2.55)		*(2.46)*		*(3.93)*		*(2.07)*
$OPTIONS_{t-1}$					−0.129	−0.154		
					(1.10)	(1.37)		
$LEVERAGE_{t-1}$	*−7.464***	*−6.791***	*−10.388****	*−9.964****	*−9.272****	*−6.881**	*−12.383****	*−11.713****
	(1.99)	*(2.02)*	*(2.92)*	*(3.04)*	*(2.82)*	*(1.81)*	*(3.84)*	*(3.80)*
ROA_{t-1}	*45.283****	*50.783****	22.912	26.468	27.921	25.147	22.143	27.126
	(3.76)	*(3.22)*	(1.46)	(1.60)	(1.48)	(1.13)	(1.26)	(1.51)
$CHARTER_{t-1}$	*−0.245****	*−0.279****	−0.143	*−0.164**	−0.095	−0.135	−0.101	−0.111
	(3.16)	*(3.04)*	(1.53)	*(1.86)*	(0.94)	(1.06)	(1.01)	(1.07)
$NONINTSHARE_{t-1}$	*−0.859***	*−0.981****	*−0.704***	*−0.848****	*−0.820***	*−0.961****	*−0.702***	*−0.849***
	(2.46)	*(3.00)*	*(2.19)*	*(2.85)*	*(2.29)*	*(2.58)*	*(2.02)*	*(2.48)*
$SIZE_{t-1}$	*0.153****	*0.164****	*0.155****	*0.166****	*0.149****	*0.127****	*0.180****	*0.199****
	(3.02)	*(3.67)*	*(3.64)*	*(3.83)*	*(3.22)*	*(2.70)*	*(3.90)*	*(4.35)*
Constant	3.204	2.503	*5.886***	*5.444***	*4.948**	*3.329*	*7.513****	*6.677****
	(1.14)	(0.98)	*(2.09)*	*(2.14)*	*(1.89)*	*(1.10)*	*(2.78)*	*(2.58)*
Observations	710	710	713	713	584	584	669	669
Number of banks	106	106	107	107	117	117		
Number of CEOs							148	148

Year dummies	Yes	Yes	Yes	Yes	Yes	Yes	Yes	Yes
Country dummies	No	No	No	No	No	No	No	No
CEO fixed effects	No	No	No	No	No	No	Yes	Yes
m_2- p-values	0.983	0.966	0.844	0.810	0,771	0.713	0.965	0.948
J-test—p-values	0.646	0.622	0.517	0.553	0.850	0.847	0.275	0.360
Difference in *J*-test p-values	0.637	0.585	0.492	0.497	0.970	0.983	0.243	0.319
Panel B : Long-term Marginal Effects								
LGBONUSt-1	*0.128****		*0.137****		*0.186****		*0.108***	
	(9.86)		*(8.61)*		*(18.67)*		*(6.16)*	
RELBONUSt-1		*1.385***		*1.370***		*2.181****		*1.060***
		(6.43)		*(6.28)*		*(14.17)*		*(4.04)*
Panel C: H0 Long-term Marginal Effects = Short-term Marginal Effects								
LGBONUSt-1	*7.44****		*7.03****		*12.45****		*4.66***	
	(0.006)		*(0.008)*		*(0.000)*		*(0.031)*	
RELBONUSt-1		*5.40***		*5.64***		*10.01****		*3.22**
		(0.020)		*(0.018)*		*(0.001)*		*(0.072)*

Table 7.6 reports regression results, obtained via the two-step system GMM estimator proposed by Blundell and Bond (1998) of the impact of cash bonuses on distance to default (DD), with Windmeijer (2005) corrected standard errors in parentheses. The model controls for CEO fixed effects, bank characteristics, time dummies, and country dummies. LGBONUS measures log (1 + cash bonus). RELBONUS is the ratio of cash bonuses to total cash compensation. OPTIONS is a dummy equal to 1 if at *t*-1 the CEO holds a portfolio of stock options and at time *t* has been granted with further stock options. LEVERAGE is equal to total liabilities over total assets, ROA is pre-tax profits scaled by total assets, CHARTER is the ratio between the market value of equity and the book value of equity. NONINTSHARE is the ratio of non-interest income over total operating income. SIZE is the log of bank total assets. The level of significance has been derived using a non-linear Wald test with χ^2-statistics reported in parentheses. The difference in *J*-test assesses the validity of the specific instruments we employ for the bonus variables, EQUITY and ROA. Panel C shows the results of a Wald test of equality between the long-term and the short-term effect. χ^2-statistics are reported with the associated p-values in parentheses.

* significant at 10%; ** significant at 5%; *** significant at 1%.

columns of Table 7.6 and confirm our finding of a positive link between cash bonuses and distance to default.

Third, in an effort to control for the role of options in shaping the incentive structure of CEOs, columns 5 and 6 re-estimate the models with a binary variable (*OPTION*), which is equal to 1 if the CEO holds stock options at *t*-1 and has received an annual option grant at time *t*. This additional control variable, introduced as an endogenous regressor to our baseline specification, does not enter the model with a significant coefficient and, more importantly, we continue to report a positive link between cash bonuses and distance to default.

Finally, we follow an approach similar to Bertrand and Schoar (2003). We re-estimate our models after replacing the bank fixed effects with CEO fixed effects. CEO fixed effects remove the impact of unobserved heterogeneity across CEOs and control for various CEO specifics such as the structure of overall CEO compensation (including its various non-cash components). Obviously, CEO fixed effects only remove the influence of unobserved CEO characteristics that do not vary over time. However, many CEO characteristics such as CEO risk aversion, talent, and reputation, which are important in determining the overall structure of CEO compensation packages, are time-invariant in the short-term. We therefore argue that CEO fixed effects should be able to capture some of the differences between CEOs in terms of their non-cash compensation. In the last two columns of Table 7.6, we estimate the models with CEO fixed effects using CEOs with at least three consecutive years of data (yielding a total of 148 CEOs). The results show that we continue to observe a risk-reducing effect of cash bonuses.[20] Notably, since CEO fixed effects also capture individual characteristics (such as managerial talent) which may correlate with bonus payments, it is not surprising that the coefficients on the bonus variables are lower under these specifications compared with the models based on bank fixed effects.

The next two subsections examine settings in which we expect the risk-reducing effects of CEO bonus compensation to no longer hold. Specifically, we examine the impact of cash bonuses on default risk when banks are highly risky and when the bank regulatory environment is weak.

[20] Furthermore, in the case of stock options, DeYoung, Peng, and Yan (2010) report that in recent years the risk-taking incentives at US banks (as measured by the sensitivity of options to bank volatility) have become less volatile compared with the early nineties. Specifically, DeYoung, Peng, and Yan (2010) show that the value of risk-taking incentives is less volatile after 2002. Therefore, we also re-estimate the models after excluding the first two years from the sample period. We continue to observe a positive impact of cash bonuses on distance to default.

Bank Default Risk and the Risk-taking Incentives of Cash Bonus Compensation

Risk-taking incentives embedded in CEO compensation contracts are likely to emerge when banks are close to default. When a bank's growth prospects are poor, shareholders gain more from high-risk activities which maximize the value of the financial safety net than from attempts to increase low levels of charter value (Keeley, 1990; Park and Peristiani, 2007). At distressed banks, shareholder-designed compensation contracts will, therefore, promote risk-shifting to bondholders and regulators. Even though CEO cash bonus payments mitigate conflicts between shareholders and creditors and lead to less risky banks under normal conditions, we expect that cash bonus payments do not exert a risk-reducing effect for risky banks and may even increase bank risk at distressed banks (see Noe, Rebello, and Wall, 1996).

To test these expectations, we introduce an interaction term between the lagged distance to default and each of our CEO bonus pay variables, such that the target distance to default at time t ($DD^*_{i,t}$) is now determined as follows:

$$DD^*_{i,t} = \gamma_1 BONUS_{i,t-1} + \gamma_2 BONUS_{i,t-1} \times DD_{i,t-1} + \beta X_{i,t-1} + B_i \qquad (7)$$

The variable descriptions are the same as before. We substitute Equation (7) into Equation (4) and report the findings in Table 7.7. The coefficients on the compensation variables (LGBONUS, RELBONUS) now capture the effect of CEO cash bonuses on the target level of bank risk when DD_{t-1} equals zero (when a bank is financially distressed). The coefficients on the interaction terms between lagged DD and the bonus variables capture the effect of CEO cash bonus payments on the target level of risk when DD_{t-1} increases (when banks become less risky).

In all model specifications, the results are in line with our intuition. The coefficients on LGBONUS and RELBONUS are negative and statistically significant at customary levels. For cash bonuses, this means that the risk-reducing impact which we observed in the general sample gives way to a risk-increasing impact at highly risky banks. We therefore conclude that when banks are financially distressed, CEO bonus pay increases default risk.

Table 7.8 reports the short-term and long-term marginal effects for each of the bonus variables on DD. We distinguish between high-risk (banks located in the lowest 5 per cent percentile of the sample distribution of DD), medium-risk (median DD), and low-risk banks (banks located in the top 5 per cent percentile of the sample distribution of DD), and compute the marginal effects of bonus payments for each of the resulting groups. As previously, short-term marginal effects capture the change in observed default risk associated with a marginal change in the bonus variables, while long-term effects capture the

Table 7.7. Distance to Default, CEO Bonus Pay, and Financial Distress

	(1)	(2)	(3)	(4)
DD_{t-1}	*0.375****	*0.376****	*0.416****	*0.390****
	(6.07)	*(5.94)*	*(6.86)*	*(5.90)*
$LGBONUS_{t-1}$	*−0.106****	*−0.105****		
	(3.24)	*(3.03)*		
$LGBONUS_{t-1}*DD_{t-1}$	*0.035****	*0.035****		
	(4.99)	*(4.70)*		
$RELBONUS_{t-1}$			*−1.519****	*−1.614****
			(3.92)	*(3.64)*
$RELBONUS_{t-1}* DD_{t-1}$			*0.436****	*0.473****
			(5.35)	*(5.10)*
$LEVERAGE_{t-1}$	*−7.507***	*−9.564***	*−7.049***	*−12.121****
	(2.02)	*(2.17)*	*(2.14)*	*(3.02)*
ROA_{t-1}	23.203	29.458*	20.921	28.310
	(1.40)	(1.73)	(1.21)	(1.47)
$CHARTER_{t-1}$	−0.156	−0.141	−0.125	−0.100
	(1.64)	(1.52)	(1.39)	(1.09)
$NONINTSHARE_{t-1}$	*−0.695***	*−0.806***	*−0.760****	*−0.986****
	(2.30)	*(2.17)*	*(2.82)*	*(2.99)*
$SIZE_{t-1}$	*0.129****	*0.122****	*0.125***	*0.139****
	(2.85)	*(2.88)*	*(2.55)*	*(3.28)*
Constant	4.365	6.511*	3.934	8.576**
	(1.48)	(1.68)	(1.54)	(2.46)
Observations	778	778	778	778
Number of banks	117	117	117	117
Year dummies	Yes	Yes	Yes	Yes
Country dummies	No	Yes	No	Yes
m_2- p-values	0.378	0.441	0.340	0.361
J-test—p-values	0.791	0.831	0.891	0.923
Difference in *J*-test p-values	0.773	0.815	0.886	0.916

Table 7.7 reports regression results, obtained via the two-step system GMM estimator proposed by Blundell and Bond (1998), of the impact of cash bonuses on distance to default (DD), with Windmeijer (2005) corrected standard errors in parentheses. The model controls for bank characteristics, time dummies, and country dummies. LGBONUS measures log (1 + cash bonus). RELBONUS is the ratio of cash bonuses to total cash compensation. LEVERAGE is equal to total liabilities over total assets, ROA is pre-tax profits scaled by total assets, CHARTER is the ratio between the market value of equity and the book value of equity. NONINTSHARE is the ratio of non-interest income over total operating income. SIZE is the log of bank total assets. The coefficients on the compensation variables capture the effect of CEO compensation on the target level of bank risk when DD_{t-1} equals zero (when the bank is financially distressed). The coefficients on the interaction terms between lagged DD and the compensation variables capture the effect of CEO compensation on the target level of risk when DD_{t-1} increases (when a bank becomes less risky). The difference in *J*-test assesses the validity of the specific instruments we employ for the bonus variables, EQUITY and ROA. When country dummies are included, there needs to be a minimum of three banks in a country.

* significant at 10%; ** significant at 5%; *** significant at 1%.

effect that marginal changes in the bonus variable have on the unobservable target level of risk.

The results of Table 7.8 confirm the main finding in Table 7.7 that the impact of CEO cash bonuses on managerial risk preferences is different for financially distressed banks compared with non-distressed banks. Both long- and the short-term marginal effects indicate that, at the least risky banks, CEO cash bonuses reduce risk, while cash bonuses are risk-increasing at the riskiest banks in our sample.

Table 7.8. Distance to Default, CEO Cash Bonus Pay, and Financial Distress: Short-Term and Long-Term Marginal Effects

	LGBONUS		RELBONUS	
	(1)	(2)	(3)	(4)
Panel A: Short-term Marginal Effects				
HIGH-risk banks	*−0.070***	*−0.070***	*−1.077****	*−1.134****
	(−2.58)	(−2.43)	(−3.32)	(−3.10)
MEDIAN	0.031	0.032	0.189	0.240
	(1.58)	(1.63)	(0.83)	(1.05)
LOW-risk banks	*0.152****	*0.151****	*1.695****	*1.875****
	(4.74)	(4.73)	(4.62)	(4.96)
Panel B: Long-term Marginal Effects				
HIGH-risk banks	*−0.113***	*−0.111***	*−1.843****	*−1.859****
	(7.24)	(6.63)	(12.32)	(11.93)
MEDIAN	0.050	0.052	0.326	0.394
	(2.50)	(2.58)	(0.415)	(1.05)
LOW-risk banks	*0.244****	*0.246****	*2.907****	*3.075****
	(26.53)	(24.45)	(19.38)	(24.20)
Panel C: H0- Long-term Marginal Effects = Short-term Marginal Effects				
HIGH-risk banks	*6.22***	*6.03***	*9.56****	*10.05****
	(0.013)	(0.014)	(0.002)	(0.001)
MEDIAN	2.25	2.19	0.62	0.92
	(0.133)	(0.139)	(0.431)	(0.337)
LOW-risk banks	*14.31****	*12.53****	*10.56****	*11.19****
	(0.000)	(0.000)	(0.001)	(0.001)

Panel A shows the short-term marginal effects of the compensation measures on distance to default estimated in the regressions in Table 7.7 for three types of banks: high risk (5th percentile of the DD distribution), medium risk (median DD), and low risk (95th percentile of the DD distribution). Robust standard errors are reported in parenthesis. Panel B reports the long-term marginal effects computed as the ratio between the short-term effect and 1, minus the coefficient of lagged DD. A non-linear Wald test is employed to assess the statistical significance of the long-term effect with χ^2-statistics reported in parentheses. Panel C shows the results on a Wald test of equality between the long-term and the short-term effect and reports the χ^2-statistics with the associated p-values in parentheses.
* significant at 10%; ** significant at 5%; *** significant at 1%.

This is further demonstrated by Figure 7.2, which plots the long-term marginal effects of LGBONUS, RELBONUS for different values of DD (risk).[21] Figure 7.2 shows that the DD threshold at which the risk-shifting incentives exerted by LGBONUS and RELBONUS are completely constrained (i.e. where the marginal effect of bonuses on DD is ≥ 0) is equal to 2.667 and 3.414 standard deviations from the default point, respectively. However, if we stipulate that any negative impact of LGBONUS (RELBONUS) on DD is statistically significant (at the 5 per cent level), the value

[21] To facilitate comparisons between the long-term effects associated with the different compensation variables in Figure 7.1, we have rescaled the long-term marginal effects so that DD = 0 corresponds to −100.

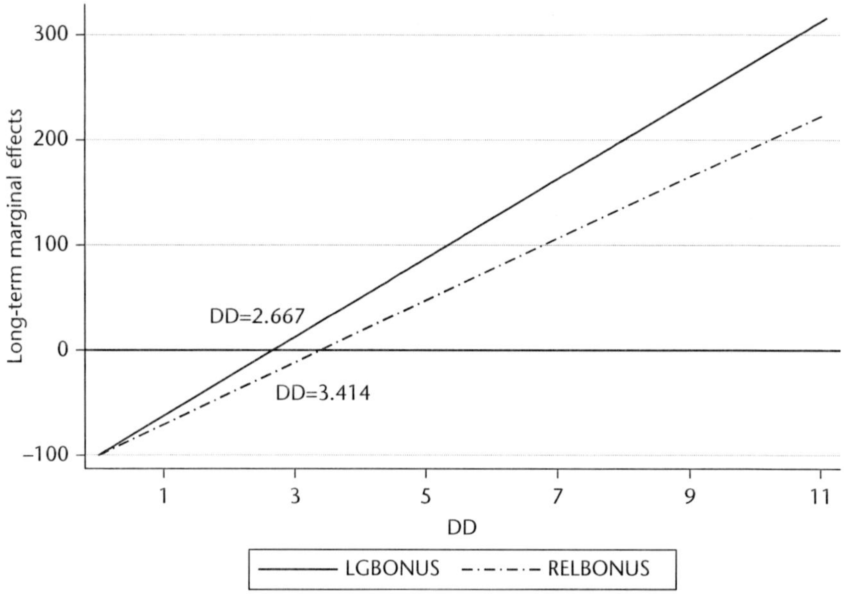

Figure 7.2. Distance to Default and the Long-Term Marginal Effects of CEO Bonus Pay Incentives

declines to 1.64 (2.32) standard deviations. Notably, only about 9 per cent (17 per cent) of banks in our sample show DD values below this value. Therefore, Figure 7.2 demonstrates that any risk-increasing effect of bonus payments is limited to the most risky banks in our sample, which approach the default point.

Conclusions and Policy Implications

In this chapter, we contribute to the ongoing debate over the optimal design of CEO remuneration policies in the banking industry. We analyse the impact of CEO cash bonuses on the distance to default of a sample of European and US banks. Our results show that banks where CEOs receive large bonus payments (both in absolute terms as well as relative to their total cash compensation) display lower levels of default risk. We interpret this finding as consistent with the shape of the CEO payoff function that underlies a typical cash bonus plan. Thus, CEO cash bonuses are solvency-contingent and, therefore, incentivize CEOs to avoid institutional failure. Additionally, the payoffs from cash bonus plans are typically linear functions of firm performance and are, therefore, not risk-rewarding for CEOs. Finally, our results show that the effect that bonuses exert on risk-taking is not confined to the short-term.

Bonus payments also affect the long-term level of default risk which bank CEOs target.

Critically, our analysis identifies a key factor which moderates the link between CEO cash bonuses and bank risk; namely, the overall riskiness of an institution determines the effectiveness of risk-taking incentives imbedded in CEO bonus contracts. We find that when banks are highly risky, CEO cash bonuses are associated with higher bank risk-taking.

Several policy implications derive from our work. First, our results suggest that increased shareholder involvement in setting executive compensation, for instance by giving shareholders a vote on compensation policy ('say on pay') as championed by the Dodd–Frank Wall Street Reform and Consumer Protection Act (Section 951), is unlikely to mitigate risk-taking incentives in the banking industry. We show evidence of increased risk-taking when banks are risky and shareholders have the most to gain from increasing the value of the safety net. When banks are highly risky, regulatory interference (e.g. with the aim of restricting certain pay practices) is the preferred alternative to more shareholder-oriented pay setting.

Second, since bonuses are linked to higher bank risk-taking at the riskiest banks, risk-shifting incentives at these institutions are only likely to be constrained if compensation practices more closely align the interests of managers and debt holders. To achieve this, Bolton, Mehran, and Shapiro (2010) suggest that CEO compensation in banking should be linked to CDS spreads on a bank's outstanding debt. Similarly, Edmans and Liu (2011) argue that increasing the share of deferred compensation and other debt-like forms of executive pay will turn executives into unsecured bondholders with a financial interest in the liquidation value of a firm and, therefore, mitigate incentives for CEOs to shift risk.

Finally, greater levels of disclosure of the terms under which CEO bonus plans are granted will clearly be beneficial. While our results convey a positive view of the role of CEO bonus payments in affecting bank risk, they can only be interpreted as first evidence. More details on the conditions of executive bonus plans (e.g. performance thresholds, caps, clawback provisions) are essential in order to better understand the link between bonus pay and bank risk. Future work should, hence, focus on the terms of executive bonus plans to derive bonus plan payoff functions for individual CEOs. A better understanding of the shape of individual CEO bonus payoff functions will be a vital stepping stone in order to understand how bonus plans should be designed to mitigate risk-taking by bank CEOs.

8

Systemic Risk Potential and Opacity in European Banks

Introduction

The global financial crisis, which erupted in the middle of 2007, has stimulated a growing debate on the importance of regulatory initiatives that increase bank transparency to safeguard against systemic instability (Beck et al., 2008; FSF, 2008). This chapter contributes to this debate by analysing how opacity impacts on the stock return co-movement and crash risk of a sample of European banks.

The regulatory view that bank transparency contributes to a safer financial system is generally supported by the existing empirical evidence by recalling the positive influence of transparency on the effectiveness of market discipline on bank risk-taking (Nier, 2005; Nier and Baumann, 2006; Bushman and Williams, 2007; Dermigüc-Kunt, Detragiache, and Tressel, 2008). Thus, the existing studies show that more transparent banks have more incentives to monitor their risk of default, by preferring a larger capital buffer for a given level of risk (Nier and Baumann, 2006), have a lower risk of large declines in market value (Nier, 2005), and lower stock return volatility (Baumann and Nier, 2004). Nevertheless, as argued later in this chapter, these studies are based on a narrow view of the effects that transparency may play on bank stability, and on a questionable definition of transparency at the firm level.

First, the focus on market discipline, and the associated benefits in terms of stability, discards an extensive set of theoretical analyses that points out how bank transparency may impact on stability well beyond the disciplining effect on the risk-taking strategies of bank managers, via acting on the distribution of information between banks and outsiders. More precisely, this distribution of information may generate sources of instability at the bank level, as it may influence a bank's exposure to market-wide (systematic) shocks (Jin and Myers, 2006; Veldkamp, 2006), its risk of crashes in the stock market (Jin and Myers, 2006), and the propagation of industry (systemic) shocks via contagion risk between banks or through correlated exposures across banks (Chen, 1999; De Bandt and Hartmann, 2000; Acharya and Yorulmazer, 2007, 2008; Acharya, 2009).

Second, the existing studies assume that an increase in the quantity of accounting disclosure reduces bank opacity, hence enhancing transparency; namely, banks that disclose a larger number of accounting items are identified as more transparent. Nevertheless, disclosure contributes to limiting opacity only when the disclosed information is available in such a way that renders banks visible and understandable. In addition, banks that provide the same set of public information to outsiders, by disclosing the same set of accounting items, may still differ in their degree of opacity when they show differences in the amount of private information retained by insiders (Cordella and Yeyati, 1998). Furthermore, although it may be valuable to improve transparency, more disclosure can also generate other (negative) effects on bank stability via information spillovers that occur when agents in the market interpret the information provided by one bank as a signal of a more general trend at the industry level (Kaufman, 1994; Tadesse, 2006). This is likely to occur especially when banks operating in the same industry have similarities in their portfolio holdings and the industry is deemed to be opaque (Wagner, 2010). Hence, information spillovers produced by public information may outweigh the benefits of transparency that may be generated by more disclosure.

This chapter extends the existing literature on opacity and stability by analysing how the distribution of information between banks and outsiders impacts on stock return co-movement and on stock price crashes for a sample of European banks. More precisely, we focus on a bank's stock return co-movement with respect to the market and with the rest of the industry. We employ these two types of co-movements as proxies, respectively, for a bank's exposure to systematic and systemic shocks. Furthermore, we extend previous studies by looking at the impact of opacity on different typologies on banking crashes; namely, we consider firm-specific stock price crashes (Jin and Myers, 2006) and crashes that occur under systematic and/or systemic stress conditions.

In our analysis, we relate bank opacity to the difficulty outside investors have in correctly evaluating bank assets (Flannery, Kwan, and Nimalendran, 2004), due to the amount of *private information* held by insiders and measured via the residual of an earnings prediction model. The analysis is based on a sample of 162 commercial banks and bank holding companies selected from 16 European countries. The European context provides an excellent frame for our tests since the banking industry is characterized by different types of banks operating in diversified institutional settings. Thus, European banks are likely to differ in terms of degree of opacity. Furthermore, over the sample period this industry has been strongly affected by technical progress, financial innovation, and global deregulation; namely, forces responsible for important changes in banking activities and their risks (De Nicolò et al., 2004; Rajan, 2005; Houston and Stiroh, 2006; Goddard et al., 2007; Boot and Thakor, 2009). As a consequence, the degree of bank opacity, as perceived by investors, is likely to have changed over time.

Our results show that the stock returns of more opaque banks tend to move more closely with the market and the rest of the industry; namely, they tend to be more exposed to systematic and systemic shocks. In the case of the co-movement with the market, however, we show that our results are entirely driven by the component of market returns correlated with industry returns. Therefore, industry factors, as suggested by the systemic risk literature (Acharya and Yorulmazer, 2008), are determining our findings. We also show that more opaque banks exhibit a higher probability of stock price crashes: the impact of opacity is particularly pronounced on bank crashes that occur under systematic/systemic stress conditions.

Two major regulatory implications can be drawn from our analysis. First, our results highlight the fact that removing bank opacity contributes to the stability of the financial sector. Second, together with the evidence of a strong positive impact of size on the exposure of banks to systematic and systemic shocks and on the likelihood of stock price crashes, these results support forms of the re-regulation of the banking industry based on limits on bank size, as invoked by several policymakers in Europe (see Dermine and Schoenmaker, 2010) and incorporated in the US Dodd–Frank Wall Street Reform and Consumer Protection Act of July 2010.

Opacity and Banking Stability—Literature Review and Hypotheses Development

Banks have been conventionally considered to be 'opaque firms', mainly due to their core business being focused on illiquid and informationally opaque loans (Morgan, 2002; Flannery, Kwan, and Nimalendran, 2004). Recent changes in the financial industry do not seem to have weakened this traditional wisdom as the financial developments of recent years seem to have encouraged banks to move into even more opaque business lines than lending activities (Rajan, 2005; Wagner, 2007). While the extant empirical literature agrees that this intrinsic opacity of banks may impact on financial stability by limiting the market discipline of risk-taking (Nier, 2005; Nier and Baumann, 2006; Bushman and Williams, 2007; Dermigüc-Kunt, Detragiache, and Tressel, 2008), an extensive set of theoretical studies suggests that the lack of transparency in banks may influence stability in many other ways.

An example is offered, outside the banking literature, by Jin and Myers (2006) that propose a model where firm opacity may contribute to increasing firm exposure to market-wide (systematic) shocks. In their model, limited information affects the division of risk between insiders and outsiders by shifting firm-specific risk to managers and increasing the co-movement of firm returns with market returns. The model also predicts that opacity increases crash risk at the firm level as managers tend to accumulate negative firm-specific information that will become suddenly available to outsiders. Hutton, Marcus, and Tehranian (2009) validate the model proposed by Jin and Myers (2006) by showing that US firms that engage in earning management practices (employed as a proxy for opacity) move more closely with the market and exhibit a higher likelihood of crashes. Overall, under the Jin and Myers (2006) framework, the stock prices of more opaque banks should move more closely with the market and should also be more prone to crashes. These results would have several relevant implications for bank stability.

First, as suggested by De Bandt and Hartmann (2000), systematic shocks may be at the root of multiple defaults in banking, leading to a systemic event; thus, bank opacity, by amplifying the co-movement with the market, may contribute to the instability of the system. Second, Pennacchi (2006) argues that existing capital requirements may have subsidized systematic risks, and concludes that as long as capital regulation and deposit insurance do not include a premium for systematic risk banks have incentives to take more systematic risks. Therefore, under the Jin and Myers (2006) framework, banks may have incentives to become more opaque to exploit the benefits associated with higher systematic risks. Third, as the risk of observing a crash in bank stock price is likely to be more pronounced in opaque institutions, regulatory initiatives aimed at reducing the opacity in the banking system may be particularly valuable to avoid bank failures and their negative systemic externalities.

The impact of opacity on bank stability may also be related to the role that the flow of information on banks plays on the magnitude of systemic risk; namely, the risk that many banks may fail together (Acharya and Yorulmazer, 2007, 2008; Acharya, 2009). This risk can arise from contagion between banks or from exposures that are correlated across banks (De Bandt and Hartmann, 2000; Acharya and Yorulmazer, 2008). Both channels of propagation of systemic shocks are affected by the presence of asymmetric information between banks and outsiders (see the surveys in Kaufman, 1994, and De Bandt and Hartmann, 2000; and Kaufman and Scott, 2003; Acharya and Yorulmazer, 2007, 2008; Acharya, 2009).

For example, a key mechanism for the propagation of shocks is information contagion, where the failure of a bank casts doubts on the solvency of others (Chen, 1999). This risk of contagion is likely to be particularly pronounced in an opaque industry where outsiders may have difficulties in distinguishing solvent from insolvent institutions. Furthermore, in the presence of informational problems, correlated exposures to aggregate risks may also arise more easily via risk shifting mechanisms. More specifically, Acharya (2009) shows that the presence of negative externalities generated by one bank's failure on the rest of the industry produces a systemic risk-shifting incentive where all banks undertake correlated investments with the effect of increasing economy-wide aggregate risk. In a similar vein, Acharya and Yorulmazer (2008) show that under the risk of information contagion, profit-maximizing bank owners are induced to herd with other banks, as the expected borrowing cost is minimized by investing in the same industry.

To recap, these theoretical arguments lead to the formulation of two testable hypotheses. First, the stock prices of more opaque banks should move more closely with the prices of the rest of the banks in the industry; in other words, more opaque banks should be more exposed to industry (systemic) shocks, as they should have more incentives to undertake correlated investments. Second, more opaque banks should be more prone to crashes under general stress conditions as they are likely to be more exposed to the negative externalities associated with stress scenarios.

The Sample

We select the banks included in our sample from the list of publicly traded banks in seventeen European countries (including the EU, Switzerland, and Norway) over the period 1991–2006. This list is drawn from Datastream International and we build the sample by focusing on banks with a primary interest in commercial banking, though they may be engaged in multiple business lines as is typical of modern financial firms. By jointly considering the specialization criteria provided by BankScope, and the primary SIC code as reported for each bank by Datastream International, we have excluded from our sample, due to their specificities in terms of core business, investment banks, banks focusing on medium/long-term credit lending, and non-banking credit institutions. Bank holding companies with an interest in commercial banking, as indicated by a primary SIC code equal to 602, have been retained within the sample. Furthermore, we have excluded from the analysis saving and cooperative banks, as they exhibit clear specificities in terms of business strategies due to their mutual ownership.

The application of the above criteria led to the identification of an initial sample of 210 banks, from which we eliminated thinly traded banks because our measures of co-movements are likely to be strongly affected by a lack of trading frequency. We identified thinly traded stocks by adopting a liquidity

Table 8.1. Sample Distribution by Country and Year

	Banks		Observations	
	Number	Percentage	Number	Percentage
Panel A: Sample distribution by country				
Austria	4	2.47	28	1.92
Belgium	6	3.70	39	2.67
Denmark	21	12.96	169	11.57
Finland	3	1.85	32	2.19
France	14	8.64	108	7.39
Germany	13	8.02	109	7.46
Greece	12	7.41	121	8.28
Ireland	3	1.85	37	2.53
Italy	27	16.67	256	17.52
Luxembourg	2	1.23	10	0.68
Netherlands	3	1.85	27	1.85
Portugal	7	4.32	68	4.65
Spain	20	12.35	205	14.03
Sweden	3	1.85	31	2.12
Switzerland	8	4.94	72	4.93
UK	16	9.88	149	10.20
Total	*162*	*100.00*	*1461*	*100.00*
Panel B: Sample distribution by year				
1994		91		6.23
1995		108		7.39
1996		113		7.73
1997		120		8.21
1998		106		7.26
1999		113		7.73
2000		121		8.28
2001		115		7.87
2002		116		7.94
2003		121		8.28
2004		116		7.94
2005		113		7.73
2006		108		7.39
Total		*1461*		*100.00*

Table 8.1 reports the number of banks and the number of yearly observations at the country level. The data refer to the sample period 1994–2006.

criterion based on the number of zero weekly returns in a year. More specifically, we require that a bank shows at least thirty-five non-zero returns (equivalent to around 70 per cent of the total returns) in a year, for at least four consecutive years over the sample period. Furthermore, this liquidity criterion has to be satisfied by at least two banks in a country. This requirement led to the removal of Norway from our sample.

The final sample includes 162 banks and a total number of 1,461 yearly observations. Panel A of Table 8.1 reports the distribution of the sample by country. This Panel shows that Italy (17.5 per cent), Spain (14.0 per cent), and Denmark (11.6 per cent) are the countries with the largest number of observations in the sample.[1] In Panel B, where we report the distribution of the sample by year, we show that the application of the selection criteria leads to a substantially stable number of observations over the sample period, especially after 1994.

Variable Construction

Measures of Stock Return Co-movement

In our analysis, we employ two measures of bank stock return co-movement that describe sources of instability in banks due to their exposure to systematic and systemic shocks.

The first measure recalls a conventional definition of systematic risk, captures the co-movement of banks with respect to the market, and is a proxy for the systematic sources of co-movement in bank stock returns. The second measure quantifies the co-movement related to banking industry factors and is used as an indicator of the systemic source of co-movement, which is generated by exposures that are correlated across banks (De Bandt and Hartmann, 2000; Acharya and Yorulmazer, 2008; Acharya, 2009). To estimate these two measures, we adopt an approach that aims to achieve two purposes. First, we employ a framework that allows us to directly compare the two measures and, second, we require the systemic co-movement to be smaller than the systematic co-movement, as the former is usually identified as a component of the latter (see, for instance, De Jonghe (2010), who defines systemic risk as an extreme form of systematic risk).

We start the estimation process by defining the market as the sum of non-financial and banking firms. Consequently, the systematic co-movement is defined as the R-square ($R^2_{M_{iT}}$) from the following regression model:

$$r_{it}=\alpha+\beta_{i_{L-NF}}r_{t_{L-NF}}+\beta_{i_{E-NF}}r_{t_{E-NF}}+\beta_{i_{I-NF}}r_{t_{I-NF}}+\beta_{i_{L-IND}}r_{t_{L-IND}}+\beta_{i_{E-IND}}r_{t_{E-IND}}+\beta_{i_{I-IND}}r_{t_{I-IND}}+\varepsilon_{it} \quad (1)$$

where the dependent variable is the return of bank i at time t, $r_{t_{L-NF}}$ is the return on the local market index of non-financial firms, $r_{t_{E-NF}}$ is the return on a European market index of non-financial firms, $r_{t_{I-NF}}$ is the return on a proxy

[1] The sample includes forty-three banks that have been delisted over the sample period in order to reduce the survivorship bias within the dataset; this bias could be particularly acute in the banking industry because of the waves of mergers and acquisitions involving European banks in the period under consideration.

for the international portfolio of non-financial firms (all the other world regions excluding Europe), while $r_{t_{L-IND}}, r_{t_{E-IND}}$, and $r_{t_{I-IND}}$ are banking industry indices observed for the same geographical contexts.[2] $\beta_{i_{L-NF}}, \beta_{i_{E-NF}}, \beta_{i_{I-NF}}$ are, respectively, a bank's sensitivity to the proxy of the local portfolio of non-financial firms, the European portfolio of non-financial firms, and the international market, while $\beta_{i_{L-IND}}, \beta_{i_{E-IND}}$, and $\beta_{i_{I-IND}}$ refer to the sensitivity to industry portfolios and ε_{it} is the residual term.[3]

The second measure of co-movement is obtained by re-estimating (1) only with banking indices. Thus, the new model assumes the following specification:

$$r_{it} = \alpha + \beta_{i_{L-IND}} r_{t_{L-IND}} + \beta_{i_{E-IND}} r_{t_{E-IND}} + \beta_{i_{I-IND}} r_{t_{I-IND}} + \varepsilon_{it} \quad (2)$$

The R-square of Equation (2), $R^2_{I_{iT}}$, is then an indicator of systemic (industry) co-movement. Notably, our approach leads to highly correlated measures of co-movement but, as explained in De Bandt and Hartmann (2000), the correlation between systematic and systemic co-movements is theoretically motivated by the presence of the broad channel of systemic risk. In other words, systematic shocks may be at the root of a systemic event as they may generate multiple defaults in the banking system. Therefore, both variables are indicators of the presence of forms of interdependency in bank stock returns and, thus, they may be interpreted as measures of the risk that shocks may simultaneously hit multiple banking institutions, putting the financial system under stress. Hence, systematic and systemic co-movements have to be correlated.[4] In an attempt to separate the relative importance of market-specific factors and industry factors for our results, we also analyse the implications of opacity on the share of systematic co-movement not correlated

[2] The use of readily available industry indices to estimate this model can generate two sources of spurious correlation in our measures of co-movement. The first is due to the inclusion of a European bank in the local industry portfolio, the second is related to the inclusion of the same bank in the European index. Therefore, to avoid spurious correlation, the local industry portfolio is constructed specifically for each bank in the sample by aggregating the remaining credit institutions operating in the same country. Furthermore, the European industry portfolio is constructed separately for each country as the value-weighted average of the remaining Datastream bank indices that compose the Datastream Bank Europe index.

[3] Our approach is inspired by the literature on synchronicity in stock returns (Morck, Yeung, and Yu, 2000; Jin and Myers, 2006) that normally estimates co-movement in stock returns via a two-index model with a local market factor and a global market portfolio (expressed by a US index). However, as banks that operate in European countries are likely to be affected by both regional and international factors (as a consequence of the increasing degree of globalization and integration of the area and the industry), we introduce, in the model, proxies for regional and international influences on bank stock return movements.

[4] This is further confirmed in the literature where indicators of systematic risk are sometimes employed as proxies for systemic risk (see Nijskens and Wagner, 2010; and Schuermann and Stiroh, 2006).

with systemic co-movement; namely, on the difference between the R-squares from Equations (1) and (2).[5]

Equations (1) and (2) are estimated via OLS at yearly intervals, and fitted on Tuesday to Tuesday weekly log stock returns.[6] Following the extant literature, we convert all the indices to local currencies and adopt the perspective of a local investor and a currency neutral framework. Furthermore, the R-squares are not directly employed in our regression analysis since they are bounded within the interval [0,1]. Thus we conduct our tests on their logistic transformation expressed as follows (Morck, Yeung, and Yu, 2000; Pietroski and Roulstone, 2004; Jin and Myers, 2006):

$$\Psi_{M_{iT}} = \ln\left(\frac{R^2_{M_{iT}}}{1 - R^2_{M_{iT}}}\right) \quad (3)$$

$$\Psi_{I_{iT}} = \ln\left(\frac{R^2_{I_{iT}}}{1 - R^2_{I_{iT}}}\right) \quad (4)$$

Table 8.2 reports the descriptive statistics for the R-square from Equations (1) and (2) and the related measures of co-movement for the full sample and by country. We draw three major conclusions from Table 8.2. First, the two models capture, on average, only around one-third of the total variation in bank stock returns: the average R-square from Equation (1) is approximately 37 per cent and declines to 31 per cent when we consider only banking indices. Second, these basic statistics highlight the presence of clear differences across European countries. For example, the average explanatory power of Equation (1) ranges from a minimum of approximately 19 per cent in Denmark to a maximum of around 59 per cent in Sweden. Focusing only on industry factors does not diminish the differences across countries, since we still observe a large gap between the minimum average value (11 per cent for Austria) and the maximum average value (54 per cent for Sweden) of the R-square. Finally, Table 8.2 shows that sizeable differences in the explanatory power of the two models are also visible within countries and this seems to indicate the influence of firm-specific characteristics on our measures of stock return co-movement.

[5] This difference is equivalent to the R-square of a regression model where the explanatory variables are the market indices that have been orthogonalized with respect to the set of industry indices.

[6] By fitting the models on weekly data we reduce the problems of non-synchronous trading and thin trading within the European context.

Table 8.2. Descriptive Statistics—Stock Return Co-movement

Panel A: R-squares

	$R^2_{M_{iT}}$ (%)					$R^2_{I_{iT}}$ (%)				
	Mean	Median	Std.dev	p1	p99	Mean	Median	Std.dev	p1	p99
Full sample	37.02	32.93	23.12	3.28	84.42	30.94	24.87	24.16	0.50	83.34
Austria	21.43	16.19	15.57	2.32	55.94	11.39	6.58	11.63	0.81	41.99
Belgium	50.38	55.33	23.52	7.30	83.64	43.93	42.49	25.94	1.76	82.86
Denmark	19.19	16.07	12.52	2.78	58.20	13.97	10.41	11.97	0.35	54.90
Finland	23.34	19.70	17.48	3.70	80.53	16.72	11.90	17.11	0.60	71.70
France	36.25	28.26	25.06	3.03	88.89	30.83	22.61	26.23	0.92	87.97
Germany	40.20	38.19	26.58	3.34	84.88	35.11	30.96	27.60	1.05	81.76
Greece	52.68	54.65	18.66	11.04	81.75	45.31	46.50	21.13	6.31	80.51
Ireland	50.60	53.36	18.65	16.47	81.61	46.49	49.67	20.12	9.80	81.29
Italy	36.38	31.32	20.67	5.39	79.44	30.57	24.89	21.95	0.39	78.94
Luxembourg	19.20	14.61	12.61	5.95	48.30	12.95	9.54	11.57	2.00	36.61
Netherlands	38.08	38.53	23.10	7.77	84.53	31.40	28.54	25.43	0.82	83.47
Portugal	33.04	26.75	18.89	4.31	72.49	26.84	21.57	18.84	1.17	69.51
Spain	31.96	26.97	22.13	3.74	88.91	23.15	13.34	22.73	1.19	86.68
Sweden	58.89	59.11	15.64	32.46	83.16	54.23	53.94	16.73	29.67	82.28
Switzerland	38.05	29.71	25.74	1.07	89.18	33.34	24.47	26.63	0.34	88.84
UK	47.62	49.96	20.82	5.84	84.00	43.32	46.20	21.99	2.15	83.34

Panel B: Co-movement measures—logistic transformation of the R-squares

	Logistic transformation of $R^2_{M_{iT}}$: $\Psi_{M_{iT}}$					Logistic transformation of $R^2_{I_{iT}}$: $\Psi_{I_{iT}}$				
	Mean	Median	Std.dev	p1	p99	Mean	Median	Std.dev	p1	P99
Full sample	−0.70	−0.71	1.22	−3.38	1.69	−1.20	−1.11	1.55	−5.29	1.61
Austria	−1.57	−1.64	1.03	−3.74	0.24	−2.53	−2.65	1.17	−4.81	−0.32
Belgium	−0.01	0.21	1.15	−2.54	1.63	−0.40	−0.30	1.40	−4.02	1.58
Denmark	−1.64	−1.65	0.85	−3.56	0.33	−2.22	−2.15	1.17	−5.66	0.20
Finland	−1.40	−1.41	1.01	−3.26	1.42	−2.11	−2.00	1.37	−5.11	0.93
France	−0.77	−0.93	1.37	−3.46	2.08	−1.26	−1.23	1.68	−4.68	1.99
Germany	−0.59	−0.48	1.42	−3.36	1.73	−1.03	−0.80	1.74	−4.54	1.50
Greece	0.11	0.19	0.85	−2.09	1.50	−0.26	−0.14	1.03	−2.70	1.42
Ireland	0.02	0.13	0.83	−1.62	1.49	−0.18	−0.01	0.92	−2.22	1.47
Italy	−0.69	−0.79	1.05	−2.86	1.35	−1.17	−1.10	1.45	−5.54	1.32
Luxembourg	−1.60	−1.77	0.78	−2.76	−0.07	−2.30	−2.26	1.13	−3.89	−0.55
Netherlands	−0.63	−0.47	1.18	−2.47	1.70	−1.34	−0.92	1.85	−4.79	1.62
Portugal	−0.85	−1.01	0.98	−3.10	0.97	−1.26	−1.29	1.14	−4.43	0.82
Spain	−0.95	−1.00	1.20	−3.25	2.08	−1.67	−1.87	1.55	−4.42	1.87
Sweden	0.40	0.37	0.70	−0.73	1.60	0.19	0.16	0.73	−0.86	1.54
Switzerland	−0.71	−0.86	1.40	−4.53	2.11	−1.16	−1.13	1.77	−5.69	2.07
UK	−0.17	0.00	1.03	−2.78	1.66	−0.45	−0.15	1.29	−3.82	1.61

Table 8.2 shows the descriptive statistics for the R-squares from Equation (1) and Equation (2) and for our measures of stock return co-movement. Specifically, $R^2_{M_{iT}}$ is the R-square of Equation (1), $R^2_{I_{iT}}$ is the R^2 of Equation (2), $\Psi_{M_{iT}}$ is the logistic transformation of $R^2_{M_{iT}}$, and $\Psi_{I_{iT}}$ is the logistic transformation of $R^2_{I_{iT}}$.

Bank Crash Risk

To measure bank crash risk we adopt an approach similar to Hutton, Marcus, and Tehranian (2009). They define a stock price crash as any firm return lower than the mean firm weekly return minus 3.09 standard deviations in a given year; this threshold is chosen because it identifies an event with a probability equal to or less than 0.1 per cent in the case of a normal distribution. In Hutton, Marcus, and Tehranian (2009) the measure of crash risk is constructed on the basis of the yearly distribution of residual returns, namely the residuals from an extended market model. They motivate the use of residual returns with the purpose of modelling the likelihood of firm-specific crashes not related to market-wide events as required by the Jin and Myers (2006) model. However, in the banking sector any type of crash is relevant for banking stability as it may determine negative externalities for other financial firms and the real economy. Furthermore, as pointed out by the systemic risk literature, the lack of transparency may affect the likelihood of crashes that are not firm-specific as they occur under extreme negative systematic and/or systemic conditions. Thus, in contrast to Hutton, Marcus, and Tehranian (2009), we initially define the crash event on the basis of the distribution of *actual* returns and only subsequently do we classify crashes via different typologies.

More precisely, similar to Hutton, Marcus, and Tehranian (2009), we start by defining a bank crash as any weekly return lower than the mean weekly bank return minus 3.09 standard deviations in a given year. Next, from the total number of crashes (*TCRASHES*), we distinguish conditional and unconditional crashes, namely, those related to *stress scenarios* as they occur simultaneously with crashes in the non-financial and/or in the banking sector (*CCRASHES*), from those that are bank-specific as they are not associated to any stress event in the non-financial and/or in the banking sector (*UCRASHES*). Thus, we consider whether a bank experiences a weekly crash simultaneously with any of the indices employed in Equation (1) and denote as a 'conditional' bank crash any extreme bank return that occurs simultaneously with an extreme return in an index. Then we classify the remaining number of crashes as unconditional (bank-specific) crashes.

For these three measures (total, conditional, and unconditional) of crash risk we create dummy variables equal to 1 when a bank experiences one or more crashes over the sample period and zero otherwise. Finally, these dummies are then employed as dependent variables in a set of logistic regressions to analyse the relationship between opacity, disclosure, and the probability that a bank suffers from one or more crashes in a given year.

Panel A of Table 8.3 reports the distribution of bank crashes. Overall, as in Hutton, Marcus, and Tehranian (2009) the frequency of crashes is much larger

Table 8.3. Crash Risk

	Total crashes (TCRASHES)		Conditional crashes (CCRASHES)		Unconditional crashes (UCRASHES)	
Panel A: Distribution of bank crashes						
Crashes in the bank year	Number	Percentage	Number	Percentage	Number	Percentage
0 Crashes	1,137	77.82	1,327	90.83	1,266	86.67
At least one crash	324	22.18	134	9.17	195	13.33
Total observations	1,461	100.00	1,461	100,00	1,461	100,00
Panel B: Bank performance in crash and non-crash weeks						
		Median		Median		Median
Bank Return Crash weeks		−13.70		−15.70		−12.26
Non-crash weeks		0.00		0.00		0.00
Panel C: Bank indices performance in crash weeks						
World bank index returns		−2.04		−6.60		−1.03
European bank index returns		−2.07		−12.71		−1.20
Country bank index		−5.81		−13.00		−2.00

[a] *Note:* Panel A shows the distribution of alternative definitions of bank crashes over the sample period. Panel B reports the median stock return in non-crash and crash weeks at the bank level. Panel C shows the returns for the set of banking indices employed in the analysis in crash weeks. Notably, the sum of conditional and unconditional crashes is not equal to the number of total crashes, as five banks suffer from both types of crashes in the same year.

than the number implied by a normal distribution.[7] This Panel indicates that around 22 per cent of bank-year observations suffered from a crash over the sample period. This frequency is larger than the percentage (17.1 per cent) identified by Hutton, Marcus, and Tehranian (2009) which have focused, however, only on unconditional crashes. When we distinguish the conditional from the unconditional crashes, we observe, in effect, that the frequency of crashes not related to stress scenarios (unconditional crashes) drops substantially to approximately 13 per cent.

Panel B of Table 8.3 confirms that our indicators indeed describe an extreme event: in all definitions of crash risk the median weekly return realized by banks in crash weeks is well below −12 per cent (with the minimum value of −15.7 per cent in the conditional crash weeks), while in non-crash weeks it is equal to zero. Thus, our crash indicator reflects a remarkable decline in bank value. Furthermore, to analyse whether conditional and unconditional crashes are capturing different typologies of extreme events in our sample, Panel C also reports the median weekly return for the banking indices during

[7] If the bank returns were normally distributed, the probability of crashes in any week should be 0.1 per cent and, in annualized terms, 5.07 per cent; namely: $1\text{-}(1\text{–}0.001)^{52}$.

both conditional and unconditional crash weeks.[8] We should expect a substantial difference in the performance of the banking indices across the different definitions of crashes, with much lower returns in the case of conditional crashes. The evidence offered by this Panel confirms this expectation: the weekly median returns for banking indices are much lower in the conditional crash weeks. This effect is particularly pronounced for the Local Country index (−13 per cent) and for the European index (−12.7 per cent): we interpret this as an indication that domestic and regional shocks, rather than international shocks, are the major sources of conditional crashes for European banks.[9]

Measuring Opacity

We define firm opacity as the difficulty outside investors have in correctly evaluating bank assets (Flannery, Kwan, and Nimalendran, 2004) and relate this difficulty to the quantity and quality of information hidden to those outside the firm (Bushman, Pietroski, and Smith, 2004). Accordingly, the degree of opacity is related to the amount of private information held by insiders that we measure through the residuals of an earnings prediction model. We argue that the degree of unpredictability of earnings is a proxy of the degree of asymmetry in the distribution of information between insiders and outsiders and, thus, of the degree of opacity of the firm as perceived by investors.

We estimate our proxies for private information following Park (1999) and Crouzille, Lepetit, and Tarazi (2004). We fit an earnings prediction model on publicly available data according to the specification described in the Appendix and employ the residuals obtained from this model to construct our proxy of private information. This proxy is the absolute value of the residual (PRIV_INF) and captures the magnitude of the asymmetric information component.

Control Variables

Our baseline models control for a set of bank-specific characteristics. First, to control for the influence of the quantity of public information on our

[8] We report only the value of the banking indices rather than all the indices in the market model to ease the exposition. Notably, only a very limited number of crashes occur when there is an indication of stress conditions in one of the market indices but not in one of the banking indices.

[9] As a further validation of our classification, we analyse the distribution of crashes by year as we expect a high degree of concentration of conditional crashes in a few time periods of extreme stress. By contrast, unconditional crashes should be more uniformly distributed over the sample period. The analysis confirms this intuition as, in the case of conditional crashes, a large share of events (68.8 per cent) is concentrated in 1997, 1998, and 2001, when the global market and the banking system suffered from extreme negative conditions.

measures of co-movement, we construct an index (*DISCLOSURE*) based on the amount of information disclosed by banks on key accounting data selected from the BankScope database. More specifically, we employ the disclosure index (DIS) originally proposed by Nier (2005) and Baumann and Nier (2004, 2006), which assesses whether a bank provides information on eighteen categories of key risk-related accounting items in its published accounts, as identified by the BankScope global format. This variable ranges from zero to one, with a higher value signalling a higher degree of accounting disclosure. We do not have a clear expectation on the direction of the impact of this variable on co-movement, as more disclosure might generate information spillovers, with an increasing effect on co-movement, or might increase transparency, resulting in a decrease in the co-movement of a bank's stock returns.

The second control variable is bank size (*SIZE*) measured as the log of bank total assets in thousands of euro. To the extent that large banks reveal or signal macroeconomic trends, their price movements can generate similar overall market and industry movements, thereby increasing co-movement (Pietroski and Roulstone, 2004). Similarly, Baele, De Jonghe, and Vander Vennet (2007) show that the largest banks are more exposed to systematic sources of risks, while De Jonghe (2010) identifies size as a key determinant of a bank exposure to systemic shocks. Outside the banking literature Hutton, Marcus, and Tehranian (2009) show that larger companies exhibit higher co-movement and crash probabilities.

Next, we control for the degree of bank functional diversification measured via the index of asset diversity (*DIVERSIFICATION*) recently proposed by Laeven and Levine (2007). The relationship between diversification and co-movement is unclear. Pietroski and Roulstone (2004) suggest that more diversified firms are less likely to track the performance of their primary industry affiliation and may be less sensitive to macroeconomic shifts. However, the departure of banks from a specialized focus is usually associated with an increasing exposure to systematic and systemic sources of risks in European banks (Baele, De Jonghe, and Vander Vennet, 2007; De Jonghe 2010).

An additional set of bank-specific control variables refer to the market-to-book ratio (*MTB*) and the growth in the size of the loan portfolio (*GROWTH*). Overall, we expect a positive relationship between the first two variables and co-movements. Specifically, as suggested by Hutton, Marcus, and Tehranian (2009) the MTB ratio places firms along a growth versus value spectrum and this is likely to be related to co-movement: growth companies tend to be more difficult to value for investors that may be tempted to use the common set of information available in the market as in the model proposed by Veldkamp (2006), with the effect of increasing the co-movement of these firms with the market and the rest of the industry. In a similar vein, faster growth in the loan portfolio leads generally to larger and more complex banks, which are likely to be more exposed to common sources of risk and to hold riskier and more opaque assets. We also control for the return on equity (*ROE*), as Hutton, Marcus, and Tehranian (2009) offer some (weak) evidence of a positive link between this variable and the co-movement of stock returns (and a negative effect on crash risk). We finally control for the impact of the organizational structure, by including a dummy equal to one for bank holding companies and zero otherwise (*BHC*).

Next, we extend the set of control variables to the features of the banking system observed at the country level. More precisely, we control for the degree of opacity of a banking system (*SYSTRANSPARENCY*), by constructing an index based on the information of banking supervision and regulation contained in the dataset originally employed by Barth, Caprio, and and Levine (2004), and further updated in 2005 and 2008.[10] More transparent countries show lower co-movement in stock returns (Morck, Yeung, and Yu, 2000; Jin and Myers, 2006) and lower crash risk (Jin and Myers, 2006). Therefore, it might be the case that more transparency in the banking system may generate positive spillover effects for individual banks and reduce co-movement and crash risk.

We then employ the log of the bank claims on the private sector, expressed in millions of euros and taken from the IMF database on international financial statistics, as a proxy for banking system size (*SYSTEMSIZE*). In the smaller sectors, banking firms are likely to have less opportunity to distance themselves from the other firms in the industry. This will probably result in an increase in the exposure of these firms to similar sources of variation, with a consequent rise in co-movement. Finally, we control for the impact of the bank market structure via the log of the number of listed banks included in our local banking market index (*LISTED*), since we predict that as the number of banks diminishes the probability to observe more synchronous prices becomes higher via an asset-based Herfindahl index of banking market concentration (*CONCENTRATION*).[11] In a more concentrated industry the degree of interdependencies between firms is likely to be higher, and news related to a firm can be perceived as more generally value relevant (Pietroski and Roulstone, 2004).

The final group of variables introduced in the regression analysis controls for country characteristics that are likely to influence the degree of

[10] From this database we combine two indices that describe the strength of external audit in banks and the transparency of bank financial statements. The banking system transparency index (SYSTRANSPARENCY) is defined as the sum of the scores assigned to a country on these two sub-indices, scaled by the sum of the maximum scores that can be achieved on each index. Hence, higher values of (SYSTRANSPARENCY) can be interpreted as a signal of higher levels of transparency (lower opacity) within a banking system.

[11] This index is computed at the country level and at yearly intervals, on the basis of information provided by the BankScope database.

co-movement in stock returns and the risk of stock price crashes (Morck, Yeung, and Yu, 2000; Jin and Myers, 2006). We employ the Good Government index (*GOODGOV*) from La Porta and colleagues (1998), following Morck, Yeung, and Yu (2000), Jin and Myers (2006), and Fernandes and Ferreira (2008); a proxy for macroeconomic instability (*MACRORISK*), the ten-year moving standard deviation of the annual growth in GDP expressed in nominal values of local currencies (Morck, Yeung, and Yu, 2000); and the domestic stock market volatility (*VOLATILITY*), measured by the annualized standard deviation of the domestic market index provided by Datastream.[12]

Descriptive Statistics and Correlation Matrix

Table 8.4 shows the basic descriptive statistics for the variables employed in the empirical analysis. For ease of exposition, in Panels A and B we replicate the summary statistics for, respectively, our measures of co-movement and crash risk.

Panel C focuses on the main explanatory variable, namely, the measure of private information. In general, the earnings prediction model performs well in predicting the future performance of banks; on average the absolute value of the residuals is small, being equal to 0.295 per cent. We interpret this finding as evidence that our proxies of asymmetric information are quite reliable in capturing the private information held by insiders, as further explained in the Appendix. Moreover, we observe substantial differences in the degree of private information across the sample; thus, the selected banks differ in their degree of opacity.

Panel D reports the descriptive statistics for the remaining variables and shows two interesting preliminary findings. First, banks show differences in terms of size and business models; thus our stringent selection criteria did not lead to a lack of variability in sample bank characteristics. Second, in spite of the trends towards integration in Europe, the descriptive statistics for SYSTRANSPARENCY suggest that there are still substantial differences across countries in terms of banking system transparency.

[12] Morck, Yeung, and Yu (2000) argue that firm-specific risk arbitrage is likely to be unattractive in countries that protect private property rights poorly and, therefore, informed trading will be correspondingly poor. Accordingly, they employ the Good Government index to capture the extent to which politicians respect private property rights at the country level, showing that synchronicity increases as this index decreases. This Good Government index is constructed as the sum of three indices measuring government corruption, the risk of expropriation of private property by the government, and the risk of the government repudiating contracts (Morck, Yeung, and Yu, 2000). Since this index is not available for Luxembourg, we assume that in this country it is equal to the score assigned to Belgium. To test whether this choice influences our results, we repeat the analyses by excluding Luxembourg from the sample; our findings remain largely unaffected.

Table 8.4. Descriptive Statistics

		N. obs.	Mean	Median	Std. dev.	P1	P99
Panel A: Co-movement							
Ψ_M	Logistic transformation of $R^2_{M_{iT}}$	1,461	−0.703	−0.711	1.216	−3.384	1.690
Ψ_I	Logistic transformation of $R^2_{I_{iT}}$	1,461	−1.195	−1.105	1.550	−5.286	1.610
Panel B: Crash risk							
TCRASHES	Dummy equal to 1 if a weekly return is lower than the annual mean—3.09 standard deviations	1,461	0.222	0.000	0.416	0.000	1.000
CCRASHES	Dummy equal to 1 if a crash occurs simultaneously with an extremely low return either in non-financial industry or the banking industry	1,461	0.092	0.000	0.289	0.000	1.000
UCRASHES	Dummy equal to 1 for bank-specific crashes	1,461	0.133	0.000	0.340	0.000	1.000
Panel C: Opacity							
PRIV_INF (%)	Absolute value of the residual of the earnings prediction model in (6)	1,461	0.295	0.189	0.434	0.005	2.011
Panel D: Control variables							
D1 Firm control variables							
DISCLOSURE (%)	Disclosure index from Nier and Baumann and (2006)	1,461	70.298	70.000	13.065	40.000	95.000
SIZE	Log of total assets in thousands of euros	1,461	16.447	16.360	2.272	11.778	20.577
DIVERSIFICATION (%)	Laeven and Levine (2007) asset diversity index	1,461	66.408	70.825	23.621	7.798	99.336
MTB	Market-to-book ratio	1,461	11.245	11.360	16.522	−27.407	34.329
GROWTH (%)	Loan growth	1,461	13.337	11.157	20.275	−40.191	83.517
ROE (%)	Return on equity	1,461	1.692	1.439	1.445	0.132	7.315
BHC	Dummy equal to 1 for bank holding Companies and zero otherwise	1,461	0.150	0.000	0.357	0.000	1.000
D2 Country control variable							
SYSTRANSPARENCY (%)	Index on banking system transparency	1,461	79.701	78.571	12.017	57.143	100.000
SYSTEMSIZE	Log of private credit in thousands of euros	1,461	12.902	13.124	1.280	9.878	14.795
LISTED	Log of the number of banks in the bank local index	1,461	2.306	2.398	0.658	0.693	3.258
CONCENTRATION	Asset-based Herfindahl index	1,461	0.121	0.094	0.089	0.025	0.349
GOODGOV	Good Government index	1,461	26.637	27.890	2.465	21.010	29.960
MACRORISK (%)	Ten-year moving standard deviation of GDP growth in nominal value	1,461	2.370	2.116	1.355	0.566	5.956
VOLATILITY (%)	Annualized domestic market volatility	1,461	3.863	3.101	3.388	0.612	16.126

The sample includes 162 banks from 16 European countries. Summary statistics on measures of co-movement and crash risk are during the period from 1994–2006, while time-varying bank characteristics are lagged one year; thus they refer to the period 1993–2005. Measures of synchronicity are computed annually on weekly returns. Measures of bank opacity are computed on the basis of the model described in the Appendix.

Table 8.5 shows the correlation matrix. To save space we omit from Table 8.5 country characteristics, with the exception of SYSTRANSPARENCY.[13] The correlation matrix does not provide any evidence in favour of our hypothesis of a positive relationship between PRIV_INF and stock return co-movement, while the impact on crash risk seems to be dependent on the definition of the extreme event adopted in the analysis. However, these preliminary findings are far from conclusive and have to be interpreted with care. For instance, our measures of stock return co-movement are clearly influenced by bank size: for both market and industry co-movement the correlation with size is well above 60 per cent. Furthermore, several other bank characteristics (i.e. diversification, ROE, and the MTB ratio) are significantly correlated with stock return co-movement. Thus, tests that do not control for differences in terms of bank fundamentals are unlikely to provide conclusive evidence.

The Impact of Opacity on Stock Return Co-Movement in Banks

The following subsections analyse the relationship between opacity and stock return co-movement. More precisely, the analysis starts from a baseline linear model that assumes the specification reported below:

$$Com_{i,j,t} = \alpha_0 + \beta_1 PRIV - INF_{i,j,t-1} + \theta' X_{i,j,t-1} + \sum_t \gamma_t Year_t + \sum_j \delta_j country_j + \varepsilon_{i,j,t} \quad (5)$$

where:

- $Com_{i,j,t}$ is either the logistic transformation of the R-square from Equation (1) or from Equation (2) or the logistic transformation of the difference between the two R-squares, for bank *i* in country *j* at time t;
- $PRIV - INF_{i,j,t-1}$ is our measure of opacity;
- $X_{i,j,t-1}$ is a $(k \times 1)$ vector of firm characteristics;
- $Year_t$ are time dummies;
- $Country_i$ are country dummies.

This initial specification is then modified in two ways with the purpose of assessing the robustness of our findings. First, we replace the country dummies with the set of country-specific characteristics previously described; second, we re-estimate the model by introducing, simultaneously, country dummies and country-specific control variables.

[13] The full correlation results are not reported for reasons of brevity.

Table 8.5. Correlation Matrix

		(1)	(2)	(3)	(4)	(5)	(6)	(7)	(8)	(9)	(10)	(11)	(12)	(13)	(14)
(1)	Ψ_M	1													
(2)	Ψ_I	0.934***	1												
(3)	TCRASHES	0.081**	0.068**	1											
(4)	CCRASHES	0.264***	0.244***	0.595***	1										
(5)	UCRASHES	−0.117***	−0.116***	0.735***	−0.090***	1									
(6)	PRIV_INF	−0.037	−0.050	0.072**	0.017	0.082**	1								
(7)	DISCLOSURE	0.367***	0.369***	0.012	0.123***	−0.089***	−0.177***	1							
(8)	SIZE	0.624***	0.621***	0.054*	0.157***	−0.066*	−0.176***	0.540***	1						
(9)	DIVERSIFICATION	0.184***	0.156***	0.083**	0.113***	0.001	−0.024	0.080**	0.244***	1					
(10)	ROE	0.082**	0.079**	0.034	0.023	0.015	0.228***	0.063*	0.046	−0.012	1				
(11)	MTB	0.111***	0.112***	0.014	0.058*	−0.017	0.049	0.099***	−0.053*	−0.128***	0.084**	1			
(12)	GROWTH	0.003	0.015	−0.009	0.010	−0.021	−0.060**	−0.035	−0.108***	−0.006	0.045	0.137***	1		
(13)	BHC	0.145***	0.155***	0.011	0.046	−0.024	−0.012	0.114***	0.212***	0.045	0.076**	−0.015	−0.015	1	
(14)	SYSTRANSPARENCY	−0.091***	−0.064*	−0.045	−0.071**	−0.001	0.001	−0.061*	0.001	−0.261***	0.035	−0.095***	−0.026	0.118***	1

Table 8.5 shows pairwise correlation coefficients computed over 1,461 observations for a sample of 162 banks. Co-movement and crash risk have been defined over the period 1994–2006, while bank characteristics are lagged one year. Thus, they refer to the period 1993–2005.

As, similar to Hutton, Marcus, and Tehranian (2009) and Haggard, Xiumin, and Pereira (2008), our focus is on the cross-sectional relationship between opacity and co-movements, we do not include bank fixed effects in the regression models. Notably, opacity is likely to be a persistent characteristic in a bank; thus, within-firm variation over a short time interval might be simply expressing noise rather than capturing effective real changes in these characteristics at the firm level. Furthermore, as suggested by Stiroh (2006) the massive consolidation process over the last two decades makes the interpretation of an unobservable fixed effect impractical for many large financial institutions.[14]

The analysis of the cross-sectional relationship between opacity and co-movements is conducted by means of two approaches. Initially, we estimate a pooled regression model via ordinary least squares with robust standard errors, clustered at the bank level to control for any firm-specific effects that lead to any dependence in the residuals over time (Petersen, 2009). This approach assigns equal importance to within and between firm variations as it treats the same banks observed in different years of the sample period as different sample units.

Then, we re-run the analysis by removing the influence of within-firm variation from our sample. Specifically, we estimate a between-regression model with robust standard errors that is equivalent to estimating Equation (5), by employing the average values of the variables and omitting year dummies. In this latter approach, therefore, the number of observations in the model is equivalent to the number of banks in the sample (162).

Pooled Regression

Panel A of Table 8.6 shows the estimation results for the pooled regression models. The first three columns report the results when the co-movement with the market is employed as the dependent variable, while the next three columns focus on our measure of industry co-movement. For both measures of stock return co-movement, we first estimate the model described in Equation (5), then we extend the analysis to consider country-specific control variables.

In all specifications, our results show that banks whose performance are more difficult to predict (captured by the PRIV_INF variable) tend to move more closely with the market and the industry. Hence, an increase in the

[14] In addition, some country control variables are constant over the sample period (for example, the variable GOODGOV) or show very low within-country variation (for example, the SYSTRANSPARENCY variable).

Table 8.6. Pooled Regression—Stock Return Co-Movement and Opacity in European Banks

	(1)	(2)	(3)	(4)	(5)	(6)	(7)	(8)	(9)
	SYSTEMATIC CO-MOVEMENT			SYSTEMIC CO-MOVEMENT			UNCORRELATED SYSTEMATIC CO-MOVEMENT		
Panel A: Regression analysis									
PRIV_INF$_{t-1}$	*22.389****	*30.181****	*22.110****	*22.712***	*33.587****	*23.072***	4.376	0.879	3.592
	(2.94)	*(3.92)*	*(2.95)*	*(2.33)*	*(3.33)*	*(2.41)*	(0.45)	(0.09)	(0.36)
DISCLOSURE $_{t-1}$	0.055	−0.165	0.033	−0.104	−0.212	−0.144	0.368	0.173	0.357
	(0.18)	(0.53)	(0.11)	(0.31)	(0.59)	(0.45)	(1.04)	(0.56)	(1.00)
SIZE $_{t-1}$	*0.353****	*0.384****	*0.366****	*0.459****	*0.490****	*0.473****	*−0.105****	*−0.101****	*−0.104****
	(16.87)	*(18.00)*	*(17.51)*	*(18.77)*	*(19.53)*	*(19.57)*	*(5.28)*	*(5.74)*	*(5.22)*
DIVERSIFICATION $_{t-1}$	−0.078	−0.098	−0.168	−0.195	−0.211	−0.274	0.078	0.087	0.079
	(0.45)	(0.51)	(0.97)	(0.99)	(0.94)	(1.37)	(0.51)	(0.60)	(0.50)
ROE $_{t-1}$	*1.181****	*1.024****	*1.302****	*1.206****	*0.983***	*1.254****	−0.236	−0.282	−0.093
	(3.69)	*(2.80)*	*(4.11)*	*(3.32)*	*(2.27)*	*(3.45)*	(0.61)	(0.71)	(0.22)
MTB $_{t-1}$	*0.119****	*0.138****	*0.110****	*0.146****	*0.170****	*0.139****	0.006	−0.004	0.006
	(2.76)	*(3.04)*	*(2.82)*	*(2.79)*	*(3.09)*	*(2.86)*	(0.20)	(0.14)	(0.19)
GROWTH $_{t-;t-1}$	0.155	0.180	0.103	*0.330***	*0.376***	*0.278**	−0.260	−0.298	−0.249
	(1.13)	(1.29)	(0.76)	*(2.06)*	*(2.18)*	*(1.77)*	(1.46)	(1.63)	(1.38)
BHC $_{t-1}$	0.111	*0.157**	0.098	0.158	*0.238***	0.148	−0.099	−0.094	−0.100
	(1.08)	*(1.71)*	(0.96)	(1.20)	*(2.06)*	(1.14)	(0.87)	(1.02)	(0.90)
SYSTRANSPARENCY$_{t-1}$		−0.562	−0.802		−0.867	−0.995		0.060	0.101
		(1.29)	(1.50)		(1.60)	(1.50)		(0.14)	(0.15)
SYSTEMSIZE $_{t-1}$		−0.021	−0.050		−0.069	0.015		*−0.057***	0.091
		(0.40)	(0.48)		(1.03)	(0.12)		*(2.27)*	(1.17)
LISTED $_{t}$		0.072	*0.536****		0.149	*0.374***		−1.020	2.878
		(0.96)	*(3.63)*		(1.45)	*(2.08)*		(0.30)	(0.53)
CONCENTRATION $_{t-1}$		*1.673***	−0.191		*2.017***	0.767		0.036	−0.057
		(2.57)	(0.23)		*(2.36)*	(0.71)		(0.71)	(0.39)

	(1)	(2)	(3)	(4)	(5)	(6)	(7)	(8)	(9)
GOODGOV		*−0.078****	−0.039		*−0.070***	*−0.153***		0.226	−1.111
		(2.89)	(0.74)		*(2.04)*	*(1.99)*		(0.39)	(1.03)
MACRORISK $_{t-1}$		0.640	−3.978		1.953	*−8.570**		*−0.139**	*0.328**
		(0.21)	(1.02)		(0.53)	*(1.71)*		*(1.83)*	*(1.76)*
VOLATILITY $_t$		*4.620****	*2.782***		*5.006***	*3.645***		−2.094	−3.233**
		(2.73)	*(2.13)*		*(2.59)*	*(2.43)*		(1.48)	(2.06)
Constant	*−7.924****	*−4.818****	*−4.899****	*−10.263****	*−6.641****	*−4.561****	*−1.321****	0.096	*−3.221***
	(25.12)	*(6.08)*	*(3.94)*	*(26.85)*	*(6.85)*	*(2.63)*	*(4.31)*	(0.14)	*(2.03)*
Observations	1461	1461	1461	1461	1461	1461	1461	1461	1461
Adjusted R-squared	0.580	0.552	0.589	0.592	0.555	0.598	0.094	0.085	0.095
Time dummies	Yes	Yes	Yes	Yes	Yes	Yes	Yes	Yes	Yes
Country dummies	Yes	No	Yes	Yes	No	Yes	Yes	No	Yes

Robust t statistics in parentheses; ***(**; *) significant at 1% (5%; 1%)

Panel B: Economic relevance on the impact of private information on R-squares (p.p)

PRIV_INF$_t$			+ 1.33			+ 1.13			

Table 8.6 reports the results of the regression model described in Equation (5). From columns 1 (4) to 3 (6) the dependent variable is the logistic transformation of the R-square of the model 1 (2). In the last three columns the dependent variable is the logistic transformation of the difference between the R-square from models 1 and the R-square from model 2. The explanatory variables include the absolute value of the residuals of the earnings prediction model (*PRIV_INF*), the disclosure index (*DISCLOSURE*), the log of total assets in thousands of euros (*SIZE*), the asset diversity index (*DIVERSIFICATION*) originally proposed by Laeven and Levine (2007), the return on equity (*ROE*), the market-to-book ratio (*MTB*), the log growth rate of loans (*GROWTH*), and a dummy equal to 1 for bank holding companies (*BHC*). Country control variables include an index of banking system transparency (*SYSTRANSPARENCY*), the log of banking credit to private sector (*SYSTEMSIZE*), the (log) number of domestic listed banks in a given country (*LISTED),* an asset-based Herfindahl index of bank concentration (*CONCENTRATION*), the Good Government index (*GOODGOV*) from La Porta and colleagues (1998), the ten-year moving window standard deviation in annual GDP growth measured in local currency (*MACRORISK*), the annualized domestic market volatility (*VOLATILITY*). The models are estimated via OLS; standard errors are robust to heteroscedasticity and clustered at the level of the firm. The dependent variables are measured over the sample period from 1994 to 2006. Lagged variables refer to the period 1993–2005. Continuous variables have been winsorized at the 1 per cent level.

asymmetric distribution of the information between insiders and outsiders produces an increase in co-movement.

In terms of the other variables, we observe a positive and highly significant influence of size on co-movement; namely, the largest banks move more closely with the market and the rest of the industry. This is consistent with the hypothesis of Pietroski and Roulstone (2004), that since large firms reveal or signal macroeconomic trends, their price movements can generate similar overall market and industry movements and this increases co-movement. Furthermore, this result confirms that the largest banks are more exposed to common shocks and, thus, are more likely to generate negative externalities on systemic stability (Baele, De Jonghe, and Vander Vennet, 2007; De Jonghe, 2010).

A positive influence on our measures of co-movement is also played by the degree of profitability (ROE) and by the MTB ratio, providing some indications that banks that benefit from larger growth opportunities seem to be more difficult to value by investors. Industry co-movements tend also to increase as banks experiment with more aggressive growth strategies.

When we introduce in the models country characteristics, we observe that only a few of these variables exercises a statistically significant influence on stock return co-movements. More precisely, when the dependent variable is the co-movement with the market ($\Psi_{M_{iT}}$), only the domestic market volatility shows, consistently, a significant and positive coefficient, while the effect played by the remaining control variables, namely the magnitude and the significance levels of their coefficients, is generally affected by the model specification. When the analysis employs the co-movement with the industry ($\Psi_{I_{iT}}$) as a dependent variable, we observe that a statistically significant coefficient is also assigned to the good governance index in both specifications; namely, a better institutional setting is associated with less co-movement in bank stock returns. This result is broadly in line with the evidence of the importance of country transparency in driving the co-movements of the stock market (Jin and Myers, 2006).

Our two measures of stock return co-movement are highly correlated. Thus, the fact that we observe similar findings for systematic and systemic co-movement may simply imply that there is a common component that is driving our results; namely, it is likely that the results for our proxy for systematic co-movement are also determined by the importance of industry factors. This would imply that bank opacity does not play any direct effect on systematic co-movement but only an indirect influence based on industry factors, as suggested by the literature on information contagion. The last three columns confirm this conjecture. In these columns we report the results for the models estimated by using as the dependent variable (the logistic transformation of) the difference between the R-square from Equation (1) and the

R-square from Equation (2). This difference thus captures the systematic co-movement uncorrelated with the systemic co-movement. These models show that our proxy for opacity does not have a significant influence on the modified systematic co-movement. Therefore, the results reported from columns 1–3 are entirely driven by the component of $\Psi_{M_{iT}}$ correlated with $\Psi_{I_{iT}}$; that is, in general our findings show that the co-movement in bank stock returns is due to industry factors, as suggested by the theoretical studies on systemic risk (Acharya, 2009; Wagner, 2010).

Finally, Panel B of Table 8.6 offers some evidence on the economic relevance of our results. Similar to Hutton, Marcus, and Tehranian (2009) we compute the change in the R-squares (co-movement) when our private information variable moves from the 25th to the 75th percentile of the sampling distribution.[15] To ease the exposition of our findings, we run this analysis only for the models with the largest set of control variables; that is, the models reported in columns 3 and 6.

This analysis shows that the effects played by bank opacity on stock return co-movement are not trivial. The shift of the private information variable produces an increase in the R-square with the total market of 1.33 percentage points and an increase in the R-square computed at the industry level of 1.13 percentage points. As noted earlier, however, both effects of opacity are driven by industry factors.[16] Notably, in a similar exercise, Hutton, Marcus, and Tehranian (2009) conclude that an increase in opacity induces an increase in the R-square of about 1.2 percentage points in their sample of US firms.

Overall, therefore, our analysis shows that bank opacity is an important determinant in driving the co-movement of a bank's stock return with the market and the rest of the industry. However, the increase in the co-movement with the market is entirely driven by the market component correlated with industry factors, that is, by the systemic component of systematic risk.

[15] As the coefficients of the regression models capture the impact of the explanatory variables on our measures of co-movement and not on the R-square, we initially derive the effect produced by a change from the 25th to the 75th percentile of a given variable on our dependent variable. Next, we add this change to the mean of the sample distribution of each dependent variable. Finally, to compute the change in terms of R-square, we convert the mean of the co-movement distribution before and after the change in the related R-squares by inverting formulas (3) and (4); namely, for each value of co-movement we derive the R-square as follows:

$$R^2_{iT} = \left[\frac{\exp(\psi)}{\exp(\psi) + 1}\right]$$

[16] The implied R-squares from the average values of ψ_M and ψ are equal, respectively, to 33.1 per cent and 22.8 per cent. As a consequence, in relative terms, the increase produced by a shift in opacity on the R-square with the market is about 4.2 per cent against a value of 5.2 per cent for the R-square computed in the industry regression.

Between Regression

In this section we extend our empirical framework by removing from our results the influence of *within*-firm variation and by focusing on cross-sectional differences *between* banks. As in the case of the pooled regression models, we present the results for varying specifications that differ in the way we control for country characteristics.[17]

Table 8.7 confirms the importance of opacity in driving the co-movement in bank stock returns: the impact of bank opacity tends to be even larger in the between regressions than when within-firm variation is maintained in the analysis. This is clearly outlined in Panel B, where we report the change in the R-squares when the private information variable moves from the 25th to 75th of the sampling distribution for the models reported in columns 3 and 6. We observe that, under the between-regression approach, the increases in the R-squares (market and industry) are systemically larger than 2 percentage points (with a maximum of 2.5 per cent in the case of industry co-movement) versus values below 1.4 percentage points when we estimate pooled regressions. Thus, by removing within-firm variation from our sample—which may be influenced by noise, especially in the short run—we obtain an even clearer picture of the importance of bank opacity on stock return co-movement. Furthermore, the last three columns of Table 8.7, where we estimate the model with the systematic component not related to industry factors as the dependent variable, confirm that the impact of opacity on the co-movement in bank stock returns is motivated by industry factors; namely, investors employ industry-related information to value more opaque banks.

In terms of the other variables, the between analysis confirms the importance of bank size on co-movement but it appears that other firm-specific characteristics do not have any significant influence on $\Psi_{M_{iT}}$ and $\Psi_{I_{iT}}$ in our sample. Similarly, this analysis does not provide any robust indication of an influence of country characteristics on co-movement. An exception is the degree of (asset) concentration in the banking industry: banks that operate in more concentrated systems tend to move more closely with the remaining banks in the industry.

In summary, this section reinforces our two major conclusions. First, bank opacity increases the degree of stock return co-movements. Second, this result is driven by industry factors rather than by market-specific factors.

[17] We also repeat the between analysis by estimating the models without country dummies, and achieve qualitatively similar results. These tests are not reported for the sake of brevity.

Table 8.7. Between Regression—Stock Return Co-Movement and Opacity in European Banks

	(1)	(2)	(3)	(4)	(5)	(6)	(7)	(8)	(9)
	SYSTEMATIC CO-MOVEMENT			SYSTEMIC CO-MOVEMENT			UNCORRELATED SYSTEMATIC CO-MOVEMENT		
Panel A: Regression analysis									
$PRIV\_INF_{t-1}$	*58.994***	*67.844****	*55.477***	*83.452****	*95.337****	*85.560***	6.379	−7.412	−1.164
	(2.28)	*(2.92)*	*(2.06)*	*(2.66)*	*(3.06)*	*(2.43)*	(0.36)	(0.41)	(0.07)
$DISCLOSURE_{t-1}$	0.122	−0.413	0.086	−0.188	−0.458	−0.279	1.003	0.240	*1.177**
	(0.20)	(0.76)	(0.14)	(0.27)	(0.71)	(0.41)	(1.57)	(0.51)	*(1.92)*
$SIZE_{t-1}$	*0.361****	*0.403****	*0.381****	*0.475****	*0.520****	*0.496****	*−0.102****	*−0.099****	*−0.107****
	(13.53)	*(14.45)*	*(12.89)*	*(14.55)*	*(14.58)*	*(13.69)*	*(3.94)*	*(4.19)*	*(4.10)*
$DIVERSIFICATION_{t-1}$	−0.187	−0.233	−0.235	−0.291	−0.459	−0.331	0.036	0.259	0.014
	(0.75)	(0.83)	(0.82)	(0.93)	(1.27)	(0.93)	(0.19)	(1.30)	(0.07)
ROE_{t-1}	0.890	0.578	0.874	1.153	0.541	0.896	−0.200	0.106	0.219
	(0.98)	(0.62)	(0.96)	(1.11)	(0.47)	(0.86)	(0.40)	(0.18)	(0.40)
MTB_{t-1}	0.048	0.075	0.051	0.056	0.094	0.065	−0.011	−0.032	−0.017
	(0.99)	(1.26)	(1.06)	(0.95)	(1.27)	(1.08)	(0.56)	(1.21)	(0.87)
$GROWTH_{t-;t-1}$	0.815	1.020	1.088	1.085	*1.517**	1.125	−0.281	−0.732	0.098
	(1.24)	(1.57)	(1.56)	(1.28)	*(1.72)*	(1.37)	(0.61)	(1.51)	(0.21)
BHC_{t-1}	0.113	0.110	0.083	0.125	0.189	0.112	−0.071	−0.108	−0.087
	(0.87)	(0.91)	(0.61)	(0.80)	(1.27)	(0.68)	(0.51)	(0.84)	(0.69)
$SYSTRANSPARENCY_{t-1}$		−0.734	1.191		−1.089	−1.945		0.591	3.246
		(0.83)	(0.30)		(0.98)	(0.37)		(0.75)	(0.97)
$SYSTEMSIZE_{t-1}$		0.085	*−0.630**		0.081	−0.258		*−0.068***	*0.293**
		(1.23)	*(1.66)*		(0.89)	(0.44)		*(2.03)*	*(1.88)*
$LISTED_{t}$		0.031	1.094		0.136	0.286		−7.292	−9.291
		(0.32)	(1.38)		(0.92)	(0.25)		(1.44)	(0.89)
$CONCENTRATION_{t-1}$		*2.945***	*4.282**		*3.784***	*5.785**		−0.034	−0.447
		(2.58)	*(1.72)*		*(2.57)*	*(1.92)*		(0.61)	(1.36)

(continued)

Table 8.7. Continued

	(1)	(2)	(3)	(4)	(5)	(6)	(7)	(8)	(9)
	SYSTEMATIC CO-MOVEMENT			SYSTEMIC CO-MOVEMENT			UNCORRELATED SYSTEMATIC CO-MOVEMENT		
GOODGOV		*−0.095***	0.117		*−0.078**	−0.176		−1.309	−3.910
		(2.55)	(0.51)		*(1.68)*	(0.55)		(1.40)	(1.24)
MACRORISK $_{t-1}$		6.498	−7.744		9.755	−3.423		*−0.198**	*0.954**
		(0.91)	(0.65)		(1.14)	(0.24)		*(1.85)*	*(1.76)*
VOLATILITY $_t$		−0.171	−8.486		0.891	−9.369		0.188	1.315
		(0.03)	(0.75)		(0.14)	(0.67)		(0.05)	(0.19)
Constant	*−7.354****	*−5.997****	−5.344	*−9.678****	*−9.005****	−1.388	*−1.911****	0.855	−7.130
	(14.48)	*(4.89)*	(0.83)	*(16.88)*	*(6.72)*	(0.17)	*(4.39)*	(0.73)	(1.36)
Observations	162	162	162	162	162	162	162	162	162
Adjusted R-squared	0.733	0.707	0.743	0.741	0.692	0.740	0.194	0.115	0.199
Time dummies	Yes	Yes	Yes	Yes	Yes	Yes	Yes	Yes	Yes
Country dummies	Yes	No	Yes	Yes	No	Yes	Yes	No	Yes

Robust t statistics in parentheses; ***(**; *) significant at 1% (5%; 1%)

Panel B: Economic relevance on the impact of private information on R-squares (p.p)									
PRIV_INF$_t$			+ 2.06			+ 2.51			

Table 8.7 reports the results of the regression model described in Equation (5), estimated as a 'between model'. Therefore, for each variable employed the analysis we compute the average value over the sample period, from 1994 to 2006, at the level of the bank. This choice, while removing within-bank variation across the sample, allows us to analyse between bank differences. The dependent variables are the logistic transformation of the R-square of the models (1) and (2). In the last three columns the dependent variable is the logistic transformation of the difference between the R-square from model 1 and the R-square from model 2. The explanatory variables include the absolute value of the residuals of the earnings prediction model (*PRIV_INF*), the disclosure index (*DISCLOSURE*), the log of total assets in thousands of euros (*SIZE*), the asset diversity index (*DIVERSIFICATION*) originally proposed by Laeven and Levine (2007), the return on equity (*ROE*), the market-to-book ratio (*MTB*), the log growth rate of loans (*GROWTH*), and a dummy equal to 1 for bank holding companies (*BHC*). Country control variables include an index of banking system transparency (*SYSTRANSPARENCY*), the log of banking credit to private sector (*SYSTEMSIZE*), the (log) number of domestic listed banks in a given country (*LISTED*), an asset-based Herfindahl index of bank concentration (*CONCENTRATION*), the Good Government index (*GOODGOV*) from La Porta and colleagues (1998), the ten-year moving window standard deviation in annual GDP growth measured in local currency (*MACRORISK*), and the annualized domestic market volatility (*VOLATILITY*). The models are estimated via OLS; standard errors are robust to heteroscedasticity and clustered at the level of the firm. The dependent variables are measured over the sample period from 1994 to 2006. Lagged variables refer to the period 1993–2005. Continuous variables have been winsorized at the 1 per cent level.

Table 8.8. Crash Risk and Opacity in European Banks—Logistic Regression

	(1)	(2)	(3)	(4)	(5)	(6)	(7)	(8)	(9)
	TCRASHES			CCRASHES			UCRASCHES		
Panel A: Regression analysis									
PRIV_INF	*74.420****	*62.339****	*74.892****	*116.464****	*96.168****	*124.636****	*48.133***	*40.320**	*46.829***
	(3.60)	*(3.14)*	*(3.67)*	*(3.35)*	*(2.78)*	*(3.41)*	*(2.21)*	*(1.86)*	*(2.10)*
DISCLOSURE	0.071	−0.131	0.074	1.771	*1.860***	1.778	−0.723	−1.171	−0.646
	(0.09)	(0.21)	(0.09)	(1.61)	*(2.12)*	(1.57)	(0.79)	(1.54)	(0.70)
SIZE	*0.072**	*0.092***	*0.089***	*0.349****	*0.347****	*0.369****	−0.062	−0.043	−0.057
	(1.68)	*(2.20)*	*(2.07)*	*(4.44)*	*(5.05)*	*(4.50)*	(1.30)	(0.92)	(1.16)
DIVERSIFICATION	*1.062****	*0.719**	*0.903***	*1.721****	*1.279***	*1.754****	0.356	0.144	0.157
	(2.97)	*(1.92)*	*(2.45)*	*(2.98)*	*(2.39)*	*(2.89)*	(0.90)	(0.36)	(0.39)
ROE	−0.622	−0.936	−0.823	0.379	−0.186	0.332	−1.044	−1.334	−1.294
	(0.72)	(1.06)	(0.91)	(0.27)	(0.14)	(0.21)	(1.15)	(1.40)	(1.36)
MTB	0.124	*0.146**	0.113	*0.272***	*0.268***	*0.267***	0.008	0.027	−0.017
	(1.57)	*(1.91)*	(1.48)	*(2.08)*	*(2.21)*	*(2.03)*	(0.11)	(0.38)	(0.23)
GROWTH	0.138	0.131	0.080	0.244	0.294	0.187	0.006	−0.056	−0.088
	(0.32)	(0.31)	(0.19)	(0.49)	(0.56)	(0.35)	(0.01)	(0.10)	(0.16)
BHC	−0.200	0.004	−0.222	0.007	0.117	0.012	−0.250	−0.057	−0.293
	(0.78)	(0.02)	(0.86)	(0.02)	(0.46)	(0.04)	(0.72)	(0.24)	(0.88)
SYSTRANSPARENCY		0.431	−0.803		−0.164	−2.800		0.086	−0.175
		(0.45)	(0.47)		(0.12)	(0.94)		(0.07)	(0.09)
SYSTEMSIZE		−0.172	−0.013		*−0.427***	*1.035**		−0.088	−0.412
		(1.40)	(0.04)		*(2.23)*	*(1.72)*		(0.63)	(1.13)
LISTED		0.024	0.101		0.311	−0.274		−0.055	0.116
		(0.15)	(0.26)		(1.20)	(0.40)		(0.29)	(0.26)
CONCENTRATION		−0.818	2.285		−0.421	5.361		−1.049	1.071
		(0.52)	(1.06)		(0.16)	(1.26)		(0.57)	(0.41)
GOODGOV		*0.084**	0.082		0.055	*−0.459**		*0.088**	0.287
		(1.77)	(0.52)		(0.71)	*(1.87)*		*(1.77)*	(1.64)
MACRORISK		−0.247	−8.260		−6.343	*−35.645**		7.153	16.611
		(0.04)	(0.76)		(0.66)	*(1.87)*		(0.98)	(1.53)

(*continued*)

Table 8.8. Continued

	(1)	(2)	(3)	(4)	(5)	(6)	(7)	(8)	(9)
	TCRASHES			CCRASHES			UCRASCHES		
VOLATILITY		*6.605**	*13.265****		1.598	*13.899***		*6.103**	*10.719***
		(1.96)	*(3.38)*		(0.30)	*(2.08)*		*(1.75)*	*(2.47)*
Constant	*−3.669****	*−4.237****	*−6.075**	*−14.522****	*−9.809****	*−13.047***	0.002	−1.778	−4.028
	(3.16)	*(3.29)*	*(1.87)*	*(7.98)*	*(4.16)*	*(1.99)*	(0.00)	(1.05)	(1.10)
Observations	1461	1461	1461	1461	1461	1461	1461	1461	1461
Pseudo R-squared	0.114	0.108	0,123	0.273	0.266	0.285	0.057	0.054	0.066
Year dummies	Yes	Yes	Yes	Yes	Yes	Yes	Yes	Yes	Yes
Country dummies	Yes	No	Yes	Yes	No	Yes	Yes	No	Yes

Robust z-statistics in parentheses; ***(**; *) significant at 1% (5%; 1%)

Panel B: Change in the probability of bank crashes

PRIV_INF	Absolute change	+ 2.99 p.p.	0.97 p.p.	1.27 p.p.
	Relative change	+ 17.96%	38.96%	11.86%

Table 8.8 reports the results of a set of logistic regressions where dependent variables are dummies equal to one if a bank has suffered in a year from a crash, and zero otherwise. The explanatory variables include the absolute value of the residuals of the earnings prediction model (*PRIV_INF*), the disclosure index (*DISCLOSURE*), the log of total assets in thousands of euros (*SIZE*), the asset diversity index (*DIVERSIFICATION*) originally proposed by Laeven and Levine (2007), the return on equity (*ROE*), the market-to-book ratio (*MTB*), the log growth rate of loans (*GROWTH*), and a dummy equal to one for bank holding companies (*BHC*). Country control variables include an index of banking system transparency (*SYSTRANSPARENCY*), the log of banking credit to private sector (*SYSTEMSIZE*), the (log) number of domestic listed banks in a given country (*LISTED*), an asset-based Herfindahl index of bank concentration (*CONCENTRATION*), the Good Government index (*GOODGOV*) from La Porta and colleagues (1998), the ten-year moving window standard deviation in annual GDP growth measured in local currency (*MACRORISK*), and the annualized domestic market volatility (*VOLATILITY*). The models are estimated via OLS; standard errors are robust to heteroscedasticity and clustered at the level of the firm. The dependent variables are measured over the sample period from 1994 to 2006. Lagged variables refer to the period 1993–2005. Continuous variables have been winsorized at the 1 per cent level.

The Impact of Opacity on Crash Risk

To analyse the relationship between crash risk in bank stock prices and opacity, we estimate a set of logistic regressions where the dependent variable is one of the proxies for crash risk previously described. Hence, the dependent variable is a dummy equal to one if a bank has suffered from a crash in a given year and zero otherwise. Furthermore, as explanatory variables, we employ the same set of controls as in the linear models discussed earlier in this chapter. Similar to the linear analysis, to assess the robustness of our findings we modify the initial basic model, which controls for bank-specific characteristics, year, and county dummies, in two ways. First, we replace the country dummies with the set of country-specific characteristics; second, we estimate the model with both country dummies and country-specific control variables.

Panel A of Table 8.8 shows that bank opacity is a key determinant of crash risk in bank stock returns; specifically, in all specifications, the coefficients assigned to PRIV_INF are positive and highly significant. Panel B of Table 8.8 provides further evidence on the impact of opacity on crash risk by reporting the effect played by PRIV_INF on crash probabilities. More precisely, this Panel shows the absolute and relative change in the probability of a crash when our proxy for bank opacity increases from the 25th to the 75th percentile of the sampling distribution, while the remaining variables are fixed at their mean values. This analysis suggests that the influence of bank opacity on bank crash risk is not minor. For instance, such an increase in opacity leads to a rise in the probability of total crashes by approximately 3 percentage points. Furthermore, the probability of conditional and unconditional crashes increases, respectively, by 1 percentage point and 1.2 percentage points. Notably, in relative terms, the effect played by bank opacity appears particularly strong in the case of conditional crashes (+ 39 per cent), namely, when we model the probability of crashes that occur simultaneously with a crash in one of the indices in Equation (1). Thus, as suggested by models of information contagion, where the degree of asymmetry in the distribution of the information between insiders and outsiders contributes to the transmission of shocks, it seems that the effect of extreme negative stress conditions tend to be strongly transmitted across opaque banks.

This is further confirmed by Figure 8.1, where we plot the (predicted) probabilities of crashes for different degrees of opacity while the other variables are fixed at their mean value. Figure 8.1 shows that, as we observe an increase in opacity, the probability of a conditional crash tends to rise at a much faster pace than the probability of an unconditional crash, up to

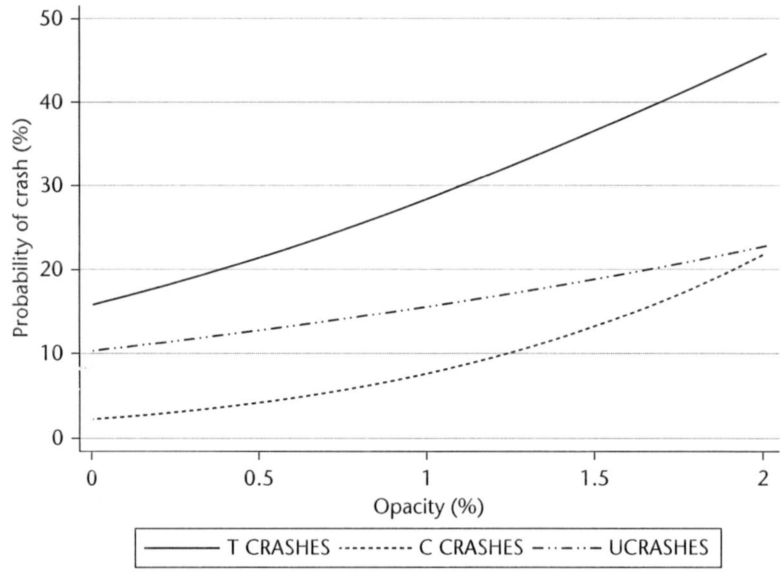

Figure 8.1. Probability of Bank Stock Price Crashes and Bank Opacity

achieving similar values in the case of an extremely high degree of opacity at the bank level.[18]

Moving onto the analysis of the set of control variables, we observe that the risk of a crash increases as banks become larger and depart from a specialized business focus. For conditional crashes, the probability of a large drop in bank price tends also to increase with the value of the MTB ratio. Overall, while total and conditional crashes seem to share similar determinants, the models based on unconditional crashes identify only bank opacity as a significant explanatory variable, as suggested by the model proposed by Jin and Myers (2006).[19]

To recap, our results confirm theoretical predictions on the impact of bank opacity on crash risk. This impact appears particularly strong on bank crashes that occurs simultaneously with a systematic/systemic crash; this finding supports, therefore, the theoretical link between the risk of information contagion and the degree of opaqueness in bank assets (Chen, 1999).

[18] Few banks experience both conditional and unconditional crashes in the same years. Thus we re-estimate the models reported in Tables 8.8 excluding these observations from the sample. Our conclusions remain qualitatively the same.

[19] The different ability of the models in predicting different types of crashes is highlighted by the large variation observed in the Pseudo R-square. This statistic achieves values systematically higher than 26 per cent when the models are aimed at predicting conditional crashes, against a maximum value of 6.7 per cent when the dependent variable is the unconditional crash.

Robustness Tests

We conducted several additional tests to check the robustness of our main findings.[20] We start by modifying the sample composition: as a large part of our sample is concentrated in Denmark, Italy, and Spain, we repeat the analysis by excluding one of these countries at a time from the sample. This reduces the number of observations employed to estimate the models between 10 per cent and 15 per cent but does not affect our main conclusions. Next, we exclude from the sample the smallest banks, those banks that are in the first quartile of the size distribution. This modification increases substantially the minimum bank size in the sample (for example, in the case of the pooled regression the smallest bank now exhibits a value of total assets larger than €2.6 billion) but does not modify our results.

A final set of robustness tests focus on the econometric methodology adopted to estimate the pooled regression. We re-estimate the models reported in columns 3, 6, and 9 of Table 8.6 by adopting the Fama and Macbeth (1973) regression approach that allows us to control for autocorrelation in the residual term. Furthermore, we re-estimate the same models with Driscoll and Kraay (1998) standard errors that assume that the error structure is heteroscedastic and autocorrelated up to some lag, and possibly correlated between the groups. Both tests confirm our findings.

Conclusions

The design of regulatory initiatives that aim to increase transparency in banks has been at the centre of the regulatory debate on how to restore financial stability after the global crisis that erupted in the middle of 2007 (Beck et al., 2008; FSF, 2008). In this chapter, we contribute to this debate by focusing on the impact of opacity on bank stability, measured in terms of stock return co-movement and crash risk, for a sample of European banks.

Our findings suggest that the co-movement of a bank's stock returns with the market and the rest of the industry increases as the degree of asymmetric information between insiders and outsiders grows; namely, as banks become more opaque they tend to be more exposed to systematic and systemic shocks. These results are driven by industry-specific factors; that is, bank opacity does not depend on the component of systematic co-movement not driven by banking industry-wide events. Furthermore, a higher degree of opacity is

[20] To save space, the results of these tests are not reported.

also associated with a higher probability of observing a stock price crash; the effect is particularly pronounced for the bank crashes conditional on general stress scenarios. Overall, our results highlight the negative implications that opacity has for the stability of banks and the importance of enhancing transparency at the firm level.

Two major regulatory implications can be drawn from our analysis. First, our results demonstrate that removing bank opacity should contribute to the stability of the financial sector. Second, together with the evidence of a strong positive impact of size on bank exposure to systematic and systemic shocks and on the probability of stock price crashes, these results add support to forms of the re-regulation of the banking industry based on limits on bank size, as those adopted in the USA with the Dodd–Frank Wall Street Reform and Consumer Protection Act of July 2010.

Appendix

Park (1999) and Crouzille, Lepetit, and Tarazi (2004) argue that the residuals from a prediction model of bank earnings can be decomposed into three parts. The first is due to the misspecification of the model, the second is produced by unexpected shocks and ignored both by insiders and outsiders, while the third component is expected by insiders but not outsiders, since it depends on the information known only inside the firm. To reduce the influence of the first component on earning predictability we introduce in the model a large set of determinants of bank earnings with the purpose of containing the bias due to omitted variables.[21] In selecting the explanatory variables, we consider previous studies by Park (1999) and Crouzille, Lepetit, and Tarazi (2004), the literature on the prediction of bank earnings (e.g. Alam and Brown, 2006), and the literature on the key drivers of bank profitability in European countries (e.g. Molyneux and Thornton, 1992; Miller and Noulas, 1997; Athanasoglou, Brissimis, and Delis, 2008).

More specifically, the explanatory variables include two earnings components, the net interest margin (MINT) and the remaining operating income (OOI), both scaled over total assets, since Alam and Brown (2006) show that disaggregated earnings contribute to improve the predictability of the next period earnings in the banking industry.[22] Furthermore, we introduce four explanatory variables drawn from Crouzille, Lepetit, and Tarazi (2004) and Park (1999). Thus, we control for the composition of a bank's portfolio through the ratio between net loans and total assets (LOANS), and

[21] Multicollinearity does not represent a problem in the context of the earnings prediction model. We are, in fact, interested only in the overall fit, namely the Adjusted R^2, of the model and not in the significance level of any specific variable.

[22] Our tests confirm these findings. The two earning components contribute, in fact, to increase systematically the adjusted R^2 of the earning prediction model.

for the relevance of core deposits on total assets (DEP). Both variables are supposed to exercise a positive influence on bank profitability since LOANS denote investments in a high profitability asset class and DEP may indicate a lower degree of funding cost for the banking firm. In addition, we employ a measure of operational efficiency defined as the ratio between operating expenses and total assets (OVHEAD) and a variable proxying for the relevance of liquid assets (LIQUY). OVHEAD and LIQUY are generally found to negatively affect banks' profits (e.g. Molyneux and Thornton, 1992). In contrast to Crouzille, Lepetit, and Tarazi (2004) and Park (1999), we also consider a measure of bank capital adequacy, that is, the equity-over-total-asset ratio (CAP), as a predictor of earnings. This choice is motivated by the fact that Molyneux and Thornton (1992) and Goddard, Molyneux, and Wilson (2004) show a significantly positive influence of capital adequacy on profitability in the major European banking markets. A similar conclusion has been achieved recently by Athanasoglou, Brissimis, and Delis (2008) for the Greek context. Finally, we control for differences in the economic conditions and in banking performance at the level of the country. Specifically, several studies find evidence for the relevance of macro variables and industry-specific variables on banking profitability (Molyneux and Thornton, 1992; Crouzille, Lepetit, and Tarazi, 2004; Athanasoglou, Brissimis, and Delis, 2008). Accordingly, for each country, we introduce in the regression the real GDP growth rate (RGDPG), the long-term interest rate (LINT), and the average ROA of the banking sector (AV_CROA).[23]

To limit the relative importance of the second component on the residuals, that is, the weight of unexpected and temporary shocks, we introduce two lags of the dependent variable as explanatory variables (Athanasoglou, Brissimis, and Delis, 2008).

The final specification of the earnings prediction model is reported below:

$$\begin{aligned} ROA_{i,t} = {} & \alpha_0 + \beta_1 ROA_{i,t-1} + \beta_2 ROA_{i,t-2} + \beta_3 MINT_{i,t-1} + \beta_4 OOI_{i,t-1} + \beta_5 OVHEAD_{i,t-1} \\ & + \beta_6 DEP_{i,t-1} + \beta_7 LOANS_{i,t-1} + \beta_8 LIQUY_{i,t-1} + \beta_9 CAD_{i,t-1} + \beta_{10} AVC - ROA_{i,t-1} \\ & + \beta_{11} RGDP_{i,t-1} + \beta_{12} LINT_{i,t-1} + u_{i,t} \end{aligned} \tag{6}$$

where the dependent variable is the ratio between net income and total assets, namely, a common measure of bank profitability.

The model is estimated at yearly intervals through OLS. This estimation strategy is motivated by need to use the set of information available for investors at the beginning of the fiscal year when we estimate the measures of opacity; namely, the residuals obtained at time *t*, and based on accounting information at time *t-1* and *t-2*, are used to construct our measures of bank opacity for the fiscal year *t + 1*.[24]

[23] To take advantage of the amount of information available in our dataset, the model is estimated using all the yearly accounting information for the 162 banks considered in the empirical analysis, even if for a specific year the synchronicity measure for that bank cannot be computed. We, therefore, employ an overall number of more than 2,500 bank-year observations.

[24] The use of a pooled (panel) regression model would lead to the use of information that is not available for investors when we compute the yearly indicator of opacity; that is, it would suffer from a forward-looking bias.

Table 8.A1. Earnings Prediction Model

	1993	1994	1995	1996	1997	1998	1999	2000	2001	2002	2003	2004	2005	2006
ROA_{t-1}	*0.559***	*0.276****	*0.244****	*0.433****	*0.879****	*0.481****	*0.327****	*0.256****	*1.182****	*0.226***	0.081	0.013	*0.204***	*0.676****
	(2.43)	*(3.46)*	*(4.22)*	*(5.75)*	*(7.17)*	*(4.66)*	*(2.75)*	*(2.93)*	*(6.29)*	*(2.51)*	(0.93)	(0.13)	*(2.31)*	*(5.54)*
ROA_{t-2}	0.142	*0.222***	0.029	0.003	−0.030	0.017	*0.218**	*0.268****	0.086	−0.119	*0.326****	*0.536****	0.096	*0.370****
	(0.44)	*(2.36)*	(0.86)	(0.07)	(0.36)	(0.39)	*(1.93)*	*(3.66)*	(1.17)	(0.70)	*(6.25)*	*(8.18)*	(1.01)	*(5.57)*
$MINT_{t-1}$	0.244	0.160	*0.228****	*0.168****	−0.068	*0.228****	0.013	0.165	0.090	*0.540****	*0.250****	*0.231****	*0.186**	*−0.253***
	(0.98)	(1.66)	*(3.64)*	*(3.20)*	(0.88)	*(2.80)*	(0.13)	(1.64)	(0.63)	*(4.45)*	*(2.73)*	*(3.03)*	*(1.94)*	*(2.07)*
$OOIT_{t-1}$	0.344	−0.045	*0.243****	*0.279****	0.062	*0.408****	0.074	0.032	−0.202	*0.393***	−0.008	*0.474****	*0.238***	−0.184
	(1.43)	(0.55)	*(4.19)*	*(4.52)*	(0.73)	*(5.03)*	(0.91)	(0.36)	(1.24)	*(2.49)*	(0.07)	*(5.34)*	*(2.13)*	(1.49)
$OVHEAD_{t-1}$	*−0.563***	0.008	*−0.178****	*−0.161***	−0.012	*−0.346****	−0.000	−0.016	0.127	*−0.511****	−0.107	*−0.513****	*−0.245***	*0.221**
	(2.00)	(0.07)	*(2.66)*	*(2.57)*	(0.13)	*(3.58)*	(0.00)	(0.14)	(0.75)	*(3.25)*	(0.91)	*(5.61)*	*(2.13)*	*(1.82)*
DEP_{t-1}	0.002	−0.004	*0.006***	−0.002	−0.001	0.004	0.002	−0.003	0.004	0.003	0.000	−0.001	−0.002	0.000
	(0.37)	(0.93)	*(2.56)*	(1.12)	(0.71)	(1.57)	(0.48)	(1.14)	(0.97)	(0.77)	(0.07)	(0.46)	(0.87)	(0.06)
$LOANS_{t-1}$	−0.012	−0.005	*−0.007**	0.002	*0.010****	0.001	0.001	*−0.012****	0.006	0.002	*−0.013****	−0.003	0.001	0.000
	(0.62)	(0.66)	*(1.76)*	(0.77)	*(2.70)*	(0.24)	(0.11)	*(2.68)*	(1.17)	(0.36)	*(3.09)*	(0.64)	(0.13)	(0.04)
$LIQUY_{t-1}$	−0.008	−0.004	−0.005	*0.006**	0.005	*0.009***	−0.000	*−0.008**	0.005	*0.018****	−0.006	0.003	0.005	0.000
	(0.44)	(0.52)	(1.42)	*(1.94)*	(1.36)	*(2.03)*	(0.05)	*(1.78)*	(0.90)	*(2.84)*	(1.15)	(0.53)	(0.81)	(0.05)
CAD_{t-1}	*0.077**	−0.032	*0.046****	0.006	*0.040****	*0.030****	0.007	−0.014	*−0.135****	0.021	*0.101****	0.029	0.016	0.029
	(1.69)	(1.16)	*(3.55)*	(0.55)	*(4.03)*	*(2.87)*	(0.38)	(0.93)	*(6.37)*	(0.76)	*(6.77)*	(1.49)	(0.96)	(1.36)
AVC_ROA_{t-1}	−0.424	−0.047	0.018	*0.040***	−0.027	−0.027	−0.104	0.033	0.022	−0.104	*0.475****	0.012	*0.359****	−0.001
	(1.39)	(0.28)	(0.94)	*(2.12)*	(1.10)	(0.22)	(1.21)	(0.33)	(0.21)	(0.46)	*(3.20)*	(0.27)	*(2.76)*	(0.14)
$RGDP_{t-1}$	0.090	*0.181****	*0.098****	*0.062****	0.042	−0.011	0.032	0.024	−0.001	−0.014	0.023	*−0.068***	0.040	0.037
	(0.93)	*(2.86)*	*(2.79)*	*(2.62)*	(1.44)	(0.37)	(0.80)	(0.80)	(0.02)	(0.26)	(0.73)	*(2.40)*	(0.96)	(1.24)
$LINT_{t-1}$	0.002	*0.043***	0.015	−0.010	0.014	*−0.094***	*0.410****	−0.054	−0.071	−0.098	−0.171	0.061	−0.043	−0.080
	(0.05)	*(2.19)*	(1.21)	(0.85)	(0.74)	*(2.38)*	*(7.27)*	(0.58)	(0.48)	(0.61)	(1.57)	(0.51)	(0.44)	(0.76)
Constant	0.008	0.003	−0.004	*−0.004**	*−0.008****	0.001	*−0.019****	*0.013***	0.000	−0.003	0.010	0.001	0.001	0.003
	(0.51)	(0.48)	(1.07)	*(1.73)*	*(2.76)*	(0.35)	*(4.16)*	*(2.48)*	(0.04)	(0.34)	(1.64)	(0.19)	(0.08)	(0.69)
Ad_R2	0.700	0.604	0.841	0.879	0.861	0.826	0.719	0.682	0.641	0.529	0.798	0.727	0.606	0.769
N. obs.	96	135	143	147	147	148	148	146	139	137	134	132	127	120

Table 8.A1 shows the estimation results for model (6). MINT is the ratio between net interest margin and total assets, OOIT is the ratio between not interest income and total assets, OVHEAD is the ratio between operating costs and operating income, DEP is the ratio between deposits and total assets, LOANS is the ratio between net loans and total assets, LIQUY is the ratio between liquid assets and total assets, CAD is the ratio between equity and total assets, AVC_ROA is the country average of the banking system ROA, RGDP is the real growth rate of GDP, LINT is the long-term interest rate at the country level.

Table 8.A1 shows the estimation results for the earnings prediction model at yearly frequency. In general, we observe that the explanatory power of the model is high, with an average adjusted R-square of 72.7 per cent over the period 1993–2006. In addition, banks' earnings tend to be highly persistent since the lag value of the return on assets is positive and significant in twelve out of fourteen years.

Part V

Conclusions and Implications for the Re-Regulation of European Banking

9

Conclusions

Introduction

In the aftermath of the financial crisis that erupted in 2007, it is not surprising that issues surrounding the size, risk, and regulation of banks have been at the centre of the policy debate across the globe. Many commentators and regulators are quite rightly questioning whether the structure, culture, and ethos of banking need a fundamental rethink, given the ongoing nature of the crisis and the unfolding number of scandals, which seem to emerge in a constant stream. The aim of this debate has been to identify the necessary interventions to restore confidence in the financial industry and limit the risk posed by future systemic events. This book has analysed these issues with a focus on the European context.

Europe offers a particularly fruitful ground for investigation as the recent and ongoing crisis has demonstrated that the European Union (EU) was institutionally ill-prepared to manage a financial crisis, especially one involving large cross-border institutions that are systemically important to a number of countries. This is particularly unfortunate as banks, especially in Europe, have grown rapidly compared to the size of the domestic economies over recent decades and have considerably expanded their activities beyond the national borders. As a consequence, for an increasing number of banks, the book value of their assets now exceeds the GDP of the economy in which they are charted. The increase in systemic size raises a number of important issues with regard to the risk-taking behaviour of banks. It is a frequently raised concern that systemic size tempts banks to maximize the value of the financial safety net by taking on more risk. The performance of many of the systemically largest European banks during the recent crisis has not dispelled such concerns. Many of these banks were forced to turn to taxpayers to fund their recapitalization efforts to some extent during the crisis.

Size and Risk

The results discussed in this book offer some support to the critics of the rapid growth in the size of the European banking industry, and highlight the importance of coordination in the regulatory landscape across Europe. Nonetheless, they also demonstrate that the negative effects associated with an increase in bank size normally materialize only under some specific circumstances which require special consideration by regulators.

In effect, we show that during the recent crisis bank default risk has increased with systemic size, which we measure by the ratio between bank total assets and country GDP. However, systemic size has not increased bank default risk during previous crises and there is no general, risk-increasing effect linked to systemic size during non-crisis periods. Our main conclusion, therefore, is that with the exception of the recent crisis banks do not take on additional risk as they grow in systemic size.

The finding that a growth in bank size produces negative effects only under some specific conditions was confirmed when we reviewed and analysed the default risk implications of M&A on acquiring banks from Europe. Essentially, we show that the average European bank merger does not affect the default risk of the acquirer; namely, an increase in bank size due to external growth does not necessarily imply an increasing risk of default for the acquiring bank. However, we also demonstrate that M&A can be detrimental for relatively safe bidders, which show an increase in their default risk in the post-merger period. Furthermore, the possibility of merger-related increases in risk is particularly pronounced for relatively safe banks when deals are diversifying and/or completed under a bank regulatory regime, in the country of the biding bank, which is relatively weak. Our results point to difficulties in achieving sustainable risk-reduction benefits from bank M&A, especially for banks that are already well-diversified. Furthermore, our finding that merger-related risk increases are particularly large for cross-border and activity-diversifying deals is consistent with a host of theoretical and empirical studies which doubt that viable diversification gains and risk benefits can be realized through bank consolidation. Yet, our finding that the default risk of the acquiring banks increase as the deal size becomes larger highlights the negative implications for banking sector stability produced by mega-mergers in the banking industry.

Nonetheless, if the impact in terms of default risk is mixed, from the results discussed in this book it appears clear that the growing expansion of banking through the integration process realized in the European banking industry has significantly changed the composition of banking system volatility during the last two decades, leading to an increase in the risk of cross-border banking crises. We argue that this evolution may reflect the growing importance of cross-border activities in European banking systems, and we provide results that point towards a positive relationship between the degree of internationalization of a banking system and the relative size of non-domestic components of banking volatility. Overall, the volatility of the European banking systems shows a rise in the relative importance of international and European non-financial components and a reduction in the contribution of country and idiosyncratic components. This growth in the relative importance of international and European non-financial components of banking system volatility has been associated with a significant upward trend in the (value-weighted average) international and European betas of the European banking systems. In general, this evolution in the composition of banking system volatility has led to a substantial increase in the degree of interdependency between banking systems that we estimate to be in the order of 2.4 per cent per year. Ultimately, the changing composition of banking system volatility demonstrates the growing relevance of the broad channel of systemic risk (De Bandt and Hartmann, 2000); that is, our results imply a rise in the likelihood that shocks can simultaneously affect a large number of institutions.

The problems posed by a large bank size during times of stress in the financial system are confirmed when we analyse the determinants of the risk that banks fail under systemic shocks, utilizing a novel empirical approach based on contingent claim analysis and the Merton (1974) distance-to-default model. Overall, while the results support the introduction of leverage and liquidity requirements, as stipulated in the Basel III Accord, they also show that the risk exposure of banks to systemic shocks increases with size (both measured in absolute and relative terms). Furthermore, the comparative analysis of the impact of different bank characteristics on bank exposure to shocks shows that, *ceteris paribus*, the Basel III interventions are likely to be less effective than imposing a cap on bank absolute size. The design of size restrictions appears, however, to be related to the size of the economy in which a bank is operating. More precisely, as the risk exposure of a bank increases with both absolute and systemic size, and in spite of the integration process of the financial industry in Europe, any regulatory intervention on size needs to be country-specific with smaller European economies needing smaller banks. In sum, how to design regulatory restrictions on bank size does not appear an easy task for regulators, although the benefits in terms of bank resilience to shocks that, *ceteris paribus*, are associated with such a regulatory restriction seem particularly pronounced.

Governance and Risk

The last part of the book has been devoted to the analysis of bank governance. Initially the attention has been on the interaction between monitoring by bank boards and regulatory regimes in the takeover market, and then we focused on the consequences generated by CEO compensation and bank opacity on bank risk-taking.

Our tests on the effectiveness of three board-monitoring mechanisms (board independence, CEO–chair duality, and board diversity) in affecting the announcement returns of bank M&A across bank regulatory environments of varying strictness show that in strict regulatory regimes board independence and board diversity are effective in improving the returns of bidding banks. Given that strict bank regulators provide monitoring and disciplinary services which are similar to those provided by board monitoring, our finding that strict regulation facilitates effective board monitoring is not consistent with the notion that regulation and firm governance are substitutes. Instead, our results point to a complementary relationship between regulation and some governance mechanisms. Our work supports earlier studies which view board monitoring and industry regulation as complements (Baxter, 2003; Becher and Frye, 2011) and has implications for theoretical work in this area in two ways. First, previous empirical work has interpreted the existence of enhanced monitoring arrangements (e.g. more independent boards) in stricter regulatory regimes as support for the complementarity hypothesis. However, the extant work makes no reference to the realized performance implications of these arrangements. By contrast, we show that interactions between regulation and board monitoring lead to more effective governance arrangements in regulated firms. We therefore advance existing theory in this area by showing that board-monitoring arrangements are associated with measurable shareholder wealth gains in strict regulatory regimes (rather than the presence of indicators of better monitoring). Second, theoretical arguments have so far stressed that regulation per se could exert strong signalling effects (Booth, Cornett, and Tehranian, 2002; Baxter, 2003). Since our study compares the effectiveness of regulation across multiple regulatory regimes, we are able to show that regulation improves the effectiveness of board monitoring only for the strictest regulatory regimes in our sample.

Next, we analyse the impact of CEO cash bonuses on the distance to default of a sample of European and US banks. Our results show that banks where CEOs receive large bonus payments (both in absolute terms as well as relative to their total cash compensation) display lower levels of default risk. We interpret this finding as consistent with the shape of the CEO payoff function, which underlies a typical cash bonus plan. Thus, CEO cash bonuses are solvency-contingent and, therefore, incentivize CEOs to avoid institutional failure. Additionally, the payoffs from cash bonus plans are typically linear functions of firm performance and are, therefore, not risk-rewarding for CEOs. Finally, our results show that the effect that bonuses exert on risk-taking is not confined to the short-term. Bonus payments also affect the long-term level of default risk which bank CEOs target. Critically, our analysis identifies a key factor that moderates the link between CEO cash bonuses and bank risk; namely, the overall riskiness of an institution determines the effectiveness of risk-taking incentives imbedded in CEO bonus contracts. We find that when banks are highly risky, CEO cash bonuses are associated with higher bank risk-taking.

Finally, we assess the importance of opacity on European bank stability, measured in terms of stock return co-movement and crash risk. We show that the co-movement of a bank's stock returns with the market and the rest of the industry increases as the degree of asymmetric information between insiders and outsiders grows; namely, as banks become more opaque they tend to be more exposed to systematic and systemic shocks. These results are driven by industry-specific factors. Furthermore, a higher degree of opacity is also associated with a higher probability of observing a stock price crash; the effect is particularly pronounced for the bank crashes conditional on general stress scenarios. Overall, our results highlight the negative implications that opacity has for the stability of banks, and the importance of enhancing transparency at the firm level.

Policy Implications

The results presented in this book lead to a number of policy implications. First, the difficulties posed by regulatory intervention on bank size, and the importance of bank size for banks' exposure to systemic shocks, speak in favour of the adoption of prudential rules designed for large and complex financial institutions. Nonetheless, our results give little justification for subjecting systemically large banks to stricter and time-invariant capital requirements than less systemically large banks (as, for instance, envisaged under Basel III via the higher capital requirements applied to global systemically important banks (GSIBs)). Instead, the results support the view that systemically large banks should issue hybrid securities such as contingent convertibles ('CoCos'), which convert into equity in the event of a systemic crisis. Flannery (2005) and Kashyap, Rajan, and Stein (2008) outline various proposals showing how contingent capital can be employed in the banking industry to increase the resilience of banks during systemic crises. The current results imply that contingent capital will be particularly effective in reducing bank risk-taking during a crisis when issued by systemically large banks.

Furthermore, the changing composition of banking system volatility and the growing international focus of large banks in Europe motivates regulatory reforms aimed at effective crisis management and resolution, or the orderly winding up of a failing cross-border bank, and these are essential to safeguarding systemic stability in Europe (see Eisenbeis and Kaufman, 2008; Krimminger, 2008; EC, 2009, 2010). The development of a European resolution framework may contribute to reducing the systemic implications of cross-border failures and may remove the need to resort to exceptional national regulatory measures in times of crisis, as those implemented during the sub-prime crisis.

As far as bank governance is concerned, our analysis is set against the background of the failure of financial institutions in the USA, Europe, and elsewhere, and debates among policymakers as regards the future of both bank regulation and bank governance. For example, a number of countries have planned to restrict the activities that banks may engage in or to introduce formal qualifications for the members of bank boards. However, an important practical implication of our work is that regulation and governance should not be viewed in isolation. Attempts to raise a board's ability to critically assess managerial risk-taking are more likely to be successful if effective bank-level governance is accompanied by strict industry regulation. Any role of government (via bank regulation) in reducing agency costs is only likely to be successful when governments signal their intent to interfere and enforce by giving powerful mandates to bank regulators. Half-measured attempts to increase the strictness of bank regulation are, thus, unlikely to improve the effectiveness of bank-level monitoring. In the same vein, for investors and practitioners, our results highlight that legislation which increases board power will, equally, be unlikely to be effective in bringing about performance gains if corporate governance arrangements at the firm level are not supported by a strict regulatory framework.

Furthermore, in terms of compensation policy our results suggest that increased shareholder involvement in setting executive compensation, for instance by giving shareholders a vote on compensation policy ('say on pay') as championed by the Dodd–Frank Wall Street Reform and Consumer Protection Act (Section 951), is unlikely to mitigate risk-taking incentives in the banking industry. We show evidence of increased risk-taking when banks are risky and shareholders have the most to gain from increasing the value of the safety net. When banks are highly risky, regulatory interference (e.g. with the aim of restricting certain pay practices) is the preferred alternative to more shareholder-oriented pay setting. Moreover, since bonuses are linked to higher bank risk-taking at the riskiest banks, risk-shifting incentives at these institutions are only likely to be constrained if compensation practices more closely align the interests of managers and debt holders. To achieve this, Bolton, Mehran, and Shapiro (2010) suggest that CEO compensation in banking should be linked to CDS spreads on a bank's outstanding debt. Similarly, Edmans and Liu (2011) argue that increasing the share of deferred compensation and other debt-like forms of executive pay will turn executives into unsecured bondholders with a financial interest in the liquidation value of a firm and, thus, mitigate incentives for CEOs to take on excessive risks. In addition, greater levels of disclosure of the terms under which CEO bonus plans are granted will clearly be beneficial. While our results convey a positive view of the role of CEO bonus payments in affecting bank risk, they can only be interpreted as first evidence. More details on the conditions of executive bonus plans (e.g. performance thresholds, caps, clawback provisions) are essential in order to better understand the link between bonus pay and bank risk. Future work should, hence, focus on the terms of executive bonus plans to derive bonus plan payoff functions for individual CEOs. A better understanding of the shape of individual CEO bonus payoff functions will be a vital stepping stone in order to understand how bonus plans should be designed to mitigate risk-taking by bank CEOs.

Finally, two major regulatory implications can be drawn from our analysis on the impact of bank opacity on bank stability. First, our results demonstrate that decreasing bank opacity should contribute to the stability of the financial sector by leading to a better flow of information between insiders and outsiders. Second, together with the evidence of a strong positive impact of size on bank exposure to systematic and systemic shocks and on the probability of stock price crashes, these results add further support to the re-regulation of the banking industry based on limits on bank size, as those adopted in the USA with the Dodd–Frank Wall Street Reform and Consumer Protection Act of July 2010.

References

Acharya, V. V. 2009. A theory of systemic risk and design of prudential regulation. *Journal of Financial Stability* 5, 224–55.

Acharya, V. V. and Thakor, S. 2011. The dark side of liquidity creation. Working Paper, Stern University.

Acharya, V. V. and Viswanathan, S. 2011. Leverage, moral hazard, and liquidity, *Journal of Finance* 66, 99–138.

Acharya, V. V. and Yorulmazer, T. 2007. Too many to fail: an analysis of time-inconsistency in bank closure policies. *Journal of Financial Intermediation* 16, 1–31.

Acharya, V. V. and Yorulmazer, T. 2008. Information contagion and bank herding. *Journal of Money, Credit and Banking* 40, 215–31.

Acharya, V. V., Hasan, I., and Saunders, A. 2006. Should banks be diversified? Evidence from individual bank loan portfolios. *Journal of Business* 79, 1355–412.

Acharya, V. V., Pedersen, L. H., Philippon, T., and Richardson, M. 2010. Measuring systemic risk. Working Paper, Stern University.

Adams, R. B. and Mehran, H. 2005. Corporate performance, board structure and its determinants in the banking industry. Working Paper, University of New South Wales.

Adams, Z., Füss, R., and Gropp, R. 2010. Modeling spillover effects among financial institutions: a state-dependent sensitivity value-at-risk (SDSVaR) approach. EBS Working Paper 10–12.

Adrian, T. and Brunnermeier, M. K. 2010. CoVaR. Federal Reserve Bank of New York, Working Paper No. 348.

Akella, S. R. and Chen, S. J. 1990. Interest rate sensitivity of bank stock returns: specification effects and structural changes. *Journal of Financial Research* 13, 147–54.

Akerlof, G. and Romer, P. 1993. Looting: the economic underworld of bankruptcy for profits. *Brookings Papers on Economic Activity* 2, 1–73.

Akhavein, J. D., Berger, A. N., and Humphrey, D. B. 1997. The effects of megamergers on efficiency and prices: evidence from a bank profit function. *Review of Industrial Organization* 12, 95–139.

Akhigbe, A., Madura, J., and Martin, A. D. 2007. Effect of Fed policy actions on the default likelihood of commercial banks. *Journal of Financial Research* 30, 147–62.

Alam, P. and Brown, C. A. 2006. Disaggregated earnings and the prediction of ROE and stock prices: a case of the banking industry. *Review of Accounting and Finance* 5, 443–63.

Allen, F. and Gale, D. 2000. Financial contagion. *Journal of Political Economy* 108, 1–33.

Allen, F. and Song, W. 2005. Financial integration and EMU. *European Financial Management Journal* 11, 7–24.

Altunbaş, Y., Manganelli, S., and Marquez-Ibanez, D. 2011. Bank risk taking during the financial crisis. ECB Working Paper 1394.

Altunbaş, Y., Carbo, S., Gardener, E. P. M., and Molyneux, P. 2007. Examining the relationships between capital, risk and efficiency in European banking. *European Financial Management Journal* 13, 49–70.

Amihud, Y., DeLong, G., and Saunders, A. 2002. The effects of cross-border bank mergers on bank risk and value. *Journal of International Money and Finance* 21, 857–77.

Anderson, C. W., Becher, D. A., and Campbell II, T. L. 2004. Bank mergers, the market for bank CEOs, and managerial incentives. *Journal of Financial Intermediation* 13, 6–27.

Arellano, M. and Bond, S. 1991. Some tests of specification for panel data: Monte Carlo evidence and an application to employment equations. *Review of Economic Studies* 58, 277–97.

Athanasoglou, P., Brissimis, S., and Delis, M. S. 2008. Bank-specific, industry-specific and macroeconomic determinants of bank profitability. *Journal of International Financial Markets, Institutions & Money* 18, 121–36.

Bae, K. H. G., Karoly, A., and Stulz, R. 2003. A new approach to measuring financial contagion. *Review of Financial Studies* 16, 717–63.

Baele, L., De Jonghe, O., and Vander Vennet, R. 2007. Does the stock market value bank diversification? *Journal of Banking & Finance* 31, 1999–2023.

Balachandran, S., Kogut, B., and Harnal, H. 2010. The probability of default, excessive risk, and executive compensation: a study of financial services firms from 1995 to 2008. Working Paper, Columbia University, New York.

Baliga, B. R., Moyer, R. C., and Rao, R. S. 1996. CEO duality and firm performance: What's the fuss? *Strategic Management Journal* 17, 41–53.

Barber, B. M. and Lyon, J. D. 1997. Detecting long-run abnormal stock returns: the empirical power and specification of test statistics. *Journal of Financial Economics* 43, 341–72.

Barth, J. R., Caprio, G., and Levine, R. 2001. Banking systems around the globe: Do regulation and ownership affect performance and stability? In *Prudential Supervision: What Works and What Doesn't*, ed. F. S. Mishkin. Chicago: University of Chicago Press, 31–97.

Barth, J. R., Caprio, G., and Levine, R., 2004. Bank regulation and supervision: What works best? *Journal of Financial Intermediation* 13, 205–48.

Bartram, S. M., Brown, G. M., and Hund, J. E. 2007. Estimating systemic risk in the international financial system. *Journal of Financial Economics* 86, 835–69.

Bartram, S. M., Taylor, S. J., and Wang, Y. H. 2006. The euro and European financial market dependence. *Journal of Banking & Finance* 31, 1461–81.

Baumann, U. and Nier, E. 2004. Disclosure, volatility and transparency: an empirical investigation into the value of bank disclosure. *Economy Policy Review* September, 31–45.

Baxter, T. C. 2003. Governing the financial or bank holding company: how legal infrastructure can facilitate consolidated risk management. *Federal Reserve Bank of New York: Current Issues in Economics and Finance* 9, 1–7.

Baysinger, B. D. and Zardkoohi, A. 1986. Technology, residual claimants, and corporate control. *Journal of Law, Economics, & Organization* 2, 339–49.

BCBS (Basel Committee on Banking Supervision). 2010a. Basel III: a global regulatory framework for more resilient banks and banking systems <http://www.bis.org/publ/bcbs189.htm>

BCBS (Basel Committee on Banking Supervision). 2011a. Range of methodologies for risk and performance alignment of remuneration. Bank for International Settlements. <http://www.bis.org/publ/bcbs194.pdf>.

BCBS (Basel Committee on Banking Supervision). 2011b. Global systemically important banks: assessment methodology and the additional loss absorbency requirement. Consultative Document, Bank for International Settlements. <http://www.bis.org/publ/bcbs207.pdf>.

Bebchuk, L. A. and Spamann, H. 2009. Regulating bankers' pay. *Georgetown Law Journal* 98, 247–87.

Becher, D. A. and Campbell, T. L. 2004. Corporate governance of bank mergers. *Proceedings, Federal Reserve Bank of Chicago* May, 267–87.

Becher, D. A. and Frye, M. 2011. Does regulation substitute or complement governance? *Journal Banking & Finance* 35, 736–51.

Beck, T., Laeven, L., Levine, R., and Pennacchi, G. 2008. Banking and bank regulation: challenges for the future. *Journal of Financial Intermediation* 17, 509–10.

Beckers, S., Grinold, R., Rudd, A., and Stefek, D. 1992. The relative importance of common factors across the European equity markets. *Journal of Banking & Finance* 16, 75–95.

Beitel, P., Schiereck, D., and Wahrenburg, M. 2004. Explaining M&A success in European banks. *European Financial Management* 10, 109–39.

Bekaert, G., Hodrick, R. J., and Zhang, X. 2008. International stock return comovements. ECB Working Paper 931.

Beltratti, A. and Stulz, R. 2012. Why did some banks perform better during the credit crisis? A cross-country study of the impact of governance and regulation. *Journal of Financial Economics* 105, 1–17.

Benston, G. and Evan, J. 2006. Performance compensation contracts and CEOs' incentive to shift risk to debtholders: an empirical analysis. *Journal of Economics and Finance* 30, 70–92.

Benston, G. J., Hunter, W. C., and Wall, L. D. 1995. Motivations for bank mergers and acquisitions: enhancing the deposit insurance in put option versus earning diversification. *Journal of Money, Credit and Banking* 27, 777–88.

Berger, A. N. and Bonaccorsi di Patti, E. 2006. Capital structure and firm performance: a new approach to testing agency theory and an application to the banking industry. *Journal of Banking & Finance* 30, 1065–102.

Berger, A. N. and Bouwman, C. H. S. 2012. How does capital affect bank performance during financial crises? Working Paper, University of South Carolina.

Berglöf, E., Fulghieri, P., Gual, J., Mayer, C., Barros, P., and Vives, X. 2005. *Integration of European Banking: The Way Forward*. London: Centre for Economic Policy Research.

Bernoth, K. and Pick, A. 2010. Forecasting the fragility of the banking and insurance sectors. *Journal of Banking & Finance*, 35, 807–18.

Bertrand, M. and Schoar, A. 2003. Managing with style: the effect of managers on firm policy. *Quarterly Journal of Economics* 118, 1169–208.

Bharath, S. T. and Shumway, T. 2008. Forecasting default with the Merton distance to default model. *Review of Financial Studies* 21, 1339–69.

Bhattacharya, S. and Takor, A. V. 1993. Contemporary banking theory. *Journal of Financial Intermediation* 3, 2–50.

Bliss, R. T. and Rosen, R. J. 2001. CEO compensation and bank mergers. *Journal of Financial Economics* 61, 107–38.

Blundell, R. and Bond, S. 1998. Initial conditions and moment restrictions in dynamic panel data models. *Journal of Econometrics* 87, 115–43.

Board of Governors of the Federal Reserve System, Federal Deposit Insurance Corporation, Office of the Comptroller of the Currency, Treasury, and Office of Thrift Supervision, 2010. Guidance on sound incentive compensation policies, 25 June. <http://www.fdic.gov/news/news/press/2010/pr10138a.pdf>.

Boehmer, E., Musumeci, J., and Poulsen, A. B. 1991. Event-study methodology under conditions of event-induced variance. *Journal of Financial Economics* 30, 253–72.

Bolton, P., Mehran, H., and Shapiro, J. 2010. Executive compensation and risk-taking. Federal Reserve Bank of New York Staff Report 456.

Boot, A. W. A. and Thakor, A.V. 2009. The accelerating integration of banks and markets and its implications for regulations. In *The Oxford Handbook of Banking*, ed. A. Berger, P. Molyneux, and J. O. S. Wilson. Oxford: Oxford University Press, 58–90.

Booth, J. R., Cornett, M. M., and Tehranian, H. 2002. Boards of directors, ownership, and regulation. *Journal of Banking & Finance* 26, 1973–96.

Bouwens, J. and Kroos, P. 2011. Target ratcheting and effort reduction. *Journal of Accounting and Economics* 51, 171–85.

Boyd, J. H. and Runkle, D. E. 1993. Size and performance of banking firms. *Journal of Monetary Economics* 31, 47–67.

Boyd, J. H., Graham, S. L., and Hewitt, R. S. 1993. Bank holding company mergers with nonbank financial firms: effects on the risk of failure. *Journal of Banking & Finance* 17, 43–63.

Boyson, N., Helwege, J., and Jindra, J. 2010. Crises, liquidity shocks, and fire sales at financial institutions. Working Paper, Northeastern University.

Brander, J. A. and Poitevin, M. 1992. Managerial compensation and the agency costs of debt finance. *Managerial and Decision Economics* 13, 1099–468.

Brewer III, E. 1989. Relationship between bank holding company risk and nonbank activity. *Journal of Economics and Business* 41, 337–53.

Brooks, R. and Del Negro, M. 2004. The rise in comovement across national stock markets: Market integration or IT bubble? *Journal of Empirical Finance* 11, 659–80.

Brown, O. C. and Dinç, I. S. 2011. Too many too fail? Evidence of regulatory forbearance when the banking sector is weak. *Review of Financial Studies* 24, 1378–405.

Brunnermeier, M. K., Dong, G., and Palia, D. 2012. Banks' non-interest income and systemic risk. Working Paper, Princeton University.

Brunnermeier, M. K., Crocket, A., Goodhart, C., Persaud, A. D., and Shin, H. S. 2009. The fundamental principles of financial regulation. Geneva Report on the World Economy 11.

Buch, C. M. and DeLong, G. 2008. Do weak supervisory systems encourage bank risk-taking? *Journal of Financial Stability* 4, 23–39.

Buch, C. and Neugebauer, K. 2009. Diversification of banks' international portfolios: evidence and policy lessons. FINESS Working Paper d.2.4.

Bushman, R. M. and Williams, C. D. 2007. Bank transparency, loan loss provisioning behavior, and risk shifting. Working Paper, University of North Carolina, Chapel Hill.

Bushman, R. M., Pietroski, J. D., and Smith, A. J. 2004. What determines corporate transparency? Journal of Accounting Research. 42, 207–52.

Byrd, J. W. and Hickman, K. A. 1992. Do outside directors monitor managers? Evidence from tender offer bids. *Journal of Financial Economics* 32, 195–221.

Campa, J. M. and Hernando, I. 2004. Shareholder value creation in European M&As. European Financial Management 10, 47–81.

Campbell, J. C. and Perron, P. 1991. Pitfall and Opportunities: What macroeconomists should know about Unit Roots. NBER Technical Working Paper No. 100.

Campbell, J. Y., Lettau, M., Malkiel, B. G., and Xu, Y. 2001. Have individual stocks become more volatile? An empirical exploration of idiosyncratic risk. *Journal of Finance* 56, 1–43.

Carlson, M. A., King, T. B., and Lewis, K. F. 2008. Distress in the financial sector and economic activity. Finance and Economics Discussion Series, Divisions of Research & Statistics and Monetary Affairs, Federal Reserve Board, Washington, DC, 2008–43.

Carter, D. A., D'Souza, F., Simkins, B. J., and Simpson, W. G. 2007. The diversity of corporate board committees and financial performance. Working Paper, Oklahoma State University.

CEBS (Committee of European Banking Supervisors). 2010. Consultation paper on guidelines on remuneration policies and practices. <http://eba.europa.eu/documents/Publications/Consultation-papers/2010/CP42/CP42.aspx>.

Cetorelli, N. and Goldberg, L. S. 2008. Banking globalization, monetary transmission, and the lending channel. NBER Working Paper Series 14101, June.

Chen, Y. 1999. Banking panics: the role of the first come, first-served rule and information externalities. *Journal of Political Economy* 107, 946–68.

Chionsini, G., Foglia, A., and Marullo-Reedtz, P. 2003. Bank mergers, diversification and risk. Working Paper, Banca d'Italia, Rome.

Clayton, J. and Mackinnon, G. 2003. The relative importance of stock, bond, and real estate factors in explaining REIT returns. *Journal of Real Estate Finance and Economics* 27, 39–60.

Coccorese, P. 2009. Market power in local banking monopolies. *Journal of Banking & Finance* 33, 1196–210.

Coles, J. L., Daniel, N. D., and Naveen, L. 2006. Managerial incentives and risk-taking. *Journal of Financial Economics* 79, 431–68.

Cordella, T. and Yeyati, E. L. 1998. Public disclosure and bank failures. IMF Staff Paper 45, 110–31.

Cornett, M. M., McNutt, J. J., and Tehranian, H. 2006. Performance changes around bank mergers: revenue enhancements versus cost reductions. *Journal of Money, Credit and Banking* 38, 1013–50.

Cornett, M. M., McNutt, J. J., and Tehranian, H. 2009. Corporate governance and earnings management at large US bank holding companies. *Journal of Corporate Finance* 15, 412–30.

Cornett, M. M., Hovakimian, G., Palia, D., and Tehranian, H. 2003. The impact of the manager–shareholder conflict on acquiring bank returns. *Journal of Banking & Finance* 27, 103–31.

Craig, B. and dos Santos, J. C. 1996. Performance and asset management effects of bank acquisitions. Federal Reserve Bank of Cleveland, Working Paper 9619.

Craig, B. and dos Santos, J. C. 1997. The risk effects of bank acquisitions. *Economic Review* Q2, 25–35.

Crouzille, C., Lepetit, L., and Tarazi, A. 2004. Bank stock volatility, news and asymmetric information in banking: an empirical investigation. *Journal of Multinational Financial Management* 14, 443–61.

Curry, T. J., Fissel, G. S., and Hanweck, G. A. 2008. Is there cyclical bias in bank holding company risk ratings? *Journal of Banking & Finance* 32, 1297–309.

De Bandt, O. and Hartmann, P. 2000. Systemic risk: a survey. ECB Working Paper Series 35.

De Jonghe, O. 2010. Back to the basics in banking? A micro-analysis of banking system stability. *Journal of Financial Intermediation* 19, 387–417.

De Nicolò, G. and Kwast, M. L. 2002. Systemic risk and financial consolidation: Are they related? *Journal of Banking & Finance* 26, 861–80.

De Nicolò, G. and Tieman, A. 2006. Economic integration and financial stability: a European perspective. IMF Working Paper 296.

De Nicolò, G., Barthlomew, P., Zaman, J., and Zephirin, M. 2004. Bank consolidation, internationalization and conglomeration: trends and implications for financial risk. *Finance Markets, Institutions & Instruments* 13, 173–217.

DeLong, G. 2001. Stockholder gains from focusing versus diversifying bank mergers. *Journal of Financial Economics* 59, 221–52.

DeLong, G. and DeYoung, R. 2007. Learning by observing: information spillovers in the execution and valuation of commercial bank M&As. *Journal of Finance* 62, 181–216.

Demirgüç-Kunt, A. and Huizinga, H. 2010. Bank activity and funding strategies: the impact on risk and return. *Journal of Financial Economics* 98, 626–50.

Demirgüç-Kunt, A. and Huizinga, H. 2011. Do we need big banks? Evidence on performance, strategy and market discipline. World Bank, Policy Research Working Paper, February.

Dermigüc-Kunt, A., Detragiache, E., and Tressel, T. 2008. Banking on the principles: compliance with Basel Core Principle and bank soundness. *Journal of Financial Intermediation* 17, 511–42.

Demsetz, H. and Lehn, K. 1985. The structure of corporate ownership: causes and consequences. *Journal of Political Economy* 93, 1155–77.

Demsetz, R. S. and Strahan, P. E. 1997. Diversification, size and risk at bank holding companies. *Journal of Money, Credit and Banking* 29, 300–13.

Dermine, J. and Schoenmaker, D. 2010. In banking, is small beautiful? *Financial Markets, Institutions & Instruments* 19, 1–19.

DeYoung, R. and Roland, K. P. 2001. Product mix and earnings volatility at commercial banks: evidence from a degree of total leverage model. *Journal of Financial Intermediation* 10, 54–84.

DeYoung, R., Peng, E. Y., and Yan, M. 2010. Executive compensation and policy choices at U.S. commercial banks. Federal Reserve Bank of Kansas City, Research Working Paper 10-02.

Dodd, P. and Warner, J. B. 1983. On corporate governance—a study of proxy contests. *Journal of Financial Economics* 11, 401–38.

Driscoll, J. C. and Kraay, A. C. 1998. Consistent covariance matrix estimation with spatially dependent panel data. *Review of Economics and Statistics* 80, 549–60.

Drummen, M. and Zimmerman, H. 1992. The structure of European stock returns. *Financial Analysts Journal* 48, 15–26.

Duru, A., Mansi, S. A., and Reeb, D. M. 2005. Earnings-based bonus plans and the agency costs of debt. *Journal of Accounting and Public Policy* 24, 431–47.

Dyck, A. and Zingales, L. 2004. Private benefits of control: an international comparison. *Journal of Finance* 59, 537–600.

EC (European Commission). 2009. An EU framework for cross-border crisis management in the banking sector. Commission Staff Working Document, October.

EC (European Commission). 2010. An EU framework for crisis management in the financial sector. Communication from the Commission to the European Parliament, the Council, the European Economic and Social Committee, the Committee of the Regions and the European Central Bank, October.

ECB (European Central Bank). 2005. Bank market discipline. Monthly Bulletin, February.

ECB (European Central Bank). 2010. EU banking structures,. <http://www.ecb.int/pub/pdf/other/eubankingstructures201009en.pdf>

Edmans, A. and Liu, Q. 2011. Inside debt. *Review of Finance* 15, 75–102.

Eiling, E. and Gerard, B. 2007. Dispersion, equity returns correlations and market integration. Working Paper, University of Toronto.

Eisenbeis, R. A. and Kaufman, G. G. 2008. Cross-border banking and financial stability in EU. *Journal of Financial Stability* 3, 168–204.

Eisenberg, T., Sundgren, S., and Wells, M. T. 1998. Larger board size and decreasing firm value in small firms. *Journal of Financial Economics* 48, 35–54.

Ekkayokkaya, M., Holmes, P., and Paudyal, K. 2009. The euro and the changing face of European banking: evidence from mergers and acquisitions. *European Financial Management* 15, 451–76.

Ely, R. J. and Thomas, D. A. 2001. Cultural diversity at work: the effects of diversity perspectives on work group processes and outcomes. *Administrative Science Quarterly* 46, 229–73.

Elyasiani, E. and Jia, J. J. 2008. Institutional ownership stability and BHC performance. *Journal of Banking & Finance* 32, 1767–81.

Emmons, W. R., Gilbert, A. R., and Yeager, T. J. 2004. Reducing the risk at small community banks: Is size or geographic diversification that matters? *Journal of Financial Services Research* 25, 259–81.

Erhardt, N. L., Werbel, J. D., and Shrader, C. B. 2003. Board of director diversity and firm financial performance. *Corporate Governance: An International Review* 11, 102–11.

Estrella, A. 2001. Mixing and matching: perspective financial sector mergers and market valuation. *Journal of Banking & Finance* 25, 2367–92.

Evanoff, D. D. and Wall, L. D. 2001. SND yield spreads as bank risk measures. *Journal of Financial Services Research* 19, 121–46.

Fahlenbrach, R. and Stulz, R. 2011. Bank CEO incentives and the credit crisis. *Journal of Financial Economics* 99, 11–26.

Fama, E. F. 1998. Market efficiency, long-term returns, and behavioral finance. *Journal of Financial Economics* 49, 283–306.

Fama, E. F. and MacBeth, J. D. 1973. Risk, return, and equilibrium: Empirical tests. *Journal of Political Economy* 81, 607–36.

Fama, E. F. and Jensen, M. C. 1983. Separation of ownership and control. *Journal of Law & Economics* 26, 301–25.

Farhi, E. and Tirole, J. 2009. Collective moral hazard, maturity mismatch and systemic bail out. NEBR Working Paper n.11698.

Farrell, K. A. and Hersch, P. L. 2005. Additions to corporate boards: the effect of gender. *Journal of Corporate Finance* 11, 85–106.

Fernandes, N. and Ferreira, M. A. 2008. Does international cross-listing improve the information environment? *Journal of Financial Economics* 88, 216–44.

Ferreira, M. and Gama, P. M. 2005. Have world, country and industry risks changed over time? An investigation of the developed stock market volatility. *Journal of Financial and Quantitative Analysis* 40, 195–222.

Fich, E. M. and Shivdasani, A. 2006. Are busy boards effective monitors? *Journal of Finance* 61, 689–724.

Flannery, M. J. 2005. No pain, no gain? Effecting market discipline via reverse convertible debentures. In *Capital Adequacy beyond Basel: Banking Securities and Insurance*, ed. H. S. Scott. Oxford: Oxford University Press, 171–97.

Flannery, M. J., Kwan S. H., and Nimalendran, M. 2004. Market evidence on the opaqueness of banking firms' assets. *Journal of Financial Economics* 71, 419–60.

Florackis, C. and Ozkan, A. 2009. The impact of managerial entrenchment on agency costs: an empirical investigation using UK panel data. *European Financial Management* 15, 497–528.

Foos, D., Norden, L., and Weber, M. 2010. Loan growth and riskiness of banks. *Journal of Banking & Finance* 12, 2929–40.

Francis, B. B. and Hunter, D. M. 2004. The impact of the euro on risk exposure of the world's major banking industries. *Journal of International Money and Finance* 21, 1011–42.

French, K. R., Schwert, W. G., and Stambaugh, R. F. 1987. Expected stock returns and volatility. *Journal of Financial Economics* 19, 3–29.

FSA (Financial Services Authority). 2009. Turner Review Conference Discussion Paper, October.

FSB (Financial Stability Board). 2009. Guidance to assess the systemic importance of financial institutions, markets and instruments: initial considerations—background paper. Report to G20 finance ministers and governors, October, Basel.

FSB (Financial Stability Board). 2010. Reducing the moral hazard posed by systemically important financial institutions. Interim report to G20 leaders, Basel.

FSF (Financial Stability Forum). 2008. Enhancing market and institutional resilience. <http://www.financialstabilityboard.org/publications/r_0804.pdf>.

Furfine, C. H. and Rosen, R. J. 2009. Mergers increase default risk. Working Paper, Kellogg School of Management.

Gatev, E., Schuermann, T., and Strahan, P. 2009. Managing bank liquidity risk: how deposit-loan synergies vary with market conditions. *Review of Financial Studies* 22, 995–1020.

Geyfman, V. and Yeager, T. 2009. On the riskiness of universal banking: evidence from banks in the investment banking business pre- and post-GLBA. *Journal of Money, Credit and Banking* 41, 1649–68.

Gibbons, R. and Murphy, K. J. 1992. Optimal incentive contracts in the presence of career concerns: theory and evidence. *Journal of Political Economy* 100, 468–505.

Goddard, J., Molyneux, P., and Wilson, J. O. S. 2004. The profitability of European banks: a cross- sectional and dynamic panel analysis. *Manchester School* 72, 363–81.

Goddard, J., Liu, H., Molyneux, P., and Wilson, J. O. S. 2011. Do bank profits converge? *European Financial Management*, forthcoming.

Goddard, J., Molyneux, P., Wilson, J. O. S., and Tavakoli, M. 2007. European banking: an overview. *Journal of Banking & Finance* 31, 1911–35.

Goetz, M., Laeven, L., and Levine, R. 2011. The private benefits of controlling complex bank holding companies. Working Paper, Federal Reserve Bank of Boston.

Goyal, V. K. and Park, C. W. 2002. Board leadership structure and CEO turnover. *Journal of Corporate Finance* 8, 49–66.

Gropp, R. and Heider, F. 2010. Determinants of bank capital structure. *Review of Finance* 14, 587–622.

Gropp, R. and Kashyap, A. 2010. A new metric for banking integration in Europe. In *Europe and the Euro*, ed. A. Alesina and F. Giavazzi. Chicago: University Chicago Press, 219–46.

Gropp, R. and Moerman, G. 2004. Measurement of contagion in bank equity prices. *Journal of International Money and Finance* 23, 405–59.

Gropp, R., Gründl, C., and Güttler, A. 2010. The impact of public guarantees on bank risk taking: evidence from a natural experiment. EBS Working Paper 10-10.

Gropp, R., Hakenes, H., and Schnabel, I. 2011. Competition, risk-shifting, and public bail-out policies. *Review of Financial Studies* 24, 2084–120.

Gropp, R., Lo Duca, M., and Vesala, J. 2009. Cross-border bank contagion in Europe. *International Journal of Central Banking* 5, 97–139.

Gropp, R., Vesala, J., and Vulpes, G. 2006. Equity and bond market signals as leading indicators of bank fragility. *Journal of Money, Credit and Banking* 38, 399–428.

Group of Thirty. 2009. Financial reform: a framework for financial stability. Special Report, Washington DC.

Guay, W. R. 1999. The sensitivity of CEO wealth to equity risk: an analysis of the magnitude and determinants. *Journal of Financial Economics* 53, 43–71.

Hadlock, C. J., Lee, D. S., and Parrino, R. 2002. Chief executive officer careers in regulated environments: evidence from electric and gas utilities. *Journal of Law and Economics* 45, 535–63.

Hagendorff, J. and Vallascas, F. 2011. CEO pay incentives and risk-taking: evidence from bank acquisitions. *Journal of Corporate Finance* 17, 1078–95.

Hagendorff, J., Collins, M., and Keasey, K. 2007. Bank governance and acquisition performance. *Corporate Governance—An International Review* 15, 957–68.

Haggard, K. S., Xiumin, M., and Pereira, R. 2008. Does voluntary disclosure improve stock price informativeness? *Financial Management* 37, 747–68.

Haq, M. and Heaney, R. 2009. European bank equity risk: 1995–2006. *Journal of International Financial Markets, Institutions & Money* 19, 274–88.

Harjoto, M. A. and Mullineaux, D. J. 2003. CEO compensation and the transformation of banking. *Journal of Financial Research* 26, 341–54.

Hartmann, P., Straetmans, S., and de Vries, C. G. 2006. Banking system stability: a cross-Atlantic perspective. In *The Risks of Financial Institutions*, ed. M. Carey and R. M. Stulz. Chicago: University of Chicago Press and NBER, 133–88.

Healy, P. M., Palepu, K. G., and Ruback, R. S. 1992. Does corporate performance improve after mergers? *Journal of Financial Economics* 31, 135–75.

Heffernan, S. A. 2003. The causes of bank failures. In *Handbook of International Banking*, ed. A. Mullineux and V. Murinde. Cheltenham: Edward Elgar.

Hellwig, M. F. 2010. Capital regulation after the crisis: Business as usual? Max Planck Institute for Research on Collective Goods, Working Paper Series 2010–31.

Hermalin, B. E. and Weisbach, M. S. 2003. Boards of directors as an endogenously determined institution: a survey of the economic literature. *Economic Policy Review* 9, 7–26.

Hernando, I., Nieto, M. J., and Wall, L. D. 2009. Determinants of domestic and cross-border bank acquisitions in the European Union. *Journal of Banking & Finance* 33, 1022–32.

Hillegeist, S. A., Keating, E., Cram, D., and Lundstedt, K. 2004. Assessing the probability of bankruptcy. *Review of Accounting Studies* 9, 5–34.

Hillman, A. J., Cannella, A. A., and Paetzold, R. L. 2000. The resource dependence role of corporate directors: strategic adaptation of board composition in response to environmental change. *Journal of Management Studies* 37, 235–56.

Holthausen, R., Larcker, D., and Sloan, R. 1995. Annual bonus schemes and the manipulation of earnings. *Journal of Accounting and Economics* 19, 29–74.

Houston, J. and Stiroth, K. J. 2006. Three decades of financial sector risk. Federal Reserve Bank of New York Staff Report 246.

Huang, R. and Ratnoviski, L. 2011. The dark side of bank wholesale funding. *Journal of Financial Intermediation*, 20, 248–63.

Huang, X., Zhou, H., and Zhu, H. 2010. Assessing the systemic risk of a heterogenous portfolio of banks during the recent financial crisis. BIS Working Paper n. 296.

Hubbard, R. G. and Palia, D. 1995. Executive pay and performance evidence from the U.S. banking industry. *Journal of Financial Economics* 39, 105–30.

Hughes, J. P., Mester, L. J., and Moon, C. G. 2001. Are scale economies in banking elusive or illusive? Evidence obtained by incorporating capital structure and risk-taking into models of bank production checking accounts and bank monitoring. *Journal of Banking & Finance* 25, 2169–208.

Hughes, J. P., Lang, W. W., Mester, L. J., and Moon, C. G. 1999. The dollars and sense of bank consolidation. *Journal of Banking & Finance* 23, 291–324.

Hutton, A., Marcus, A. J., and Tehranian, H. 2009. Opaque financial reports, R-square, and crash risk. *Journal of Financial Economics* 94, 67–86.

Ibragimov, R., Jaffee, D., and Walden, J. 2011. Diversification disasters. *Journal of Financial Economics* 99, 333–48.

IMF (International Monetary Fund). 2009a. Responding to financial crisis and measuring systemic risk. Global Financial Stability Report. Washington, DC: International Monetary Fund.

IMF (International Monetary Fund). 2009b. The State of Public Finances: A Cross-Country Fiscal Monitor, International Monetary Fund, Report, Washington D.C.

IMF (International Monetary Fund). 2009c. World economic outlook: crisis and recovery, April, Report, Washington DC.

IMF (International Monetary Fund). 2010. A fair and substantial contribution by the financial sector. Report for the G-20. Washington, DC: International Monetary Fund.

Indjejikian, R., Matějka, M., Merchant, K., and Van Der Stede, W. 2011. Earnings targets and annual bonus incentives. Working Paper, Arizona State University, Metro Phoenix.

Jensen, M. C. 1986. Agency costs of free cash flow, corporate finance, and takeovers. *American Economic Review* 76, 323–9.

Jensen, M. C. 1993. The modern industrial revolution, exit, and the failure of internal control systems. *Journal of Finance* 48, 831–80.

Jensen, M. C. and Meckling, W. H. 1976. Theory of the firm: managerial behavior, agency costs and ownership structure. *Journal of Financial Economics* 3, 305–60.

Jin, L. and Myers, S. C. 2006. R2 around the world: new theory and news tests. *Journal of Financial Economics* 79, 257–92.

John, K., John, T. A., and Senbet, L. W. 1991. Risk-shifting incentives of deposit insurance: a new perspective on federal deposit insurance reform. *Journal of Banking & Finance* 15, 895–915.

John, K., Mehran, H., and Qian, Y. 2010. Outside monitoring and CEO compensation in the banking industry. *Journal of Corporate Finance* 16, 383–99.

John, K., Saunders, A., and Senbet, L. W. 2000. A theory of bank regulation and management compensation. *Review of Financial Studies* 13, 95–125.

John, T. A. and John, K. 1993. Top-management compensation and capital structure. *Journal of Finance* 48, 949–74.

Jokipii, T. and Milne, A. 2011. Bank capital buffer and risk adjustment decisions. *Journal of Financial Stability* 7, 165–78.

Kashyap, A. K., Rajan, R. G., and Stein, J. 2002. Banks as liquidity providers: an explanation for the coexistence of lending and deposit-taking. *Journal of Finance* 57, 33–73.

Kashyap, A. K., Rajan, R., and Stein, R. 2008. Rethinking capital regulation. Working Paper, University of Chicago.

Kaufman, G. G. 1994. Bank contagion: a review of the theory and evidence. *Journal of Financial Services Research* 8, 123–50.

Kaufman, G. G. and Scott, K. E. 2003. What is systemic risk and do bank regulators retard or contribute to it? *Independent Review* 7, 372–91.

Kearney, C. and Potì, V. 2008. Have European stocks become more volatile? An empirical investigation of idiosyncratic risk and market risk in the Euro area. *European Financial Management* 14, 419–44.

Keeley, M. C. 1990. Deposit insurance, risk, and market power in banking. *American Economic Review* 80, 1183–200.

Keys, B., Makherjee, T., Seru, A., and Vig, V. 2009. Financial regulation and securitization: evidence from subprime loan. *Journal of Monetary Economics* 56, 700–20.

Kim, Y. S., Nam, J., Thornton Jr, J. H. 2008. The effect of managerial bonus plans on corporate derivatives usage. *Journal of Multinational Financial Management* 18, 229–43.

Knapp, M., Gart, A., and Becher, D. 2005. Post-merger performance of bank holding companies, 1987–1998. *Financial Review* 40, 549–74.

Knaup, M. and Wagner, W. 2012. Forward-looking tail risk exposures at U.S. bank holding companies. *Journal of Financial Services Research* 42, 35–54.

Koenker, R. and Hallock, K. F. 2001. Quantile regression. *Journal of Economic Perspective* 15, 143–56.

Koetter, M., Bos, J. W. B., Heid, F., Kolari, J. W., Kool, C. J. M., and Porath, D. 2007. Accounting for distress in bank mergers. *Journal of Banking & Finance* 31, 3200–17.

Kole, S. R. and Lehn, K. M. 1999. Deregulation and the adaptation of governance structure: the case of the US airline industry. *Journal of Financial Economics* 52, 79–117.

Kosnik, R. D. 1990. Effects of board demography and directors' incentives on corporate greenmail decisions. *Academy of Management Journal* 33, 129–50.

Krimminger, M. H. 2008. The resolution of cross-border banks: issues for deposit insurers and proposals for cooperation. *Journal of Financial Stability* 4, 376–90.

La Porta, R., Lopez-de-Silanes, F., Shleifer, A., and Vishny, R. 1998. Law and finance. *Journal of Political Economy* 106, 1113–55.

La Porta, R., Lopez-de-Silanes, F., Shleifer, A., and Vishny, R. 2000. Investor protection and corporate governance. *Journal of Financial Economics* 58, 3–27.

Laeven, L. and Levine, R. 2007. Is there a diversification discount in financial conglomerates? *Journal of Financial Economics* 85, 331–67.

Laeven, L. and Levine, R. 2009. Bank governance, regulation and risk taking. *Journal of Financial Economics* 93, 259–75.

Laeven, L. and Valencia, F. 2008. Systemic banking crises: a new database. IMF Working Paper 08/224.

Leone, A. J., Wu, J. S., and Zimmerman, J. L. 2006. Asymmetric sensitivity of CEO cash compensation to stock returns. *Journal of Accounting and Economics* 42, 167–92.

Lepetit, L., Nys, E., Rous, P., and Tarazi, A. 2008. Bank income structure and risk: an empirical analysis of European banks. *Journal of Banking & Finance* 32, 1452–67.

MacKinnon, J. G. 1994. Approximate asymptotic distribution functions for unit-root and cointegration tests. *Journal of Business and Economic Statistics* 12, 167–76.

Mahoney, P. G. 2001. The common law and economic growth: Hayek might be right. *Journal of Legal Studies* 30, 503–25.

Mallin, C., Mullineux, A., and Wihlborg, C. 2005. The financial sector and corporate governance: the UK case. *Corporate Governance: An International Review* 13, 532–41.

Masulis, R. W., Wang, C., and Xie, F. E. I. 2007. Corporate governance and acquirer returns. *Journal of Finance* 62, 1851–89.

McAllister, P. H. and McManus, D. 1993. Resolving the scale efficiency puzzle in banking. *Journal of Banking & Finance* 17, 389–405.

Mehran, H. and Rosenberg, J. V. 2007. The effect of employee stock options on bank investment choice, borrowing, and capital. Federal Reserve Bank of New York Staff Report 305.

Mercieca, S., Schaeck, K., and Wolfe, S. 2007. Small European banks: Benefits from diversification? *Journal of Banking & Finance* 31, 1975–98.

Merton, R. C. 1974. On the pricing of corporate debt: the risk structure of interest rates. *Journal of Finance* 29, 449–70.

Mester, L. J. 2005. Optimal industrial structure in banking. Federal Reserve Bank of Philadelphia, Research Department Working Paper 08–2.

Miller, S. M. and Noulas, A. G. 1997. Portfolio mix and large-bank profitability in the USA. *Applied Economics* 29, 505–12.

Mishra, S., Prakash, A. J., and Peterson, M. 2005. Bank mergers and components of risk: an evaluation. *Journal of Economics and Business* 29, 84–6.

Molyneux, P. and Thornton, J. 1992. Determinants of European bank profitability: a note. *Journal of Banking & Finance* 16, 1173–8.

Molyneux, P. and Wilson, J. O. S. 2007. Developments in European banking. *Journal of Banking & Finance* 31, 1907–10.

Morck, R., Shleifer, A., and Vishny, R. W. 1990. Do managerial objectives drive bad acquisitions? *Journal of Finance* 45, 31–48.

Morck, R., Yeung, B., and Yu, W. 2000. The information content of stock markets: Why do emerging markets have synchronous stock price movements? *Journal of Financial Economics* 58, 215–60.

Morgan, D. P. 2002. Rating banks: risk and uncertainty in an opaque industry. *American Economic Review* 88, 874–88.

Morgan, D. P., Rime, B., and Strahan, P. E. 2004. Bank integration and state business cycles. *Quarterly Journal of Economics* 119, 1555–84.

Morris, S. and Shin, H. S. 2008. Financial regulation in a system context. *Brookings Papers on Economic Activities* 32, 229–74.

Moshirian, F. and Wu, Q. 2009. Banking industry volatility and banking crises. *Journal of International Financial Markets, Institutions & Money* 19, 351–70.

Murphy, K. J. 2000. Performance standards in incentive contracts. *Journal of Accounting and Economics* 30, 245–78.

Nier, E. 2005. Bank stability and transparency. *Journal of Financial Stability* 1, 342–54.

Nier, E. and Baumann, U. 2006. Market discipline, disclosure and moral hazard in banking. *Journal of Financial Intermediation* 15, 332–61.

Nijskens, R. and Wagner, W. 2011. Credit risk transfer activities and systemic risk: how banks became less risky individually but posed greater risks to the financial system at the same time. *Journal of Banking & Finance* 35, 1391–98.

Noe, T. H., Rebello, M. J., and Wall, L. D. 1996. Managerial rents and regulatory intervention in troubled banks. *Journal of Banking & Finance* 20, 331–50.

Outreville, J. F. 2010. Internationalization, performance and volatility: the world largest financial groups. *Journal of Financial Services Research* 38, 115–34.

Pais, A. and Stork, P. A. 2011. Bank size and systemic risk. *European Financial Management*, forthcoming.

Park, S. 1999. Effects of risk-based capital requirements and asymmetric information on banks' portfolio decisions. *Journal of Regulatory Economics* 16, 135–50.

Park, S. and Peristiani, S. 2007. Are bank shareholders enemies of regulators or a potential source of market discipline? *Journal of Banking & Finance* 31, 2493–515.

Pathan, S. 2009. Strong boards, CEO power and bank risk-taking. *Journal of Banking & Finance* 33, 1340–50.

Penas, M. F. and Unal, H. 2004. Gains in bank mergers: evidence from the bond markets. *Journal of Financial Economics* 74, 149–79.

Pennacchi, G. 2006. Deposit insurance, bank regulation, and financial system risks. *Journal of Monetary Economics* 53, 1–30.

Petersen, M. A. 2009. Estimating standard errors in finance panel data sets: comparing approaches. *Review of Financial Studies* 22, 435–80.

Pietroski, J. D. and Roulstone, D. T. 2004. The influence of analysts, institutional investors, and insiders, on the incorporation of market, industry, and firm-specific information into stock prices. *Accounting Review* 79, 1119–51.

Pilloff, S. J. 1996. Performance changes and shareholder wealth creation associated with mergers of publicly traded banking institutions. *Journal of Money, Credit and Banking* 28, 294–310.

Rajan, R. 2005. Has financial development made the world riskier? NBER Working Paper Series 11728.

Rechner, P. L. and Dalton, D. R. 1991. CEO duality and organizational performance—a longitudinal analysis. *Strategic Management Journal* 12, 155–60.

Richard, O. C. 2000. Racial diversity, business strategy, and firm performance: a resource-based view. *Academy of Management Journal* 43, 164–77.

Rime, B. 2001. Capital requirements and bank behaviour: empirical evidence for Switzerland. *Journal of Banking & Finance* 25, 789–805.

Roe, M. J. 2003. *Political Determinants of Corporate Governance: Political Context, Corporate Impact*. Oxford: Oxford University Press.

Rossi, S. and Volpin, P. F. 2004. Cross-country determinants of mergers and acquisitions. *Journal of Financial Economics* 74, 277–304.

Saunders, A. and Wilson, B. 2001. An analysis of bank charter value and its risk-constraining incentives. *Journal of Financial Services Research* 19, 185–95.

Scharfstein, D. and Stein, J. 2000. The dark side of internal capital markets: divisional rent-seeking and inefficient investment. *Journal of Finance* 55, 2537–64.

Schuermann, T. and Stiroh, K. J. 2006. Visible and hidden risk factors for banks. Federal Reserve Bank of New York Staff Report 252.

Schüler, M. 2002. The threat of systemic risk in European banking. *Quarterly Journal of Business & Economics* 41, 145–65.

Schwert, G. W. 1989. Why does stock market volatility change over time? *Journal of Finance* 44, 1115–53.

Schwert, G. W. 2002. Stock volatility in the new millennium: How wacky is Nasdaq? *Journal of Monetary Economics* 49, 3–26.

Shaffer, S. 1994. Pooling intensifies joint failure risk. *Research in Financial Services* 6, 249–80.

Shaw, K. W. and Zhang, M. H. 2010. Is CEO cash compensation punished for poor firm performance? *Accounting Review* 85, 1065–93.

Shleifer, A. and Vishny, R. W. 1997. A survey of corporate governance. *Journal of Finance* 52, 737–83.

Shleifer, A. and Vishny, R. W. 2003. Stock market driven acquisitions. *Journal of Financial Economics* 70, 295–311.

Shleifer, A. and Vishny, R. W. 2010. Unstable banking. *Journal of Financial Economics* 97, 306–18.

Shrader, C. B., Blackburn, V. B., and Iles, P. 1997. Women in management and firm financial performance: an exploratory study. *Journal of Managerial Issues* 9, 355–72.

Shrieves, R.E. and Dahl, D. 1992. The relationship between risk and capital in commercial banks. *Journal of Banking & Finance* 16, 439–57.

Sirower, M. 1997. *The Synergy Trap: How Companies Lose the Acquisition Game*. New York: Free Press.

Smith, C. W. and Stulz, R. M. 1985. The determinants of firms' hedging policies. *Journal of Financial and Quantitative Analysis* 20, 391–405.

Song, M. H. and Walkling, R. A. 2006. Anticipation, acquisitions and bidder returns. Working paper, San Diego State University.

Stern, G. H. and Feldman, R. 2009. Addressing TBTF by shrinking financial institutions: an initial assessment. Federal Reserve Bank of Minneapolis, *The Region* June issue.

Stiroh, K. J. 2004a. Diversification in banking: Is noninterest income the answer? *Journal of Moaney, Credit and Banking* 36, 853–82.

Stiroh, K. J. 2004. Do community banks benefit from diversification? *Journal of Financial Services Research* 25, 135–60.

Stiroh, K. J. 2006a. A portfolio view of banking with interest and noninterest activities. *Journal of Money, Credit and Banking* 5, 1351–61.

Stiroh, K. J. 2006b. New evidence on the determinants of bank risk. *Journal of Financial Services Research* 30, 237–67.

Stiroh, K. J. 2009. Diversification in banking. In *The Oxford Handbook of Banking*, ed. A. Berger, P. Molyneux, and J. O. S. Wilson. Oxford: Oxford University Press, 146–71.

Stiroh, K. J. and Rumble, A. 2006. The dark side of diversification: the case of U.S. financial holding companies. *Journal of Banking & Finance* 30, 2131–61.

Subrahmanyam, V., Rangan, N., and Rosenstein, S. 1997. The role of outside directors in bank acquisitions. *Financial Management* 26, 23–36.

Sundaram, R. K. and Yermack, D. L. 2007. Pay me later: inside debt and its role in managerial compensation. *Journal of Finance* 62, 1551–88.

Tadesse, S. 2006. The economic value of regulated disclosure: evidence from the banking sector. *Journal of Accounting and Public Policy* 25, 32–70.

Uhde, A. and Heimeshoff, U. 2009. Consolidation in banking and financial stability in Europe: empirical evidence. *Journal of Banking & Finance* 33, 1299–311.

Vafeas, N. 1999. Board meeting frequency and firm performance. *Journal of Financial Economics* 53, 113–42.

Van Hoose, D. 2009. *The Industrial Organization of Banking: Bank Behavior, Market Structure, and Regulation*. Heidelberg: Springer.

Van Lelyveld, I. and Knot, K. 2009. Do financial conglomerates create or destroy value? Evidence for the EU. *Journal of Banking & Finance* 33, 2312–21.

Vassalou, M. and Xing, Y. 2004. Default risk in equity returns. *Journal of Finance* 59, 831–68.

Veldkamp, L. L. 2006. Information markets and the comovement of asset prices. *Review of Economic Studies* 73, 823–45.

Vogelsang, T. 1998. Trend function hypothesis testing in the presence of serial correlation. *Econometrica* 66, 123–48.

Vogelsang, T. 2001. Testing for a shift in trend when serial correlation is of unknown form. Working Paper, Cornell University.

Vulpes, G. and Brasili, A. 2006. Banking integration and co-movements in EU banks' fragility. MIPRA Paper No. 1964.

Wagner, W. 2007. Financial development and the opacity of banks, 2007. *Economic Letters* 97, 6–10.

Wagner, W. 2008. The homogenization of the financial system and financial crises. *Journal of Financial Intermediation* 17, 330–56.

Wagner, W. 2010a. Diversification at financial institutions and systemic crises. *Journal of Financial Intermediation* 19, 373–86.

Wagner, W. 2010b. In the quest of systemic externalities: a review of the literature. *CESifo Economic Studies* 56, 96–111.

Webb, E. 2008. Regulator scrutiny and bank CEO incentives. *Journal of Financial Services Research* 33, 5–20.

Wei, K. C. J. 1988. An asset pricing theory unifying the CAPM and APT. *Journal of Finance* 43, 881–92.

Wei, S. and Zhang, C. 2006. Why did individual stocks become more volatile? *Journal of Business* 79, 259–91.

Weisbach, M. S. 1988. Outside directors and CEO turnover. *Journal of Financial Economics* 20, 431–60.

Wheelock, D. C. and Wilson, P. W. 2012. Do large banks have lower costs? New estimates of returns to scale for U.S. banks. *Journal of Money, Credit and Banking* 44, 171–99.

Windmeijer, F. 2005. A finite sample correction for the variance of linear efficient two-step GMM estimators. *Journal of Econometrics* 126, 25–51.

Wintoki, M., Linck, J., and Netter, J. 2011. Endogeneity and the dynamics of internal corporate governance. *Journal of Financial Economics* 105, 581–606.
Yermack, D. 1996. Higher market valuation of companies with a small board of directors. *Journal of Financial Economics* 40, 185–211.
Zambrana, M. S. 2010. Systemic risk analysis using forward-looking distance to default. Federal Reserve Bank of Cleveland, Working Paper 10/05.

Index